Too Near for Dreams

Too Near for Dreams

The Story of Cleveland Abbe, America's First Weather Forecaster

SEAN POTTER

American Meteorological Society

Too Near for Dreams: The Story of Cleveland Abbe, America's First Weather Forecaster

Published by the American Meteorological Society
45 Beacon Street, Boston, Massachusetts 02108

Frontispiece: Portrait of Cleveland Abbe
published in *The Popular Science Monthly*. Wikimedia Commons.

The mission of the American Meteorological Society is to advance the atmospheric and related sciences, technologies, applications, and services for the benefit of society. Founded in 1919, the AMS is the premier scientific and professional society serving the atmospheric and related sciences. Additional information regarding society activities and membership can be found at www.ametsoc.org.

Library of Congress Control Number: 2019920324
ISBN: 978-1-944970-56-7
eISBN: 978-1-944970-57-4

For Sarah and Ethan, whose unending love and support sustain me,
and in loving memory of my father, Charles Potter, whose own writing
and appreciation for weather continue to inspire me

We may dream of the immensity of space as we contemplate the star-lit sky at night, for the stars are far, far away and men are always dreaming of them—but we can not merely *dream* of the clouds, the weather and the storms; the atmosphere is too near at hand for mere dreams; it forces us to action; it is close to us; we are in it and of it. It rouses us to both study and do; we must know its moods and also its motive forces; we must conquer it in our struggle for existence.

—Cleveland Abbe

Contents

Author's Note

This book relies heavily on the use of original source material, much of it handwritten and dating to the mid-nineteenth century. Every attempt has been made to be as true as possible to the original sources in terms of spelling, punctuation, and grammar. While this may at times lead to passages that are somewhat cumbersome in their readability, I hope readers will forgive any difficulty encountered in remaining faithful to letters and other material as they were written. One example is the use of the archaic form of "&c" rather than the more familiar "etc." to abbreviate "et cetera." This is especially common in letters written by Cleveland Abbe's mother. For this reason, I have opted not to use the customary notation "[sic]" following errors that are reprinted here from letters, diaries, and other unpublished sources, except in a few cases where the errors are especially conspicuous. I have also employed "[sic]" with errors that appear in published material that is quoted or excerpted.

I have chosen to, for the most part, refer to Cleveland by his first name only. This not only creates a sense of familiarity with him as the central figure in this story, but also helps avoid any ambiguity in sections discussing other members of the Abbe family. Both first and last names are used for Cleveland—and other major figures—on the first instance of each chapter.

In the sections discussing Cleveland's time spent in Russia, I have chosen to use the widely accepted spelling of "Pulkovo" when referring to the village and observatory south of St. Petersburg, where Cleveland lived and studied. However, when directly quoting original sources, I have retained the spelling used by the creator of the source material, which may appear as "Poulkova," "Poulkowa," "Pulkowa," or "Pulkova." References to dates during this period are given primarily according to the Gregorian calendar, or "New Style," with the equivalent "Old Style" dates, according to the Julian calendar used in Imperial Russia, given in parentheses as "O.S."

The terms "Signal Service" and "Signal Corps" often are used interchangeably when referring to the branch of the Army responsible for taking meteorological observations and issuing forecasts and warnings from 1870–1891. According to one source, "The Signal Service had been organized June 27, 1860, was renamed Signal Corps on February 24, 1880, lost the civilian meteorological work by transfer to the newly constituted Weather Bureau on June 30, 1891, and continues in existence to-day."[1] For the sake of consistency, I have chosen primarily to use the term "Signal Service" throughout but have retained the term "Signal Corps" when used in a quote. Likewise, if a quote uses the term "Weather Bureau" or "Weather Service" when referring to the Signal Service, I have retained the original wording for the sake of accuracy. I have occasionally used the term "weather service" generically when referring to the meteorological work performed by the predecessor agencies of the National Weather Service.

Key Figures in the Life of Cleveland Abbe

Cleveland Abbe (1838–1916) Astronomer and, later, meteorologist; the first person in America to successfully provide regular, practical weather forecasts for the public, based on reports from a network of observers

George Waldo Abbe (1811–1879) Cleveland's father; a prosperous dry goods and commission merchant in New York City and prominent philanthropist

Charlotte Colgate Abbe (1817–1885) Cleveland's mother; daughter of Bowles Colgate, cofounder of the Colgate Soap Company

Walter Abbe (1841–1924) Cleveland's brother; served in 37th New York Militia during the Civil War and later worked as head chemist for Atlantic White Lead Works

William Colgate Abbe (1843–1879) Cleveland's brother, also known as Willie; served in 37th New York Militia during the Civil War; later worked as a traveling salesman for Colgate & Co.; died as the result of a wound received at Gettysburg

Charles Colgate Abbe (1849–1917) Cleveland's brother, also known as Charlie; civil and mechanical engineer and inventor; also worked as assistant examiner in the U.S. Patent Office

Dr. Robert Abbe (1851–1928) Cleveland's brother, also known as Bob; surgeon and pioneer in radium therapy

Helen Abbe (1853–1925) Cleveland's sister; an educator and founder of the City History Club of New York

Harriet Colgate Abbe (1855–1938) Cleveland's sister, also known as Hattie; active in social and philanthropic activities

Frances Martha Neal Abbe (1838–1908) Cleveland's first wife, also known as Fanny

Cleveland Abbe Jr. (1872–1934) Eldest son of Cleveland and Fanny, also known as Cleve; geographer and meteorologist who served as assistant editor of *Monthly Weather Review*

Dr. Truman Abbe (1873–1955) Second son of Cleveland and Fanny; surgeon and chronicler of Cleveland's life

William Abbe (1877–1928) Youngest son of Cleveland and Fanny; patent attorney

Margaret Augusta Percival Abbe (1865–1936) Cleveland's second wife

Dr. Benjamin Apthorp Gould Jr. (1824–1896) Astronomer and head of the longitude department of the Coast Survey during Cleveland's time there; founder of the *Astronomical Journal*

Albert Smith Bickmore (1839–1914) Close friend and confidant of Cleveland; founder and first director of American Museum of Natural History

Friedrich Georg Wilhelm Struve (1793–1864) Known as Wilhelm; German astronomer who served as the first director of the Nicholas Central Observatory at Pulkovo, Russia

Otto Struve (1819–1905) Wilhelm's son, who succeeded him as director of the Pulkovo Observatory

Nikolai Struve (1842–1917) Otto Struve's half-brother and a close friend of Cleveland during his time at Pulkovo; a student of theology at the University of Dorpat

Emilie Struve (1834–1912) Otto Struve's younger sister and the youngest daughter of Wilhelm Struve; the object of Cleveland's romantic interest during the latter part of his stay in Pulkovo

Simon Newcomb (1835–1909) Astronomer and professor of mathematics at the U.S. Naval Observatory, under whose direction Cleveland worked from 1867–1868

William Hooper (1812–1894) President of the Central National Bank of Cincinnati and secretary of the Cincinnati Astronomical Society

John Armstrong Gano (1826–1898) Cincinnati businessman and civic leader; editor of *The Cincinnati Commercial* and president of the Cincinnati Chamber of Commerce in 1869, when Cleveland began his series of weather bulletins as director of the Cincinnati Observatory

Increase Allen Lapham (1811–1875) Civil engineer, surveyor of canals, and self-taught scientist; petitioned General Halbert Paine, congressman from Milwaukee, to take action to prevent losses from storms

General Halbert Eleazer Paine (1826–1905) U.S. representative from Wisconsin's First District; at Lapham's urging introduced a joint resolution in Congress authorizing the secretary of war to take meteorological observations at military posts across the country

General Albert James Myer (1828–1880) Chief signal officer of the U.S. Army, under whose command the first government weather service was placed, beginning in 1870, until his death in 1880

General William Babcock Hazen (1830–1887) Succeeded Myer as chief signal officer in 1880, serving until his death in 1887

General Adolphus Washington Greely (1844–1935) Succeeded Hazen as chief signal officer; oversaw the transition of the weather service to the Department of Agriculture in 1891

Professor Mark Walrod Harrington (1848–1926) First civilian chief of the U.S. Weather Bureau, a position he held from 1891 until 1895

Professor Willis Luther Moore (1856–1927) Succeeded Harrington as chief of the Weather Bureau, serving from 1895 until 1913

Professor Charles Frederick Marvin (1858–1943) Succeeded Moore as chief of the Weather Bureau, serving from 1913 until 1934

Thomas Corwin Mendenhall (1841–1924) Close friend of Cleveland who taught physics at various institutions in Ohio and served briefly as a professor in the Signal Service from 1884 until 1886

Preface

Why Cleveland Abbe? In an age when weather forecasts are so ubiquitous and easily accessible that one need only look at an app on a smartphone to gauge the current and predicted state of the atmosphere, it is easy to forget there was once a time when accurate and precise weather forecasts were less than commonplace. It may be said that all weather forecasters today—certainly all government forecasters—can trace the roots of their scientific profession to Cleveland Abbe.

A modest, self-effacing man of strong scientific principles and religious convictions, Cleveland Abbe did more than any other person to help lay the foundation for modern weather forecasting in the United States. In establishing a system for creating daily weather forecasts, first while director of the Cincinnati Observatory and later as a civilian employee of the newly established forecast and storm warning division of the U.S. Army Signal Service (which later became the U.S. Weather Bureau), he became the first person in America to issue official, regularly scheduled weather forecasts, which he originally called "probabilities."

As the editor for many years of the journal *Monthly Weather Review*, Abbe also worked tirelessly to help disseminate knowledge in the area of meteorology and related fields. His dedication as a scientist and pioneer in his field was exceeded only by his humility and character as a human being. In a tribute to Abbe following his death in 1916, Weather Bureau Chief Charles F. Marvin remembered him as "a man of gentle and generous ways and a spirit refined and purified by his unselfish promotion of the pleasure and welfare of all around him."[1] Writing in 1930, more than a decade after Abbe's death, meteorologist Alfred J. Henry said Abbe possessed "that particular form of genius that enabled him quickly to teach others to equal and even to improve upon his own work as a forecaster."[2] He has been described as "a pathfinder on this continent," worthy of being "ranked in his sphere amongst Champlain, La Salle, Lewis & Clark, Freemont."[3]

Yet, Cleveland Abbe's story is not one made up solely of achievements or accolades. His struggles with depression and self-doubt early in life helped form a man whose introspective nature informed not only his treatment of himself, but also of those around him. His innate desire to help his fellow human beings manifested itself in a life as devoted to charity and self-sacrifice as to scientific pursuits. His work to help African Americans—especially during the years of Reconstruction—seems at odds with his descriptions of native Africans and other peoples he encountered during his travels. And his deep-seated interest in genealogy and pride in his own heredity have led some to link him to the growing eugenics movement in the United States during the early twentieth century.

This book strives to serve as a single, authoritative, objective history of the life and career of Cleveland Abbe that goes beyond the typical biographical sketch that can be found elsewhere, mainly in encyclopedias and other books. The only other full-length biography of Abbe's life is the book written by his son Truman, published in 1955, more than half a century ago.[4] While still a valuable reference, it has been described as a "work of filial piety"[5] and is based on mostly first- and secondhand accounts and lacks the objectivity a biography such as this deserves. The goal of this book is to tell the story of Cleveland Abbe through the events of his life as well as those taking place around him, both in the world of meteorology and the world at large. In doing so, it covers not only his many successes but also his shortcomings. It is as much about Cleveland Abbe the person as it is about Cleveland Abbe the scientist.

Prologue: "What Hath God Wrought?"

On January 6, 1838, a group of curious onlookers gathered in a room at the Speedwell Ironworks in Morristown, New Jersey, to witness history being made. There, an event took place that would forever change how people communicate and serve as a defining moment in the development of technology. At the center of the room stood a forty-six-year-old painter-turned-inventor named Samuel F. B. Morse, who, along with his assistant, Alfred Vail, successfully demonstrated for the first time that messages could be transmitted between distant locations by sending pulses of electromagnetic current along copper wires between two locations. Five days later, on January 11, Morse and Vail performed a more public demonstration by sending the first telegram in America across two miles of wire at Speedwell Ironworks.

Morse was motivated not so much by ambition as by tragedy. In 1825, he was in Washington, D.C., working on a portrait he had been commissioned to paint of the Revolutionary War hero General Gilbert du Motier, better known as the Marquis de Lafayette. While he was working on the portrait, a messenger arrived on horseback, informing Morse that his wife had taken ill at their home, in New Haven, Connecticut. Morse immediately set off for New Haven, but when he arrived, he found that not only had his wife died but she had already been buried. In his frustration and despair, Morse found the inspiration to develop the electromagnetic telegraph as a means of more rapid communication across great distances.

It would take several more years following the demonstration in Morristown before Morse's dream of sending messages between distant locations would become a reality. In 1840, he obtained a patent for his invention. Three years later, he asked Congress to appropriate funds to install a telegraph line from Washington to Baltimore—some thirty-eight miles away. Another year was consumed by logistics, including the laying of copper wire between the two cities.

Finally, on Friday, May 24, 1844, Morse was ready to send the first message across the new line. At 8:45 a.m., he sat down at a desk in the Supreme Court Chamber in the U.S. Capitol and began tapping away at the telegraph key. The message he sent was simple yet poignant: "What hath God wrought?"[1]

In the press, Morse's achievement was hailed as nothing short of phenomenal. "The miracle of the annihilation of space is at length performed," declared the *New York Daily Tribune* in reporting the news.[2] In the coming years, the widespread use of the telegraph would not only transform the physical landscape of America—with its ubiquitous wooden poles dotting the countryside—but also the cultural landscape. It would provide a faster and more practical means of communicating with friends, family, and businesses. It would reshape the newspaper and railroad industries. It would even help win wars. While providing a means for bringing humanity closer together, it also gave us the ability to fully realize our meteorological manifest destiny. The invention of the telegraph would pave the way for the practical use of weather observations—not just as a record of what had happened at a particular time and location but as necessary elements to make possible the age-old quest of predicting what *would* happen. It was the telegraph that would make possible the transmission of simultaneously collected weather observations, something a thirty-year-old New Yorker living in Ohio named Cleveland Abbe—who was born the same year as Morse's first demonstrations—would take full advantage of decades later.

CHAPTER ONE

Early Years (1838–1860)

> My boyhood life in New York City had impressed me with popular ignorance and also with the great need of something better than local lore and weather proverbs.
>
> —Cleveland Abbe, 1916

By all accounts, Monday, December 3, 1838, was a cool but pleasant day across the northeastern United States. Although no official weather service existed at the time to either forecast or later preserve a record of this, a picture of the meteorological conditions across the region can be gleaned through accounts memorialized in the diaries and journals of weather-savvy citizens, as well as records kept at military installations around the country.[1]

In Cambridge, Massachusetts, astronomer William Bond recorded a temperature of 29 degrees at half past six that morning, with winds out of the west at force one on the Beaufort scale and no cloud cover.[2] Some fifty miles to the south, in New Bedford, whaling merchant and diarist Samuel Rodman also reported a temperature of 29 degrees that morning, at sunrise, which rose to 36 degrees by two o'clock in the afternoon. The air pressure, according to his barometer, ranged from 29.88 to 30.29 inches, and skies were clear throughout the day.[3]

About sixty-five miles north of New York City, in a village known as Fishkill Landing, a former slave named James F. Brown recorded his impression of the day's weather in his diary. "Today the weather has been very fine for the season."[4] Brown, who had escaped from Maryland, worked for the Verplanck family at their picturesque estate, Mount Gulian, on the banks of the Hudson River.

In New York, an Army surgeon at Fort Columbus (which later became Fort Jay), on Governor's Island, reported a temperature of 27 degrees that morning and 37 degrees in the afternoon, with fair weather.[5] Similar conditions were reported in nearby Brooklyn Heights, as well as at Erasmus Hall Academy, in the Flatbush neighborhood of Brooklyn, and at the U.S. Army hospital at Fort Hamilton, on the Brooklyn side of the Narrows, the tidal strait separating Brooklyn from Staten Island.

At his home at 179 Chambers Street, in Manhattan, William Redfield, who had dutifully been making observations of weather conditions for several years, recorded a temperature of 28 degrees at six o'clock that morning, with a rising barometer at 30.17 inches. Redfield's thermometer showed a modest increase to 36 degrees by two o'clock that afternoon. He noted winds were out of the west-northwest or northwest at moderate strength throughout the day and skies were either "clear" or "fair."[6]

Half a mile to the southeast, in a three-story brick home at number 7 Dutch Street[7] in lower Manhattan, George Waldo Abbe and his wife, Charlotte Colgate Abbe, were likely not concerned about the intricacies of the day's weather as they welcomed into the world early that morning, around four o'clock, their firstborn child—a son—whom they named Cleveland, after his paternal grandfather. The first of seven children for the Abbes, Cleveland would eventually make his mark on the world in a way that would indelibly link him to the weather. By the end of the century, he would become arguably the most famous—and celebrated—meteorologist in America, if not the world.

Beginnings

From the beginning, Cleveland enjoyed a home life full of warmth and love, surrounded by members of a large extended family and instilled with the devotion of his staunch Baptist roots. "My earliest remembrance," he recalled years later,[8] "is of a dear old house and garden with its altheas, lilac bushes and box hedges, on the east side of Dutch street—the very humblest old street in New York City." He also recalled his nanny (or "nurse") who hailed from the Isle of Man and who regaled young Cleveland, or "Cleve" as he was known, with "wonderful stories of life in that quaint spot." Other early memories include "the great garret upstairs" in the family's house on Dutch Street, "the cold water baths in the morning" (indoor plumbing did not become a fixture of New York City homes until the completion of the Croton Aqueduct and Reservoir in 1842 and private baths did not become widespread across the city until the 1850s[9]), and his "busy mother stopping her work to play battledore[10] or cut out paper pictures."

Cleveland's mother would be a constant source of comfort and solace in his early years. "I found my pleasures at her side or in my books," he said. Early memories of her dominated his recollection of childhood, including those of her "playing or singing at the piano," as well as his "admiration of her requisite watercolor paintings of flowers." It is clear that Cleveland's parents had a positive influence on him from an early age. "The guiding spirit in that house was the gentle patient and loving mother," he wrote, adding "she was our Queen of Hearts, and the upright youthful and spirited father was not less the King of Hearts. He was always very cheerful and perfectly self reliant, while mother's daily refuge was in secret prayer."[11]

George's habit of daily prayer was also a source of comfort and inspiration to Cleveland and his siblings growing up. "Father's habit of family prayers after breakfast was a steadying influence," Cleveland's brother Robert recalled years later. One phrase that especially resonated with young Robert was the original aphorism, "We are all prone to evil, as the sparks are to fly upward." As Robert recalled, "It seemed to be so ingenious an illustration and so clearly true to our childish minds, that it was truth personified, and its daily repetition must have left an indelible impression which without reiteration would be lost."[12]

In writing about his father, Cleveland's son Truman suggested an equally strong influence by both his parents. "In his boyhood in that house, Cleveland must have listened to his father's stories as eagerly as he absorbed his mother's. And his father's memories must have dealt with the hard lot of farmers in nearby Connecticut, of their crop losses due to early frosts and delayed winter cold spells, and from droughts and floods."[13]

Cleveland also cherished the extended family—many of them on his mother's side—who lived with them (including two of his great-aunts and their mother, his great-grandmother) or in neighboring residences on Dutch Street. "Nowadays I often pity the homes that have no old people in them," he recalled at a time when indeed he was approaching his later years, adding, "to me the old folks always seemed to be a necessity."

Cleveland had a great interest in genealogy and spent a good portion of his life—some sixty years—carefully researching and documenting his family's history. The material collected was assembled, with the help of editor Josephine Genung Nichols, into a massive volume spanning more than five hundred pages that was published in 1916, the year of Cleveland's death.[14] On his father's side, Cleveland was able to trace his ancestry back to John Abbe, who was born in England around 1613 and immigrated to Salem, Massachusetts, in 1635. John's son Samuel lived in Salem during the infamous witch trials of the 1690s. Samuel and his wife, Mary, were among those opposed to the "fanaticism" that took place and even testified as witnesses at the trial of one of their neighbors.[15] The family eventually settled in Windham, Connecticut, where Cleveland's grandfather and namesake, Moses Cleveland Abbe, had bought land and homesteaded in 1818. Cleveland's father, George Waldo Abbe, was born in Ashford, Connecticut, on October 20, 1811, the second child of Moses Cleveland Abbe and Talitha Waldo Abbe.

George moved to New York City around age fourteen to work for his cousin, Giles Taintor, a dry goods wholesaler in Manhattan.[16] By 1835, George struck out on his own and eventually formed a dry goods business with partners Austin F. Williams and John D. Camp, operating under the name Williams, Camp & Abbe. George's partner Williams, a prominent abolitionist who served as a conductor on the Underground Railroad, would later play a role in the repatriation of several dozen African slaves who revolted aboard their slave ship, *Amistad*, off the coast of Cuba in 1839.[17]

George was prominent in the Baptist Church, serving as a deacon at the Madison Avenue Baptist Church, and cofounded the American Bible Union. He was also active in a number of charitable organizations, including the New York Association for Improving the Condition of the Poor, where he served as an officer for four decades. He was a manager of the Hospital for the Ruptured and Crippled (now the Hospital for Special Surgery) and served as a governor of New York Hospital (now New York-Presbyterian Hospital). Despite being a staunch abolitionist, he was unable to serve during the Civil War, due to an ankle injury.[18]

Charlotte Colgate Abbe, Cleveland's mother, was born in New York City on March 23, 1817. Her father, Bowles Colgate, was a cofounder, along with his brother William, of the Colgate Soap Company (which would eventually become Colgate-Palmolive Company), originally located at number 6 on the narrow, one-block lane known as Dutch Street.[19]

Both of Cleveland's parents were deeply religious and instilled in him a devotion that would not only inform his character but remain with him his entire life. In fact, his parents had intended that Cleveland pursue a life of ministry—that is, until science and his own curiosity for the world around him intervened.[20] "The vivid interest in chemistry, comparative philology, history, archaeology and theology, that I had inherited remained (and still remains)," he said, "but the conviction that I ought to become a preacher of the gospel gave way to the ~~more~~ very reasonable conclusion that [a] layman could also do good in the world and that the physical sciences, astronomy, meteorology, chemistry and optics gradually took precedence in my thoughts."[21]

Nevertheless, Sundays growing up in the Abbe household were reserved for worship. "In those days a strong religious interest pervaded New York and the atmosphere of the city was from all accounts purer than now a days," Cleveland recalled half a century later. "The picture of our opposite neighbor Mr. Barnes, with his large family, remains deeply impressed on my memory because of the regularity with which every Sunday morning they were to be seen as a body starting for their Sunday School." Abbe's family, by his own account, presented a similar model of punctuality and piousness. "As for ourselves, we made up an equally large family party and with almost equal promptness and regularity set out weekly for the Tabernacle Baptist Sunday School, half a mile distant in Mulberry Street," he said, noting "how well I remember the impressions made upon me by the open shops of the Jews as I walked past them those Sunday mornings and wondered as to whether it ever could have been right to disobey the Fourth Commandment in order to keep the first day of the week holy."

Their devout adherence to the Sabbath did not preclude the Abbes from the occasional Sunday stroll down the streets of Lower Manhattan. "In those days there was some question as to the propriety of taking a pleasant quiet walk Sunday afternoon as contrasted with the duty of church going or other form of religious service," Cleveland would later recall. "Fortunately our father often decided in our favor as little children, so that I remember many a pleasant Sunday afternoon walk with brothers and cousins down Broadway past Bowling Green to the Battery." Those walks left an indelible impression on the young boy's mind. "The Battery itself with its sailors and emigrants from every land, its green grass and salt ocean breezes, the Bay with its white sailed ships going and coming, the glimpse of the ocean beyond the Narrows," he recalled, "all made a little world that awakened lifelong yearnings to see more of the great world beyond."[22]

The world Cleveland saw during his childhood years, however, was marred by the fact that he was severely nearsighted—something neither he nor his parents nor teachers would discover until his teenage years. "When mother had taken me on her lap singing 'Twinkle, twinkle little star,' I had looked up at the sky and wondered but saw nothing," he later lamented. Aware that something was not right, but unable to pinpoint the cause during those early years, young Cleveland did his best to fit in and make sense of the world around him. "When my great-aunts and grandmother had gazed with awe at the blaring comet of 1843 I had listened to their tales and wondered why I could not see it more clearly," he said. "Probably I did see some faint blur for I remember saying 'yes,' though what I saw did not at all correspond with their descriptions." This led to "a habit that afterward troubled me greatly," he admitted, "that of saying 'Yes I see,' when I did not half comprehend what my teachers were explaining to me." The effect of his poor eyesight was felt not only in the classroom but in the forms of recreation that satisfied Cleveland, who, by his own admission, "took little comfort in flying kites, shooting marbles, playing ball, hunting or fishing or anything that required distinct vision at long distances."[23]

On May 1, 1847, George moved his growing family uptown to a more spacious townhouse at number 37 (which later changed to number 32) East 20th Street. At that time, all New Yorkers looking to change residences moved on the same day of the year, May 1, known simply as "Moving Day."[24] The Abbes' new home was just two houses down the street from the five-story townhouse Cornelius Van Schaack Roosevelt purchased in 1850 as a wedding present for his son and daughter-in-law, Theodore Roosevelt Sr. and Martha Bulloch. The Roosevelts would raise four children at their home on East 20th Street, including their youngest son, Theodore Jr., who was born in the house in 1858—when Cleveland was nearly twenty years old—and who would go on to become the twenty-sixth president of the United States.[25] It was through the eldest Roosevelt child, Anna, or "Bamie" as she was known, that the younger Abbe children "ventured to climb up a rear two-story wooden porch to interview a monkey,"[26] which was kept for the Roosevelt children by their aunt Lizzie, who lived next door. The monkey, "Topsy," had a nasty habit of biting whomever came too near it and Bamie Roosevelt became one of its victims.[27] Another neighbor, Peter Goelet, kept a collection of animals that included several kinds of birds—pigeons, jackdaws, peacocks—as well as "a jackass which brayed and heehawed at regular intervals." The jackdaws, in particular, were known as the source of mischief throughout the neighborhood. One day when Cleveland was in his twenties, one of the mischievous birds entered the window of Cleveland's bedroom and absconded with several sheets of paper from his table, which contained mathematical and astronomical computations "of incalculable value," according to Cleveland's younger brother Robert. "We were at breakfast, and all noticed white papers fluttering out of a large ailanthus tree that grew in our backyard," Robert recalled. "Cleve jumped from the table and rushed upstairs to find the jackdaw had flown in at the open window and taken quantities of those loose sheets from Cleve's table and flown with them to the tree to see them scatter."[28]

Cleveland was born at a time when America was coming of age politically. The concept of political parties was beginning to take hold and the first national political conventions had recently taken place. The Jacksonian Democracy that dominated the 1830s brought with it an increase in voting rights—at least among white males who were not property owners—a strengthening of the executive branch of the federal government, and the promise of Westward Expansion that would eventually lead to Manifest Destiny. The midterm elections of 1838 saw a modest increase in the number of Whig members of Congress to challenge Democrat Martin Van Buren's policies, especially when it came to the economy, following the Panic of 1837.

The year of Cleveland's birth, 1838, also saw the launching of the Wilkes Expedition, a nearly four-year-long scientific voyage led by the U.S. government to explore the Pacific Ocean and surrounding lands. In addition to collecting valuable scientific information, the expedition brought back numerous specimens that contributed to the early collection of the Smithsonian Institution. Also that year, exactly two months before Cleveland was born, twenty-year-old Frederick Douglass escaped from the bondage in which he was held as a slave in Maryland, beginning a new life as a free man, dedicated to civil rights and social reform.

During much of Cleveland's childhood, New York City remained largely undeveloped outside of lower Manhattan. "At that time open squares and green grass greeted us everywhere," he recalled of his new environs. "Dr. Hawks Church[29] at 21st Street had just been opened; the Harlem R.R. Depot was at 28th Street; the telegraph, gas and water were novelties or modern improvements." Robert, who was born April 13, 1851, recalled the warm, amiable atmosphere of the Abbe home on East 20th Street, which became a focal point for social gatherings. "Father's home seemed to attract every sort of worthwhile person, especially clergymen and editors. It seems to me as though the mohair sofa was always occupied on Sunday. They always seemed to relish our big roast beef dinners."[30] Robert also recalled time spent at the home of their maternal grandmother, Lourina Townsend Colgate, who lived nearby on East 16th Street. "Like all large families we small children were sent away to stay at grandmother Colgate's, 137 East 16th Street, when some had contagious diseases or when a new baby came," he said. "Well I remember the delight of these new experiences. We slept in grandmother's room where a big four poster bed had a trundle bed under it which disappeared in the daytime and was trundled out at night."[31]

The Abbes were a close-knit family who remained close even when apart through frequent correspondence, the subject of which often included the children. In a letter dated March 18, 1840, George's mother, Talitha, wrote asking her son and daughter-in-law to "write & tell us how Cleveland is whether he finds any thing to do." Writing to her husband at his work address in the city several months later—on August 22—Charlotte described life with relatives in the country and provided updates on Cleveland, who was just over twenty months old at the time:[32]

Mr. George W. Abbe
No. 6 Cedar St.
N. York

Windham — Aug. 22nd 1840 —

My dear husband,

I have received two welcome letters from you since I last wrote to you, in which you said you expected me at home to day. You know my dear George I told you when you left, I should be at home three weeks from that day. — But the girls have pursuaded me to wait till after the wedding which is the second Tuesday in September. & then Eliza will be ready to come on Wednesday home with me. I am very sorry to have you left alone for two weeks to come yet, but my dear George, you know the meeting will be sweeter & you will prize me the more (perhaps) when you get me back again, not that I would insinuate that you did not prize me enough before. Cleve has gone out riding on horseback with Andrew[33]. He has been out riding every pleasant day since we have been here, for you know I am still staying with Eliza — Henry[34] & Andrew have tried their best to entertain me. & I have been delighted with my visit. They take Cleve up and walk off with him & play with [him?] almost equal to his father & save me a wonderful sight of trouble. Cleve grows as fat & brown: every ride he takes he looks better after it. The doctor only called that once & the blue pill had the desired effect. — I never saw a child so crazy after the horse & horsewhip & wagon as he is. We went yesterday to Chaplin to see the paper mill. — The day before we went to N Boston & saw the cotton mill, then round to Aunt Binghams & spent the day. — The day before we called on Giles[35] & his wife & aunt Taintor & aunt Charlotte. The day before that we had uncle Levi & his wife here to dinner, & in the afternoon took them down to your mothers to a tea party, & we have kept up visiting in this style since you left, & are likely to, till I go — Eliza says I shall only have time to go the rounds — aunt Charlotte is going to send [?] next week, & we are going to ride down to uncle Lack's one day — Mary says I must certainly go over there and spend a week, & Andrew & mother both say I have not finished their visit yet, so you see my dear George I am at the mercy of the community. Every time we meet we wish you were here with us, you know I wish you were here oftener then that, but your friends all regret they cannot see more of you — I am afraid Cleve will get the whooping cough, for I think Eliza has it. But if he does we must be patient. His tooth is through & he is a good boy. If he does not get sick I shall bring him home good and fat. — Tell Abby I received her letter, & was glad enough to hear the news, & shall answer it soon — have all the family got home. I hope so, & you must visit them often & my dear husband will not be so lonely. I am sorry to have you alone, but two weeks will soon go now. — You said I should probably not hear from you again. Dont pray let it be so — for it is one great thing that keeps me from being homesick, receiving your letters. Do write to me often while I stay. — I told ma that you thought Grosvenor had better wait another year — She was very willing. But it will be a damper to Grosvenor, for he overheard his mother & father talking the matter over, & he was on his high heeled shoes at the idea, & he told some one that he hoped you would send for him before he got through ploughing. — I have not seen him since. — Your mother is rather better than she was, as also Eliza & the rest of the invalids. Give my love to all, & do go out visiting & dispel all melancholy if such should be the case. & I will come back & cheer you up one of these days; it has been exceedingly warm here this last week, so that I thought it would not be *exhilierating* in N. York, as it was when you wrote to me. Do take care of yourself & dont get sick. If anything should happen write me immediately, & I can be ready in two hours to start for home. — Cleve has just got back from his ride & *says he has had a good one*, that is by looks — I must leave off & take care of him — Do write to me — Dont think I am too engaged to care nothing about it for you must know to the contrary. Keep up your spirits & think often of your affectionate wife

CHARLOTTE —

As Cleveland's granddaughter Elfriede Abbe wrote, "the spirit of the family, as reflected in the letters, was one of cheerful freedom and even of exuberance on the part of the children."[36]

In addition to Cleveland and Robert, George and Charlotte had five other children, three sons—Walter (born June 20, 1841), William (born June 9, 1843), and Charles (born February 12, 1849)—as well as two daughters—Helen (born June 15, 1853) and Harriet (born July 17, 1855). Together with their children, George and Charlotte were "at the center of the beginnings of great commercial enterprises in a great city, the rise of unprecedented affluence in America, and the philanthropic extensions of that wealth toward educational, charitable, and religious goals," as their great-granddaughter (and Cleveland's granddaughter) Elfriede would describe years later, adding, "and their sons fulfilled the intellectual promise and vigorous forward-looking spirit in their professional lives."[37]

Early Education

From 1845 until 1850, Cleveland attended The Misses Pine's Preparatory School, located on 19th Street, near Union Square. It was a private school run by Charlotte Pine, along with her sister, Elizabeth, and Maria and Lydia Colgate—all relations of young Cleveland.[38] In October 1850, he entered public school at Ward School No. 25, located on East 20th Street, between First and Second Avenues, just a few blocks from the Abbe home. A brand-new school in 1850, the county superintendent of common schools for New York City described it as a "large and commodious school house."[39] The school's principal, David B. Scott, would make a name for himself with his 1852 textbook, *A Manual of History of the United States*. Abbe would remember Scott, however, for the influence he had on him and his ultimate choice of career. "There, under the energetic tuition of that prince of teachers David B. Scott, the first and only rap on his knuckles from Scott's lively rattan aroused him," Cleveland said, referring to himself in the third person. "The first experiments by Scott in electricity and the thunder storms turned him towards meteorology." Cleveland would go on to say, "The United States Weather Bureau had a beginning at Ward School No. 25."[40]

Young Cleveland's formal education was supplemented at home by books on a variety of subjects. One book, *The Telescope and Microscope*, was written by Thomas Dick, a Scottish minister, teacher, and science writer whose works sought to create a "God-centered account of nature within an evangelical and devotional framework."[41] The book's opening passage holds true to that principle:

> God has been pleased, in various ages, to guide men to those discoveries which have enlarged their views of his perfections, and increased their knowledge and happiness. Among these discoveries may be placed the construction and the uses of the telescope.

The balance between religion and science would be a constant force in Cleveland's life, driving him toward a career that simultaneously—and equally—hinged upon an understanding of the physical world (and universe) and service to his fellow man. "His appreciation of the infinite care that controls this immense universe was deeply imbedded in his mind as a small boy," his son Truman wrote. "The proper use of these devices for the benefit of mankind was almost his religion, at least, the goal for which he must strive."[42] As Cleveland put it, "It was perfectly possible for me to study the Holy Scriptures at one time reverently hoping to get clearer views of my own personal duty or to achieve a more intimate spiritual sympathy and unity between myself and Jesus—but at another time to study the Scriptures critically hoping to deduce from them some fragments of truth relative to the history and development of the human race and its gradual emancipation from the thraldom of superstition, ignorance and priestcraft." Cleveland's incessant quest for knowledge—and the truth—about nature and the world in which he lived created an epistemological mind-set, informing not only how he viewed the world but how he interacted with it. Early examples of his attempts to understand and unravel the mysteries he encountered indicate a multidisciplinary approach that he would continue to embrace throughout his life:

> With my growing love for nature, there developed an equally absorbing interest in history, especially of the ancient time, in archaeology, theology and hieroglyphic inscriptions, all of which may perhaps be philosophically explained as due to a great development of wonder and veneration; certain it is, however, that days and weeks were spent copying and poring over the hieroglyphic inscriptions in Abbott's Museum of Egyptian Antiquities.[43] Vivid dreams about the Mound Builders led me to dig for supposed remains in various spots in the country. There was a perpetual study going on in my thoughts as to the origin of nations and languages, as to Assyrian remains, as to the reconciliation of the Bible and geology, and many other questions that will vex the world of scholars, and on which in my own boyish way I was seeking more light, conscious only of the on determination to attain a result if possible without being too much affected by the hypotheses or the theories of ignorance; desirous always of drawing a clear line between what we know or may reasonably assume as certain and what we do not know.[44]

Just before his eighth birthday, Cleveland's mother presented him with a copy of *Praise and Principle*, a book by Maria J. McIntosh, first published in 1845.[45] It tells the contrasting stories of two school companions who, based on their respective values, pursue much different lives. Protagonist Frank

Derwent, through "a steadfast adherence to truth and principle," finds success as a lawyer and "wins an honourable name and a happy home." Meanwhile his competitor, Charles Ellersby, seeks "the praise that Frank discards for the love of the dearer right" and, as a result, "receives, as bitter punishment, that curse of manhood, a fashionable wife, and in a year is ruined."[46]

Cleveland's most treasured book, however, was *The Philosophy of Natural History*, by William Smellie, presented to him by his mother when he was eight.[47] First published in 1790, it became a popular text on the subject, with revisions published well after Smellie's death in 1795. The 1846 edition includes chapters on "the Nature of Living Bodies and the Distinction between Animals and Vegetables"; the habitations, hostilities, society, and docility of animals; and "the progressive Scale or Chain of Beginnings in the Universe." The chapter titled "Of the Transformations of Animals," however, is perhaps most noteworthy, as it discussed the theory of evolution long before Charles Darwin published his seminal work, *On the Origin of Species*. As Smellie states, "In the animal world, every successive change is a new approach to the perfection of the individuals." Cleveland would refer to this small volume again and again over the years as he developed his own understanding of the world around him. "Often now as I peruse its pages, I wonder how at that tender age I could possibly have drawn any instruction from such a mature work, or what my mother thought me made of that she should have put it into my hands," he pondered, "but certain it is that every where through its solid sentences I found food for thought and when at thirty I found myself agreeing with ~~Darwin and Huxley~~ the evolutionists, it seemed simply because I had always thought that way."[48] Cleveland treasured his copy of Smellie's book so much, it was laid to rest with him upon his death, tucked neatly in his hands as if to provide him with both a sense of comfort and wisdom in the hereafter.[49]

Young Cleveland's scientific curiosity grew immensely when, at age twelve or thirteen, he received a compound microscope as a birthday present. "Probably my greatest pleasure in the way of personal and accurate observation was found in the use of [that] compound microscope," he would later recall, noting how he "spent many hours dissecting vegetable and animal tissues." His greatest fascination, however, came from the optical properties of the microscope's lenses themselves. Equipped with several references—including Dick's treatise on telescopes and microscopes—and his own desire to learn more, he began "reading whatever was accessible bearing on the properties of lenses. The result was of course a desire to have a still more powerful instrument, and after viewing with longing eyes in immensely expensive microscopes displayed in the window of Benjamin Pike, the Optician, I made up my mind that the only hope for me would be to make one as best I could myself."[50]

Summers growing up were spent outside the city, on his grandfather's farm, Dog Hill, in Windham County, Connecticut. Cleveland described his summers there as "the halcyon days of youth" and recalled lessons learned during the summer of 1849, when he spent time at a factory that manufactured wooden type used in printing presses. The wooden type served not only as convenient playthings for young Cleveland but also gave him an opportunity to practice spelling. Two years later, during the summer of 1851, when he was twelve years old, Cleveland attended classes at Pine Hill Seminary in South Windham, run by Dr. Jabez C. Fitch, a devout Baptist who had abandoned medicine to pursue teaching.[51] Cleveland would later describe Fitch as a "driving school master," noting that his grandfather "did sometimes resent Doctor Fitch's methods of punishment." Nevertheless, Cleveland recalled the experience as a pleasant one, noting that Fitch "is still held in reverence by those who passed under his tuition, those who have now for many years lived happy married lives, wiser and better than they would have been without his influence. Since those days I have passed under many teachers, and learned many lessons, but none more important than those picked up during happy summer days in Windham."[52]

Summers at Dog Hill also provided Cleveland with an opportunity to develop his first passion in science, astronomy. It was there, in the summer of 1853, that Cleveland found himself with his cousin in the machine shop of his cousin's father, in South Windham, constructing first a microscope and then a telescope. "The telescope was his hobby I believe," Cleveland said, "but I am sure I wanted one as bad as he, and so we helped each other as best we could." The process involved making their own castings, grinding and polishing mirrors, and polishing the reflecting surface, which, as it turned out, "was not sufficient to really repay us for all our work." This ultimately led Cleveland to proclaim, "I do not think that I should recommend a boy who has the money where with to buy a good instrument, to spend his time making a poor one." When he returned to New York that fall, Cleveland tried using his new homemade telescope to observe the heavens above the sprawling city, but after several futile attempts he abandoned the subpar instrument. He was fortunate, instead, to be able to borrow a much better specimen—"an excellent four-inch Cassegrainian reflector of London workmanship"—from a local college professor. This telescope, which he mounted on the roof of his family's home on East 20th Street, did him "a good service until the following spring." As his son Truman later wrote, "This was his first recorded experiment in meteorology and astronomy"[53] and ultimately led Cleveland to the conclusion that "[w]hether one makes his own instrument or whether he buys a better one matters little, if only, having got one he will overcome the further difficulties and obstacles and persevere till he educates himself into becoming a good observer and successful investigator."[54]

Taking this idea a step further—and perhaps postulating on the theoretical problems in meteorology with which he and others would ultimately grapple—Cleveland proclaimed, "The object that we aim at in science lies beyond the mere observing and measuring; that is simply the process of collecting the data preparatory to the next important step which is to get at the laws behind the data."

At the Free Academy

In 1851, Cleveland entered the Free Academy of New York (now City College of New York), where he would continue his education until his graduation in 1857. As he put it, "I entered in 1851 with Able, Baker, etc., but chose to take the 1853 year over again, to my great advantage as a student."[55] One of his classmates described him as "a young man who was interested in his work, and anxious to learn. As he went through college his ability in mathematical and mathematico-physical science became more and more apparent, and, at the close of the college course, there could be no question of his superiority."[56]

Established in 1847 in an effort to make advanced education accessible to New York's growing middle class, the Free Academy became the first institution of higher education in the country to offer tuition-free instruction to its students. Thus, it offered a viable alternative to the city's two existing postsecondary schools at the time, the University of the City of New York (now New York University) and the elite Columbia College (now Columbia University). In comparison to its rivals, the Free Academy "was unique in that it did not charge tuition while offering a curriculum that was not only strong in practical subjects but also provided an opportunity to study classical languages and literature."[57]

Cleveland exemplified this ideal program of study. In his final year alone, he pursued studies in religion, physics, ancient languages, civil engineering, typographical drawing and field exercises, oratory, original English composition, French (including pronunciation, grammar, and regular and irregular verbs), and chemistry. By his own admission, mathematics and science were among his favorite subjects, and his performance earned him medals in each. When not attending to his studies, Cleveland competed on the academy's debate team, the Phrenocosmia, and honed his skills in public speaking, which would assist him later in life, despite his inherent modesty.

While at the Free Academy, Cleveland applied himself to his studies but also affirmed his commitment to religious doctrine by formally joining the Baptist Church in January 1853 and attending regular student prayer meetings, which several upperclassmen led Friday afternoons. "Undoubtedly every tendency of my nature both by inheritance and education led me to admire his teachings and his life who said 'Be ye perfect as I am perfect,'" he would later write. "Nothing would have shocked me more than to feel that the study of nature could in any way lessen my admiration and love of Him." Cleveland believed religion was "an active power for good" and described it as a necessity both of everyday life "and of the ideal fully developed man."

Writing to his mother a dozen years later, Cleveland recalled with satisfaction the experience of repeating his first year at the academy and how it informed the sense of duty that came with his newly embraced religious faith:

> I shall never forget the summer of 1853. It was in the preceding winter that I had been baptized. At the end of the academy examinations Dr. Webster very kindly showed me that for two years I had not been doing my duty and that I must try to do better. All through the vacation I trembled with fear lest I might find myself dismissed for poor scholarship. My conscience was upbraiding me all the time and I could hardly believe my ears when I found that I had only got to go over the past year again with the new Freshman class. As the students would not be entirely new to me this gave me an advantage and I began to study having really only two desires: to do well for the sake of my parents and for the sake of my Christian influence.[58]

In September 1853, Cleveland obtained his first pair of eyeglasses, at the age of fourteen. For the first time, he could see the world around him clearly and in focus. "Not until he was a student at the Free Academy did he fully realize the extent to which his nearsightedness had prevented him from seeing much of the blackboard work in grammar school, and had kept him from playing baseball and even seeing the stars," his son Truman would later write. "He often said that he had never seen a star until after he had entered the Free Academy." Cleveland himself recalled the incident that finally led to his realization that the world he had seen up until that point was—much like the shadowy figures described by Plato in his Allegory of the Cave—only a blurry reflection of reality. "Strange to say I was nearly fifteen years old before it occurred to me one day that mine were near sighted eyes; this happened on the occasion of the appearance of the comet discovered by Klinkerfues[59] and visible to the naked eye for a few days in August and Sept. 1853." While on summer vacation at his relatives' farm near Windham, Cleveland became frustrated that others were able to see the comet clearly, while he could not. "I took my grandmother's spectacles to see if they would help me," he said. "I found they made matters worse and in an instant I recognized the fact that a concave glass would have helped me and that I was nearsighted."[60] Upon his return to the city that fall, he paid a visit to Benjamin Pike, "the well-known optician, then on Broadway near John Street," and was fitted for his first pair of glasses. The clarity of the world that opened up around him both enthralled and amazed him. "I walked down to the Battery with a heart too full for utterance," he said of the experience. "The most distant objects were sharply defined, the faces of people and their very eyes, the names of the streets, the birds in the air were for the first time clearly seen, and the Battery on that bright sunny day with the Bay and the Narrows beyond, seemed little short of heaven." As Truman further explained, "Thus, until that time Father had spent a very quiet and serious boyhood, his activities conditioned by a strong religious influence, and his play limited by his myopia."[61] With his new outlook on the world around him came a renewed interest in astronomy. "I think my interest in the stars had been waning a little because I could not see them," he would explain, "and because objects near at hand had made themselves so attractive through the microscope, but now that I could see the celestial bodies, they resumed their intense interest for me."

On July 21, 1857, Cleveland graduated from the Free Academy with a Bachelor of Arts degree, one of twenty-one students in his class. He had already identified astronomy as the subject of professional interest he wished to pursue, much to the discouragement of his father, who told him, "Gazing at the moon and the stars might be a pleasant recreation on a moonlight summer's night, but is scarcely preparatory for the support of a wife and family."[62] Nevertheless, upon graduation, Cleveland's father presented him with a gold pocket watch, with sailing ships beautifully engraved on the back of it. Inside the case, Cleveland's name was engraved, but somehow misspelled as "Cleaveland."[63]

As quoted in a biographical sketch of Cleveland that appeared in *The Popular Science Monthly* in January 1888, one of his classmates at the Free Academy summarized his character and aptitude by stating, "Everybody liked Cleveland Abbe thirty years ago, as I suppose everybody likes him now. He was unselfish, modest, kindly then, and, in disposition, though only twenty years old, a scientific man, a lover of scientific truth."[64]

Meteorology in Mid-Nineteenth Century America

While it would be decades before Cleveland would fully realize his calling as a meteorologist, the nascent field held his interest from an early age, as evidenced by an account written at the end of his life and read before members of the National Academy of Sciences:

> My boyhood life in New York City had impressed me with the popular ignorance and also with the great need of something better than local lore and weather proverbs. The knowledge of the sailors and farmers whom I met seemed to me unsatisfactory. The popular articles in the New York daily papers, by Merriam, Espy, Joseph Henry, and others—notably Redfield and Loomis—had by 1857 convinced me that man should and must overcome our ignorance of the destructive winds and rains.[65]

Meteorology was beginning to emerge as a scientific field—both in theoretical and practical terms—around the time Cleveland was born. Observations and studies conducted up to that time focused mainly on climatological or other aspects, with little attempt for serious, systematic collection of weather observations for the purposes of predicting the weather. While there was a tradition among weather-savvy citizen scientists—including several Founding Fathers, such as George Washington, Thomas Jefferson, and Benjamin Franklin—to keep weather diaries and journals, systematic observations of weather conditions on a national level did not begin until 1814, when the U.S. Surgeon General James Tilton directed Army surgeons stationed at forts around the country to take regular measurements of weather conditions.[66] Other observational networks were established in the following decades, with varying lengths of record and station densities. In 1848, the newly established Smithsonian Institution, under the direction of Joseph Henry, appropriated a sum of $1,000 for the establishment of a network of 150 volunteer observers, who began reporting conditions from posts around the country the following year. A decade later, under Henry's direction, the Smithsonian network had expanded to more than 600 observers, at various locations including Canada, Mexico, Latin America, and the Caribbean. Henry even went so far as to take the observations and plot them on a large map of the United States he displayed in the central hall of the institution's castle-like building in Washington, D.C. Henry once remarked that visitors from out of town "all appear to be specially interested in knowing the condition of weather to which their friends at home are subjected at the time."[67]

On the theoretical front, this was, as mathematician Maxime Bôcher noted in 1888, "a formative period during which the scientific world was divided between the most opposite theories, a period characterized, in this science, by the use of no mathematics higher than arithmetic."[68] Two notable figures emerged by the mid-1830s to put forth explanations for the structure and nature of storms—each with differing viewpoints that would pit the rivals against each other in a decades-long dispute known as "The Storm Controversy."[69]

One of the rivals was William Redfield, a New Yorker who managed a line of boats on the Hudson River for the Steam Navigation Company. Redfield devoted his spare time, however, to his passion of meteorology, especially in relation to the direction of winds in cyclonic storms. In 1821, he observed the damage caused by a hurricane that struck Connecticut, noting the circular pattern of trees scattered by the storm. A decade later, he summarized his findings in an article in the *American Journal of Science and Arts*, stating, "This storm was exhibited in the form of a great whirlwind."[70] Redfield argued, based on his own observations and eyewitness accounts he collected over the years, that winds blew in a circular, counterclockwise motion around the center of a storm. While he generally remained out of the spotlight, seldom giving public lectures or presenting papers at scientific meetings, Redfield devoted the rest of his life to the study of hurricanes and was active in scientific organizations, becoming the first president of the American Association for the Advancement of Science in 1848.

Redfield did have his opponents in the storm theory arena. Chief among them was James Pollard Espy, who in 1817 moved to Philadelphia, where he became an instructor of classical literature and mathematics, eventually joining the faculty of the Franklin Institute after its founding in 1824. Around this time, he became interested in atmospheric phenomena, which led to his 1834 appointment as chairman of the Joint Committee on Meteorology of the American Philosophical Society and the Franklin Institute. Among other contributions, Espy formulated a theory for the structure and formation of storms. After studying the work of John Dalton on the evaporation and condensation of water vapor in the air, Espy became convinced that this was the key to understanding the storms—the "lever with which the meteorologist was to move the world," as he said in the preface of his seminal work, *Philosophy of Storms*, published in 1841.[71]

Unlike Redfield, Espy theorized that air, warmed by the heat of convection, moved vertically up the center of a storm like the air in a chimney, stoked by the heat of a fire. Espy referred to his theory as the "centripetal motion" of storms and began popularizing it through publications and lectures. He eventually caught the attention of the secretary of war, who in 1842 appointed Espy to become the first official meteorologist in the United States, charged with collecting reports from volunteer weather observers—known as "meteorological correspondents"—around the country and preparing maps and reports based on them. Espy continued this work under the direction of the secretary of the Navy, who also directed Espy to assist Henry with his burgeoning meteorological work at the Smithsonian Institution.

Espy first publicly criticized Redfield's work in 1834, in a note that appeared in the *Journal of the Franklin Institute*. Under the heading "Notes of an Observer—Meteorology," Espy wrote:

> In the American Journal of Science and Arts for October, 1833, there are two well written articles, by Mr. Redfield, on Meteorology. They contain a most laborious collection of facts, which, if well authenticated, will be of immense importance to meteorological science. Some of them, however, are so anomalous and inconsistant [sic] with received theories, that I hesitate to put entire confidence in them, and shall continue to doubt until I have the most certain evidence of the facts.

Throughout the 1840s, Espy and Redfield would challenge, if not outright attack, each other's theories on the structure of cyclonic storms. In 1839, for example, the *Journal of the Franklin Institute* published a rebuttal of Espy's work by Redfield, under the heading "Remarks on Mr. Espy's Theory of Centripetal Storms, including a Refutation of his Positions Relative to the Storm of September 3rd, 1821: with some Notice of the Fallacies which appear in his Examinations of other Storms." The dispute continued until 1853, when Espy and Redfield essentially "agreed to disagree," as Professor Alexander D. Bache, superintendent of the Coast Survey (and great-grandson of Benjamin Franklin), declared at a meeting of the American Association for the Advancement of Science in Cleveland, Ohio. Bache noted that "facts alone [are] to be established; whether they are consistent with theories is another thing."[72] In reflecting on the impression made when he first encountered these two pioneers, Cleveland noted, "I first studied Espy and Redfield [and] I quickly recognized how true to nature were those earlier leaders in meteorology."[73]

Other notable leaders in the field of meteorology at the time included Elias Loomis, who, after surveying the damage left by two tornadoes in 1842, found evidence that indicated both Espy and Redfield were partially correct in their theories. The winds whirling around cyclonic storms did so in a counterclockwise manner but spiraling inward toward the center of the storm. Loomis theorized that Earth's rotation caused this inward, counterclockwise spiral.

Meanwhile, William Ferrel further contributed to the burgeoning field by applying mathematical formulae to the study of winds, paving the way for meteorology to establish itself as a serious scientific subject. It was Ferrel's seminal paper, "The Motions of Fluids and Solids, Relative to the Earth's Surface," appearing in the journal *Mathematical Monthly* in 1858, that captured Cleveland's attention. "I realized that he had overcome many of the hidden difficulties of the theories of storms and winds," Cleveland recalled years later. "From that day on he was my guide and authority."[74]

Michigan Bound

In March 1857, resolute in his conviction that his future lay in the pursuit of astronomy, Cleveland "wrote to every astronomer in the country, inquiring about courses of study and work, and was told that he must study astronomy in Ann Arbor if he could not go to European universities."[75] Although he considered the response to be "not a very encouraging one," Cleveland took solace in the fact that "the letters of so many eminent and good men gave me a realizing sense of the fact that the astronomers were human beings like myself and not genii or mysterious pundits."[76]

The encouragement—and opportunity—Cleveland sought arrived with a handwritten letter from Dr. Franz Brünnow, a German astronomer who came to America in 1854, at the recruitment of University of Michigan President Henry Tappen, to lead the university's new observatory.[77]

> Ann Arbor Dec 31st 1856
>
> Dear Sir,
>
> It is not in my power to appoint any Assistant for the observatory at present, but it is the intention of the Regents, to appoint several, which shall be selected from the most talented of our students. I shall be very happy, to see you here and I should advise you, to come the 1st of October and to attend the astronomical lectures in this University, which embrace a course of four

years. You will make thus a thorough Astronomer of yourselves. From the 1st of October I can employ you also at the observatory, you will have an opportunity to work observations and calculations and if you do well I can give you a recommendation for your services. The lectures in the University are free, though I think you have to pay an entrance fee of 10 dollars.

Respectfully
Yours
Dr. Brünnow

The letter must have come as a welcome relief to Cleveland, whose admiration for the esteemed professor persisted well beyond the years he spent under his instruction. Brünnow's "arrival and the opening of his course of lectures on the higher practical astronomy form a brilliant epoch in the history of that science in this country," Cleveland wrote in 1903, adding that "Ann Arbor was *the* place to study astronomy" at the time.[78] "Dr. Brünnow was one of the small number of men, who at that early time gave the University its high character for scientific instruction," proclaimed a history of the university's observatory, published in 1912.[79] "On his arrival he immediately planned advanced courses in Theoretical and Practical Astronomy, extending over two and a half years, in continuation of the elementary course which was then required of all students in the first semester of the Junior year."

Cleveland's academic pilgrimage to Ann Arbor, however, would have to wait until he secured sufficient funds to support the endeavor. Upon his graduation from the Free Academy, he spent a year as a tutor of mathematics at Trinity School, which dates to 1709 and today is considered one of the top elite prep schools in New York City. He taught in the "grammar school" section, which consisted of fifth through eighth grades, with a curriculum that may have resembled the following:

> In the grammar school, fifth graders in arithmetic took on decimal fractions, greatest common divisors, and least common multiples. Rapid oral drill was the favored teaching technique. Then came more decimals, and work with weights and measures. Seventh graders learned about the metric system, compound numbers, and percentages.[80]

This was during the days of the Great Panic of 1857, a financial downturn that affected the United States for several years and from which the country would not fully recover until after the Civil War. Money was tight for many families in New York, including the Abbes, whose patriarch, George, was forced out of business. George and his partners "settled honorably with their creditors and later paid all claims in full, but thereafter he was engaged as a commission merchant and broker for the remainder of his life."[81] In a letter dated October 19, 1857, Charlotte Abbe wrote to her husband, "We are trying to be as economical as possible, these awful hard times," she said, "but I trust you will not allow money pressures to weigh on your mind at all heavy, for you have many blessings left, more than we deserve, even if all the money goes—our boys can soon take care of themselves & us too if it comes to that . . ."[82]

When he wasn't tutoring at Trinity, Cleveland furthered his own education at home, studying German, mathematics, and astronomy. "Astronomy had taken a very firm hold upon my admiration and in my desire to devote my life to it," he said. He also indulged, despite the economic hardships of the time, in occasional entertainment. In January 1858, he spent four dollars on the opera.[83] That same month, Cleveland invited his mother to go with him to hear the composer and pianist Sigismond Thalberg perform at the Academy of Music, on the corner of 14th Street and Irving Place. "I don't think Cleve was as much pleased as he expected to be with Italian opera music," his mother wrote in a letter to her husband, "but he gets his eyes opened a little with all these things."[84] Cleveland also noted in his account book a visit to see "Hermann—Prestidigitator." This was likely the legendary magician Alexander Herrmann, otherwise known as "Herrmann the Great," who was known for performing his tricks without the aid of elaborate props, relying solely on sleight of hand.

It was also around this time that Cleveland began a practice, which he would continue for the next decade, of donating nearly a third of his income "to church and benevolence." Some of his charitable contributions included nineteen cents to a "colored preacher" in 1858; fifty cents "to a beggar man" in 1859; and two separate donations—of twenty-five and ten dollars—to "Rev. Freeman" in 1860. In 1862 he gave twenty-five cents "to a slave buying his freedom." He would lament decades later, near the end of his life, that inflation and a rising cost of living limited such charitable contributions to one-tenth of what he had previously given. "How the times have changed!" he exclaimed. "Prices and expenses have gone up but I still enjoy my cornmeal pudding as much as ever."[85]

In the fall of 1858, with the money he earned from teaching at Trinity School, Cleveland set off for Ann Arbor. Despite the reputation of the university and Dr. Brünnow, Cleveland found it unusual to have to venture so far from the cosmopolitan and centuries-old academic institutions of New York and New England in order to further his education. "In those days it did seem an anomaly," he later wrote, "that one should go so far west into a state known mostly as the scene of one of the Leather Stocking Tales[86] and imagined to be a pathless forest separating Detroit from Chicago."[87] Instead, what he found was a university full of "charm and history" and Dr. Tappen's theories on the "proper function and development of a University quite carried me away," he said. In Dr. Brünnow he found "an able and promising astronomer, familiar with all the methods of observation, skilled in the computation of the orbits of the heavenly bodies and every way likely to awaken intelligent enthusiasm in the minds of the students."

In addition to his studies under Brünnow, Cleveland worked as an instructor of physics and civil engineering at the University of Michigan, earning a salary of $500.[88] He worked under the direction of Professor Joseph Warren Wood. Cleveland also lived with Wood and his wife, Mary, and their two children. Beginning September 23, 1858, Cleveland paid the Woods $2.50 a week for room and board but was responsible, as he put it, for "finding my own fuel, lights, and washing."[89] According to detailed entries he made in his account book, he paid seventy-five cents for a fluid lamp made of glass, thirty-two cents for a fluid can, and twenty cents for a quart of burning fluid.[90] While he didn't specify what kind of burning fluid he used at the time, later entries during the winter of 1859 and spring of 1860 indicate that he used lard oil. It would not be until October 1860 when he began using kerosene in his lamps, which had begun to overtake lard, whale oil, and other burning fluids as the preferred fuel for lamps.[91] A week later, he paid $1.62 for a load of wood.

In recalling the situation years later, Cleveland said the Woods "formed one of the happiest families of Ann Arbor. He was simple and honest, modest, fearless and a student, as was his admirable wife. The names and lives of both will always be a bright spot in my memory." Cleveland added that he always admired Joseph "for his love of knowledge and his perseverance in getting it."[92]

In the spring and early summer of 1859, Cleveland took a break from his studies at the University of Michigan to pursue other activities. "I believe that in America it is not so much what a man knows as what he can do that determines his career, and marks him as [a] successful or useful man," he wrote, "and thus it very soon happened that my friend Dr. John M. Gregory, then Superintendent of Public Instruction for the state of Michigan, finding that I could talk and teach as well as study, proposed that I take a vacation from the University work and undertake mathematical and other teaching in the State Agricultural College at Lansing, Mich."

On April 6, 1859, the Michigan Board of Education voted "that Mr. Cleveland Abbe be employed as tutor at the Agricultural College to teach civil engineering, etc."[93] It was also here that, as Cleveland put it, "meteorology seemed forced upon my attention" while serving as a meteorological observer for the Smithsonian Institution.[94] "The record kept by me will be found full of minute observations on minor local phenomena," he would later confess.[95]

His activities in Lansing, however, were cut short after just a few months when "a severe attack of malarial fever" struck him. Nevertheless, the time he spent in Lansing forever remained "a most profitable epoch"[96] in his life. Years later, Cleveland received an invitation to attend a ceremony on June 22, 1892, to lay the cornerstone of a new botanical laboratory at the Agricultural College. In sending his regrets for not being able to attend, he said, "I often think with pleasure of the summer that I spent at the Agricultural College," adding as he closed his letter, "With the kindest remembrances to those in Lansing who may still remember me."

In the fall of 1859, following brief visits to New York and the family farm in Windham, Cleveland returned to Ann Arbor as a tutor under Professor Wood in the Department of Scientific Civil Engineering. During his final year in Ann Arbor, he lived at the residence of James Robinson Boise, professor of the Greek language and literature at the University of Michigan, whom Cleveland described as the "happiest acquaintance during that year in Ann Arbor." It was at Boise's residence, on the south side of Ypsilanti Street, that an assistant U.S. marshal named N. B. Nye encountered Cleveland, among other residents, in discharging his duties as part of the eighth decennial U.S. Census, while working his way across Ann Arbor's First Ward. At the time, the responsibility of carrying out the census every ten years fell upon U.S. marshals and their assistants.[97] Under the "Profession, Occupation, or Trade" column of form Schedule 1—Free Inhabitants, Nye wrote "Tutor in Mich. University" next to Cleveland's name, noting a value of personal estate of $500. "His was the very ideal of an intellectual family and himself the model critical scholar," Cleveland said of Boise.[98]

Professor Brünnow's friendship also provided Cleveland with "a great stimulus," according to Truman, "but after a year the professor left Ann Arbor for the Dudley Observatory in Albany. As he had also been able to provide remunerative work for his student admirer, his departure was a double setback." Succumbing to pressure from the astronomical community in Ann

Arbor, the Michigan Board of Regents offered Brünnow a reappointment, at a higher salary of $1,500, beginning October 1, 1860.[99] Cleveland's fate as Brünnow's assistant, however, remained uncertain, as Cleveland learned via a letter from Brünnow he received that summer[100] while staying with his family in New York:

Ann Arbor Aug 9 1860

Cleveland Abbe Esq

Dear Sir

There was a meeting of the Executive Committee of the Regents yesterday, but I found, they had no power to do anything. Nothing will be decided about an Assistant before the meeting of the Board next October and therefore, although I should like it very much to have you here as Assistant, I cannot hold out any promise, as I do not know, what arrangements the Regents are willing to make. I expected to raise a good deal of money in Detroit and thus to make the observatory near independent, but the time is very unfavorable and I shall not succeed before spring. In case the Regents are willing to give me an Assistant, I will recommend you and Mr. Hall[101] of Cambridge. What salary they would be willing to give, I do not know, but I am afraid, it would not be more than $500, which may be too little to support a family.

I was sorry, that you did not come a day sooner to Albany; I intended at first to stay longer, but I wished to pay a visit to Dr. Peters[102] at Clinton before coming here and to attend the commencement at Hamilton College.

Very Truly
Yours,
F. Brünnow

In the end, Brünnow's return to Michigan "prompted a reshuffle of the staff that left no slot for Abbe, and the Regents were forced to terminate his appointment at the end of the academic year."[103] Cleveland's time in Michigan had come to an abrupt end, but he was left with experiences—both personal and professional—that would remain with him the rest of his life. By his own account, however, he was nascent in his professional development, noting years later that at the time of Brünnow's departure from—and subsequent return to—Michigan, he was "absorbed in [his] work and still a boy in all that pertained to the world of men & human nature."[104] Naïve, perhaps, to the politics that could dictate the path of one's career as much as scientific knowledge or acumen, Cleveland acknowledged his ignorance. "I was utterly unconscious of the great tension of feeling then existing among these very elders whose astronomical fame I would emulate," he admitted.[105]

Among other things, Cleveland's sojourn in Michigan also afforded him the opportunity to solidify his formal education in astronomy and add to his academic credentials. On July 17, 1860, the faculty of the Free Academy recommended to the New York City Board of Education that the degree of Master of Arts be conferred upon nearly a dozen students, including Cleveland, who had successfully "given the Faculty evidence that they have prosecuted some branch of learning" during the three years since obtaining their bachelor's degrees. Cleveland's work—and studies—in the three years since obtaining his bachelor's degree in 1857 satisfied the board's conditions, as described in the academy's annual report:

> A Bachelor of Arts, or of Sciences, of three years' standing, may be admitted to the degree of *Master of Arts*, or to that of *Master of Sciences*, provided he show, to the satisfaction of the Faculty, that in the interval he has been engaged in some literary or scientific pursuit, and has sustained a good moral character; application to be made either personally or by letter, at least one month before Commencement, accompanied by an original paper on any subject, and certified under his own hand to be his own composition, written within six months before his application.[106]

Remaining in New York through the summer and early fall, Cleveland devoted himself to his studies while taking time to enjoy such simple pleasures as a giant watermelon, which became a recurring theme in a series of letters, dated August 29, 1860, from Cleveland, his brother Walter, and their father, George, to Charlotte Abbe, who was staying with relatives in Windham.

From George:

> Cleve takes good care of us and gives us a great variety. He gets what he pleases — we had for dinner yesterday chops — sweet and Irish Potatoes, Tomatoes — Corn — Baked apples, stewed Plumbs, Pudding, Water mellon etc — Walter is satisfied with the fare — Sarah[107] dont want any thing wasted & if there is any corn left she puts it on cold for breakfast — several days since we had a water mellon — I told Cleve he had better get a larger one next time as they are best. So last Saturday he bought the largest one I think

> I ever saw, it would not go in the refrigerator, so he stood it on end & as the cover would not shut down I rather think Sarah brought her weight to bear on it, it had to come of course & burst open on both ends, it was a good one. We had it Sunday & ever since & may last till you get home.

From Walter:

> We are revelling in a decayed watermelon that Cleve bought Saturday & which we wish to save.

And from Cleveland:

> I have been very well notwithstanding that during the past three or four days we three unaided and alone have devoured demolished and caused to disappear one of the most hugest of watermelons measuring two feet from the big end to the little end and two feet one inch from the little end to the big making the grand sum total four feet 1 inch. Was that not a whop-hop-per?

Cleveland closed the letter to his mother by stating that he had been studying and enjoying himself very much. "It is very pleasant to have the house so quiet," he added, reflecting in the solitude of what might have been had he remained in Michigan and what would be as he looked forward toward the next chapter of his life.

CHAPTER TWO

Cambridge (1860–1864)

> Now that years have passed I can the more easily see the advantage of growth in such an atmosphere of scientific learning as then pervaded Cambridge and my only regret must be that owing to my ambition in work and study and to an innate shyness of society my time was too fully occupied to fully profit by the personal acquaintances that were at hand.
>
> —Cleveland Abbe, c. 1888

In October 1860, Cleveland Abbe stepped off a boat in Boston Harbor and made his way through the old town to nearby Cambridge, where, as he put it, "for the first time in my life I walked through the grounds of Harvard College."[1] There, he met Dr. Benjamin Apthorp Gould, a noted astronomer who headed up the longitude department of the Coast Survey. Cleveland had been corresponding with Gould since December 1856, when the young, aspiring astronomer wrote his elder counterpart, seeking advice and inquiring about possible employment in the field. At the time, Gould served as director of the Dudley Observatory in Albany, New York, where Cleveland's Michigan mentor, Dr. Franz Brünnow, would eventually succeed him. From the beginning, Gould displayed a distant, if not discouraging, attitude toward Cleveland, as shown in a letter he sent in 1857[2]:

> Cambridge 1857 July 25
>
> Dear Sir
>
> My absence from home has delayed the reception of your letter of the 16th, so that I have not been able to reply until now.
>
> The period of organization of the Dudley Observatory is as undecided now as it was when I wrote you last. The Observatory requires $75,000 before

we can begin, with propriety. My advice to the trustees has uniformly been to wait until the beginning could be made on a proper scale. Whether this will require five weeks or five years, must depend on circumstances alike beyond my control & my judgement. — What steps will then be taken for using the instruments it is of course impossible to say, and I should be reluctant to give you any advice predicated on the prospect of employment there. In general however to prepare yourself for future usefulness as an astronomer, I know no better course than that which I pointed out before.

The relation between director and assistant may be considered in one sense analogous to that of teacher and pupil, in so far as it may demand instruction relative to the performance of new duty, or to the especial mode of doing it; but only so far, if only for the reason that with the best will in the world it would demand too large an amount of time & attention. The less it is necessary to be taught, the more valuable of course are the services rendered. I am inclined to think that you erred in not seizing the opportunity for a situation in the Nautical Almanac, the place being now filled.

If you incline (as I certainly think advisable) to devote the coming year to preparation for usefulness in astronomy, I see no better course than for you to carry out the plan already proposed, which will surely give you occupation enough, I do not know that there is any better opportunity for study in Michigan than in New York or Massachusetts with the single exception of the meridian circle at Ann Arbor; and it is hardly probably that Dr. Brünnow would give a tyro the privilege of observing with so costly and delicate an instrument.

Still if he is willing, his advice and instruction would be very useful, — and you must judge whether the practical instruction or the theoretical study are most needed. (He is at present in Europe.)

Under any circumstances you understand that if employed in any scientific work your position would be an extremely humble one at first, and only advanced as you prepare yourself capable of performing duties of a higher order.

Very truly yours
B.A. Gould

Mr. Cleveland Abbe
No. 37 E. 20th St. N.Y.

Gould took a more amiable, if not apologetic, tone three years later, when he wrote to Cleveland in July of 1860, following Cleveland's scholarship in Michigan, which clearly impressed Gould. "The events of the last three years have long since given you the explanations which of course I could not give at the time," Gould wrote, "of my hesitance & willingness in 1856 & 7 to commit you to the Dudley Observatory!"[3]

Cleveland's persistence in periodically writing Gould to inquire about employment opportunities paid off in October 1860, when he received the following letter[4]:

Cambridge 1860 Oct. 15

Dear Sir

I have this day received authority from the Superintendent of the Coast Survey to engage you for three months at the usual rate for Coast Survey Aids, viz $15.00 a month and 60 cts a day for subsistence.

Should this be acceptable to you, I should be pleased to receive information to that effect by first opportunity, and to see you here at early convenience, — within the present week if possible. Of course your fare hither is at the expense of the C. Survey

Yours respectfully
B.A. Gould
Asst U.S. Coast Survey

C. Abbe Esq

Gould followed this letter with another drafted the same day, in which he apologized to Cleveland for the apparently paltry salary he could offer him and encouraging him to think of his employment with him as temporary.[5]

Cambridge 1860 Oct. 15

My Dear Sir

I am sorry that I am not able to offer you any higher remuneration; but I am not without hopes that before the three months shall have expired, something better may turn up for you. — If you will let me know when you are likely to arrive, I will have some one ready to help you about finding accommodations for board & lodging. You would find it convenient I think to take the night-boat if the weather should be favorable, — then leaving your baggage in Boston for a while to come out in the horse-cars which pass my door. — I live in Little's Block, Harvard Square.

Yours very truly
B.A. Gould

C. Abbe Esq

Despite the meager wages and certainly not owing to Gould's disposition, Cleveland deemed himself "fortunate in obtaining what I supposed was a temporary position"[6] assisting Gould.

Gould was a complicated individual. Born in Boston in 1824, he was a precocious child prodigy, "reading aloud by the age of three, composing odes in Latin at five years, and giving lectures on electricity, illustrated with machines of his own construction by the time he was ten years old."[7] These traits certainly informed Gould's personality, which has been described as arrogant and obsessive, with the implication that he suffered from what at the time was labeled "manic depression."[8]

Graduating from Harvard in 1844, Gould spent a year teaching at the Boston Latin School while obtaining his master's degree before departing for Europe to continue his studies amid the great European astronomers of the time. He spent a year at the Berlin Observatory, working as an assistant, and was present when German astronomer Johann Galle discovered the planet Neptune, on September 23, 1846. While in Berlin he became friends with the scholar Alexander von Humboldt, and later in Göttingen, Carl Friedrich Gauss, who has been described as "one of the great mathematical astronomers of all times."[9] Gould became a disciple of Gauss and, in 1848, received his Ph.D. from the University of Göttingen, the first American to receive a doctorate in astronomy. Gould returned to America in 1848 and, a year later, founded the *Astronomical Journal*, still published today as one of the premier peer-reviewed journals of its field. Despite being offered a professorship at Göttingen by Gauss—along with directorship of the observatory there—Gould remained in his homeland, determined to take what he had learned and witnessed in Europe and create a new scientific tradition in America. His efforts would fall short of his expectations, however, and his career would eventually be marred by controversy.

In 1852, Gould took up work with the Coast Survey, leading the division in charge of determining the longitudes of various locations through the use of telegraphic lines. In 1855, he accepted the position of director of the recently established Dudley Observatory and relocated to Albany. His tenure was short-lived and came to an abrupt end when, in 1859, a dispute erupted between the trustees of the observatory and its Scientific Council, of which Gould was a member, over Gould's administration of the fledgling institution. This included what amounted to "charges of incompetence, disloyalty, and sloth"[10] made against Gould by the trustees. The Scientific Council—whose members besides Gould included such scientific luminaries as Joseph Henry (director of the Smithsonian Institution), Benjamin Pierce (a professor at Harvard), and Alexander Bache (superintendent of the Coast Survey)—came to Gould's defense, but to no avail. At one point, Henry even tried to enlist the help of Jefferson Davis, then a U.S. senator from Mississippi.[11] The trustees ultimately voted to terminate Gould's appointment, but the beleaguered director dug in his heels, refusing to leave his residence at the observatory. Eventually, Gould was forcibly ejected from his residence, his professional papers and personal belongings strewn about. In a lengthy statement published in his own defense, Gould claimed, "I was driven from my dwelling by a hired band of rioters, acting without form or pretence [sic] of law,—a mere brute force, which left me no other choice than a passive endurance of the high-handed outrage, or an employment of similar agencies for protection in my position."[12]

The Dudley Observatory controversy created a rift in the astronomical community and, at one point, pitted Gould squarely against Brünnow. In July 1858, Brünnow penned a scathing letter of recrimination to Gould. "I feel sorry for you individually, but I must say that you brought on all this difficulty by your own imprudence," Brünnow scornfully wrote. "I also regret that this has chilled the friendly feelings I had towards you since our first acquaintance."

Gould returned to Cambridge in 1859 and resumed his work with the Coast Survey. When Cleveland joined him the following year, Gould had recently returned from an expedition to Washington Territory, in the Pacific Northwest, to observe the total solar eclipse of July 18, 1860.

Cleveland's duties would be more mundane by comparison. The accurate determination of a location's longitude had long plagued astronomers and others who relied on such measurements. Unlike its cartographic counterpart, latitude, calculations of longitude relied on the knowledge of how local time differed between two locations—one with a known longitude and one without. The advent of the telegraph in the mid-nineteenth century helped overcome one of the major obstacles in this effort by allowing observers at distant locations to easily compare the relative times at which a celestial object appeared in their telescopes. The basic methodology was summarized in a historical survey of longitude determination published in 1956 in the journal *Monthly Notes of the Astronomical Society of South Africa*:

> The procedure was to make several determinations of local time over a short period at the two stations with transit instruments mounted in the respective meridians. As the stars crossed the fixed vertical wires of the telescope, the observer tapped a key and recordings were made on the same chronograph as the beats of a clock. Between determinations of local time, the observers at both ends tapped out sets of signals in turn which were sent over the telegraph line connecting them and registered on both chronographs. The local times at a common epoch were easily deduced.[13]

The Coast Survey took up the practice of longitude determination in 1846 and by the time Gould took over the work in 1852, the survey had already used the telegraph to determine the longitude of New York City Hall, the Philadelphia Observatory, several locations in Washington, D.C., including the Capitol, and the observatory in Charleston, South Carolina, among other locations.[14] For his work, Cleveland received credit and praise in the summaries Gould submitted to Bache for inclusion in his annual report as superintendent of the Coast Survey, including in 1863 when Gould thanked Cleveland for his "assiduous, conscientious, and most serviceable aid."

Whatever his professional stance toward his superior, it is evident that Cleveland did not always hold Gould in high esteem. In July 1862, after learning that Gould had rejected a friend from the Phi Beta Kappa honor society, Cleveland made mention of it in his diary, noting his displeasure by scrawling a single word: "Detestable."[15] Cleveland also referred despairingly to his employment under Gould several years later, in a letter to his mother in which he recalled his time in Cambridge, "when I tried during the first year to work enough to satisfy my employer and signally failed."[16] Nevertheless, when describing the 1856 dedication of the Dudley Observatory in an undated memoir he wrote some years later, Cleveland referred to Gould, albeit indirectly, as someone he "was soon to know as a life long friend," only to later strike out the words in the typed manuscript by hand.[17]

When he wasn't engaged in his duties with the Coast Survey, Cleveland found pleasure in the wealth of academic resources available to him, as well as the close association of colleagues, professors, and other academics who were regular fixtures in the houses of Harvard Square. "My chief scientific delights were found in the astronomical works of the College Library and of

Dr. Gould's private library," he proclaimed, "and in the regular Wednesday afternoon mathematical club which held its meetings in the rooms of Prof. Benjamin Peirce."

Cleveland recalled his memories of Peirce as "very dear" to him, noting how the elder professor would encourage him in his professional development. "I used to think he took especial delight in encouraging me to special advances in mathematical work," he said, "more likely is it that this was his uniform kindly treatment of all young men and that it merely seemed the more grateful to me because of the contrast in my own mind between him who knew so much and one who knew so little."[18]

Those Wednesday afternoon mathematical club meetings to which Cleveland alluded consisted of the members sharing special problems in determinants, notes on higher algebra, or "computations relative to astronomical precession and nutation." Cleveland presented a paper of his own titled "The Motions of the Billiard Ball," which he said was "suggested by some pretty tall stories that were told as to wonderful curving shots by famous experts."

What made the most vivid impression on Cleveland, however, were the ideas Professor Peirce put forth on the structure of Saturn's rings. First observed by Galileo in 1610, astronomers had debated the nature and structure of the rings of Saturn for centuries. In 1859, Scottish astronomer James Clerk Maxwell published an essay in which, as opposed to theories of a solid ring as others had suggested, he sought to "consider the case of a ring, the parts of which are not rigidly connected, as in the case of a ring of independent satellites, or a fluid ring."[19] In summarizing Peirce's ideas, Cleveland referred to "the great probability that they are simply ropes of sand, streams of gravel, a multitude of small masses perpetually disturbing each other in their movements, so that the gravitation towards Saturn and the tidal action gives rise to first to mutual shocks and friction, then to heat and its loss by radiation, then to the gradual settling of the rind down toward the planet and its dissipation in meteoric dust."[20]

In the fall of 1861, Peirce gave a series of post-graduate lectures on the nebular hypothesis, explaining the formation and evolution of the solar system, as well as the various theories of creation put forth at the time. Cleveland was among those who applied for admission and the demand easily ensured the course would be held. "In fact," Cleveland noted, "many a cultivated Cambridge lady attended." Cleveland described the series of lectures as "a brilliant plea for some form of evolutionary hypothesis," but noted that while Peirce "examined in detail the difficulties attending every specific hypothesis that had thus far been made and amended them when possible so as to advance a step nearer the truth there could be but one final conclusion that we have not yet attained to a satisfactory solution of the problem."[21]

During his four years in Cambridge, Cleveland had opportunities to interact and develop relationships with a variety of individuals, some of whom would go on to make important contributions to their respective fields. One of the most influential was Louis Agassiz, the Swiss-American biologist and geologist whose pioneering work on the theory of ice ages helped give birth to the field of glaciology. It was through Agassiz's teachings that Cleveland saw the interconnections between the slow advances and retreats of glaciers and the climatic variations that were an extension of meteorology, even if he had yet to realize the latter field would become his life's calling:

> The great importance of glacial phenomena was not appreciated until in 1860, when I came to live at Cambridge and was associated with the working members of Agassiz's school of geology and zoology and then I recognized at once that the glacier was but an extension of the atmospheric influences that had been so deeply impressed upon my thoughts. In those days I did not know that I was a meteorologist, and the enthusiasm of Agassiz might well have turned me into the paths of geology, had I not determined to look upon my studies upon the atmosphere as simply contributing to the perfection of work in astronomy, for to the astronomer the atmosphere is an obstacle always injuring his views of the heavenly bodies and of ofttimes obscuring views altogether and always a source of error.[22]

The "working members" of Agassiz's group with whom Cleveland became associated were a close-knit cadre of young men who have been described as "a lively group of astronomers, mathematicians, and other physical scientists from Harvard University, the Nautical Almanac Office, and the Coast Survey."[23] In Cleveland's words, "we were all young together and we soon found that a common sentiment animated us all, the advancement of our respective sciences as such, irrespective of personal aggrandizement and the desire to avoid all personal feuds and jealousies. It seemed to us enthusiastic young men, as though the world was wide enough to afford room for all without interfering with each other, that science needed workers and co-workers not dissensions."[24]

One of these men among Agassiz's inner circle was Albert S. Bickmore, who worked for him at the Museum of Comparative Zoology and who would go on several years later to become the founder of the American Museum of Natural History in New York. Born three months after Cleveland, Bickmore—"a man of simple and deep religious faith[25]"—became one of Cleveland's closest friends, with the pair meeting at a church service just a few months after Cleveland's arrival in Cambridge. The two shared much in common, including a childhood filled with imagination and wonder about the natural world. In fact, for Bickmore, it was a tragic event brought on by severe weather that would help shape his worldview and provide him with a deep appreciation—and a healthy respect—for the forces of nature. In his autobiography, Bickmore tells the story of one fateful night during his childhood when a storm raged off Midcoast Maine, just a few hundred feet from his family's house. "From the rocky point between our beach and the adjoining harbor there came one night, in the midst of a heavy storm, the alarming cry that a vessel of a neighbor had been cast away, and that both ship and crew were in the greatest peril and would be lost unless immediate aid could be rendered." Bickmore's father and two uncles rushed to the ocean in a frantic effort to save their storm-swept neighbor. A rogue wave, however, overcame one of his uncles, who "found a watery grave only a few moments after he had started out from our house," Bickmore recalled. "My uncle's heroic death sanctified the cruel ledges, over which we could hear the sea moaning during the heavy storms as we sat by our own comfortable fireside. And in like manner every rocky islet and sunken ledge near and far had its own story of shipwreck and of the brave deeds of daring seamen which were especially adapted to arouse a child's imagination and admiration."[26]

It was Bickmore, whom Cleveland described as "a very enterprising young man and delightful companion," who introduced Cleveland to the Agassiz inner circle. Bickmore described the period during which Cleveland was in Cambridge—from 1860 to 1864—as being "included in the lyceum period of our American culture, when ablest thinkers willingly accepted invitations to lecture and present orally and personally their instruction to our citizens." Some of the more noted speakers who presented in Cambridge during this period were Edward Everett, Oliver Wendell Holmes, and Ralph Waldo Emerson.

The Civil War

On November 6, 1860, Abraham Lincoln—a self-proclaimed "prairie lawyer" from Springfield, Illinois—was elected sixteenth president of the United States. The following month, George Abbe sent a letter[27] to Cleveland, relaying news from home and expressing the family's growing concern—undoubtedly shared by many—of the fate of the Union:

New York Dec 14/60

My dear Son

I received your letter some time since and as your mother has heretofore done all the correspondence I have not answered it as promptly as I should. I judge that you are out of the reach of panics & political trouble that our country is involved in. What the end is to be, no one can tell but we are hopeful there will be no dissolution of the Union —

As you were only engaged there for three months, do you know what you are to do when your time is up. Will you be wanted longer or can you get a better place? There are many out of employment & it may be difficult to find a place — since you heard from home your mother has been quite sick but is up again — the rest of the family are well. — I went to Windham Thanksgiving & had a good time. Our friends are well & enjoy themselves. They expected to see you. Uncle Harry is here & is quite well. Mother will answer your letter when she has time.

We are getting along with our church edifice quite well & hope to get into it this month — or next at farthermost. I hope you will get your pay from government & have no doubt you will. Let us know what the prospect is of your staying there.

Affectionately Your Father

G. W. Abbe

Four days after George drafted his letter to Cleveland, South Carolina seceded from the Union. Within two months, Mississippi, Florida, Alabama, Georgia, Louisiana, and Texas followed suit. On March 4, 1861, Lincoln was sworn in as commander-in-chief by Chief Justice Roger B. Taney of the Supreme Court. In his inaugural speech, the new president did his best to assuage fears and preserve the Union. In closing, he said:

> We are not enemies, but friends. We must not be enemies. Though passion may have strained it must not break our bonds of affection. The mystic chords of memory, stretching from every battlefield and patriot grave to every living heart and hearthstone all over this broad land, will yet swell the chorus of the Union, when again touched, as surely they will be, by the better angels of our nature.[28]

Despite Lincoln's efforts, war was inevitable. Less than six weeks after his inauguration, on April 12, 1861, Confederate troops, under the command of General Pierre Gustave Toutant-Beauregard, opened fire on Fort Sumter, in Charleston Harbor, ushering in four years of battle, bloodshed, and bombardment in what Cleveland referred to as our country's "first great struggle for existence." The American Civil War had begun.

In Cambridge, Cleveland, like many young men, felt the struggle of weighing his own responsibilities at the time against the patriotic call for duty that seemed to cry out from every corner of his conscience. "[A]lthough I was well nigh buried in my own pursuits yet I could not be wholly unconscious of my privileges and duties as a citizen," he said. While Cleveland stayed in Cambridge during Lincoln's initial calls for volunteer troops in 1861—when the president asked for seventy-five thousand troops to serve for three months—he finally relented in the summer of 1862, after Lincoln put out another call for volunteers to defend the Union. This time the call was for three hundred thousand men to enlist for nine months of service—a group that became known as "nine months men"—and whose patriotic spirit could be heard in recruitment halls and training camps throughout the land:

> We are coming, we are coming,
> Our country to restore;
> We are coming, Father Abraham,
> Three hundred thousand more.[29]

After attending a meeting "for stirring up recruits" held on July 12 at Cambridge City Hall, Cleveland made up his mind. "It had not been easy to persuade myself to stay at home when the first and second calls for volunteers were issued by President Lincoln," he said, "but when finally in 1862 the call for 300,000 nine months men was made I in common with so many other enlisted for the field of battle."[30] On what Cleveland described as "a pleasant day," August 13, 1862, he added his name to a list of members of the 4th Battalion of the Massachusetts Infantry, led by Captain Charles Storrow, which would eventually become part of the 44th Regiment of the Massachusetts Volunteer Militia. The following day, Cleveland took a steamboat on the Fall River Line to New York, where he met his father to discuss the matter of enlisting. Receiving no objection from his father, he said goodbye to numerous friends before boarding a boat on August 15 to Norwich, Connecticut, and then on to Cambridge. On August 18, he officially enlisted and met with Captain Storrow. His enrollment was recorded by the city clerk five days later.

The men of the 44th Regiment were a mixed lot. They came from a variety of backgrounds and their interests and habits were equally varied. Professionally, they were farmers, merchants, lawyers, physicians, printers, cabinet makers, musicians, blacksmiths, druggists, bookkeepers, and students, among others. Politically, they aligned themselves with the various factions of the Republican Party at the time—moderate, conservative, and "radical" (the latter group advocating a complete abolition of slavery without compromise)—as well as the Democratic Party, the Constitutional Union Party, and the Abolitionist movement. They worshiped at Unitarian, Congregationalist, Methodist, Episcopal, Baptist, and Universalist churches. They were husbands, fiancés, and widowers. They were smokers, drinkers, and every combination thereof—including those who drank nothing stronger than cider and ale and those who abstained from "ardent spirits of any shape."[31] What they did share in common what a sense of patriotism and a desire to serve that transcended political, professional, or other boundaries. "No promises were held out to us," recalled one of the men years later, "that we would not be put to as severe tests of courage, or have a chance to achieve as great deeds of heroism, as any who had preceded us."[32]

The initial activities of the battalion took place in Cambridge and involved drills, parading through the streets, and the election of company officers. Abbe was joined by several friends, including Albert Bickmore, who had just returned from Bermuda, where he had been collecting specimens for the showman P. T. Barnum.[33] At three o'clock on the afternoon of August 29, the new recruits boarded a train and headed to a training camp at Readville, Massachusetts, south of Boston. The details of life in the camp at Readville are revealed in the diary of a fellow recruit from the 44th Regiment:

> Each man was told to carry rations enough for two meals. We formed company for the first time, out of doors, on the Boylston Street Mall; marched to the Boston and Providence Depot, and after hand-shaking with our friends, went aboard the cars, arriving at Readville, ten miles out, at four o'clock; and here the troubles and tribulations of many a fine young man began. We found that either the regiment had come too soon or the carpenters had been lazy, for only three of the ten barracks were roofed, and some were not even boarded in, so while the carpenters went at work outside, we went at it inside, putting up and fixing the bunks.[34]

"Matters were in pretty rough shape even for a military camp," Cleveland noted upon reaching Readville, "but gradually order was brought about."

That day, he and Bickmore stood guard duty, their barracks half-completed.[35] The following day, August 30, Cleveland underwent his first exam by the camp surgeon to determine his readiness as a soldier. He did not pass. His severe myopia again impacted his life in ways he could not have anticipated.

The next day, August 31, Cleveland and his fellow recruits from the 44th Massachusetts Volunteers decided to take advantage of the day's heat—and the fact that they were free to do what they wanted that Sunday afternoon—and went swimming in a half-acre pond near their camp, along a railroad embankment. "I could swim a little and struck out boldly for the centre of the pond on a race with the others," Cleveland recalled, "but when we turned round to come back I went under and was a long time coming up; in fact I found that I couldn't get up and that if I was to reach the shore at all I must walk as fast as possible along the bottom." Luckily, Cleveland had made a point of practicing walking along the bottom of the pond while swimming underwater in the past. What he did not anticipate, however, was that he was soon about to lose consciousness. "They say that a drowning person recalls at a glance all the events of his life," he would say later, as he often did when telling the story to his children. "This was not my case and I doubt whether it is a general rule for so few drowned persons ever come back to tell us what they thought of." Thanks to the quick thinking and action of one of his comrades, Private W. A. Simmons of Chelsea, Massachusetts, Cleveland was saved before he completely passed out. "The most embarrassing result of this adventure was the loss of my spectacles," he admitted. "Imagine a near-sighted soldier with spectacles and you can get an idea of about how useful I should have been at any critical time in the field during a campaign." When the examining surgeon visited the camp the following day, Cleveland reckoned this image is what he had in mind, as well, "for it seems," Cleveland said, "that although we were all acceptable as state militia, yet we were not all to be accepted for the use of the United States Government—at least I was not to sing 'We're coming Father Abraham, Three Hundred Thousand Strong.'"

Poor eyesight was not necessarily an impediment to serving in the Army at that time. "During the Civil War a great many men were enlisted who had defective sight and disease of the eye," according to a brief note that appeared in the *American Journal of Ophthalmology* in 1898.[36] Severe myopia—or nearsightedness—however, was enough of a concern that, in 1864, the Army codified that its existence, while not ordinarily grounds for rejection, could be considered so in extreme cases, according to its *Manual of Instructions for Enlisting and Discharging Soldiers*: "Myopia, unless very decided or depending upon some structural change in the eye, is not a cause for exemption."[37]

The surgeon's decision left Cleveland feeling disillusioned and unfulfilled, as he was determined to do his patriotic duty to answer Lincoln's call and help save the Union, even if it meant risking his own life. "This was a severe disappointment for I had fully made up my mind that I should be just as good if not a little better soldier and just as acceptable as a target for the enemy's bullets as any other one," he lamented.[38] Undeterred, Cleveland went to Boston on September 1 to get a second opinion at the regiment's headquarters and even saw the governor at the state house. The surgeon he saw made the same assessment and, when the governor asked him, "What would you do with a nearsighted man?" the surgeon's response was emphatic. "I should reject him."[39]

Disheartened, Cleveland returned to camp to gather his belongings and say goodbye to his comrades before returning to Cambridge to resume his life as he had known it several weeks prior. Determination—or tenacity—got the better of him, however, and he made two more attempts to appeal the medical ruling, to no avail. The doctors assured him he could not pass muster as a private but could possibly get in as an officer. Cleveland disregarded this possibility, however, "for it seems that the army was really more in need of intelligent engineers, commissaries, surgeons and other officers than it was in need of privates but I did not then fully realize this and knew that to a certain extent, as Dr. Gould had said, the work that I was doing for him in the Coast Survey was also of value to the Government."

On September 19, Charlotte Abbe wrote a letter to her son in which she expressed her relief in his rejection as a soldier. "I was glad when you wrote me, that you were not accepted as a Volunteer," she said, "for I am sure you are not fitted for a soldier."[40] She then added, "How disappointed Bickmore must feel at the loss of your company." It was clear to Cleveland's mother that his friendship with Albert Bickmore was a close one. A few weeks later, on October 14, Cleveland made a trip to Readville to visit his friend at the training camp. There he found Bickmore "sick and homesick." Later that month, Bickmore, along with the other members of the 44th Massachusetts Volunteers, boarded a steamer for North Carolina, where they would spend the next eight months defending the Union against the rebel forces of the Confederacy. It was from his post in Beaufort, North Carolina, that Bickmore wrote to Cleveland in April 1863, expressing contentment for his current condition but also a longing for the comradery and companionship of his Cambridge-bound friend. "I feel as happy and hopeful as ever I did, and wish you were here with me now in my pleasant room to talk over the many things that have occurred in Cambridge and North Carolina since I last bid you adieu," he confessed, adding, "A beautiful jonquil near this desk on which I write has been pouring out its rich fragrance."[41]

Matters of the Heart

The closeness of Cleveland and Bickmore's relationship is evident in the diary entries Cleveland made during his years in Cambridge, revealing a level of intimacy that, while not uncommon at the time, seems out of place by contemporary standards. Cleveland mentions numerous occasions between 1862 and 1864 when the two men not only spent time together but often slept together and even, on occasion, bathed together. While it is impossible to know the exact nature of Cleveland and Bickmore's relationship, many historians have suggested that this type of behavior, given the historical context, is less indicative of homoerotic tendencies as it is a close, intimate type of male friendship common at the time, known as "fraternal love." As historian Donald Yacovone writes:

> A remarkably constant language of fraternal love appears in the rhetoric and writings of Americans from the Puritan settlement until the second decade in the twentieth century. Regardless of age, race, class, geographic location, or occupation, American men possessed the freedom to form affectionate relations. This language of fraternal love, no mere passing phase of youth, represented a pervasive cultural ideal. More common than expressions of "traditional manly virtues" of independence, force, will, and power, fraternal love was, in the nineteenth century, the true measure of a man. The nineteenth century created a sentimentalized ideal of manhood, enshrined in both private and public correspondence and by lithographers and photographers, that employs virtues we commonly associate with women and is completely at odds with our understanding of what constitutes a man.[42]

According to Yacovone, modern notions of gender "have little or no bearing on the history of sexuality and gender before the era of Freud," adding that "attempts to impose modern categories and labels on a world gone by perpetuates misunderstanding, if not complete mystification."[43] Yacovone argues that we should not "be perplexed by or suspicious of motives when the rhetoric of fraternal love passed into more overt physical manifestations," citing several factors that "encouraged intimacy and physical contact" at that time. "From the earliest years of childhood, males shared beds—as had been the practice for centuries—and continued to do so throughout their lives, without homoerotic desire or the suspicion of homoerotic intent. Men from all classes and from every section of the country regularly slept together, particularly when illness or personal tragedies were involved."[44]

Examples of fraternal love are found among several famous contemporaries of Cleveland, including Presidents James Buchanan, James Garfield, and Abraham Lincoln.[45] For Cleveland and Bickmore, their relationship was one that Cleveland's son Truman—in noting the numerous instances of the two sleeping together—described as simply a "close friendship."[46] Several months after they parted ways, Cleveland wrote to his mother in New York, confessing to her, "I have missed Bickmore very much because he so often has cheered me and set me to rights."[47]

Romantic relationships did not come easily for Cleveland and this may have been the result—at least in part—of the close, idyllic relationships he formed with his mother and other female family members growing up. "My mother often said that his associations at home with his mother, his aunts, and his sisters had been so idealistic that he imagined everyone who wore skirts was an angel," Truman confided. "There were some things he could learn only along the hard road of experience."[48] His first love affair proved that point. While he was living in Michigan, Cleveland began a relationship with a woman named Thirza Rothwell Dodsley. The daughter of a straw hat maker and a cotton lace maker, Thirza was born in Nottinghamshire, England, in 1837. Her family immigrated to the United States sometime between 1840 and 1850 and settled in Ann Arbor, Michigan, where, according to the 1860 U.S. Census, she was working as a milliner, making women's hats. Cleveland's correspondence records show letters to and from her beginning in May 1859 and increasing in frequency after his move to Cambridge in 1860.[49] Sometimes as many as four or five letters a month each traversed between them. In addition to letters, Cleveland sent her money—usually nine or ten dollars each month—beginning in June 1862 and continuing through July 1863. The exact details of what happened next are unclear, but in July 1863, Thirza traveled from Ann Arbor to Cambridge and was received at Cleveland's room at Harvard's Divinity Hall. There, she met his mother, a sister, and two brothers. On July 14, Cleveland's diary indicates that he "talked Thirza" with his father, from whom he borrowed $746, apparently to help settle a claim.[50] According to Truman, "she appeared before a notary in Cambridge, Massachusetts, and for the sum of one thousand dollars gave Father a full release from any kind of claim she might have upon him."[51] In all likelihood, this was a case of "breach of promise to marry," which was common cause for legal action at the time. According to one explanation for the practice:

> The nineteenth-century plaintiff claiming a breach of promise to marry was typically a female. The average nineteenth-century American woman depended on marriage for her very survival, and the breaking of an engagement promise often left the aggrieved female less desirable in the marriage market. Thus, it is understandable that society and the courts, given those social conditions, allowed women to make breach-of-promise claims that would place them in the financial position in which they would have been had the marriage taken place. In effect, the courts treated the plaintiff as if the marriage had taken place and failed, and the court was now figuring out what alimony should be paid.[52]

In one such case, reported in *The New York Times* in 1860, the plaintiff, who was seeking $10,000 in damages, claimed "that after a series of visits and attentions, the defendant, in June, 1857, promised to marry her, she accepting him and his offer."[53] In Cleveland's case, this turned out to be an expensive lesson in love, as his annual salary from the Coast Survey at the time was only $500—half what he paid Thirza to release him from any claims. It's possible that Cleveland's parents were unaware of Thirza—and any promises their son might have made to her—until the end of the affair. In April 1863, just a few months before the matter with Thriza was settled, Cleveland's mother wrote to him on the very subject of entering seriously into such a relationship without first seeking her counsel. "Tell me about some young ladies you visit, but beware how you get entangled in any love scrapes—ask my advice before you think seriously of such a thing—I can not feel as if you were too old to come to your parents for advice yet."[54] In another letter, dated July 30, Charlotte wrote Cleveland expressing concern that he was about to surrender his heart again. "Be careful how you let your affections become too much drawn out," she cautioned. "Perhaps I am wrong thus writing, but your past experience makes me feel as if I wanted to warn you & yet I would not hurt your feelings for any thing. Unless a person is in a situation to be married, they ought to conquer all serious thoughts, but what am I writing, forgive me."[55] Several years later, Cleveland referred to Thirza in a letter to his mother, indicating that the experience had left him both jilted and jaded and reluctant to ever begin pursuing another romantic relationship. "I am not too old to need sober, wise advice, nor too headstrong to heed it," he said. "When I think of Thirza I do so shudder with a cold shiver and am so filled with dread of the recurrence of any similar experience, that I find for me to fall in love is something quite impossible and any talk of hearts and Cupid's darts is quite absurd."[56]

William Is Wounded, Walter Maltreated

The Civil War had profound effects on families on both sides of the Mason Dixon Line and the Abbes were no exception. Although Cleveland's eyesight rendered him unfit for service in the 44th Massachusetts Regiment, two of his brothers, Walter and William, enlisted in the 37th New York Militia in 1862, both initially stationed at Baltimore. William's "military spirit moved him to re-enlist in 1863," and he received a commission as second lieutenant in a regiment of African American soldiers. In July 1863, William was wounded during the Battle of Gettysburg. Cleveland received the news in a letter from his mother, dated July 6, 1863.[57] "We have had exciting times the last week, which I suppose you have escaped amongst the port towns of Maine," she wrote. "You may not have heard of Willie being shot in the neck in a slight skirmish about 7 miles from Harrisburg. It was a very narrow escape." She told Cleveland that his brother was in "splendid spirits," despite his injury, and then went on to express hope based on this turning point of the war. "If this great victory can only be followed by the surrender of Lee's army shall we not have reason to rejoice," she wondered. Charlotte's letter was followed closely by one written by Cleveland's sister Helen,[58] then ten years old, who, despite an abundance of spelling errors one might expect for a writer of that age, described the incident involving their brother William in much greater detail:

> July 6th, 1863
>
> Dear Brother,
>
> I should like to know weather you have heard that Willie is wounded, as I suppose you have not I will tell you. A ball struc him in the neck, just behind the jugular vain and came out by the vertibrae, the Docter said that he would be well if he did not get cold in it. He is in the hospital at Harrisburg now. Father went on to see him last Friday and he said that he was in good spirits, but his neck was very stif. Mother bought the pioneer boy which refers to Abe Lincoln. I was head of my clas in school and Miss Haines gave me a gold brestpin with a coral in the middle of it, we have vacation now. We had a very

pleasant day for the fourth except it was a little rainy in the morning. Walter enjoyed the torpetoes as much as I did. Walter took Hattie and I to see the fireworks in the evening but they were very poor. We have just had a letter from Willie and he said that the young ladys send him boquets and he said that one had just invited him to tea. I am afraid that they will spoil him. We are all very well. I think that Walter will go away this week. Willie got the pistol that Father sent him.

your affectionate
sister Helen

One week later, while in New York, Cleveland noted in his diary, "Riotous burning of 29th St. & Broadway & orphan asylum. Walter maltreated & robbed." His account of the vandalism and violence refers to the infamous draft riots that took place in New York City from July 13 to 16, 1863.

For three days, rowdy mobs consisting of thousands of people—mostly Irish immigrants—took to the streets, protesting the federal draft signed into law by President Lincoln earlier that year, with the first draft lottery held in New York on July 11. The mob, which roamed freely due to the limited police force and lack of federal troops, many of whom had been sent to fight in Gettysburg, took out its collective frustration on those it deemed responsible for their conscription. This included the wealthy, who could buy their way out of the draft for $300—nearly a year's wages for working-class citizens—as well as African Americans, who were exempt from the draft and whom many of the rioters saw as the reason for the war in the first place. This latter idea had become galvanized in the minds of many following Lincoln's Emancipation Proclamation, which became law on January 1 of that year. Among the buildings they destroyed was the 8th District provost marshal's office, which stood at the corner of 29th Street and Broadway and served as one of the locations of the draft lottery. Another target was the Colored Orphan Asylum on Fifth Avenue, between 43rd and 44th Streets.

On July 30, Charlotte wrote a letter to Cleveland, recalling the events from earlier that month, noting the anxious feeling that permeated the city. "I forgot to say any thing about our city riots," she wrote. "We felt very uneasy for a while after you left, but after the sabbath sermons by the priests—I felt that that portion of our population would be more quiet, & our militia & state troops being on hand we felt as safe as usual. Some anticipate more trouble & some do not. We can only wait and & hope."[59] She did not mention anything about the incident involving Walter, other than to say he had resumed work. According to Cleveland and Walter's brother Robert, Walter "ventured out one night to Madison Square, was attacked by a gang, clubbed on the head and came home with a bloody cut on his scalp." For at least a week, Walter kept an African American man who worked for him—driving a team of horses for his business—secretly hidden in a pile of hay at his store, on Eighth Avenue, near 33rd Street. "It would have been death to the driver had he been discovered or ventured out," according to Robert.[60] Several weeks later, on August 8, he filed a formal claim with the city comptroller for damages amounting to $216.80. The episode of the draft riots remains the largest and most violent insurrection in U.S. history other than the Civil War itself.

A Change of Pace

Back in Cambridge, the tedium of his work for Gould began to take a toll on Cleveland by 1864, when, as he put it, "a succession of headaches and utter inability to work satisfactorily convinced me that something was wrong and that I must make a complete change in my habits."[61] Believing that a change in both work duty and environment would do him some good, he asked to be reassigned to field work with the Coast Survey. Gould complied and on July 28 assigned Cleveland to take part in a coast survey in Maine that would perform hydrographic work along the St. George's River. It was a welcome relief for Cleveland, who boarded the schooner *Bailey*, under the command of his friend, F. P. Webber. From late August until early November, the *Bailey*, with its crew of eight, sailed up and down the coast of Maine, exploring the river and its approaches. Cleveland's duties included procuring food for the crew, which consisted, among other things, of berries, ice, milk, lamb, and lobster.[62]

In addition to providing him with a welcome relief from his office job in Cambridge, the Coast Survey experience gave Cleveland a chance to connect with a part of New England familiar to him, as cousins on his father's side, the Fessendens, lived in nearby Rockland. The patriarch of the family, Samuel C. Fessenden, was an ordained minister at the Second Congregational Church in Rockland and later served as a U.S. representative from Maine. Samuel and his wife, Mary Abigail Grosvenor Abbe, had a dozen children between the years 1839 and 1859, all but one of whom survived to adulthood.

Cleveland had spent the previous Christmas with the Fessendens at their home in Rockland, where he enjoyed skating and sleigh riding with his cousins Marcia, Lucia, and Debby.[63] It was his cousin Marcia, however, with whom he was closest. Over the course of that year, they exchanged nearly a dozen letters and Cleveland noted several occasions during his time in Maine when they took walks together and shared a goodnight kiss.[64] Later that fall, he would receive two photographs of her—an ambrotype and a tintype.

In addition to the Fessendens, Cleveland was able to spend time in Maine with his friend Bickmore, whose parents lived in St. George, also near the site of the survey. Cleveland had spent time with Bickmore and his family the previous summer, a visit that brought great joy in anticipation to Bickmore. In a letter dated May 25, 1863, he told Cleveland, "I have been anticipating the pleasure I shall take in having you go down with me to my home in Maine and shall depend on you going with out fail." Excerpts from Cleveland's diary entries from that visit show the camaraderie and companionship that underscored his time in Maine:

> July 4, 1863: Capture of nest of Golden headed woodpeckers for Albert. After dinner walked to Turkey Cove. Striae, sparrows nest, Indian Shell Mound, two seals.
>
> July 4, 1863: Rode to Thomaston. Visited State Prison. Copperhead Quarries. Studied surrounding geology. With Bickmore rode to Rockland. We call and stay at Mr. S. C. Fessenden's.
>
> July 7, 1863: I (not Bick) get to Thomaston, to Blockington Quarry. . . . Bonfire and celebration over fall of Vicksburg.
>
> July 8, 1863: Males go to Owl's Head Lighthouse and fishing. Married folks go to ride. Copy Abbe Coat of Arms. Reading to Marcia. Evening sing and frolic. Marcia plays and sings.

Russia Bound

By the time Cleveland returned to Cambridge in November 1864, plans were already underway for the next chapter in his life—an unprecedented journey that would take him from the familiarity of his fatherland to the far-flung reaches of the realms of scientific thought and civilized society. It would also test him—both personally and professionally—in ways he could not have anticipated.

Ever since his time studying under Brünnow in Michigan, Cleveland had grown to appreciate the European tradition of astronomy and longed to be a part of it. Reflecting on the nearly complete collection of the journal *Astronomische Nachrichten* his father had given him as a present ("the most valuable present that I had ever received"), he remarked, "The more I delved in this mine of scientific wealth the more I realized the perfection with which astronomy was cultivated in Europe."[65] Brünnow and Gould had taught Cleveland to revere the works of such eminent European astronomers as Friedrich Wilhelm Bessel, a contemporary of Carl Friedrich Gauss, Gould's mentor, as well as Friedrich Georg Wilhelm Struve (known to his family and colleagues simply as "Wilhelm"), a German astronomer who, in 1839, became the director of the newly established Nicholas Central Observatory at Pulkovo, just south of St. Petersburg, Russia—a facility Gould would later proclaim "the astronomical capital of the world."[66]

One of the most renowned astronomers of his time, Struve was patriarch of a dynasty of astronomers that spanned five generations. His son Otto followed in his footsteps as an astronomer and took over as director of the Pulkovo Observatory in 1862, two years before the elder Struve's death. In the summer of 1859, Charles Piazzi Smyth, who served as Astronomer Royal for Scotland, traveled to Russia and visited Pulkovo. He later wrote about his experiences in a two-volume book, *Three Cities in Russia*, which Cleveland "quickly bought and devoured, for it told me much about Struve's home in Poulkova and inflamed my ardent desires."[67]

On May 5, 1864, Cleveland wrote a "modest letter of inquiry" to the elder Struve, asking about the possibility of going to Pulkovo to gain practical experience in the field of astronomy. On July 15, while he was on the surveying expedition in Maine, Cleveland received a reply from Otto Struve, with an offer that would change the course of his life forever.[68]

Pulkowa 1864 June 25

Dear Sir,

In reply to your letter I have the honour to inform you that we shall be pleased to see you here and offer you all facilities for becoming intimately acquainted with the different branches of practical astronomy, in use at the Observatory.

You will get here free lodgings with furniture, fire and light; with that the average expense of a years residence at Pulkowa might be estimated to 300 dollars.

Perhaps it might be recommended to you to enter here for a limited time in the position of a supernumerary astronomer. If this suggestion appears worth your consideration, apply to Dr. Gould or Prof. Bond and try to get from them my last years annual report, to which there are added the regulations of the Observatory. You will learn there what position those voluntary assistants occupy in our organization.

Considering your question if you should devote yourselves more to computation or observation, I must suspend my answer until becoming more acquainted with your own talents and disposition. On the whole it might be said that, as long as you have not to your disposition a first-rate instrument you will have more chances to promote astronomy by investigation and computation than by observation.

I am particularly pleased with your desire to further our knowledge of the proper motions. In this respect you will find here a great many materials prepared; for that same object has formed a principal part of the aims, to which the activity of our Observatory has been directed since 25 years.

I hope to hear soon from you. Let me know what time we may expect your arrival.

Faithfully yours,
Otto Struve

Mr Cleveland Abbe
Cambridge, U.S.

Struve's offer "overwhelmed" Cleveland with the assurance that a place for him existed at Pulkovo. With financial help from his father (". . . and for my part I determined that he should have no cause to regret it"), Cleveland began making the necessary preparations, having secured, with Gould's blessing, a two-year leave of absence from the Coast Survey. Recalling the experience years later, he was reminded of a verse from a song from his student days:

> Whom God will gracious favor show, Him sends He out, the wide world traveling o'er.

In early November, Cleveland made his way back to Cambridge and then on to New York, via Windham, with heartfelt goodbyes delivered at each stop to family, friends, and colleagues. "All New York seems cold and cheerless," he complained. "My first two afternoons here were spent on Broadway & Fifth Avenue and the rain & clouds added to my dolefulness. Just in the nick of time Walter drove over and took me over the Central Park."[69]

In New York, he completed final preparations for his journey abroad. On November 23, he paid a visit to Brooks Brothers, on the corner of Broadway and Grand Street, where he purchased an overcoat for forty dollars.[70] The next day, he applied for a passport. According to the application, Cleveland stood five feet, eight and one-quarter inches tall. The document further described him as having blue eyes, light-colored hair, light complexion, a "medium" mouth, round chin, oval face, high forehead, and a "prominent" nose.

On November 24, Cleveland wrote to his cousin Marcia. "I have been making what few preparations are necessary for leaving and now expect to sail for Bremen on the 3rd of December and hope to reach Pulkova before Christmas," he explained. "As the 3rd is my birthday I shall in accordance with the advice of the best astrologers deem this a lucky day and I hope (in the midst of my fears) that my sojourn abroad will be for my good." Cleveland confided in Marcia his trepidation of communicating with foreigners during his time in Europe. "My heart still fails me when I think of having to speak German and French—if only somebody else would do it for me! However I console myself with the reflection that all troubles & trials come simply and a stout heart will overcome—the trials of housecleaning only excepted."[71]

On the third of December, his twenty-sixth birthday, Cleveland took a ferry across New York Bay and boarded the *Bremen*, a 265-foot long, 2,300-ton steamer that was part of German shipping company Norddeutscher Lloyd's line. The next day the ship was forced to return to New York, as one of the flanges of the screw propeller broke off. After several days in dock—which allowed Cleveland more time to spend with family and friends—the *Bremen*, having been "thoroughly overhauled,"[72] set off once again for Europe on December 10. Cleveland noted a snowstorm early that day before leaving his parents' home in New York and that the precipitation had changed to sleet as the ship made its way across the bay. He settled in for the night, having overindulged in supper. Among the other forty or so passengers, Cleveland noted, were a young wife of eighteen, a mother of five children, a young naval officer, and an army private.[73] His cabin mates drank gin to pass the time and offered him some, which he likely refused. He preferred to spend his time observing the sun from the ship's deck (assuming it was not obscured by clouds) or talking astronomy with the occasional fellow passenger or crew member. The two-week passage to Europe went by relatively uneventfully, with Cleveland noting that "the westerly gales helped us on our course."[74]

"I do not know that I have experienced any of that loneliness that one expects to feel at sea," he wrote in a letter to his parents. "There is so much going on, on shipboard, and one gets so tired of that continual rolling and the noise of the revolving screw that I have looked with some satisfaction away over the blank blue sea."[75]

Although he experienced some anxiety—manifesting itself one night, about halfway into the voyage, in a dream of arriving at Pulkovo to a cold reception by Struve[76]—for the most part Cleveland felt optimistic in contemplating what lay before him. "All human hearts are moved by similar emotions when we first experience the realization of long delayed hopes,"[77] he said. With great anticipation, Cleveland's Russian adventure was about to begin.

CHAPTER THREE

Pulkovo (1864–1866)

Beloved Poulkova. Beloved Friends. My heart is with thee always.

—Cleveland Abbe, writing in his diary, 1889

It was Saturday, December 24, 1864—Christmas Eve—when the steamer *Bremen* arrived at the German port of Bremerhaven, on the North Sea. Large shards of ice were visible along the banks as the ship entered the mouth of the river Weser, which connects the port city of Bremerhaven with the larger, commercial city of Bremen, about sixty kilometers to the south. Cleveland Abbe disembarked the ship that had been his home for two weeks and boarded a smaller steamer that broke through the river ice, at times sliding over it and at other times diving under it. Cleveland, who had never been on such a vessel before, proclaimed he "liked the fun amazingly."[1] Upon reaching the railway station, he boarded a second-class train for Bremen, where he found the restaurants in the waiting hall to be "most complete and excellent," noting that anything a hungry traveler desired "he could have cooked and served in the best style."[2]

At seven o'clock that evening, he boarded a train for Berlin. The journey would take twelve hours, with a two-hour stopover in Hanover.[3] In Berlin, he checked into his hotel, where he would spend the next three nights before completing his journey to Russia. On Christmas Day, Cleveland did not pass up the opportunity to find a church where he could attend service, especially given it was a Sunday. He had hoped to visit the Berliner Dom, or cathedral, located on Museum Island near the center of the city, to hear the music there, but, as he told his parents in a letter, "it seemed so revolting to my tastes and feelings that I enquired for an English service, meaning in the English language, so they directed me to the Schloss Bijou where I found the Church of England service."[4]

He was also searching the city for his Michigan mentor, Dr. Franz Brünnow, who was in Berlin at the time. After several unsuccessful attempts, he was finally able to connect with him, as well as with several other prominent astronomers and professional acquaintances, including Wilhelm Förster, professor of astronomy at the University of Berlin, who would go on to become director of the Berlin Observatory.

Cleveland also had the opportunity to take in some of the local culture during his brief stay in Berlin. While searching for Brünnow on Christmas night, he found himself "in a gentlemans parlor . . . where they were just beginning the Christmas festivities & the Christmas tree had been shown."[5] One of his acquaintances, a graduate student from Harvard named S. F. Emmons, who was staying at the same hotel, accompanied him to the opera house, where they heard the Norwegian violin virtuoso Ole Bull perform the ballet *Das schlecht bewachte Mädchen*, by the German composer Peter Ludwig Hertel. Cleveland took note that "the applause was very subdued and without any stamping of the feet," adding, "very little clapping of the hands seemed sufficient for an encore." Cleveland seemed less than pleased with the performance, however, telling his parents that "the magnificence of the scenery & dresses and the hosts of actors and choruses almost made me forget the music." He added, "I was strongly inclined to think that Berliners cared as much or more for ballet dancing & fine shows as they do for music and was in this respect disappointed with the musical world."[6]

The pair also visited a beer garden, which seemed to Cleveland to be a novelty reserved for the *hoi polloi* of German society. "You have the same in New York but they are hardly considered reputable," he told his parents. "No stigma of this kind attaches to them here and they are certainly a most peculiarly German institution. A large hall held four hundred people sitting at little tables drinking beer, smoking, talking, reading, playing cards. At the further end a platform held some musicians. A very novel sight, and so long as the masses spend their evening in such a senseless way, the country must make very slow progress in improving itself."[7]

Before leaving Berlin, Cleveland purchased, for the sum of thirty-seven thalers (a type of silver coin in use in Germany at the time; this amount was equivalent to sixty-five U.S. dollars), several items to keep him warm while in Russia, including "a pair of overboots of foxskin and an enormous cloak of sheepskin black wool very warm good black cloth outside and fox collar & cuffs."[8] Although the cloak was too large in size for his modest frame ("I put it on over my overcoat and am quite lost in it."), he found it to be very warm and was confident it would meet his needs. "Muffled in this I hardly felt any cold until the last six hours before reaching St. P.," he said, adding, "indeed the ladies in the coupé wished the window open and so we had it half the time. For it was not cold weather and the frost on the window prevented our seeing anything outside."[9]

Cleveland passed the time by conversing with fellow passengers, when he could, and practicing his Russian. "On the route I began in earnest to study the Russian letters and numerals and learned to call for tchee soups &c & to pay my roubles & copeks," he wrote his parents after having arrived in Russia. "They have here almost entirely paper money for all sums of 1 rouble and more. Less than that they have silver coins and a good deal of copper. There is quite a presence of gold here. As the finances Russia are in a worse state than another European nation I get for £10 bill on London 80 Roubles and this costs me in N.Y. $50 in gold."[10]

Russia

"It was Wednesday evening, December 28th, 1864, that I wrapped my impatient soul in a huge black astrakhan cloak, seated myself in a corner of the Express for St. Petersburg and fell asleep as the wheel rumbled over the frozen ground."[11] With his sojourn in Berlin at an end, Cleveland embarked on the final leg of his journey to Russia, a land few Americans of his time would ever visit. About halfway between Berlin and St. Petersburg, the train's engine broke down near the Prussian settlement of Eydtkuhnen (now Chernyshevskoye, in the Russian exclave of Kaliningrad). "Der Maschine ist krank,"[12] the German conductor told Cleveland. They would remain on the frontier overnight before resuming, at a slower pace. As the train crossed the border into Russian territory, Cleveland's first impressions were of a land—and people—unlike any he had ever seen before:

> The minute we passed into Russia the new & strange things began to attract attention. I was in a coupé with a Frenchman who had lived many years in St. P. and spoke Russian so I got on nicely. Almost every station had a guard of six soldiers drawn up to receive us. There was just snow enough to make good sledding and a fine snow was falling so that over the vast plains flat and trackless I saw an occasional serf with [a] little horse and big hoop over his

head, dragging along loads of hay grain &c. All of these & the soldiers have a close fitting coat reaching to the knees of sheepskin wool inside and a belt around the waist. Nobody here is ever cold. I think they keep so warm as to be over delicate.[13]

Finally, on Saturday evening, during a snowstorm, the train pulled into the station in St. Petersburg. After checking into his room at the Hôtel de Russie, an establishment one contemporary guidebook recommended "tourists accustomed to foreign hotels, and who can make themselves understood in French or German, should ask for,"[14] Cleveland settled in for the night. The hotel, located on the Place Michel, or Mikhailovsky Square (now Arts Square), in the center of the city, featured approximately two hundred rooms, dinners by a French cook, not to mention "cold, warm, and shower-baths on the premises, as well as the indispensable tub." English, French, and American newspapers were also available.

On Sunday, Cleveland awoke to the "incessant but musical ding of the innumerable cathedral bells"[15] that populated the city. After breakfast, he called on a couple of acquaintances who happened to be in the city before spending the afternoon taking in some of the sights, including the Michaeloff Palace, the Admiralty building, and the imposing St. Isaac's Cathedral, with its neoclassical exterior and impressive gilded dome of pure gold. The cathedral, built on the orders of Tsar Alexander I, took forty years to complete and stood as the largest church in Russia when it opened in 1858. Cleveland took it all in, enchanted by the majesty and magnificence of what he saw.

This was the Russia of Tchaikovsky, Tolstoy, and Dostoevsky, who was just a year away from publishing his novel *Crime and Punishment*. In it, he paints a less-than-cheerful picture of Russia's Imperial capital. "There are few places where you can find so many gloomy, harsh, and strange influences on man's soul as you can in Petersburg," he wrote.[16] In fact, St. Petersburg and all of Russia were witness to incredible social and political upheavals in the 1860s. Less than four years before Cleveland's arrival, Tsar Alexander II changed the course of Russian history when he signed the Emancipation Reform of 1861, ending centuries of serfdom and effectively liberating some twenty-three million people across the vast Russian Empire. This, along with other sweeping reforms, including those to the judiciary and armed forces, helped make Alexander one of the most popular tsars of the Romanov dynasty[17] and prompted his brother, Grand Duke Konstantin Nikolayevich, to proclaim, "This may be the most important era in the thousand-year existence of Russia."[18] Despite his popular reforms, however, the tsar had his political detractors, as well as revolutionist enemies. Several attempts were made on Alexander's life, including one in the spring of 1866, while Cleveland was in Russia.[19] In 1881, members of the revolutionary group Narodnaya Volya (People's Will) succeeded in assassinating Tsar Alexander II, thus ending a period of reform and restructuring in Russia.

The changes that took place under Alexander's rule were evident to Cleveland as he entered the new, exotic land. "Every thing here is changing the whole nation is preparing to make great strides. The serf emancipation is the leaven that is working mightily. Every leading mind here now can make deep and lasting impressions. Especially I think the people need more of the American principle of saving time."[20]

Among all the nuances of Russian life that impressed upon Cleveland, none seemed to take as great a hold on his spirit as that of the bells that adorned the onion-domed churches and cathedrals of the Russian Orthodox faith. The effect the bells' medley had on him "was as I were suddenly transplanted among Nature's own sweet fields where the grass is interspersed with daisies, where butterflies flit over the sunny spots, and the quiet shades are filled with violets . . . a beautiful landscape swims before my eyes, everything harsh is transformed into beauty and harmony; the liquid notes seem not so much to raise one to heaven, as rather to serve to beatify the earth."[21] Enchanted by the bells' melodic effect, he further compared their tones to the works of classical musicians:

> The bell ringers of Russia do not attempt chimes or complicated pieces of music, artificial and tasteless; they make a bold stroke down through form and show to our fundamental love of tone; they simply fill the air with a pleasing bewildering flood of mellow notes, so that through our sense of hearing the mind is charmed and all nervous activity is hushed. As dance music affects the muscles and moves the feet—as Sebastian Bach makes one hold his breath oblivious to this world while soaring to higher realms—as Wagner stirs every emotion of human love—as Beethoven fills us with peace and purity—the bells of Russia without artifice by a perfectly natural appeal to our simplest mode of enjoyment of musical tones, are able to do for the uneducated ear all that the most famous composers have done for the cultivated musical world.[22]

While Cleveland's love for classical music and poetry is clearly evident in his description of Russian church bells, he reminded himself that the purpose of his visit was more scientific than artistic in nature. "I did not go to Russia to study poetry, music and art," he said, "or rather the poetry and art that I was to study was of the more precise kind known as 'mathematics and astronomy.'"[23]

Pulkovo

On Monday, January 2, Cleveland departed St. Petersburg for Pulkovo, located about eighteen kilometers due south of the city, among rolling hills. He employed a droshky—the type of low, four-wheeled, horse-drawn carriages ubiquitous in Russia at the time. He found it "neither convenient, comfortable or economical," yet noted it was the primary mode of transportation, despite its obvious drawbacks. "The seat is rarely large enough for two and the wheels are so small that the inexperienced one riding over a good cobblestone pavement feels that certainly the next bump will land him on terra firma."[24] As he left the splendor of the city—with its palaces, cathedrals, and elegant houses lining the boulevards—and made his way to the village that was Pulkovo, Cleveland noted how well laid out the route was, once his driver found the right road, that is.[25] "A broad straight avenue leads from the heart of the city southward, under a triumphal arch, straight to the door of our astronomical palace."[26] About ten kilometers to the southeast was the village of Tsarskoye Selo (Tsar's Village), home to the lavish Catherine Palace that served as the summer residence of the Romanovs. Aside from the observatory, Pulkovo itself was not much to speak of. Writing to his parents in New York, Cleveland described it as "a serf village," noting "how completely shut out from the world we are."[27] He later added:

> Here in Pulkova we have the best of Russian serf villages—a town of two thousand without any store or post office—no signs of life & energy compared with what we should expect in an American place of ¼ its size. Yet as it is a good specimen of the best of serf towns we are bound to look as much as possible at its good features. They certainly are noticeable. All the houses being of logs one and a half stories high and most of those that are ten years old in a tumble down condition are yet ornamented in a high degree with gingerbread filigree and paint. The Russians are decidedly fond of coloration. It is an essential in their idea of beauty and naturally so. Here, with snow on the ground five months and the sun very much obscured by clouds bare walls and the grand beauty of chaste Grecian marble are out of place being chilling and monotonous. Stuccoed walls and wooden walls must be painted. A rich yellow like gold or butter or cream is the favorite and it certainly is most refreshing to the eye. In the days when the air is filled with snow all the time this yellow seems

> very warm. Today with an atmosphere of almost unnatural clearness the sun gives this yellow stucco a glow and richness that is perfectly delighting to the eye by its contrast with the sparkling white snow. So also do I sympathize with the taste of the women who put on the richest red and orange and blue with white furs if possible for the sake of additional contrast. Not gaudy but rich.[28]

Upon arriving at the observatory, Cleveland met Dr. Wilhelm Döllen, one of the two senior astronomers, who showed him to his room. Dr. Friedrich Winnecke, who served as vice director of the observatory, stopped by Cleveland's room while he was unpacking to welcome him and explain some of the finer points of living there. Cleveland learned that "every thing must be brought from St. P. and every thing in St. P. is imported."[29] He was free to dine with the observatory's intendent, Mr. Heintz, which was the practice of the other unmarried men in residence at Pulkovo. He would have to provide his other meals for himself. He was advised, therefore, to keep a "bachelor's hall in high style" though Döllen warned him that it was "quite impossible" for someone to live alone there for more than a few years. "If he does not marry he will overwork and sicken."[30]

Cleveland was disappointed that the observatory's director, Dr. Otto Struve, who had extended him the invitation to come to Pulkovo, was not there to greet him. The famed astronomer had taken ill prior to Cleveland's arrival and decided to spend the winter in southern Europe to recuperate. Acting on Struve's behalf, Döllen wrote of Cleveland's arrival in the observatory's annual report, published two and a half months into his stay:

> Toward the end of the year the remaining free vacancy for a supernumerary astronomer was assigned, namely to the citizen of the United States from North America, Mr. Cleveland Abbe from New York, who in December arrived with the intention to spend some time here to further his education in practical astronomy. We have received with particular joy this visit from a country that is so far away from us, but in terms of observational methods is closer to us than many others, yet at the same time presents several unique features. Mr. Abbe already has several years of practical experience working for the Coast Survey, and his current stay with us is for us so fortunate in that, since the visits of the famous astronomers Gould and Bond, in 1848 and 1852, no personal interaction with our American colleagues has taken place.[31]

Cleveland found Döllen to be a "kind-hearted man" and spent many hours with him and his wife, Charlotte, the eldest daughter of Wilhelm Struve, and their children. Although Cleveland never got the opportunity to meet the elder Struve, who died just a few weeks before his arrival, he imagined him to be "an unusually open hearted affable gentleman." His impressions of the new director of the observatory, however, were less than glowing. "Otto Struve is about 47 and not a handsome man but tall and I think pleasant, at least he is to me though I find others are not much drawn out towards him but perhaps he will change," Cleveland told his mother, before proceeding to describe Otto's children. "Wilhelm is studying Mathematics at Dorpat. He is about twenty four. Marie is about twenty very pleasant & speaks English very well—you see I am sure to find out who speaks English. The little children are also pleasant so that we have an addition to Pulkova society."[32]

Cleveland quickly became acquainted with the remainder of the staff and their families—approximately 125 in all—who lived at the observatory. Among them were two young men, close to Cleveland in age, with whom he became close friends. One of these men was Nikolai Struve, Otto's half-brother, who went by "Kolla" (or "Colla," as Cleveland referred to him). The other, Victor Fuss, was, like Cleveland, a supernumerary astronomer whose father, Georg, was a regular staff astronomer at the observatory. When Cleveland wrote his mother that summer telling her how much he missed Bickmore, he added that he had found the void "partially filled by Colla Struve & Victor Fuss & others." It was in Nikolai that Cleveland found an especially kindred spirit, as the young Struve was studying theology at the University of Dorpat (now the University of Tartu, in Estonia), with the goal of becoming a Lutheran pastor. Along with the Döllens' governess, Miss Helwig (which Cleveland sometimes spelled "Helwigh"), "a young lady of a very decidedly religious disposition,"[33] Cleveland and Fuss had formed an informal English study group, which also fulfilled Cleveland's need for a modest amount of social interaction. "We form what may be denominated the English society as Colla reads with me quite regularly and Fraulein Hildebrand[34] speaks, whilst Miss Helwigh being too timid to speak only listens and reads, but she is an excellent scholar," he said in a letter to his parents. "Meanwhile I find it of course the best way to learn German."[35] Learning German was not just an academic or recreational pastime for Cleveland, it was a necessity, as it was the lingua franca of the observatory. "I must learn German and Russian as soon as possible," he wrote his parents soon after arriving at Pulkovo.

Another custom to which Cleveland had to adjust during his stay in Pulkovo was that, like all of Russia during the nineteenth century, the observatory and its residents still relied on the Julian calendar, which lagged twelve days behind the more modern Gregorian calendar that much of Europe had adopted shortly after its introduction in 1582. Thus, in many of his letters and diary entries written while in Pulkovo, Cleveland denoted two versions of any given date—the "New Style" and "Old Style." This also meant that, shortly after his arrival in early January 1865 (New Style), the residents at Pulkovo were about to celebrate Christmas, as December 25 (Old Style) fell just a few days after his arrival. To celebrate, Dr. Döllen invited Cleveland to dine with him and his family. Afterward, they joined the other members of the observatory and their families for the lighting of the Christmas tree. "The tree and the surrounding tables were brilliantly lighted but the lights did not give satisfaction," Cleveland said. "They were little glass lamps for burning kerosene oil: so after a while they were exchanged for the little wax candles."[36] Cleveland was surprised and "quite overwhelmed" to receive as gifts a copy of the observatory's library catalogue, as well as a Russian samovar, used to boil water for making tea. "This is a truly Russian invention," he told his parents, "is a necessity in every home and I thought it a very splendid present." The samovar remained a treasured possession of Cleveland's well after his stay in Pulkovo.[37]

On Wednesday, January 11 (O.S. December 30), Cleveland walked to Tsarskoye Selo to visit the "Emperor's Summer Palace," which he described in a letter to his parents as being "a copy of that at Versailles and being the finest one I had particularly noticed of course I was much interested in every particular."[38] Cleveland described the ride to the palace "through a very large park which is I presume very beautiful in summer. On the roadside I noticed a facility in which I understood that there was kept an elephant for the emperor's use."[39] His tour of the palace included a visit to the famed Amber Room, with its stunning panels of polished amber, pieced together like a giant jigsaw puzzle to form a room of breathtaking opulence. The beauty of this remarkable room—a gift from King Frederick William I of Prussia to Peter the Great—so enchanted Cleveland that he later made note of it in his diary.

Back at Pulkovo, Cleveland began to settle into his work as a supernumerary astronomer, where he and the other astronomers in residence at the time who occupied this position—including Victor Fuss—were "at liberty to devote their whole time to their own studies, they yet generally choose to contribute several hours daily to the regular work of the observatory, receiving a small compensation therefor."[40] For his part, Cleveland received twenty-five rubles per month,[41] equivalent to approximately $21 at the time, or about $331 in 2019.[42] This proved to be a challenge for him, as he wrote his parents soon after arriving that he "shall try to squeeze through on it"[43] and eventually had to ask his father to send additional funds to subsidize his stay. "What His Excellency Otto Struve meant by writing me that one could live in Poulkova for $300 I do not know," he later wrote his parents. "I guess he never tried it on."[44]

Cleveland kept busy studying "the atmospheric phenomena that affect astronomical observation and was hoping to unravel the irregularities of refraction near the zenith."[45] Such an achievement was something he "knew that the eyes of Practical Astronomers were searching for and would criticise severely whoever should undertake it."[46] Cleveland, with his characteristic modesty, told his parents, "It will be a work of years and I may not have the talent to do it properly, but I shall try and when well done I believe it will be a lasting monument." This meant long hours and little time for recreation or other activities during his early days at Pulkovo. As he wrote to his parents about two weeks after his arrival:

> Our life is so very monotonous that there is absolutely nothing to do but to study and I am buried in Astronomy. In this respect these are the Halcyon days. I rise at 7 & retire at 11 and just now it is 8 1/2 PM. I have taken my tea and after this letter shall read some astronomy then a German Fairy Tale by Hans Andersen then my Bible & to bed.[47]

Cleveland viewed his time in Pulkovo not just as an opportunity to further his career at one of the finest astronomical institutions of its time but also as a chance to experience a people and culture far different from his own. He saw this as a way to broaden his horizons. "I don't think it is well for any one who wishes to avoid narrowminded ideas to stay in one place & see nothing of others," he wrote his mother. "Besides I think it one of the strong bonds of the union of our states that the people travel so much and that every one feels therefore that he is & ought to feel at home & welcome in any part of the country."[48] He told his parents he hoped "to see more of the pure Russia"[49] during visits to St. Petersburg and Moscow, though he never made it to the latter. "Your father says you must see all you can, & tell us about it," his mother urged him. "It may be a long time before you visit Europe again, & you must make the best use of your eyes & ears."[50]

Cleveland's schedule allowed him to observe not only the stars above but some of the goings-on of the local society around him. "This Morning about five o'clock I was up to observe some stars about six I was interested to observe a procession of six women & five men each good naturedly dressed & bearing rakes coarse brooms &c," he wrote his parents in the spring of 1865.[51] "They disappeared from my sight but I afterward found them brushing off the winter's collection of leaves sticks &c from our grass so as to give the young blades a chance to sprout. They make a merry group laughing & happy in this glorious sunlight. I hate to see women working out of doors—they seem so happy but they look so robust & strong that it offends my idea of delicacy. However it would be quite a mistake to attribute to these peasants the delicacy of a gentleman."[52]

Appearances aside, Cleveland's notion of a stratified society, combined with his strict religious principles, led him to form harsh judgments toward those whose lifestyles did not confirm to his worldview. "But here more than in all Europe (unless I except Ireland Turkey & Greece which are about on the same level) the people high & low seem to really regard life as an animal existence to be enjoyed to its utmost," he told his parents. "Everyone argues that we know nothing of the future from observation or history and why should we be anxious about it? There is certainly no high spiritual standard to which all are trying to conform."[53]

Nowhere did this sententious attitude manifest itself more than when it came to the practice of drinking. "Now the height of happiness for the middle & lower classes is found in drinking & carousing & especially with the peasants the sober ones are rare exceptions," he said.[54] While strolling around the streets of St. Petersburg on Easter Sunday, Cleveland noticed how happy the locals seemed. "As the day wore on it became more & more painfully evident that the commoner people consider themselves truly happy only when they are drunk," he lamented. "Brandy is the staple drink and the source of one third of the government revenue. Every minute I saw a soldier or istrostichike peasant or other going along perhaps a wife or child on one side but certainly a two gallon jug of brandy on the other."[55] In his disgust, Cleveland could hardly comprehend the scene before him. "Not in all my life—adding together all that I have ever seen have I seen so many men tipsy & reeling or else dead drunk. Really the whole city had gone off on a great spree. To be sure I did see plenty of sober gentlemen & some sober workmen. Had I been in Pulkova Wagner[56] tells me that I could not have seen a single sober man." Cleveland's abhorrence left him feeling revulsed for days afterward:

> I was thoroughly disgusted with St. P. and have not yet recovered from the influence of that days sights. The Police seemed to have no orders to arrest tipsy men nor to prevent their going where they would. On the pleasantest promenades where were gentlemen and ladies of at least exterior decency—were intermingling the tipsy reelers as freely as though they were all on the

> same level. And indeed I began to think they were sober. Men appeared not in the least pained at this to me distressing exhibition of animal nature. Gentle ladies looked on with as much unconcern as the Spanish ladies would look on a bull fight. And where all were so much hardened having frequently seen such spectacles—I thought all must be essentially equally lowered.[57]

Still, Cleveland was able to enjoy himself socially from time to time. Just a few weeks after his arrival, on February 15 (O.S. February 3), he attended a formal ball in St. Petersburg, held at the residence of the American minister to Russia, General Cassius Marcellus Clay, a Kentucky politician and abolitionist. "I got my white cravat and white kids (such kids as I never knew in America) and made my appearance," Cleveland recalled in a letter to his mother. "The Emperor had not yet arrived and I learned that he had had an unfortunate previous engagement to go out hunting so that he came not at all. However his family &c were there—the two grand dukes Constantine & ——— also."[58] Cleveland enjoyed conversing with several of the other guests, including Grand Duke Constantine and Admiral Lisianski—who invited Cleveland to call on him at his house. The highlight, however, was an activity in which Cleveland was a neophyte, but in which he found much delight:

> But to me the charm of the evening after all lay not in the delicious champagne, nor the brilliant uniforms nor the decorations of delicious flowers nor the illustrious personages Ghortschakoff & the would-be King of Greece nor in the feeling that I was privileged to look upon such an assembly—But I found my delight in dwelling upon the beauty and inimitable grace of the younger ladies who were the dancers. In America I have but rarely seen any grace & good taste that could not be subject to some more or less severe criticism. And I have rarely allowed myself to criticize it except to say that so & so did not suit me. But here every thing was far beyond my powers of criticism. I had only to drink in the pleasure of watching such graceful movements and to admire the tasteful dresses. Especially was I surprised at the perfect absolute absence of all constraint. In all American parties one can see more or less stiffness each seems to be thinking of himself or herself & making more or less unpleasant comparisons. Here each appeared to forget himself and to only enjoy. I had looked for some form & formality—but there was none. I suppose that each had been dressed by her waiting maid & knew that all had been done that could be done & so gave herself no further trouble but abandoned herself to the enjoyment of the dance. I have read of the delicious ease & politeness of the noble families but it was better to

have seen it & to know how perfectly delightful is such grace: it is probably somewhat the result of education & companionship and partly natural—but it appears perfectly natural.[59]

Cleveland's enjoyment of the scene quickly turned to anxiety when one of the women—later revealed to be Princess Suvorov[60]—invited him to take part in one particular dance. "The lady collects her own partners and my heart quite went bumpety bump when the prettiest having already two came to me for her third & special one," he reminisced. "Ah mother—you don't know how much you have deprived me of by not sending me to dancing school—However I think it best that I do not know how to dance for the pleasures of gay life are very fascinating—probably all the more so to me because I see so little of them and they offer so fine & complete a relaxation from study."[61]

Cleveland's mother responded several weeks later, addressing her son as "My dear Cleveland Georgeovitch," assigning him his "new Russian cognomen" that followed the pattern of the patronymic used by Russians, who referred to Cleveland as such. In reference to Cleveland's observations at the ball, Charlotte reminded her son, "I know the beautiful ladies in their becoming dresses &c were very fascinating, but you must hold on to your heart." She added, "Don't regret that you can't dance—I know it seems hard when fascinating young ladies want you for a partner, but in the end, it will be as well. Did that young lady ask you in German or French, or only motion to you?—to dance."[62]

The episode also caught the attention of Cleveland's younger brother Walter, who wrote wanting to know more of Cleveland's social life in St. Petersburg. "I say Cleve are you getting up in the world," Walter wrote. "Aren't your swallowtails[63] most worn out, going to see the girls & noble men so often. I guess you get more to eat than you did here, you go out so often after it." Walter then asked, "Was that charming creature that lovely Russian—a young Bear unmarried or married—I refer to the animal that wanted you to dance."[64]

The day after the ball, Cleveland wrote his mother, telling her they had been experiencing "both cold & warm weather here this past month. The first two weeks & this present week are quite warm the thermometer being above freezing at noon. But the interim has been cold -20 to -30 Fahrenheit. The sky & atmosphere are perfectly clear and sometimes a strong wind. I have enjoyed this dry cold weather very much almost every one would prefer it to the present warm muggy cloudy atmosphere."[65]

Another Russian tradition which Cleveland found amusing was the celebration of Maslenitsa, or "Butter Week," as he referred to the carnival-like festival that takes place during the last week before Lent in the Russian Orthodox Church. Cleveland described it as "a week of days in which every one gives himself up to amusements."[66] In St. Petersburg, Cleveland marveled at the temporary wooden structures erected in the public squares throughout the city, where "pantomime theater" and other shows took place. He was especially fascinated at the two "ice mountains," forming great curved slides—some thirty feet high and three hundred feet long—covered with ice on which "one can slide down most easily & delightfully." It was the children who walked the streets selling hot tea that Cleveland found to be among "the oddest sights to notice," however. They walked throughout the crowds "with great jugs bound in clothes which they carry about under their arms to pour out a cup of hot tea (Russian tchée) for a few copkecks." He was also interested to see a group of "Laplanders" (most likely Sami people from the Arkhangelsk region of northern Russia) camped along the banks of the Neva with reindeer. "They do a good business by giving the curious ones a ride behind their reindeer on their original sleds and of course I indulged myself so as to say that I had ridden like Santa Claus."[67]

As he observed the local peasantry enjoying themselves, Cleveland was surprised at how the richness and joviality with which they expressed themselves seemed to belie the relatively simple lives they led:

> On every day but particular Sunday of this past week the Russian maidens are out of doors riding & singing. They are a very happy people I think certainly they appear far more so than any clan in America. I do not admire their singing though I like to hear it in the absence of all other noise. The whole village was out on Sunday afternoon. Every horse & sled was in requisition every one loaded with its full complement of lads & lasses. But when one looks beyond the apparent happiness & the gaudy colors he experiences a great shock at finding that these have not any education. They may almost be said to know less than nothing. Education & perhaps religion is making progress here among the serfs but has not elevated them apparently as yet very far above the beasts.[68]

In St. Petersburg, Cleveland found a world of cosmopolitan culture and society that provided a welcome escape from the isolation and monotony of life at Pulkovo. He made several trips to the city in the spring of 1865, including a visit on Saturday, April 15 (O.S. April 3), "to stay several days to see the

Russian manner of enjoying the Easter Holidays and hoping also to drive off a very unpleasant attack of inability to study & compute."[69] He marveled at the sights and sounds of the strange city, which was so different from his native New York. He especially enjoyed a visit to the Bolshoy Gostiny Dvor,[70] a vast shopping complex along St. Petersburg's Nevsky Prospekt:

> On Saturday I said I first wandered into the Gostini Dvor. This is a block of little stores one of its sides facing on the Nevski Prospkekt. The sidewalk surrounding it is covered by an arch and in terms of holdings is full of small stands with all things for sale. This Gostini Dvor is I believe the principal shopping place for respectable people. The Apraksini Dvor is much more extensive and very fine looking having been lately rebuilt—but it is filled mostly with shops for poorer people. I found in the Gostini Dvor a multitude of buyers & sellers. Easter eggs of every style from hard boiled & dyed red eggs at 20 copecks up to elegant imitation with gold & paintings at two or five roubles. Holy pictures & shrines & candles of equally diverse styles. Fruit & candies are in one store. Books & music in another. Toys for children and useful articles for the household. Very much such a mixture as you will find in a Sanitary Commission Fair.[71] I saw something that looked so queer that I determined to buy & eat some of it—that I might have an intelligent idea of the taste thereof. The seller was a Greek from Constantinople and I afterward saw two others with the same Oriental look & dress & commodity. They must have travelled together all the way over land & ice & snow as do very many of these nations of the interior of this continent.[72]

Several months later, Cleveland had an opportunity to visit the Hermitage Museum, which had opened to the public in 1852 and, the same month Cleveland arrived in Russia, had acquired the painting *Madonna and Child* (*The Madonna Litta*), created by Leonardo da Vinci in 1490.[73] Cleveland had planned to get a general overview of the vast collection during his initial visit, in hopes of returning later. "This is a very famous collection being large & having some fine paintings," he described. "The collection of sculptures & ancient antiquities is also extensive. I expected here to find a very great treat of course I was doomed to a little disappointment but there were some things that pleased me much."[74] Among the works that Cleveland found most pleasing were the massive oil paintings *Sacrifice of Isaac*, by Rembrandt, and *Liberation of St. Peter*, by Bartolomé Esteban Murillo.

Above all, he found the section of the museum along the embankment of the river Neva to be the most pleasing. "The paintings were good the rooms old & antique and above all the view of the river & the opposite bank the Fortress Bourse Academy Observatory University &c all were to me more interesting than anything else especially as I could imagine to myself the Empress Catherine who founded the Hermitage as she enjoyed the scene in the good old days," he said. "But she was a very corrupt wicked woman so I did not take much pleasure in thinking of her."[75]

In April 1866, Cleveland had the opportunity to observe the ceremonies in St. Petersburg celebrating the twenty-fifth anniversary of Tsar Alexander II and Tsarina Maria Alexandrovna. "Sunday a week ago was the Silver Wedding day of the Czar and as I did not see the inside of affairs I can only narrate of the outside," he wrote his mother shortly after the event. "Sunday was [a] high holiday every poor man dressed in his best rags and the rich in their richest. Of course I put on my every day suit and my rose colored spectacles my high heeled caloshes and my walking stick—But notwithstanding my best efforts I did not see much for Petersburg is a large place and the Russians are tall."[76]

His frequent visits to St. Petersburg provided Cleveland with an opportunity to experience the many opulent and exquisite features the city had to offer, as well as features that were less than refined. During an excursion with Kolla Struve in August 1865, the pair found themselves on a steamer traversing the Neva that Cleveland described as "a row boat with a kettle in the middle." In addition to a noisy whistle that went off every few minutes to announce the boat's presence, he complained of its unusual smoke pipe "which bows its head at every bridge" allowing it to spit a "black mud"—a combination of steam and smoke—on the passengers. This happened, Cleveland said, "to the great profit of my washerwoman and the distress of my tailor & friends. For my summer suit has so shrunken after the washing to which it was necessary to submit it that I am made to appear like a monkey in baby's clothes."[77]

A Depressive State

Back at Pulkovo, Cleveland threw himself wholly into his work but often found himself despondent and discouraged, sometimes to the point of wanting to abandon astronomy altogether. "Ofttimes I have my old fits of longing to give up astronomy & all hard work but I suppose it will not do," he wrote his parents. "There is much that I want to do and that I can do. I hope I may be able to maintain the American reputation for energy & activity though sometimes I think I have lost all power of studying or investigating & am hardly fit to be a mechanical computer."[78] When his mother read this, she responded by suggesting a change of pace—and scenery. "I hope your health is not going to give out," she wrote. "You speak of yourself as if you were not strong—according to the book I read on Russia, you will have some charming weather soon, & you must take some of your companions & roam the country & drink in the fresh air."[79]

As spring settled in and the first signs of summer began to appear, Cleveland found his mother's prediction held true. "During this past week our spring grass & leaves & flowers have finally come and it is very pleasant indeed," he wrote her in late May.[80] "Nightingales & skylarks are also here with many other birds." It was a period during which Cleveland became entranced by the atmospheric phenomena he observed. "The weather here is however the most treacherous of all that I have known. Clouds come & go without warning and one must always be on his watch not to lose a valuable hour or two," he reported two weeks later.[81] By late July, as summer firmly took hold, Cleveland found that the warm weather—while too much for others—was a welcome relief from the typical sweltering summers he was used to in New York. "It is now twelve noon and having just arisen and finished my bread & milk breakfast I will write you & tell you how hot warm weather can be so near the North Pole," he wrote his mother in late July. "It is now 86 Fahrenheit and is called insufferable, of course as I am accustomed to 96 I do not find myself at all melted. Indeed the past month of cloudless & warm weather is to me quite a godsend and I have improved it to the utmost observing all night & day, with occasional intermissions to play croquet sleep & drink coffee."[82]

While his astronomical work dominated his time at Pulkovo, Cleveland did find time to enjoy occasional recreation, as well as the company of others, as his late-July letter to his mother alluded. His favorite pastime during the summer months was croquet, which he described as "a very excellent game for young & old."[83] To Cleveland, the game added a certain egalitarianism to the stratified life[84] at the observatory. "It certainly is the point of all outdoor plays as yet invented where men & women can play together and if it absorbs too much time it is better for us and is a testimony to the excellence of the game."[85] Even this, however, provided but a brief distraction to his observing. "I find it quite delightful after dinner to go over to the West side of the observatory when Mrs. Döllen & the children come out to sit under the shade trees & enjoy the cool breeze," he wrote his mother. "There we all ten or fifteen lie on the grass & play to our hearts content: after 7 o'clock it is pleasant to play croquet for an hour after that I observe but the others take walks and become very romantic, I suppose."[86]

While he may not have taken part in romantic walks, Cleveland did appreciate the company of the young women at Pulkovo. "Miss Helwigh a young lady a new teacher for Mr. Döllen's children and Miss Hildebrand added very much to the pleasure of our society & were in continual demand," he told his mother.[87] "They tell me that on most of the fine evenings the two young ladies and some of the gentlemen have made very pleasant walks here in the ground, or the park as it is called but I have only heard their voices—which disrupt my observations."[88]

Miss Hildebrand, in particular, seemed to be the object of Cleveland's affection during the early part of his stay at Pulkovo. He maintained a certain degree of modesty when describing her to his mother:

> She came here as a governess for Mr. Hintze's family some two weeks after I did. As she speaks English of course it is rational that I should speak with her rather than with the Russians at our dinner table. And sometimes when I am reading the paper I must go to her for assistance and sometimes at the table when I don't understand the others they must get her to be interpreter. Being young & fair with a multitude of blushes of course there's a fine chance for flirtation but as Bickmore says I am too much in earnest for that so I like not to perceive her so well pleased with me. I am quite sure that on the evening of the baptism she wanted me to dance with her but I don't dance and I presume shall not learn. Mr. Hintze & Dr. Gyldén take great delight in seeing us together each blushing and awkward but I don't think that their expectations will be realized.[89]

One "very pleasant and cool" day in March 1865, Cleveland took time out of his day to show Miss Hildebrand the view of St. Petersburg "through a small spyglass from the steps of the main entrance" of the observatory. While atmospheric conditions were not ideal for looking at the distant city, Cleveland noted they had "a very clear view of the church & houses & domes. It is a very unique & beautiful sight to point the glass along the road from the foot of the hill 12 miles northward and then see the triumphal arch & the spire of the fortress church." Later, he showed Miss Hildebrand portraits that hung in the main hall of the observatory, including those of Tsar Alexander II and his father, Nicholas I, as well as of various astronomers. "The portrait of the Elder Struve which hangs in the Director's room is a very fine picture and I hope to be able to send you a photograph from it as also views of the observatory itself," he wrote his mother.[90]

Still, Cleveland found it difficult to maintain an active social life and keep up with his astronomical work and studies, which clearly were his priority.

"You will wonder whether I have not yet outgrown my fancy for girls and whether I am not so absorbed in study as not to think of them," he told his mother. "Neither is true and for the sake of my astronomy I could wish not to see another young lady whilst I am here. As for enjoying their society one hour and forgetting them the next in order to study that is wellneigh impossible."[91] To this, his mother replied, "I see you are not without young ladies in your establishment—all I can say is take care you know your weakness."[92]

In the spring of 1865, Cleveland went through what he later referred to as "a bleak & gloomy time."[93] In writing his mother, he said:

> If I seem—as I know I am—often low spirited and deprived of all energy to do astronomical work—you must attribute it not to my failure to have what I want—for father has enabled me to perfectly satisfy the reasonable desires of any astronomer—but to the fact that in the midst of said work as I delight to do and can do well there come days & weeks when all thoughts of it are repulsive when I lose all power to do original thinking or computing and can only perform such mechanical work as I have before done. It makes anyone sad and dejected when he sees that in a few years his mind on which he depends will be gone. I have attributed any trouble to the excessive over work that I have done since I was fifteen and especially in Cambridge—but now I know that besides this and equally suicidal—there has been another cause. However I have not lost all hope—on the contrary when it is pleasant & I am as happy as I am today no one could seem in better spirits—and I do confidently expect that in a few years I shall have overcome and shall have regained what now I have lost.[94]

The depression, Cleveland said, had affected him "too often these past five or six years," making him feel "terribly lonesome and sick of life."[95] When he was in Cambridge, he said, he often felt "in such a mood" that he would not write at all. In Pulkovo, he told his mother, he "endeavored to write regularly and this may to some extent explain why I have written in so many unhappy moods."[96] These mood swings were nothing new to Cleveland, as he had dealt with them since he was a teenager. Writing his mother in the fall of 1865, he asked:

> I wonder whether you have ever such days of happy sadness as I sometimes have had. I remember the first ones that I experienced it was when I was fifteen and used on Sunday almost regularly to go alone by myself to read my Bible and pray and cry. Perhaps I then formed the habit—but certain it

is that still I find times when nothing but a good cry makes me happy. A spirit of unsatisfied longing comes over me and I grow discontented until by thinking & reading my faith in the goodness of God returns. I swallow down the transient unpleasant realities of life my murmurs are washed away with my tears and the calmness of resignation comes over me. So often is this my experience that I am loth to stop the tears but will rather welcome them heartily because of their salutary effect.[97]

Cleveland tried to brush aside his bouts of melancholy as a passing phase. "Perhaps all my trouble is imaginary and will disappear as I grow older," he hoped. "I am very thankful that it is not deep melancholy for it only lasts a day or two. Today I have had a real good Sunday: the first for a long interval."[98]

News from Home

While Cleveland was in Russia, his alma mater in New York, the Free Academy, was undergoing a transformation. Owing to pressure by some of its alumni that the term "academy" did not convey an appropriate level of academic achievement, the state legislature adopted a measure—which the governor signed—officially changing the name of the institution to the "College of the City of New York." While some, including the academy's president, Horace Webster, did not immediately embrace the new name, the student body overwhelmingly did. So much so that they celebrated with a torchlight mock funeral procession through the streets of New York, carrying a coffin filled with textbooks, which they buried in the front yard of the academy. Among those taking part in this demonstration was Cleveland's brother Robert, then a sub-freshman. "Let us recall the forming of classes in procession—each man with his torch—marching and counter-marching, shouting and echoing, crowding and jostling, within and without that old iron railing; thronging the streets, bullying policemen, anathematizing Columbians. We owned the town that night."[99]

Charlotte relayed the news of the academy's name change—as well as the latest goings-on of the Abbe family—to her son in one of the many letters she wrote Cleveland while he was in Russia. "At home, all moves on as usual—Willie to his cousins, the girls to school & the boys to College—For you know the name of the academy is changed. The boys had a gay time one evening & buried the old academy, with speeches & songs &c They then serenaded Drs. Webster & Doremus & Mrs. Haines' girls—I don't know how she liked that—of course they did not show themselves."[100]

While Cleveland absorbed himself in his astronomical pursuits, his parents kept him abreast of other news from back home, including the latest on the rebellion, which weighed on the hearts and minds of the Abbes, both at home and abroad. "I am glad you find the best men are in favor of putting down the Rebellion and slavery," his father wrote to him soon after Cleveland arrived in Russia, "and that they sympathize with the North in having had great successes lately and a few more victories will do up the Confederacy & slavery."[101] Several weeks later, Cleveland's mother wrote to him with an update:

> You say you have heard none of our late news.— Since you left, our army have taken fort Fisher, & stopped the port of Wilmington—Sherman has marched across Georgia, & come out, & took the fort that protected Savanah, & caused that to be evacuated, & marched north, cut all the railroads, taken Columbia the capital of S. Carolina, keeps right on, & today we hear Charleston is evacuated, & our troops are in possession, our flag floats from Ft. Sumter, & he will not stop till Richmond is taken—We are ready to hear any thing now; all this has been without a battle—Has not God been on our side?"[102]

The war had officially come to an end with Lee's surrender to Grant at Appomattox Court House in Virginia on April 9. On April 13, Cleveland's mother wrote him a letter in which she described the mood back home with the war finally at an end. "By this time you have heard of the great success of our armies, & the rejoicings we have—Every one wears a joyous face, & you would be so pleased to see the flags floating all through our streets."[103]

The next day, in Washington, D.C., President Abraham Lincoln awoke for what was to be a long day of meetings with his cabinet and others. Secretary of War Edwin Stanton later recalled that Lincoln appeared "more cheerful and happy" than he ever had during a cabinet meeting, with "the near prospect of firm and durable peace at home and abroad."[104] It was Good Friday and the president decided to unwind that evening at the theater. The comedy *Our American Cousin* was playing at Ford's Theatre on 10th Street, just a few blocks from the White House. The play was already underway when Lincoln, his wife, Mary, and their guests, Major Henry Rathbone and Miss Clara Harris, entered the theater. The actors on stage paused mid-scene as the presidential party made its way to the state box that James Ford, brother of theater owner John Ford, had hastily adorned that afternoon with American flags borrowed from the Treasury Department,[105] along with a portrait of George Washington, upon learning that Lincoln would be in attendance that evening. As the orchestra played "Hail to the Chief," audience members stood and turned to get a glimpse of the man who had led the Union to victory through four years of civil war. Lincoln took his seat and the play resumed. The third act was in its second scene when actor John Wilkes Booth ascended the stairway and made his way to the presidential box. Familiar to the theater staff, Booth moved freely past the seats of the second-floor balcony to the door of the box that separated him from his target. He waited until just the right moment before bursting in and shooting Lincoln in the back of the head with his small Derringer pistol, just as actor Harry Hawk delivered one of the most humorous lines of the play, sure to bring big laughs from the audience that would muffle the sound of the fatal gunshot.

The news of Lincoln's death stunned a nation already wounded by war, but it took two weeks to reach Cleveland, cloistered away in the relative isolation of Pulkovo. "Last night the St. Petersburg paper brings one very short dispatch saying that 'Lincoln is murdered Seward dangerously wounded & gold 147,'" he wrote to his mother on April 28. "I cannot believe it. It must be a gold speculator's last resort to save himself from bankruptcy. But it must be several days before the arrival of later news can confirm or deny this statement & I begin to be quite feverish with hopes & fear."[106] He went on to discuss other matters, but as he closed his letter, Cleveland added a statement of hope that perhaps the reports by the St. Petersburg press were simply rumors that ultimately would prove to be untrue. "May I soon hear that Lincoln & Seward are not assassinated and that the Union is triumphant," he said. The following day, however, amid other notations about washing the floor of his new room and the consecration of a church in Tsarskoe Selo, Cleveland wrote the words "**Lincoln is dead**" with extra ink and a double underline in his diary. He also went back to his entry for April 14 and similarly added the following line at the bottom:

This day is Lincoln murdered

Charlotte had continued composing her letter of Thursday, April 13, the following day, describing the joyful mood that prevailed across New York—and throughout the Union—that Friday evening, following Lee's surrender, just as the devastating events in Washington were taking place. Stricken with grief, she added a much more somber note to the letter Saturday morning. "I little thought when I wrote this letter last evening of the awful event taking place when I was penning it—our president was assassinated last night—shot down in his box in the theatre surrounded by wife & friends.—He was insensate from that time & is now in eternity." She continued, "God help this nation—what will become of us—We have trusted to our good moral society, & our free institutions & thought he was safe. Our trust is in God that he will bring good out of this seeming evil."[107] Cleveland would not receive his mother's letter until May 4. The following day, May 5, Charlotte penned another letter to her son in which she wrote of the rejoicing taking place, in spite of the continued mourning for "our good Presidents death," as she put it. "Now we are happy in the prospect of no more battles—as the armies of the South are mostly surrounded, we feel that the war is over," she wrote. "Jeff Davis is still fleeing & we fear will escape. A great reward is offered for him, as being implicated in the murder of Lincoln. Can it be possible? Our city is still draped in mourning, & it is astonishing how quickly we have taken the good news poured in upon us."[108]

Cleveland wrote his mother back on May 9 (O.S. April 27). "I had been expecting & almost dreading the paper containing the details of the murder of President Lincoln," he said. "Everywhere in Europe the event provides a most profound sensation and a revulsion in the opinion of the admirers of the South. It covers the Southern cause with the blackest pall." In his grief, he tried to make sense of the senseless tragedy that had befallen his homeland:

> When the first burst of passionate resentment passes we turn to inquire what does this mean. Certainly God in causing this to be done has a purpose. Everyone acknowledges that the tending on the part of many loyalists was toward great leniency to the conquered rebels. We see this tendency at once checked and we learn that it was not pleasing to God who demands justice first & then lenience. Our lenience is the more culpable because it is desired by many men from sordid & selfish motives—from love of ease & peace from a vain desire to show how great magnanimity can be exhibited by a great nation. We should have boasted for ever of the greatness of the American name. We are only men with like passions & faith—but we should have come to think ourselves very nearly angels in forgiveness.[109]

As he went on, Cleveland expressed his beliefs that, through the powers of the federal government, the nation would be healed and justice would be served. "We are much more truly one nation than ever before in our history. We love our Union we acknowledge our central federal national government as our supreme head & that all other authorities in the land must bow to it," he wrote. "Andrew Johnson is right in thinking & saying that treason must be punished as the law directs—leniency to traitors is treason to the state."

In his convictions, Cleveland expressed hope that history would not repeat itself. "The horrible days of the ignorant, blind fanaticisms of the French Revolution need not be repeated in America: our streets need not flow with the blood of thousands of rebels else we may cause more bloodshed than is necessary to render treason odious."[110]

With four years of bloody conflict at an end, Cleveland felt a renewed sense of resolve in his faith that divine providence had struck down the rebellion. "It strengthens me mightily to reflect that this is the righteous wrath of God revealed from heaven against all ungodliness and unrighteousness of men." Yet when it came to the fate of Lincoln's assassin, his feelings were somewhat mixed. "When I reflect on what Booth must have suffered during the last week of his life I quite pity him," he said. "I am glad Corbett shot him. There were few men who were so worthy or would have done it in so noble a spirit. His death & burial suit my taste better than if either had been more public."[111]

Cleveland also received accounts of the aftermath of the assassination from his friend Asaph Hall, whom he knew from his Cambridge days and who had taken a position at the U.S. Naval Observatory in Washington, D.C. Among other things, Hall told a grisly tale of the fate that befell a Southern sympathizer shortly after Lincoln's death. "At one of the public bars in Washington an individual drank to the health of Lincoln's spirit and added that he ought to have been killed four years ago," he wrote Cleveland. "As he lifted his glass to drink to the diabolical sentiment the bar keeper stabbed him in the throat, killing him almost instantly." Hall also detailed his experience in seeing Lincoln's funeral procession as it made its way up Pennsylvania Avenue to the Capitol from the White House, where the body of the slain leader was taken after he died. Beneath the majestic marble columns of the Capitol rotunda, Lincoln's body lay in state before boarding a funeral train that made stops in several cities in the eastern and central United States en route to its final destination of Springfield, Illinois. "I saw the funeral of the President at Washington," Hall recalled. "The absence of the army rendered the number of persons in the ranks small, not more than thirty thousand all told. The bystanders wept as the coffin passed. I noticed one a rough looking, sea faring man apparently who made no effort to restrain his tears, as the body of our martyred patriot was drawn slowly by him."[112]

Hall also informed Cleveland of the fate of African American slaves following the signing of the Emancipation Proclamation and the end of the Civil War. "Ultimately entire emancipation and political rights equal to those enjoyed by the whites will be given to the blacks," Hall said. "The government, however, seems determined to let public sentiment acquire a decided tone before they will venture upon anything." This was a subject in which Cleveland expressed much interest, having written to his mother in late 1865 with questions, which he did not expect her to be able to answer. "I don't yet understand the condition & prospects of the negros in the amendment abolishing slavery [as the] law of the land. Can negros vote for Federal offices. Can they in any state vote for state offices. Please ask Walter or Father or Will to answer."[113]

With Reconstruction underway, Charlotte felt a renewed desire to travel—something she had expressed to Cleveland in February 1865. "You almost give me a desire to follow you, & see something of the world, & I cherish the hope that, one day, I may do so. But I must see more of my own country, before I search out the beauties & riches of the old world—I want to go west & to Washington, & if ever this 'cruel war is over', I want to go south."[114]

A year later, in February 1866, Cleveland's parents made a trip to Washington, D.C., during which they visited the U.S. Capitol, among other sites. Charlotte's description of the building, with its recently completed dome, certainly piqued the interest of Cleveland, who had yet to visit the city:

> Truly there can be no handsomer building, in the old world, than our Capitol, or indeed any of the public buildings in Washington. The Capitol is on a high hill, & overlooks Washington, in every direction, as well as across the Potomac to Arlington Heights—The building is magnificent, in proportions—at first I was struck with the vastness, & extent of the galleries, the spacious room, the immense number of steps the columns &c But the details of the finish of it is beautiful—The large paintings in the Rotunda, which we so often read of, are grand in size but do not strike you as so beautiful. The "Embarkation of the Pilgrims," was my favorite—"Westward the Course of Empire Takes its Way," by Leutze as you ascend one of the grand stair cases, was the favorite of all. Some of the long corridors on the basement floors, were one continuous gallery, of landscapes, flowers & animals, as well as heads & figures all finely painted in fresco—The Senate & House of Representatives were charming rooms, —large, handsomely finished & carpeted—but the Presidents room, & receiving room, off the Senate Chamber, were perfect gems—The Presidents room, was the most exquisite frescoing & pannelling I ever saw—The ceiling & sides, were equal to the finest oil painting—Representation, of Religion & Justice Legislation, & other subjects,—with flowers, wreaths, & portraits of Washington & all his cabinet, together with the elegant furniture & carpets, were more than my pen can describe. The Retiring

Chamber, was next to this, & was in panels of chocolate colored marble, with white fluted pillars, & beams of white marble over head & panels of chocolate marble beneath—both sides & ceiling were all marble, except where immense mirrors fitted in—It is said to be the finest room in the world, & I cant conceive of any thing more elegant.[115]

They also visited the White House, where everything "was in a grand scale," Charlotte wrote. "The East room almost a hundred feet long, & fifty wide was spacious—The conservatory was beautiful & many choice flowers in bloom." While President Johnson was not there that day, they did see his daughters, Martha and Mary, each in their thirties at the time. "The daughters were quite ordinary looking ladies, but received us gracefully, which was not a difficult task."

As impressed as she was with the White House, Charlotte seemed particularly interested in the activity taking place on the Senate floor, where debates were taking place over Johnson's recent veto of a bill that sought to extend the Bureau of Refugees, Freedmen and Abandoned Lands (otherwise known as the Freedmen's Bureau)—which had been established the year before by Lincoln to provide relief and services, including education, health care, and employment—to freed slaves and poor whites following the Civil War. "We spent the most of our time in the Senate—It is very exciting to hear the speeches, especially just now, for there is much excitement on the subject of the Freedmens Bureau, & the Presidents veto of it—Still the country is settling down, & I think good will come of the veto after all. President Johnson will come out right I think after all."

Upon returning to New York, Charlotte noted that she was happy to be home but was somewhat surprised at the behavior of Cleveland's younger sisters, who at the time were ten and twelve. "The children did prove when we were gone, that when 'the cats away the mice will play,'" she told Cleveland. "They had parties, & candy pullings, & dressed up in boys cloths, & went to the circus, & I cant tell what else—I find it hard for them to settle down again—Hattie & Helen are about as wild as need be." [116]

A Break from Work

Back at Pulkovo, Cleveland's work ethic began to catch up with him after his first few months there. "I have today told Dr. Döllen who is acting director that I must for the present give up my place as supernumerary,"[117] he wrote his father in late May 1865, noting that his duties in this position required three hours of computing daily, a task that easily wore on him. Döllen told Cleveland to do as he felt best and agreed that it would be for the best if Cleveland were to take all his "time and strength" for himself. This put Cleveland in the somewhat unfortunate position of having to ask his father to subsidize his stay at the observatory. "I am sorry to have to do this because it will necessitate my asking you for four or five hundred roubles, say 60 £ yearly, but for the present I think it must be necessary," he explained, adding that perhaps by the following winter he would feel up to resuming his position. "You are already familiar with my excessive over work in Cambridge," he explained, "and how my six months recreation served to restore me so that when I arrived here I felt again like myself with the strength that I had years ago but two months of hard work (and I may have done too much, though I tried to be moderate) took it all away."[118] For his part, George Abbe seemed understanding and willing to support his son however he could. "You state that you have resigned your position as assistant astronomer with the pay and will need assistance to continue your studies there," he wrote Cleveland. "If it is to be of great advantage to you to remain there I will assist you to the needs any funds."[119]

Grateful for his father's assistance, Cleveland nonetheless hoped to find a way to be self-sufficient and, at the same time, advance his career at the observatory. "I lead a very different life from what I have and as my progress here must be slower than I had hoped I am quite desirous to stay here three or four years and to do so neither at father's expense nor as the Observatory's guest but independently, which I believe there is some prospect of my being able to do," he told his mother. "It was intimated to me the other day that I might be offered a permanent position as adjunct astronomer but this I hardly think probable at least I shall not at present so consider it."[120]

Cleveland's mother, wishing to express support for her son's efforts, found that she was limited in the professional advice she could offer. "To me the other position of adjunct astronomer, if that were obtainable, should suit you better," she wrote. "But I am a timid woman, & don't know much about these things."[121] Charlotte did try to reassure her son that, despite his protestations that his talents had left him, he need not be so despondent. "You grieve me in saying your talent has left you—It cannot be. It must be, you are desponding, & will overcome it. If talent consists in endurance of hard work, that is different. You have tired yourself, & time will overcome it." She went on to tell him, somewhat admonishingly, that she felt it impossible for him to be devoid of all talent or ambition at his young age. "I am not willing to believe, that at twenty-six years old, you are worn out, if so, the mechanics must have been very weak. Now don't let yourself to thinking, that I underrate you & grow low spirited; cheer up; go more into the society of those around you, & don't sit & brood over what has past, & cannot be restored or I should say recalled—If I recollect—you wrote to Robby to learn Longfellows 'Psalm of Life,' I would say to you study it, & practice on it.—But I won't preach to you any more."

Charlotte's mention of Henry Wadsworth Longfellow's poem "A Psalm of Life"—which inspires readers to take charge of their destinies, reminding them that "Life is real! Life is earnest!"—refers to a letter Cleveland wrote to his brother Robert in May 1865.[122] In it, Cleveland attempted to impart his knowledge and wisdom to his younger brother, who was fifteen years old at the time, encouraging him to pursue a life of righteousness in which he could have some influence over others. In doing so, Cleveland put forth a sort of manifesto of his own life and ambition:

May 1, 1865
Poulkowa near St. Petersburg

My Dear Robby:

Sometime ago I thought that I would try to write often to my brothers & sisters as well as to father and mother. This is in fact a subject that has been to me of growing importance for three or four years—for I dared nothing so much as that ~~you~~ we should feel like strangers and should not take an intelligent interest in each other. In union is strength.

Charley will perhaps have expected to have heard from me but my present disposition is rather to write now to you.

You are so much younger than I that you do not realize how very short a time it is since I was in your place going to school like you, playing like you, studying the same books, with the same teachers perhaps. Do you ever wish to go back a year & live it over again? Do you ever regret what you have done or left undone and think that, could you have known before what you now know you would have done differently? So also with other men—but the wish can not, never, be granted. There are but three courses often—you may do that which your reason tells you will probably lead to a desired result—or, you may do that which your past experience tells you will most probably lead to this result—or you may do that which the actual experience of others tells you will almost certainly lead to the desired end.

As we cannot live our lives over again and have but imperfect powers of reasoning & of forseeing perhaps our best guide in general will be the experience of others. But it is often difficult to come at a precise knowledge of their experience.

You will therefore find it a very valuable exercise to reflect much on your own past experience and to question others as to theirs—the comparison will teach you everything.

Add to this worldly wisdom those reliable maxims of the Holy Bible and you will have formed a code of rules for your daily conduct—applicable both to private and public life—such as will finally reward you with success here and happiness hereafter.

But "success" implies that you have an object for which you are striving. I hope that I have not mistaken in supposing that already you begin to have some idea of what you would like to be and to do in the world. You have most probably about forty years before you—to be spent here among millions of men and women. The first ten you may devote entirely to your education & to the beginning of an independent manly life—what shall you do with the remaining thirty?? And how can you best employ your time during these first ten years.

These are serious and to you important questions—if you are wise you will seek to have them settled at once: if possible decide them alone by yourself and then have that decision ratified & confirmed by your best friends or modified as may seem best.

If I were to write to Charley such advice as this perhaps he would smile incredulously and not think again of what I say—but do you not do thus. Remember that whatever you now decide to do & to be—that, you <u>can</u> accomplish—only you must persevere & never give up your determination—no matter how little hope you have left. Nil desperandum: perseverantia vincit.[123] Always seek the easiest & best way—for we all have hard work enough—he who saves his strength is by so much stronger than he who wastes.

In trying to decide as to what you will aim for I will only say <u>aim very high</u>. Are there not millions whose aims are all on one low level? What or who has said that you must not think of doing more than they? Nobody. Nothing prevents you from aspiring to the highest attainments. Were you fifty or seventy years old you might be excused (but <u>never</u> justified) for saying I cannot do this, I dare not think of attempting that. But you are young every week and day you are learning something new do you not <u>feel</u> that you know more than you did a year ago? Just so will you feel a year hence and so every year of your life you may say I am still studying & learning.—if you only will. In a few years you will begin to find out that there is much for you to learn that is not printed in books and you may study through all eternity without learning all that there is in heaven and earth, in men's hearts and God's laws. Energy is what you want it is what we all need. With it men do all things without it man is a machine. Energy and Enthusiasm are divine principles. You cannot afford to live and die without them, and without cultivating them. I beg you to commit to memory Longfellow's Psalm of Life and live up to it.

I say then that of all imaginable ~~things~~ objects whatever one seems to you most worthy of living for—that one choose and never let it be forgotten. Marry yourself to it let it be always present with you and in the end you will attain to your desire. Your choice is only limited by these considerations i.e. you must not desire that which is intrinsically wrong—all your acts must be approved off by your pure conscience—your final, great and all controlling desire must be for God's honor and the triumph of justice.

If then you have at any time neglected to love God and our savior—if you have broken his commandments and have not done to others as you would wish them to do to you. It is now your first duty to repent of these sins. God is kind he will forgive if you are ready to live for him—to give your life to him.

Consecrated to the honor of our Father in Heaven your life must be a success if you do not fritter it away by attempting too many things. Let all things be made to contribute to your success in the one work you have marked out for yourself.

Read the lives of distinguished men. You have read Washington Banks Lincoln Hamilton Napoleon Slater etc.—do you not see how plain it is that what a youth aims for that he will attain?

There are many cases of so called failure—these are generally misnamed—the truth is that the unfortunate man had too many aims—tried to do too many things and succeeded only in doing each partially well. You may hunt a long time before you will find one who has failed in an honest attempt to do only one thing well.

You have not perhaps wished me to suggest what you should live for and yet I cannot forbear calling to your mind a few things.

During the past four years you have seen very many thousands of soldiers and have read of terribly bloody battles and have seen riots & soldiers & cannon in New York City. You ~~heard~~ remember the firebells of last November.[124] You will never forget the murder of President Lincoln.

Do you know what all this means? Do you realize that although you love to obey the laws yet there are tens of thousands who do not.

These bloody times were foreseen of Old. Washington and Hamilton feared that they themselves would see them. Five times have the black war clouds come close down upon us until it seemed that they must burst out upon us—five times have they passed ~~without~~ by harmlessly until now in our times the flood of blood ~~is poured~~ flows over the land.

As a final sacrifice the death of our pure minded President expiates the nation's guilt. May his blood be the last to be shed.

Does God rule the world? Is this his doing? or by his permission?

In ancient times He required free will offerings of his people and so have we willingly given money time friends & lives. We had ~~expiated~~ atoned for the wickedness of seventy five years and how this lightning stroke is to probe us to the very bottom to see whether we be truly humble and submissive.

I would that in all coming time (for there are many ages yet in the future) we may never again need such terrible punishments—I wish that many men of eloquence and influence might arise—statesmen and judges and senators of wisdom and truthfulness—who by their integrity might guide us into peaceful waters and plant our whole government on foundations of righteousness.

If I were such an one—if you were such an one—whoever is such an one—is blessed here—"and their works do follow them."

Oh Robb I beg of you to seek for influence over men—that by using it you may be a ~~statesman~~ blessing to the whole nation & the whole world.

Is this desirable to you? Would you be willing to make this your work?—that you may thereby honor God and bless the land.

You can have it.

Ask every one who has any influence from each you will get an idea and you may in a few months begin to ~~feel~~ see your influence spreading—may it spread ~~and~~ until it includes many and blesses all.

When you enter the Free Academy I want you very soon to become acquainted with Prof. Barton from whom you can learn much that is profitable. After you graduate I hope that in some higher university you may come into contact with men of experience so that you may not have narrow views and wherever you are you can always profit by learning from those about you—men of age and experience are always ready to communicate their knowledge—and with ~~from~~ youth of your own age you will always find it profitable to interchange opinions.

Compare your reasons for your opinion with their reasons for their opinion.

Finally and firstly—you must—you can, make your own destiny. "What thy hand findeth to do—do it with thy might."

Your affectionate brother,
Cleve

Meanwhile, with a less demanding schedule, Cleveland set out to make the most of his time at Pulkovo without running the risk of overexerting himself. He knew his experience was unique. No American astronomer before him had traveled to Russia to study and gain practical experience in his field. "I feel more & more the importance of my situation in respect to American astronomy," he told his father. "No one in the U.S. has had my advantages nor anything like them."[125] As he plodded away with his work at the observatory, Cleveland felt a sense of satisfaction, though his inherent modesty tempered any feelings of pride. "My computations & studies are progressing famously," he wrote his mother later that year. "You were glad to hear that the Director is pleased with my work. However I am not trying particularly to please him but rather to satisfy myself [as] one who is accustomed to mathematical studies learns soon enough that he can afford to be quite independent of other men & has enough to do if he honestly tries to live up to his own ideal." In telling his mother that he had striven for years to achieve the "highest usefulness in astronomy and in all my relations to the world," he pointed out that there must be "a distinction between those who strive to add something to the stock of human knowledge and those who try to diffuse knowledge more widely among men." In Cleveland's mind, there was no doubt as to which group he belonged. "These two work together in harmony but neither can do the work of the other they are two distinct professions and the former is my choice."[126]

When Cleveland told his mother that "nothing in the world is farther from my thoughts than to wish for honors and praises,"[127] she later told him, "Don't seek honors too much, let them seek you."[128] Cleveland scoffed at the idea that, despite his advantages and achievements, he would ever seek any sort of laudation. "Your idea of my reaching out for honors is to me quite laughable. I have never yet had any honor except the privilege that father gave me of coming here. Nor do I go for them. If I did I should have been long ago renowned in the world as most astronomers make themselves known before they are 27."[129]

Still, Cleveland could not shake the incessant feeling that his "talents" as an astronomer had left him and that he was wasting his time. "Were I ten years younger, with my slow head, I would give up all idea of being an astronomer," he confessed to his mother in August 1865, "but now it is too late and I must drag on as best I can and hope that in years I shall find my strength of former years returned."[130] In another letter, he lamented, "Oh if I were only not an astronomer but a poet or business man I believe I would write some poetry—but it takes all the little strength I have to do my computing & mathematical theory."[131] While he felt it was "not worth while to make so long a journey without accomplishing something," he also believed the experience would prove worthwhile in the end. "I should have been even more profited—by this sojourn—but there are many exterior circumstances that combine to show me that on the whole this will prove to have been my best occasion."[132]

A Change in Seasons and an Offer

As summer gave way to fall, the transition in seasons resulted in weather that Cleveland found quite fickle. "The day has been unusually warm and after dinner I have just now changed my winter clothing for a thinner suit, whilst doing so a thunder storm of ten minutes passed over us—the first we have had for two months," he wrote his mother in early September 1865. "The weather is at present extremely variable quite in contrast with what I have here hitherto seen. The never ending clouds keep us warm but the minute that they clear off for a few hours it grows cool cooler coolest & freezes."[133] Despite the warm afternoon weather, the cool air that morning provided a refreshing atmosphere for Cleveland as he took an early morning walk in the observatory's park. "Reminds me as well as the falling leaves that you also must begin to think of Autumn," he told his mother. "September with its golden apples and October with its gorgeous leaves find but a sorry representation here so far away from New England. I believe Massachusetts & New Hampshire must be the happiest parts of the world."[134]

In November 1865, Charlotte wrote to Cleveland, telling him that his father had received a letter of introduction from a professor at the University of Chicago, A. H. Mixer, indicating that Cleveland had been appointed assistant professor at the university's Dearborn Observatory. "I suppose if they want you they will write to you themselves," she said.[135] Cleveland's initial reaction was one of skepticism and disbelief. "I know nothing of the Chicago appointment further than what you have written so presume it is all rumor or a gold fish net," he wrote to his mother.[136] Over the course of the next several months—and with his parents serving at times as intermediaries—Cleveland learned that Professor Mixer, who represented the interests of the Chicago Astronomical Society, was interested in retaining Cleveland for such a position, though there remained a question of his salary. "He says nothing about salary—except that everything is on an economical basis—where I suppose that they have not funds enough to pay any one except Mr. Safford,"[137] Cleveland wrote his father, referring to Truman Henry

Safford, Cleveland's friend from Cambridge and director of the observatory. "Probably they wish to publish me in the Catalogue as 'pursuing preparatory studies at the Imperial Central Observatory Pulkova Russia'—a distinction of which I am not at all desirous."

The change in seasons once again provided a subject of interest, as Cleveland shared with his mother in early November. "Three weeks ago as I received your letter of Sept. 1st we were having our first real snow. Of course it only lasted an hour but at least the ground was white," he wrote. "Now for a month we have had only clouds & so long as it is cloudy it is warm. If it clears off for five hours the radiation of heat through the clear sky cools us down to five or ten degrees below freezing. Generally it has been rainy or at least muddy: two days ago there fell an inch of snow that will probably not be melted away until May 1866."[138] Late one night in mid-November, Cleveland heard the distinctive howl of a wolf as he made his way back to Pulkovo from St. Petersburg.[139] The canine animal was quite prevalent in the region at that time. "They are to be found in considerable numbers in the immediate neighbourhood of St. Petersburg, as well as all over Russia, and, unless hard pressed by hunger and in packs, are seldom dangerous," reported one travel guide from the period.[140]

As 1865 drew to a close, Cleveland found himself feeling despondent and wistful. Despite the festive season, he found little reason to celebrate. Even the weather left him disappointed. "I wish I could give you some account of a Russian winter," he wrote his mother, "but as yet I cannot. It is very unpleasant to have so much unseasonable warm weather as we are having the thermometer is half of the time above freezing and the snow that came one week is washed away the next by a warm drizzle."[141] Cleveland observed his twenty-seventh birthday in relative isolation, much to the dismay of those around him. "Last Sunday was my birthday and all were shocked to hear that I had run away from it early in the morning," he told his mother. "Perhaps they thought or wished to congratulate me as the custom is—but I preferred to have somebody else who expected to see me." Who that "somebody else" was would remain a mystery, though clues would emerge later suggesting an identity. In his diary entry for December 31 (O.S. December 19), Cleveland wrote, "Today I hope I have begun to learn the principle of what is love & what it is to say I love. May my doubts & fears & timidity soon be dissipated. An unhappy year is unhappily ended. May Otto Struve's wish 'a prosperous new year' be realized."[142] The next day, Cleveland had tea with his friend Victor Fuss. The two spoke for four hours during which Cleveland both confided and learned much. He came home "hopeful and happy," writing in his diary, "Oh grant Good Lord that I may not do wrong or foolishly and bless Thou the end of my hopes."[143]

To Find a Wife

January 2, 1866 (O.S. December 21), saw the first anniversary of Cleveland's arrival at Pulkovo. He bought some wine "in order to call the young men together in my room to celebrate the end of my first year." Before they left the city, however, two of the others insisted Cleveland drink with them. "The whole proceeding so disgusted me that my own wine still lies untouched in the cellar & there it will stay at least until the 4th July. I count this day as the turning point in my acquaintance with these two gentlemen."[144]

Cleveland wrote his mother shortly after the event, reminding her that in the midst of all the drinking and carousing that surrounded him he remained steadfast in his principles of abstinence and restraint. "Your advice as to wine &c is indeed neither unnecessary nor unwelcome," he reassured her. "I have in America always been in such company as scarcely to know anything of temptation and have not been prepared steadfastly and absolutely to resist all trials. During the last week of the old year I frequently contemplated the decided influence that my Pulkova life has had upon my thoughts heart & actions and concluded that self preservation demands that I go regularly to an evangelical church."[145]

Around this time, Cleveland also began teaching a Sunday school class at the American Chapel in St. Petersburg. Following the first week's class, he dined with the pastor, took coffee with the school's superintendent, and "returned home quite contented and happy."[146] In a letter to his mother, Cleveland said that despite the two-hour ride each way (which he described as "healthy work") he looked forward to the obligation. "This regularity will I hope keep off any low spirits that may arise from all work and no play." He also said the labor would "keep me warm in my Christianity & the opportunity will be given me to make acquaintances in the city."[147]

"Our winter weather is at last come," Cleveland wrote his mother in February. "There is no snow to speak of but it has now been clear for nearly three weeks and the thermometer every morning at -10° Fahr. so that the cold begins to be felt through the thick walls & double windows. But tomorrow it will be cloudy & we shall thaw out." He also noted that the days were getting longer and that "soon the true spring time will come here we learn how to be thoroughly thankful for the summer its long days & fairy like twilight. I do not know what at home I shall be often longing for the sweet June nights that can only be found in Pulkova."[148]

As spring arrived, Cleveland found reason to rejoice. "I write now from the midst of spring rains & mud clouds & fogs—but it will soon clear away & warm genial summer be with us," he told his mother. "Early this morning the birds began their music and even yesterday I stood & listened to the skylarks 'Type of the wise who soar but never roam—True to the kindred points of Heaven and Home,'" he added, borrowing the words of poet William Wordsworth.[149] Cleveland felt a renewed sense of purpose to assess the priorities in his life. He had decided to delay giving an answer to Mixer about the Chicago position while he considered other possibilities. "Until I know whether there is any opening for me at Rochester I shall not think it best to decide upon the invitation of the Chicago Ast. Society," he wrote his father. "To come back to the old question however—the first thing in importance is for me to find a wife and the beginning of a home and the necessary requisite is a salary."[150]

The subject of marriage was one that had been on Cleveland's mind for some time. On August 10, 1865, he received a letter from his friend and confidant Albert Bickmore, who was sailing around the East Indian Archipelago, collecting specimens for the natural history museum he hoped to establish in New York. Bickmore had penned the letter more than six months earlier, on January 31, as he was sailing in the Atlantic Ocean, about six hundred miles southwest of the Cape Verde Islands, on his way to Batavia, in the Dutch East Indies. In the letter, Bickmore wrote of his desire to hear from his friend and to relive their days together in Cambridge. "It seems a long time since I saw you last and feeling anxious to have a chat with you I betake myself to my only resource—the pen," he wrote. "I hope you have found pleasant companions in your new home. I have come to believe however that those whom we can safely and properly make our confidential friends are very few in this world. I hope you have not forgotten me because so great a distance separates us." Bickmore continued:

> I have lately read in the book I have referred to, that "however long a woman's letter may be, she always keeps what she wishes to say most till the last"—that mine may not have the same failing I think I will write what's in my head now.—Perhaps you have already walked down Harvard St. in your imagination & perchance stopped before you reached Mr. Merrill's—if so you have anticipated my thoughts completely—such imaginings you know are always

allowable at sea. I am inclined to believe that sea life is peculiarly favorable to day dreams. How often do you find yourself in Rockland at least in head & heart if not in the body! Many times I guess—but I do not speak this at all in a chiding way.[151]

Just nine days later, Cleveland was pleased to find another letter from Bickmore had arrived; this one written much later, on May 28, as Bickmore was recovering from "a slight attack of fever" and just after he had left the hospital. "Now I am in my room in a private boarding house, and though it is Sunday morning I cannot think it very wrong, as I cannot go to church, to sit down & talk with you through the medium of my pen." Bickmore wrote about his travels and expressed happiness in Cleveland's desire to travel to Sweden, Paris, and other parts of Europe while he was in Russia (a trip he did not take) before turning his thoughts to more personal matters. "I must confess I was a little surprised not to find in your letter a mention of something I still believe is in your heart & I dare say occupies more than one of your stray thoughts, namely of miss M."[152] He was referring to Cleveland's cousin Marcia Fessenden, with whom Cleveland had kindled a relationship two years earlier while visiting her family in Maine.

Whatever his feelings for Marcia may have been at one time, Cleveland's attitude had cooled during his stay in Russia, to the point where he looked down at the implication that his mother had suggested a relationship between the two cousins while visiting family in Windham. "I spoke of you, as I would of any of my children, & never intimated, that I know of any thing ever passing between you & Marcia," Charlotte wrote to her son, defending her actions. "I think her a quiet nice girl, but with such a large family & all so fond of visiting, I think, whoever marries into it, will have a house full all the time."[153] By the spring of 1866, Cleveland had given up the thought of anything further developing between him and Marcia. As he explained to his mother, he had very specific ideas in mind of what a wife should be to him:

What I have to say is merely that I cannot bear to think of having a selfish wife. I want one with the least possible taint of this disposition—Such an one will not only be necessary to my own satisfaction but to the maintenance of proper friendly relations with others. The director of such an observatory as Pulkova or Greenwich if the observatory is isolated from the city as is very necessary must first of all look out for the maintenance of a happy state of society—He destroys & nullifies every thing if he indulges the arrogant & and satirical nature that many of us have. To control oneself as to words, actions & appearances is not sufficient. He and his wife must have learned to control their hearts & thoughts.[154]

Marcia, it seemed, did not fit this mold. "I have found my admiration of Marcia so cooled on a future acquaintance," he told his mother. "Now I am afraid that Marcia in her contentedness at home and willingness to sacrifice herself for the enjoyment of her friends & brothers has so far obliterated her own self as to have no real wishes & longings left has become so passive that she is <u>only</u> passive and with not enough energy & will left to know & to say that this or that would please her best."[155]

Cleveland's desire—if not intent—to get married was complicated by several factors, including his self-described lack of preparation for such an endeavor, a deficiency that he blamed, at least to some degree, on his mother. "You feared that I had been too gallant in my attention to the ladies—but I think not. On the contrary the wish is frequently expressed to see me often so that I think I am not going beyond moderate limits," he told her. "Oh I wish I had a nice little wife."[156] Cleveland told his mother that she had not adequately prepared him or his brothers in finding suitable partners. "All us boys have very susceptible sensitive sensible hearts and if we govern our tongues that is as much as you can expect," he wrote. "Now I would be pleased if instead of giving us all three such impracticable advice as the above you teach us how to decide what sort of wives we each of us want where we shall find them how we may win them. Teach us to be cautious & to examine the character of our acquaintances very carefully but do not advise us to shut our eyes and go blindly risking the whole of our future happiness."[157] Cleveland went on to describe how the love he had experienced so far in his life was not enough:

Now Mother I can not live without loving and you must have known that when I was a little boy. I know what it is to love all that is good & pure and to hate what I see in others & in myself that is low and impure. I love God & Jesus & the angels and the sainted dead. I love children and good men & women. I love my friends, and almost every one of my acquaintance is my friend. I love my brothers & sisters & parents. I love you all better than I do myself and yet I am not satisfied. My business and my devotions do not satisfy me—and I know what will satisfy me that is a good wife & a happy home. So that I do not believe that it is right for me to follow your advice to the letter & let the girls alone—that is keep out of their society. On the contrary just as soon as I accept the Chicago or any other position that will give me a competency I shall seek a wife—to which end I am now looking around with very inquisitive eyes.[158]

Cleveland knew that in order to be successful in finding and keeping a suitable companion, he would first have to rethink his attitudes surrounding the concepts of friendship and love. "I have come to the sober conclusion that I have never before realized or understood the difference between kind hearted sympathy & love for all and a special enduring love," he lamented. "Certainly I have never before so learned to prize that friendship which is founded upon thorough knowledge of one's friend and that love which is founded upon and grows out of this friendship."[159]

Perhaps recalling his experience with Thirza Dodsley—or some other ill-fated dalliance—Cleveland began to recognize the shortcomings in his past experiences with romantic love and sought to learn from them. "I hope to be able to control myself and never again mistake an unstable passion & longing for the enduring affection," he asserted. "I have been very simple and childish in my life—instead of being a full grown man at fourteen I was a boy at twenty four and so I shall ever be. Hereafter I will try to be wiser & cooler. But oh it is so pleasant to let the blood course freely and give the heart up to the excitement of being absorbed in someone else."[160]

In the summer of 1865, Cleveland wrote both to his father and to Bickmore, seeking advice on a matter of a very personal nature that seemed to interfere with his ability to find fulfillment in his personal life. The response from his father was one of shock and dismay. "I must confess that I was very greatly surprised at the contents of your letter so far as it related to yourself the subject I don't care to refer to, it is entirely personal and I have no advice to give and I am not a little surprised that you should soon write to any one or even consult a physician on the subject," his father wrote. "I know or rather suppose that persons of sedentary habits are more liable to brood over their desires than those of more active pursuits but your solitary habits are low and should not be tolerated and of the two, are more debasing than associating with women."[161] In a similar letter a year later, Cleveland's father admonished him for writing to his doctor in New York, seeking medical advice for matters he considered too personal to be discussed, even with medical professionals. "Your letter to Doctor Herrick was open and I read it and tore it up so you will know why you don't hear from him," he wrote. "I was mortified that you should make known to him your habits, besides the information you seek you can obtain from any doctor there or your own common sense will tell you. I think you had better keep such things to yourself and if you are married it will be the end of such low desires." Later, in the same letter, George did offer some advice—and a stern warning—to his son. "I will add in reference to the question you ask Doctor Herrick that I do not think you need have any fears from your habits, about children providing the union is not too old. If you don't get married you must break off your vile habits."[162]

Bickmore was more candid in his response but had little advice to offer. "You tell me the facts and the Doctor's advice, as a manner of asking my opinion I suppose, but after thinking over the matter I can come to no decided judgement, except to say do what you yourself think is best. If the evil cannot be stopped then it will be best to guide it, is all the decision I can come to, and how that had better be done you can tell better than I."[163] Bickmore, who was at the time in the Spice Islands, told Cleveland, "Every man who is not married—and of these there are few—keeps a native woman sometimes two. As for me, I have kept Paul's example in view and have not yet fallen into any snare, though temptations to such evil here are vastly more potent than in our cold climate." Bickmore was referring to a passage from the Bible in which Saint Paul advises the Corinthians on the principles of marriage.[164] "Paul says it 'is better to marry than to burn' and if you can remain continent until you are married I believe it will very greatly increase the happiness of yourself and your wife—an object worth much self-denial." Bickmore also suggested that Cleveland's desires were not uncommon. "This evil is one that many are subject to, I imagine," he said. "I believe that anxiety of mothers to have their daughters married, quite frequently arises from no other cause—though this at first may seem to you quite startling." Bickmore seemed concerned, however, whether marriage would be the solution to Cleveland's apparent problem. "I do not believe that marrying will altogether do away with the evil from which you have suffered—for I have heard that that is but the beginning with many men." He followed this up, however, by reaffirming his conviction that Cleveland's cousin Marcia would be an ideal match who could help in easing his suffering. "A glance at the whole matter makes me wish very much that when you do marry, it may be to Marcia, for I believe there are very few women who could take such good care of you, as she would, and I think you will find yourself considerably under the influence of your wife if you marry chiefly to avoid or mollify the evil alluded to."[165]

While George destroyed the letter to Dr. Herrick that Cleveland wrote in the summer of 1865, it was not the first time Cleveland had written to his physician on the subject. In November 1863, while he was toiling away in Gould's office in Cambridge, Cleveland sent a letter to Dr. Herrick, seeking his advice on the matter. Herrick's reply two weeks later offered concrete suggestions to help quell the pent-up frustrations with which Cleveland struggled.

New England Soldier's Relief Association
No. 194 Broadway
New York

Dec. 1, 1863

Dear Cleve,

I received your letter and should have answered it before, but as your case was not very urgent have allowed other things to crowd it aside.

I have been considering how best to advise you, and am hardly clear yet how to do it.

Probably you know how to manage yourself as well as any one can tell you. I have no doubt that change of almost any sort will benefit you—that which involve most physical fatigue probably the most. If you would get your body well tired every day, the demand upon the nervous system for physical recuperation, would perhaps give you release from that excitement which you so much deprecate & dread. Two hours solid gymnastics every evening, rowing, billiards, bowling, either or all alternated, games of any kind which would give you powerful diversion, would accomplish the object. A military campaign active full of difficulty & danger would result in more radical diversion, even, than you would relish.

While you regard the army with so much favor, you must remember that the army sometimes for months, lies in camp utterly indolent, with no excitement & no labor, fraught with more temptation to the indulgence from which you are escaping, than almost any other conceivable position. I have seen very many young soldiers the last two years utterly mired by the ennui of camp idleness. I do not think the army the place for you. I am sure you are coming out "all right." Your idea of a term of physical labor is sound in theory—You undoubtedly need release from "computation," if you cannot "strike a balance" with it. But it seems to me that you need not abandon intellectual work, if you will weigh with it sufficient muscular fatigue. I do not know that I can say more and you knew it all before—In the winter you can get tired enough skating, if you relish it as much as I do. Your conscientiousness good sense & resolution will yet carry you among the stays to your heart's content.

Very truly yours
Everett Herrick

Dr. Herrick's advice is reminiscent of that of Dr. John Harvey Kellogg, the nineteenth-century doctor and health advocate who became famous for his invention of Corn Flakes, which he promoted as part of the strict vegetarian diet he prescribed patients at his Battle Creek Sanitarium in Michigan. In his treatise on sexuality, *Plain Facts for Old and Young*, Kellogg sought "to call attention to the great prevalence of sexual excesses of all kinds and the heinous crimes resulting from some forms of sexual transgression." He wrote:

> Physical exercise is a most powerful aid to pure thoughts. When unchaste ideas intrude, engage at one in something which will demand energetic muscular exercise. Pursue the effort until fatigued, if necessary, making, all the while, a powerful mental effort to control the mind. Of course, evil thoughts will not be expelled by thinking of them, but by displacing them by pure thoughts. Exercise aids this greatly.[166]

Emilie Struve

By the late spring of 1866, as he pondered his future, Cleveland became more and more convinced that he must find a wife as soon as was practicable—a sentiment shared by the observatory's physician. "Every time Dr. Konradi sees me he repeats his advice 'Mr. Abbe get married at once,'" he told his father, asking for his help in finding permanent position for him. "The words, the tone, the earnestness rings in my ears for I realize thoroughly that it will be my only salvation. This consideration at times so overpowers me that I would beg you to secure for me the first chance that offers no matter what or where it is—yet now in a soberer moment I shrink from binding myself to any place where I must for years stay."[167] Cleveland explained to his father that Dr. Konradi had "pointed me out to two young ladies either one of whom I could easily win & marry" and whose union would ensure a permanent place for him at Pulkovo. "To marry one of them would bring me into too intimate relations with Otto Struve. To marry the other will be highly delightful for she is as good & prudent & experienced a woman as I can desire for a wife."[168]

One of the women was Emilie Struve, Otto's younger sister and the youngest daughter of the Elder Struve, Wilhelm, and his first wife, also named Emilie. The younger Emilie (whose name Cleveland sometimes spelled as "Aemilie" or "Emilia") was born January 13 (O.S. January 1), 1834. The day after her birth, her brother Alfred succumbed to a ten-month-long struggle with a diseased hip and died. The shock of his death was simply too much for their mother, who became fraught with grief and began developing violent pains and spasms throughout her body. Unable to overcome this, she passed away February 1 (O.S. January 20), 1834, with her husband, Wilhelm, and eldest surviving son, Otto, at her side.[169] A year later, Wilhelm married his second wife, Johanna Henrietta Francisca Barthels, the daughter of a prominent German mathematician. Together, they had six children (four of whom survived to adulthood). This—in addition to the twelve children Wilhelm had with his first wife (eight of whom survived to adulthood)—ensured the Struve dynasty would endure for years to come. After her mother's death, young Emilie lived with her stepmother, Johanna, in St. Petersburg, but she made frequent visits to Pulkovo.

Cleveland first wrote to his mother of Emilie in August 1865. "Miss Emilie Struve is Colla's half sister and next to the youngest daughter of the Elder Struve—she is about 28 30, I should think, and of an unusually sweet disposition sings very well and is indeed of great use to us when she is here."[170] Among his favorite activities during his free time, Cleveland enjoyed singing German hymns and choral music with Emilie. During one of the many celebrations that took place during his stay at Pulkovo—in honor of the baptism of the son of August Wagner, senior astronomer and vice-director of the observatory—Cleveland had an opportunity to practice his dancing with the young ladies present, including Emilie. "In the early part of the evening, Mr. Wagner had lighted a piece of magnesium wire which gives a light too bright to look at and this inaugurated the evening," he wrote, describing the festivities to his mother. "After the congratulations & some tea drinking somebody began to play on the piano & the young people made themselves as gay as they could considering the heat & closeness of the rooms. I believed that I danced considerably notwithstanding a headache that two cups of chocolate gave me. Whether I danced too much with any particular lady Miss Aemilia Struve or Miss Helwig must be left for the future to decide."[171]

This type of merriment and entertainment, however, was secondary to Cleveland's work at the observatory. "I am not trying to enjoy myself, but to study & compute & learn to use instruments in order to fit myself for the highest usefulness hereafter," he told his mother. "But in order to accomplish this you well know that I must be free from headaches & those terrible despondencies which have of late years grown upon me." To this end, he credited Emilie with improving his spirits and relieving him of the "despondencies" that had so often gripped him. "I feel now as though I should never again have them & hopefulness is the foundation of my happiness. I think I am very much indebted to Miss Aemilia Struve for this improvement in my condition & out of gratitude if nothing else I like to call there when I am in the city."[172]

Cleveland told his family back home of his desire to marry Emilie and possibly remain at Pulkovo for an extended period of time. "So far as my personal feelings indicate I would rather have Miss Struve* for my wife than any other whom I know," he said, writing to his father in April 1866, "but I am neither engaged nor do I propose to be until I see my way clear. I have been foolish & hot enough in my life and if a few words from you can keep me cool & cautious* I shall be thankful to the end of my days." The asterisks he included were tied to a footnote he added to the bottom of his letter, which read: "*as for being constant I will be so hereafter if I can be—possibly."[173]

Cleveland's news of his intent to marry Emilie was met with mixed reaction from his family. "All I know to say is if you marry her I hope [she] will prove a good wife. You are old enough and had experience enough to judge," his father wrote, adding, "I trust you will not get married on any uncertainty about supporting yourself."[174] His mother, perhaps having misgivings for having said too much about Cleveland's romantic interests in the past, told him she could "give no advice—you have asked none." She added, "If all goes right & she makes you happy I am satisfied."[175] Later, when the prospect of marriage seemed even more certain, Charlotte could not contain her concern. "You seem a great way off, & if you marry, you will seem farther," she wrote. "I imagine from what you say, that your engagement is a settled fact, though I may be mistaken. You say you may not settle there—Will the lady be willing to come here for life?—Can she speak English at all; you know I can not speak any thing else, & feel almost too old to learn."[176]

The most critical response, however, came from Cleveland's brother William, then twenty-two. In responding to the news, he wrote a scathing letter to his brother, urging him to reconsider his proposed marriage. "We judge here at home that you have hit upon some maid of the mist, she may be old for aught we know, and have either popped the question, or are on the point of doing so," he said. "No doubt the German or Russian lassies are robust, hearty, thrifty and able women—and are an interesting set of angels to look upon, but you have no idea yourself how easily a woman controls your heart-strings, and how your pure sympathetic nature, coincides always with the ladies. . . ." Insisting he was not trying to hurt Cleveland's feelings, William went on to tell Cleveland that the fact that he was "in a foreign clime, under foreign influences" left him susceptible to "ideas very different from those which you would receive, were you within reach of the kindly influences of the home circle. . . ." With a nationalistic and somewhat xenophobic tone, he added, "we do not want any foreign elements introduced in our midst, and if your heart goes pit a pat, for any of these dear creatures, then you have our request and pleadings to seek something which is slightly Americanized and not something which we shall have to use the deaf & dumb language to." In closing his letter, William asked Cleveland to "keep in mind that there are better girls here than you ever saw in Russia."[177]

As summer approached and the "white nights" began to return to the region, bathing St. Petersburg and Pulkovo in the glow of the midnight sun, Cleveland wrote his father with an update on his situation. "It is by no means certain that Miss S. gives her consent to a marriage under any circumstances least of all with the expectation of being taken away from friends & relatives to whom she is very dearly bound and from a stepmother to whom she feels herself by a strong sense of duty bound for life," he reported. "Such a feeling as this is too sacred & I honor it & admire it too much to dare to disturb it—But as I do not wish to think of being permanently separated from her I have been contemplating the possibility of my settling here for an indefinitely long time—that is at least until the death of Madame von Struve removes the chief obstacle to our return to America."[178]

With Emilie indelibly tied to her stepmother, Cleveland considered the possibility of remaining at Pulkovo, at least for the immediate future. "Should I settle here there will be no valid objection to our marriage so far as I can see," he told his father, adding that the observatory's director, Otto Struve, "seems by no means displeased at the idea of my staying here permanently—at least for some years as one of the official members of the corps of astronomers."[179] Struve went so far as to propose to the committee overseeing the observatory to approve the addition of a temporary adjunct astronomer, with the understanding that "in a proper time" the position would become one of a full senior astronomer. Cleveland felt confident that "when this proposition is confirmed by the Minister of Public Instruction as it probably will be [Struve] will give the post to me," though he noted that the "salary of 750 Roubles is not sufficient to allow one to be married but 1500 is more than enough."[180] Cleveland felt that should such an arrangement be possible it would allow him to enter into marriage with Emilie without reservation. "If there were any certainty or great probability that I should in a year receive the advanced post there would then be no great risk in entering into a marriage engagement." He went so far as to imagine their living arrangements as husband and wife, telling his father that "furnishing our simple rooms is not so expensive here as furnishing a house is with us at home and simple as the living expenses are with the Pulkova families they will be still more economized by Miss Emilia who is accustomed to a simplicity that would be very distasteful at home in New York."[181]

One day in late May, Cleveland and several others went to the observatory grounds to play croquet after dinner. Later, Cleveland noted he felt "much too dejected by not having heard a word from anyone as to my stay here," adding that Emilie was "very much shocked at my moodiness."[182] A few days later, on May 31 (O.S. May 19), he took a long walk with Emilie's stepmother, Madame Struve. She gave him "good advice," he noted in his diary, adding, "I will wait patiently for events."[183] On June 12 (O.S. May 31), he met with Madame Struve again. This time "Miss Emilia [was] also consulted." By this point, Cleveland's patience had worn thin. "Now this conflict must be decided & the storm cease," he wrote in his diary.[184] It would be another two and a half months, however, before any resolution would be had. Finally, on August 23 (O.S. August 11), he had his answer. "The consolation letter written," Cleveland wrote in his diary that day, also making note of "the three o'clock meeting—the seven o'clock parting." It was not to be. Feeling dejected and detested, Cleveland wondered, "Have I been loved? Or am I loved? Or shall I be? No!" He then added a note of resentment to his diary entry for the day: "Despised and scorned—Remembered only as der Persecutor."[185]

The next day Emilie departed Pulkovo for Karlsruhe. "The last glimpses of each other," Cleveland solemnly recorded in his diary. They would never see each other again. Three days later, on August 27, Cleveland received a letter from Safford. "Chicago not in condition to give funds," he said. Cleveland's prospects had dwindled. His future seemed uncertain. One thing he knew for sure—he could not remain at Pulkovo. Upon hearing this, Otto Struve expressed his regret. "I am very sorry that this heart affair has so disturbed your plans and overthrown our hopes," he said.[186] When the news reached Cleveland's father in New York, he wrote expressing his surprise, but also offered reassurance to his son. "I believe however it is all for the best," he wrote. "We shall be glad to see you home and here no doubt you will soon find a better position than the Coast Survey," adding, "if you cannot, it would hardly have supported you married."[187]

Cleveland began packing his steamer trunk full of his books and other belongings. He exchanged photographs with those closest to him at the observatory and, on September 24, he said goodbye to his friends and colleagues at Pulkovo—many of whom had been like a second family to him over the previous two years—and quickly made his way to the railroad station, where he boarded a train for Dorpat. After staying there a week, he made his way to Germany, where he made stops in Berlin, Leipzig, Dresden, Mannheim, and Heidelberg. By late October, he was in Holland—Utrecht and Rotterdam—before visiting London, Greenwich, and, finally, Liverpool.

On the last day of October 1866, he boarded a steamer for New York, having paid an "Emigrant's fare" and agreeing to wash dishes in the ship's kitchen to help subsidize his passage. On November 1, the ship arrived in Queenstown (now Cobh), in southern Ireland, where 150 emigrants boarded. As the last view of Ireland slipped out of sight, Cleveland settled into a life at sea for the next two weeks. He spent his days reading poetry and the novel *Graziella*—about a young Frenchman who falls in love with the granddaughter of an Italian fisherman while traveling to Naples, only to lose her—and his nights observing Venus, Jupiter, and the moon. He worked sanding the kitchen floor and visited a sick boy, whom he tried to comfort by reading to him.

One Sunday, after working, he took a walk on the deck with several other passengers, including a woman he referred to only as "Madame _____," who was bound for Cincinnati.[188] They spent many hours together on the ship, discussing topics that included astronomy and his work at Pulkovo. He told her of his hopes and dreams—including his desire to head an observatory similar to that in Greenwich. Cleveland knew nothing of this woman—or of the influence she would have on his future. She would not forget him, however.[189]

On November 16, Cleveland returned home to New York and his family. Shortly after his arrival, he received a letter from Otto Struve, who expressed his hope—almost apologetically—that Cleveland would find some happiness in reflecting on his time at Pulkovo:

> While I write this you will probably have reached your home since more than a week and your stay at Pulkowa will appear you like a dream. I am afraid this dream might not be throughout a pleasant one; for certainly these two years that you have spent with us were the least favourable by exterior circumstances that Pulkowa ever has witnessed. My father's death, my own illness those of Winnecke, Döllen etc.; together with many other displeasing

> circumstances, were not qualified to make your stay here a pleasant one. With all that I hope you will have taken with you a friendly recollection of the inhabitants of the Observatory and be satisfied with the general character of our working and proceeding.[190]

Cleveland's time in Russia was behind him, but the experience left an indelible mark on his mind and heart. Nearly a quarter century later, in his diary entry for August 19, 1889, he wrote, "August 7 Old Style 50 Anniversary of the Inauguration of Poulkova obs$^{\underline{ty}}$." [191] He then paused, dropped a line on the page, and added:

> Beloved Poulkova Beloved Friends
> My heart is with thee always

CHAPTER FOUR

Cincinnati (1867–1870)

I have started that which the country will not willingly let die.

—Cleveland Abbe, in a letter to his father, 1869

When he arrived home in New York in November 1866, Cleveland Abbe set out to find a way to take the knowledge and experiences he had acquired in Pulkovo and apply them to the founding of a similar institution in America, which he would lead. "I left Poulkova full of courage in the determination to enlarge upon these generous ideas so similar to what had long been growing in my own mind and when I landed in New York," he later recalled. "I had already begun to elaborate a sketch of the 'Astronomical Institution' that I hoped to see develop from such beginnings as I might be able to make."[1]

A few weeks after his return home, Cleveland wrote to Professor Elias Loomis, whose interest and work in meteorology had placed him near the center of the Redfield-Espy "Storm Controversy" several decades earlier. Now a professor of natural philosophy and astronomy at Yale University, Loomis, Cleveland thought, seemed an obvious choice to be the beneficiary of his ideas and ambitions. "I desire very much to make a determined effort for the establishment of an active useful Astronomical Institution in this city—which would have for its object to add to our knowledge & to make that knowledge practically useful," Cleveland wrote, adding that such an institution "should be to navigation what Greenwich has been & is and to geodesy what Poulkova is and more than this should lead on in new and most refined investigations."[2]

Loomis responded disparagingly, recalling efforts made in 1859 to establish an astronomical observatory in New York, which he said had likely been "abandoned as a hopeless undertaking."[3] He did, however, suggest that Cleveland might pick up where others had left off. "If you have the requisite energy and perseverance, you may carry the enterprise to a successful termination, and I hope you may be able to do so," Loomis ended his letter. Without the needed support—or funds—however, Cleveland was left to put his dreams of establishing a world-class astronomical institution on hold.

Cleveland began writing to several of his friends and former colleagues, looking for whatever opportunities might be available to him. His friend Asaph Hall wrote to him from Washington, where he worked as an assistant astronomer at the U.S. Naval Observatory, under the supervision of Professor Simon Newcomb. "Probably you can get a position here if you desire it," Hall wrote, "as Prof. Newcomb has spoken of you and under the present direction of Observatory matters things are arranged pretty much in accordance with his wishes."[4] Cleveland wrote to Newcomb on December 17, 1866, and, two days later, received a reply. "Thinking you would be a very desirable candidate for a position here, I asked Hall to suggest the matter to you," Newcomb confessed.[5] "At present there is no vacancy and, seemingly, no way in which we could employ you. But as a vacancy may occur at any moment, and I want the best man I can get to fill it, I will explain the case to you with a view of your making up your mind whether you would come if a vacancy occurred." Newcomb explained that the only position he could offer Cleveland at the time was that of "aid" (what Newcomb described as being an "assistant"), which carried with it a salary of $1,333. "Promotion not yet provided for, but must come for all whose services become valuable," he added. Newcomb went on to describe the ideal attributes of an observatory aid:

1. Good health, so as to stand night work.
2. Good eyesight for observing faint objects by day & night.
3. An expert computer.[6]

While "great talents for mathematics & astronomy" would not be of immediate importance, these qualities "would go very far in securing future advancement."[7] Though it was far from what he envisioned for his future, Newcomb's offer did interest Cleveland and he wrote back to find out more, including the possibility for advancement. "There is no great prospect of promotion of an aid before 5 years service," Newcomb explained in a subsequent letter, adding that after such a period aids could likely expect a raise.

"After serving that long with satisfaction I don't think Congress would refuse to increase their salary."[8]

Expecting that Cleveland would come to Washington around the beginning of the year to accept the position, Newcomb wrote at the end of January 1867 that he "was disappointed not to see" Cleveland "on or about New Years."[9] He attempted to further entice him with the promise of temporary work for a colleague in the Coast Survey later that year, which he said could be performed at the observatory in Washington. Cleveland and Newcomb continued to correspond into March, when Newcomb informed him that one of the aids at the observatory had announced his intention to resign. "If, therefore, you would still like to try the position, you had better put in an application, with recommendations from prominent men, into my hands forthwith, and I will make the best use of it I can, and send it in to the [Navy] Department at a proper moment."[10] He added that if Cleveland were to include a recommendation from Otto Struve, it would "be one of the best," but not to wait for it if he did not already have it in hand. Newcomb also mentioned that the pay for civil servants in Washington had increased for the fiscal year by 20 percent, to $1,600 per year.

Cleveland responded, asking for more time. In the meantime, he had written to Benjamin Peirce, superintendent of the Coast Survey, to ask for a continuation of his employment there. Noting that he was "entirely unacquainted with the nature of your past services," Peirce found it necessary to contact Benjamin Gould, under whose supervision Cleveland had worked in Cambridge prior to his sojourn in Pulkovo.[11] In writing to Peirce of his experience with Cleveland, Gould stated that he had "no hesitation in bearing witness to his character as a young man of strict moral integrity, & of excellent principles." He added that Struve "speaks favorably of his industry & zeal."[12]

In early April, Newcomb again wrote to Cleveland, further persuading him to accept the position he had offered. "I think you would find a position at the observatory more to your liking than you have judged from my letters," he said. He also suggested the experience would be valuable in giving Cleveland "the acquaintance of men of influence in the scientific affairs of the government" and that he "would also learn some of the foibles of human nature which display themselves in the feelings of that class of men."[13] Cleveland finally agreed and on April 13 boarded an express train to Washington[14] to begin his new job.

Initially, Cleveland stayed with his cousin Samuel Fessenden, who had served as a U.S. representative from Maine from 1861 to 1863, and who, in

1865, became an examiner at the U.S. Patent Office. Fessenden had written Cleveland several months earlier, giving him advice as far as lodging in the nation's capital. "For a longer or shorter period, room and board can be obtained from $40 to $60 per month. Usually room & board for ten days or so in a good private family is $2 per day," he said, adding, "I have no doubt that I can make satisfactory arrangements, at a very reasonable rate, for your stay in the house where I am, when you decide to visit Washington. To go to a public house—these days, is ruinous—unless you have a pocket-full of green-backs."[15]

Washington, D.C., was a thriving, progressive city in the years following the Civil War. In January 1867, just three months before Cleveland arrived, black men in the city became the first African Americans in the nation to achieve the right to vote. That same month, workers removed scaffolding from the inside of the newly constructed dome of the U.S. Capitol, officially marking its completion.

In the third-floor rooms of an otherwise nondescript, red-brick building at 437 ½ 7th Street, NW, Clara Barton, who had spent years helping Union troops during the Civil War, operated the Missing Soldiers Office, where she helped friends and families of those lost during the war find information on their missing loved ones. Often, relatives wrote letters to Barton, who had been sanctioned by President Lincoln to become the official keeper of the rolls of the war's dead. On January 17, 1867, two months before he relocated to Washington, Cleveland wrote a letter to Barton on behalf of a "Scotch family" who lived in St. Petersburg, Russia, and whose son immigrated to New York in 1863 "without the consent of his family" to enlist in a New York regiment. Barton replied that she had no information on the missing soldier about whom Cleveland had inquired and suggested he contact the "Soldiers Messenger" in Philadelphia.[16]

In the years following the Civil War, Washington had also begun to establish itself as the scientific heart of the nation. Federal agencies such as the Coast Survey and the Hydrographic Office were conducting research and other work on a variety of topics and laying the groundwork for future scientific agencies within the federal government. The National Academy of Sciences, which President Lincoln signed into existence in 1863, served as a consulting body on scientific matters within the federal government. And the Smithsonian Institution—which had suffered a serious setback with a devastating fire in January 1865[17] that destroyed part of its castle-like building—was finally recovering and resuming its work to increase the diffusion of knowledge. By 1867, the institution boasted some 385 meteorological observers around the country, a number it hoped to increase "so that a more rapid and accurate accumulation of data relative to the meteorology of this country will be obtained than at any time heretofore."[18]

"Washington was at that time beginning to surpass in importance as a scientific centre either Cambridge or New Haven and since then it has come to over-shadow all other cities in the country in the eminence and activity of its scientific men and societies," Cleveland would later write. "In those days we had only the scientific club, a small gathering usually meeting at Dr. Peter Parker's, at least whenever I was invited to attend its meetings and I believe without any formal organization; it was in fact a club for natural improvement and the interchange of ideas upon novelties in science, not an active association for the advancement of science such as the Philosophical Society of Washington soon came to be after its organization in 1871."[19]

At the Naval Observatory

One of the oldest scientific agencies in the country, the U.S. Naval Observatory dates back to 1830, when the Navy established the Depot of Charts and Instruments, whose primary mission was to maintain the collection of charts, chronometers, and other instruments used by the Navy. In 1844, the Navy expanded the work of the depot and created a fully functional observatory near the banks of the Potomac River in the Foggy Bottom section of Washington. It would remain at that location for nearly half a century, performing work on such astronomical phenomena as the speed of light, solar eclipses, and transits of Venus. It was also home to the *Nautical Almanac*, which began publication in 1855.[20]

At the observatory, Cleveland was assigned to work as an assistant in the *Nautical Almanac* Office—which had moved to Washington from Cambridge the year before—eventually coming under the direction of Simon Newcomb. Newcomb had been placed in charge of the observatory's new Transit Circle, a large instrument consisting of a telescope specially mounted on a horizontal axis. Cleveland also made a few observations in May using the prime vertical transit instrument, which had been used in a five-year-long series of observations of the star Alpha Lyrae—also known as Vega—completed two months earlier.[21] Newcomb was among the most accomplished and well-known American scientists of his time and his writings included works on such diverse subjects as astronomy, economics, and even "The Outlook for the Flying Machine" (in which he concluded, just two months before the Wright brothers made their first successful flight at Kitty

Hawk, that "aerial flight is one of that great class of problems with which man can never cope").[22] Despite his "sometimes abrasive nature" (he is rumored to have single-handedly destroyed the career of Charles Sanders Peirce, the son of Coast Survey Superintendent Benjamin Peirce),[23] Newcomb would become Cleveland's close friend for years to come.[24]

As Cleveland labored in his observations and computations—much in the same way he had during his time at Pulkovo—he began to develop a disdain for the military organization and administration of a scientific institution, such as the Naval Observatory. As he later recalled:

> Such thoughts as these were forced upon my attention at every hand during the years 1867–68 that I first spent in Washington and years have strongly confirmed the convictions then formed that the scientific men throughout the country if they really intend to maintain the dignity of their profession must take a lead in the scientific legislation of the country. As a rule these men are quiet students of nature and of books in the laboratory and in the observatory; they have little to do with man and most to do with the laws of inanimate nature. They shrink from the ambitions, rivalries jealousies and deceptions practiced by men among themselves and are only animated by the search for truth; to ask for a position in which they may carry out some scientific research seems to them like asking for a personal favor, and yet they of all others know the wide value of the results that they are aiming at. Thus it happens that large representation of Army and Navy officers always living at Washington and always cooperating as with a single mind; always well acquainted with Members of Congress and well organized in their own clubs; are continually found offering their services at the right time, ready to carry on some newly proposed work of applied science and if need be employ the shrinking student where ever they can find him, to do the work.[25]

Over the course of the next year, Cleveland made the most of his time in Washington not spent at the observatory, in terms of cultivating professional contacts and devoting himself to his faith. Among those with whom he maintained professional relationships were Joseph Henry, secretary of the Smithsonian Institution, and General Oliver Otis Howard, former head of the Freedmen's Bureau, whose efforts to improve conditions for African Americans during Reconstruction led to the establishment of Howard University. Cleveland was also active in the YMCA and attended the organization's convention in the fall of 1867, noting in his diary entry for October 30 that there were "very few delegates" and that there was "Negro representation," which led to protests and the withdrawal of the delegates from Baltimore.[26] On Sundays, Cleveland volunteered his time at the Colored Sunday School on 13th and D Streets, NW, in a seedy section of Washington known as Murder Bay that the *Washington Post* described in 1888 as "a dreaded spot where for many years disorder and crime flourished without let or hindrance."[27]

On Monday, December 16, Cleveland penned an entry in his diary noting that Bickmore—who had just returned to the United States after spending three years traveling throughout the East Indian Archipelago, Siberia, and Europe—had arrived for a brief visit. Following Bickmore's departure the next day, Cleveland recorded:

> Remember the Sabbath Day
> to Keep it Holy

That evening Cleveland was back at work at the observatory—a good night for observing, he noted.[28]

When the weather was nice, Cleveland would set aside time to play croquet with friends. Sometimes he would play with Joseph Henry on the Smithsonian grounds. On occasion he was known to play on the lawn of the Capitol.[29]

According to his son Truman, Cleveland's work at the Naval Observatory was merely a stopgap. "He had taken it as a means of livelihood until he could find an observatory position where he could use his training to advance in the career he had chosen."[30] That opportunity began to unfold shortly after Cleveland's return from Pulkovo.

Cincinnati

"Although I had always thought that New York City as my final resting place, yet a slight circumstance turned my thoughts toward the Queen City of the West as Cincinnati had been called for many years," Cleveland recalled years later, as he reflected on the path his career had taken. "I had namely while on the steamer from Liverpool to New York been led to make the acquaintance of an elderly lady—a stranger—who after great suffering had by the middle of the voyage recovered sufficiently to sit on the deck and bask in the sunshine. Cleveland befriended the kindly, older woman and the two began to converse. "If my lonesomeness made me sympathetic, hers made her slightly trusting and I learned that in her old age she was for the first time leaving her home in Yorkshire, and was traveling alone to meet a brother and a sister in

Cincinnati," he said. "I experienced the same astonishment and interest that those in Poulkova had so lately expressed in the fact that I should travel all alone from America to Russia."[31]

A few days after the woman arrived in Cincinnati, her sister, Anne Emory, wrote a letter to Cleveland, thanking him for the kindness he had shown her sister during their voyage.[32] That letter never arrived, but another one dated January 7, 1867, did.[33] In addition, Cleveland had written to Anne's husband, the Rev. Joseph Emery, and the two began corresponding. Emery was a "humble Baptist missionary in the western portion of that city" to whom Abbe said he "owed the information that subsequently led me thither."[34] In a letter dated January 15, 1867, Emery thanked Cleveland "for the kindness shown my wife's sister" and provided him with important information on the Cincinnati Observatory, which, although no longer operational, served as the residence of its former director, William Davis.[35] "After many inquiries concerning our Observatory I find Wm H. Davis is residing there, and but little interest is taken either in Astronomy or the Observatory," Emery wrote, adding that William Hooper, president of the Central National Bank and secretary of the Cincinnati Astronomical Society, was "the proper person to write to on the subject."[36] That same day, Cleveland drafted a letter to Hooper and posted it. Two weeks later he received a reply. "In regard to the Observatory, I regret to say that nothing has been done in carrying out its objects since Prof. Mitchel left here and went to Albany," Hooper wrote.[37]

"The Cincinnati Observatory had been the pride of the Western States," Cleveland would later write. "It had been founded simultaneously with the Washington Observatory in 1842, a year before the great comet of 1843." In Cleveland's view, "the eloquence of its founder, O. M. Mitchel had been given it a world-wide fame; his popular journal the 'Sidereal Messenger' had penetrated every where; his eloquent lectures were for sale in cheap editions."[38] The observatory, which began operations in 1845, was the brainchild of Ormsby MacKnight Mitchel, a Cincinnati astronomer who served as its first director until 1860, when he became director of the Dudley Observatory in Albany.[39] When the Civil War broke out, Mitchel—a graduate of West Point—fought for the Union but contracted yellow fever and died in 1862.[40] The observatory sat dormant for several years. In his letter, Hooper also advised Cleveland that "the site has become unfit for perfect observation owing to the smoke which arises from many furnaces causing vibration in the atmosphere." Nevertheless, Hooper remained optimistic about the observatory's future. "For my own part I shall be very happy to take an active interest in the resuscitation," he said.

In June, Hooper wrote Cleveland that he was attempting to "ascertain something of the probabilities of reviving an interest in the Observatory among its former friends." Hooper hoped that renewed interest in the institution might lead to increased funding, and a position for Cleveland. "My idea has been that if we could realise the value of the present property we might secure something towards a fund to support a director," he said.[41]

A month later, Hooper wrote explaining that he had called together a meeting of the observatory's board of trustees and, among other things, read them excerpts of Cleveland's letters "to show that some interest was still felt, in behalf of science, that our observatory should take its part in the astronomical field of use."[42]

In September, Hooper wrote from Boston, saying he would be in New York the following week. "If you should have any occasion to be in New York at that time I shall be very glad to meet you," he told Cleveland. "I think we can talk over matters to advantage."[43] Cleveland decided immediately that he would meet Hooper. He left for New York on September 26 and, the following day, met him at the Fifth Avenue Hotel, a luxury establishment located between 23rd and 24th Streets. The two men spoke for two hours.[44] Following the meeting, Hooper promised to convene a meeting of the board of trustees of the Cincinnati Observatory. Several months passed with Hooper unsuccessful in getting the board to meet. On January 6, 1868, he wrote Cleveland with an update. "I have tried to get a meeting in the holidays, and again only yesterday but failed of a quorum," Hooper explained. "I shall be glad if you will intimate to me privately what compensation you would be willing to accept for the first year or two as Director of the Observatory in case I should find the Board willing to make the appointment."[45]

Two and a half weeks later, on January 24, Hooper wrote again, this time with the news Cleveland had been anxiously awaiting. "Yesterday I had the pleasure to propose your name to our observatory Board," Hooper wrote enthusiastically. "I have the gratification to announce that you were elected Director by a vote of 6 members," he added. "Being wholly without a dollar in the treasury they made no appropriation for your salary," he added.[46]

Cleveland was elated but had reservations. The observatory had essentially lain dormant since the onset of the Civil War. Would such a place—which would clearly need much in the way of repairs and renovation—be the right location to put into motion his grand scheme for a first-class astronomical institution? There was also the matter of salary. Hooper, along with seventeen other men—including several members of the observatory's board—signed a pledge of support, in hopes of further enticing Cleveland to come. "To revive the observatory, that it may resume its former position among the scientific Institutions of the Country, and be of its former advantage and renown to our city," it read, "the undersigned agree to advance annually for three years the sums below, to pay the salary of Mr. Cleveland Abbe, lately elected Director, & other incidental expenses."[47] Each man agreed to pay $100 annually for up to three years to "to make the much-needed repairs of the building, and to conduct the Observatory, until some plan for the endowment and proper support of the institution could be matured."[48]

Cleveland consulted his parents in New York on his impending decision. "I am glad you write in better spirits—I wish I were competent to give you good advice, but cannot," his mother wrote. "I think you can be a good Christian & still an astronomer," she added.[49] Cleveland's father was more direct in his response. "I don't think you ought to go to Cincinatti [sic] for just enough to support you just for the reason the institution is firm if they want you they ought to pay a decent salary," he wrote, adding, "you have prepared yourself by long study and expense, and that is your capital and I think you ought to make it available to your pecuniary benefit, as well as honor."[50]

Taking all the advice into consideration, Cleveland weighed his options. Then, on February 1, he sent a long, detailed letter to Hooper with his decision. "The honor thus conferred is inferior only to the responsibility of the position and it is with earnest that I accept the invitation of the Board of Trustees," he wrote. His acceptance, however, came with stipulations. Chief among these was the matter of salary. "Very desirous as I am to see our Observatory enter upon a career of activity, I must however hesitate to leave my present position and remove to Cincinnati until a definite and sure provision for my support is made," Cleveland argued. "The Trustees will doubtless agree with me that the permanent salary of the Director ought to be at least $2000 and if he accepts a less sum it should be a merely temporary arrangement with which both parties will become rightfully dissatisfied if it continues longer than two or three years."

Cleveland also laid out several recommendations he wished the board of trustees to consider. "It is evident that our Observatory has yet much to do before realizing the high hopes of its many friends," he said. "Henceforth we must never lose sight of our ideal and it may be allowed me now to indicate some of the points to which it is vitally important that we should attain within four or five years." Among these recommendations was the securing of "a larger endowment in money, land &c," as an observatory, Cleveland insisted, "is not a money making institution." Likewise, he contended that an observatory "is not an Institution for instruction nor for promoting the general diffusion of knowledge," which he claimed were the responsibilities of schools and colleges, teachers and lecturers. "We are to go deeper and rank among those who lay the foundation stones of all true material progress," he wrote.

Considering that "carrying on systematic observations according to a prearranged plan" results in the accumulation of "isolated facts which are generally useless and meaningless until after gathering much material," Cleveland suggested that the observatory should strive to "make its usefulness felt by its geodetic labors, tending to improve the maps of our country, since geography is probably next to navigation the most useful of all the practical applications of astronomy." While stipulating this, Cleveland did acknowledge that "the increase of our knowledge of the heavenly bodies is to be the first business of our Observatory."

"In the future activity and growth of the observatory," Cleveland said, "it will become important to extend out observations into the departments of meteorology and magnetism for which we may now prepare the way by making no such expenditures restrictions or changes as will impede future enlargement." In addition, Cleveland insisted that the results of observations made "should always be considered as open to the use of the scientific world, since investigators all have one common interest in the Truth."

Cleveland asked that any permanent assistants "who will share in the labors and responsibilities of the Director" be solicited "from among the accomplished young men of the land." And, perhaps reflecting on his own role as a supernumerary astronomer at Pulkovo, Cleveland asked that he "be allowed to gather about him a few young men who intend devoting their lives to astronomy."

Finally, with regard to the acquisition of new instruments, Cleveland pointed out that "there are but two or three firms in the world who make instruments fit for the finest astronomical and geodetic work." For reasons of "economy as well as convenience," Cleveland recommended that instead of looking to Europe for instruments, a "first class Mechanical Institute" be established in Cincinnati "in connection with the Observatory."

"In conclusion," Cleveland wrote, "I must be allowed to express the hope that the future years of our scientific prosperity may fully reward the zeal with which you have labored for the resuscitation of the Cincinnati Observatory."[51]

Hooper wrote back on February 19, telling Cleveland he agreed with him "in regard to future compensation,"[52] and again on March 13 to say he had "secured sufficient contribution towards the Observatory expenses,"[53] expressing enthusiasm for Cleveland's anticipated arrival in Cincinnati. "Whenever you may find it convenient to come we shall be happy to welcome you."

A Mother's Concern, A President Impeached

In late February, Cleveland received a letter from his mother, who was unaware of the news of his election to director of the Cincinnati Observatory. "Do you hear any thing from Cincinnati," she wrote, "and have they acceded to your propositions?" She also mentioned Cleveland's brother William, who had told her that Cleveland "advised him to have nothing to do with the ladies—odd advice for you to give, who think so much of them," she wrote. "'Practice before you preach,' is an old motto, & pray don't forget it," she said admonishingly. Then she added, "I hope I have not hurt your feelings, by these remarks, if I have forgive me, I meant no harm."[54] Earlier that month, Charlotte wrote her son of the impending visit by several of his cousins to Washington, encouraging him to take time from his professional activities to entertain them. "I wish you could go to some of the receptions with them, & change the current of your thoughts," she said "'All work & no play, makes Jack a dull boy,' & it is as true as any saying ever said."[55] While on the subject of family, Charlotte asked if Cleveland had ever called on Senator Cornelius Cole, her second cousin. "I don't think you need any letter of introduction," she assured him, "your card & your mothers name is sufficient." Then she added, "I feel sorry for him, as regards his brother Gen. Cole—who is shortly to be tried for murder."[56] She was referring to the scandalous incident the year before in which George W. Cole, who had served as a major general in the Union Army, shot New York State Assemblyman L. Harris Hiscock in the head at point-blank range for having allegedly "dishonored his simple, 'innocent wife.'"[57]

In the end, Charlotte was supportive of her son's decision to move to Cincinnati but had reservations about his taking on so important a role as director of the observatory there. "Will you not have more anxiety—& care when at the head & leading others, than as an assistant?" she asked, admitting that it was not her "makeup" to manage others. "I have no executive ability," she confessed, "I could never see two moves ahead either in checkers or chess."[58]

As Cleveland was preoccupied with his impending move and new job, he had little time to concern himself with the political events taking place in Washington, where President Andrew Johnson stood trial in the Senate for attempting "to bring into disgrace, ridicule, hatred, contempt and reproach, the Congress of the United States."[59] The charges resulted from his clashing with Congress over Reconstruction legislation aimed at protecting the rights of freed slaves, as well as his defiance to uphold the Tenure of Office Act when he ordered the removal of Secretary of War Edwin Stanton. In New York, Charlotte read the newspaper accounts of the impeachment trial, which lasted from March through May, and expressed her wishes that Cleveland could have witnessed it firsthand. "You ought to have gone & heard some of the speechifying, in this great impeachment case, for we may never live to see another of its kind," she wrote him.[60]

Move to Cincinnati

In April 1868, Cleveland traveled to Cincinnati for two weeks "to look over the equipment of the observatory and meet its board of directors."[61] On May 19, he wrote a letter to Secretary of the Navy Gideon Welles, tendering his resignation from his position at the U.S. Naval Observatory in Washington, effective June 1. Welles wrote back the next day, accepting his resignation.[62] A week later, as he was preparing to depart Washington for Cincinnati, Cleveland encountered "a most interesting incident." In reviewing the revised list of the principal astronomical observatories of the world, he noticed that the Cincinnati Observatory had been omitted. This seemingly inauspicious sign, he thought, was "partly due to the fact that the position of this observatory with reference to others of the world is only very roughly known."[63] Nevertheless, Cleveland recorded this in his diary entry for May 27,[64] with this notation, followed by five giant exclamation points:

> Cincinnati struck off from the
> List of principal observatories !!!!!

Cincinnati, which derives its name from the Society of the Cincinnati, a hereditary society founded by officers of the Continental Army at the end of the Revolutionary War,[65] had grown to a population of more than one hundred sixty thousand by 1860.[66] Its location on the Ohio River and the completion of the Miami and Erie Canal, which connected the river with Lake Erie, helped spur industrial progress. The Cincinnati-Covington Bridge, spanning the Ohio River between the two cities, opened on January 1, 1867, as the longest suspension bridge in the world. Known as a leading manufacturer of goods as far-ranging as carriages and beer, the city became best known during the mid-nineteenth century for its pork trade, which earned it the nickname Porkopolis. The city also became home, in 1869, to the nation's first professional baseball team, the Cincinnati Red Stockings.

The team reorganized and, in 1890, shortened its name to simply the Cincinnati Reds. Cincinnati had established itself scientifically through the efforts of several of its early citizens, including Professor Mitchel, whose observatory Cleveland was about to direct.

In early June, Cleveland left Washington for his new home. Following brief visits with his family and friends in New York and Windham, he arrived in Cincinnati on June 10, full of ambition and ideas and ready to get to work. He would have his work cut out for him, however, as his son Truman explained:

> Father's first weeks at the Cincinnati Observatory were busy ones. He had taken over the directorship of a virtually deserted observatory building in which precious instruments had lain long in disuse. His first task was to clean the great equatorial telescope and set up the instruments which he had induced the Navy Department and the Hydrographic Office to loan or donate. Next, he unpacked his boxes of books and charts.[67]

In addition to dealing with logistical issues, including unpacking and getting settled, Cleveland had to contend, in his early days in Cincinnati, with the very thing for which he would become famous—the weather. On June 18, a thunderstorm—the third in as many days—inundated the city with heavy rain, causing damage to the observatory and Cleveland's belongings. It was the "greatest storm for years," he recorded in his diary, with six and a half inches of rain falling over the course of twelve hours, leaving his books "all afloat."[68] Not long after arriving in Cincinnati, Cleveland received a letter from his sister Helen in New York, asking him, among other things, about the weather. "Do you find it warmer in Cincinnati than in Washington?" she wrote. "The weather has been quite summerish this last week, but today it rains."[69]

In taking stock of the observatory—which would serve as both his home and place of business—Cleveland noted the deteriorating effects that time, neglect, and other factors had on the physical structures of the institution. He was frank in presenting his assessment to the board of trustees in his inaugural report as director of the observatory, dated June 30. "It can not be said that the Observatory building is in good repair," he wrote, "nor would it be possible to make it a comfortable winter residence without considerable expense."[70] Among other things, Cleveland noted that the entire roof needed to be rolled off when the equatorial instrument was used, which he said "gives much trouble." Exposing the observatory room in this way, he argued, presented "many disadvantages, and, especially puts the instrument at the mercy of the least breeze that may spring up." He also noted that, due to the exposure, accurate observations could only be taken "when there is no wind and no dew."

When Cleveland examined the observatory's library, he was appalled to find it in a "fragmentary condition." It seemed that when Professor Mitchel left for the Dudley Observatory in Albany, he took most of the library with him. Cleveland insisted that "all possible means be taken to render it as complete and serviceable as possible," stressing that "without proper books, it is generally a waste of time to attempt any independent astronomical work." While he sought to negotiate with Mitchel's heirs to reclaim the missing volumes, he also appealed to the superintendent of the Naval Observatory in Washington, who happily loaned out duplicate copies of titles on hand. "The volumes thus loaned to us form a most welcome addition to our library, for which we must hope to make due return by our contributions to knowledge," Cleveland said.[71]

Before he left Washington, Cleveland began identifying himself as director of the Cincinnati Observatory in his correspondence and using the title "Professor," a term used by his peers at observatories across the country, but one he had easily dismissed as "too much an honor" just two years earlier, when writing to his mother from Pulkovo, after she told him he should wait for such an honor to come to him. "But in my eyes such a name is only an empty sham," he told her. "You will find all kinds of men in all kinds of institutions who have all grades of proficiency & learning dubbed Professor. So that it was perfectly in keeping when our negro whitewasher told us that he was Professor Jones."[72]

Meteorology

In discussing future activities of the observatory, Cleveland suggested that if he were to "be sustained in the general endeavor to make the Observatory useful," he should seek to extend the observatory's work "so as to embrace, on the one hand, scientific astronomy, meteorology, and magnetism, and, on the other, the application of these sciences to geography and geodesy, to storm predictions and to the wants of the citizen and the land surveyor."[73] It was an aggressive agenda for Cleveland to pursue, especially given his meager budget and limited staff. Among other tasks before him, Cleveland was faced with the prospect of using astronomical data to lay out a meridian line for a "certain county" in Ohio; furnishing the necessary information to establish more accurate longitude and latitude data for "prominent points in Kentucky and Tennessee," not to mention the observatory itself (to address its recent omission from the "list of the positions of the principal astronomical observatories of the world"); and undertaking the necessary work to address the "inconvenience . . . felt in the city from the want of standard mean time." In addition, he proposed to utilize "a complete set of costly self-recording magnetic instruments in the possession of the Coast Survey," which would be made available to the observatory, as long as it was willing to provide an observer and a shelter for the instruments."[74]

Despite being, in his own words, "severely tasked by the many calls upon my time and strength," Cleveland took advantage of the pleasant weather that prevailed during much of June and made the necessary observations "to determine with approximate accuracy the errors in the position of the equatorial." While the "inconvenience of the movable roof" prevented him from obtaining the best results possible, he nonetheless felt confident to proceed with the examination of the southern sky for double stars—a specialty of Wilhelm and Otto Struve in Pulkovo, whose "insistence on the practical utility of scientific research" influenced Cleveland greatly.[75]

Nowhere else in Cleveland's career did such practical utility manifest itself as in his efforts to make meteorology a major focus of the Cincinnati Observatory. In his inaugural report as director, Cleveland laid out a plan to make weather observations—and forecasting—a priority, thus laying the groundwork for transforming the observatory into a center of meteorological activity. Cleveland had already ensured that within his first three weeks as director daily meteorological observations were systematically made and recorded—something he considered to be "a necessary part of the work of an Observatory."[76] He further asserted that the observatory should commit itself to providing a "daily bulletin of telegraph dispatches from the meteorological observers of the country being necessary to the prediction of storms." To this end, he had already secured the support of several other necessary institutions. "I have received the promise of the hearty cooperation of the Smithsonian observers, and also of those of the army, as well as of certain of the telegraph companies," he said.[77]

Cleveland also enlisted the support of local businessman and civic leader John A. Gano, whom he later proclaimed "should be remembered by American scientists as the one who most efficiently encouraged the establishment of a system of daily weather predictions for the benefit of business men."[78] Gano's influence initially stemmed from the newspaper he edited, *The Cincinnati Commercial*. He also served as president of the Cincinnati Chamber of Commerce. In late July, Cleveland wrote a letter to Gano,[79] detailing his plan and appealing to him for cooperation:

Cincinnati Observatory, July 29, 1868

Dear Sir—I take the liberty of bringing to your attention, and through you to that of the Associated Press, a plan of operations looking to a system of storm warnings such as will, I believe, be highly appreciated by the public.

It cannot have escaped your notice that during the past twenty years very many endeavors have been made by various nations to utilize the science of meteorology. From the Paris Observatory daily bulletins are published showing the state of the weather in Western Europe. In England storm warnings are published many hours in advance and sent to the ports that are threatened.

The great value of such storm warnings long ago suggested the importance of the study of the phenomena of our own climate, and these labors have met with commensurate success. But such endeavors must be long continued and not spasmodic, and in view of their importance, I take the liberty of suggesting a simple plan by which the Associated Press may contribute much towards the progress of the science of meteorology as well as towards its utilization.

The Cincinnati Observatory, because of its central position with reference to the railroad and the telegraph systems of our country, may, with special propriety, be made the central station for meteorological dispatches from all parts of the country.

The newspapers daily publish such dispatches for from ten to fifty stations, and it is suggested that if the Associated Press will substitute for these far more accurate and valuable observations of the trained meteorological observers stationed all over our country, and will forward them to this observatory, we will submit them to a careful discussion and will within a few hours return them systematically arranged and condensed to the Associated Press. In this shape they will be of increased value to all who consult them.

We shall, moreover, ourselves enter these observations upon an appropriate manuscript chart, and propose that when we send the daily digest of the weather to the Associated Press, we accompany it with such general predictions of the weather for the next two days, as we may seem authorized to venture upon.

It seems certain that, at least in the case of a great storm, we may arrive at a greater degree of certainty in these predictions than is obtained in England and France where only seven-tenths of the predictions are verified.

Such a system as is proposed would, it is believed, powerfully contribute to advance scientific and practical meteorology. We have received promise of the hearty co-operation of the observers of the Smithsonian Institution and of the army, in case the systematic daily publication of good observations and storm warnings is attempted.

To render these meteorological reports as simple and brief as possible, consistent with accuracy, a series of blanks will be issued to each observer, who will each day at an appointed minute (8 a.m., Cincinnati mean time) record the following data:

a. Barometer reduced to 32° and to a common standard.
b. Temperature of the free air.
c. Amount of moisture in the free air.
d. Direction and force of the surface wind.
e. Quantity of lower clouds, kind, and direction of motion.
f. Quantity of upper clouds, kind, and direction of motion.
g. Amount of rain or snow during the past 24 hours.
h. Condition of the atmosphere (clear, hazy, foggy, &c.).

Further instructions will be given the observers by which the dispatch from each will average twenty or twenty-five numbers or letters. Observers of the requisite experience can be readily found in all desired localities. They should be distributed widely over the country—If not to be found at any desirable point, then the telegraph office at that point will be supplied with the proper instruments, and some employee of the company instructed in their use—the company being responsible to the extent of $100 for the value of the instruments.

The observers will send their blanks to the nearest telegraph office, addressed to the "Cincinnati Observatory," and we must receive them all at the Cincinnati office of the Western Union Telegraph by 12 o'clock, noon. Should there be no communication with any station we are to be informed of the fact and the delayed dispatches are to be forwarded at the earliest opportunity. These dispatches are to remain at and to be the property of the Cincinnati Observatory.

The observers will furnish their observations gratis, receiving in return a copy of the Daily Bulletin or summary in a form convenient for preservation.

The daily digest and the weather predictions are to be furnished by the Cincinnati Observatory gratis to the Associated Press and to such institutions as unite with us in the undertaking.

At least 100 stations ought to be thus occupied and report daily. If the Associated Press will assume the expense of fifty daily dispatches, it will not be difficult for us to secure the co-operation of other interested parties who will afford the means of largely increasing the number of daily dispatches.

Hoping that this or some improved plan may commend itself to your attention.

I remain very respectfully yours,
Cleveland Abbe, Director.

John A. Gano, Esq.,
Ed. Cin. Commercial & President C. Chamber of Commerce.

Cleveland's plan was nothing short of revolutionary. Where others—including the U.S. Army and the Smithsonian Institution—had tried and failed, Cleveland saw a way forward to creating a network of observers who would take regular, systematic observations of the weather from disparate points, hundreds of miles distant, and transmit them to a central location, in a timely enough manner that they may be used to make predictions of the future state of the weather. In his annual report for 1869, Cleveland described the essence of his vision, with supporting evidence to justify its capability and utility as a benefit to commerce and society:

> The science of meteorology is slowly advancing to that point at which it will begin to yield most valuable results to the general community. Although we can not yet predict the weather for a week in advance, yet we are safe in saying that, with a proper arrangement of outposts, we can generally predict three days in advance any extended storm, and six hours in advance any violent hurricane. This may be effected simply by constituting the observatory a central station, to which telegraphic reports of the weather are regularly daily transmitted. The careful study of these dispatches enables the meteorologist safely to make the predictions mentioned, which can be at once disseminated through the public papers or otherwise. In France, Italy and England, and on our own eastern coast, such storm warnings are considered of very great importance.[80]

Gano urged Cleveland to revise his proposal and resubmit it to the Chamber of Commerce, leaving out the part about the Associated Press.[81] Cleveland's revised proposal made the case succinctly and convincingly. "I propose to inaugurate such a system, by publishing in the daily papers, a weather bulletin, which shall give the probable state of the weather and river for Cincinnati and vicinity one or two days in advance," he said, adding that the accuracy of the predictions "will increase from month to month and year to year, in proportion as we are able to increase the number of our stations."[82] Suggesting that it was "most probable" that as many as 90 percent of the predictions would verify, he assured his would-be benefactors that his system would rely on science rather than soothsaying. "It is thus evident that we do not propose to guess at the weather (leaving that to the almanac makers), but we shall be able to assert with confidence the nature of the weather for one, two or four days in advance, as well as the stand of the water in the river." Appealing to the businessmen's sense of economy and desire to benefit commerce, Cleveland estimated that total expenses for the endeavor "will not exceed $750 or $1,000 per year."[83]

The chamber's board of officers approved a motion to authorize a committee "to confer with Prof. Abbe, and make such arrangements as may be necessary." The committee, which consisted of Samuel Covington, S. C. Newton, and George Graham, issued its report on July 17, 1869. The committee noted that Cleveland had expressed "the fullest confidence that necessary observations can be made and prepared for transmission . . . by competent parties at a trifling charge, at least for an experimental test." In doing so, the committee expressed its confidence that the enterprise would "result beneficially to our entire community."[84] Secretary George McLaughlin conveyed the committee's findings to Cleveland in the form of a letter:[85]

July 17, 1869

Prof Cleveland Abbe

Dear Sir,

At a meeting of the Board of Officers of the Chamber held this day the Report of the Committee heretofore appointed in reference to your communication in regard to a system of observations of the state of the weather, was adopted and you are hereby authorized to make the necessary arrangements to carry the scheme into effect, in the manner suggested, for a period of three months from Sept. 1st, 1869.

Yours Truly,
Geo. McLaughlin
Sec.

With Cleveland's assistance, the committee made a "thorough examination of the subject" and decided in order to test the practicability of his plan, it would "be advisable to embrace an area equal to the extreme distance of travel in twenty-four hours of a clearly developed storm, and which may be named at about six hundred miles."[86] As Cleveland later explained, "I believed, once the general direction of a storm was ascertained, the probabilities were that the storm, traveling at a measured speed, would reach certain localities at a time that could be computed."[87]

To support his experiment, Cleveland would need to recruit a cadre of competent weather observers, capable of adhering to the rigor of daily observations and whose locations would provide the necessary spatial distribution for him to adequately make his forecasts. The most desirable cities considered were: Memphis and Nashville, Tennessee; St. Louis, Missouri; Leavenworth, Kansas; Omaha, Nebraska; St. Paul, Minnesota; Chicago, Springfield, and Cairo, Illinois; Indianapolis, Indiana; Pittsburgh, Pennsylvania; and Louisville, Kentucky.[88] Cleveland wasted no time in drafting letters to prospective observers in these and other locations, hoping to enlist their support. The letter he sent to the prospective observer in St. Paul[89] illustrates both the degree of certainty that Cleveland possessed in making his request and the hopefulness he held that, in the name of science, his recipients would comply:

Cincinnati Observatory
July 20/69

Dear Sir

I have been requested by the Chamber of Commerce in this city to prepare for the use of that body a daily bulletin of the weather to be compiled from telegraphic dispatches sent to this observatory between the hours of 10 & 11 A.M. or earlier.

This undertaking is in some measure an experiment and I have tendered my services without remuneration for 3 months beginning on the 1st of September.

I am in hopes that the meteorological observers throughout the country will be animated by the same desire to further the advancement of our science, and will be disposed to heartily cooperate in this undertaking.

I can hardly doubt but that the result of the first three months experience will be to establish beyond all dispute the utility of this system of weather reports. If I am correct in this I shall at once proceed to widely extend the system of observers and shall publish a daily bulletin of observations, predictions, &c, &c accompanied by charts presenting the same in a graphic manner to the eye.

At present I am not authorized to offer any considerable sum for such daily dispatches as we desire, the telegraphic companies offer us the use of their wires for 3 months and other parties have made equally generous offers.

I would like to inquire on what terms you would be willing to furnish me with daily report (Sunday's report to be sent on Monday morning) for the Barometer, Wet and dry Therm. Wind, Rain, clouds, &c.

If you could for the present at least accept a copy of some one of the daily papers of this city (to be chosen by yourself) containing a tabular view of all the reports furnished me as a sufficient return for your own contribution this would be particularly acceptable to me.

I have the honor to remain
Very respectfully yours
Cleveland Abbe
Dir. Cin. Obs.

John W. Heimstreet
St. Paul

The response to Cleveland's request for volunteers was overwhelmingly positive. His would-be observers were generally enthusiastic, though in some cases logistical issues or other practicalities prevented them from carrying out their duties as completely or faithfully as they—or Cleveland—would have liked. One notable example is that of Eliza Young, a farmwife in rural Springdale, Kentucky, twelve miles east of Louisville. Her husband, Lawrence Young, was a farmer and ran a profitable nursery that supplied apples, peaches, and pears to customers throughout Kentucky and Tennessee.[90] Mrs. Young had been a regular observer for the Smithsonian for years and maintained one of the most complete meteorological records of the time in Kentucky.[91] Lawrence wrote to Cleveland on July 26, 1869, on Eliza's behalf. "Mrs. Young bids me say, that it will be impossible for her punctually to respond to you as you indicate," he said, "because our residence is several miles from any telegraphic Station and two miles off the Rail Road." As an alternative, the Youngs proposed that a neighbor "by rail go daily to Louisville during next winter leaving at 7 am—On days when inclement weather or sickness did not prevent the trip we should report for 7 am and have the report left at any telegraph office in Louisville and could begin on the 1st of Sep."[92] Apparently, this arrangement did not go as well as planned, as the Youngs soon discovered their reports were piling up at the telegraph office, unsent. On October 4, Eliza herself wrote to Cleveland, apologizing for the lack of observations he received. "We stated to you some time ago that our ability to furnish a daily Bulletin of the Weather depended upon the assistance of one of the pupils in a city school and write now only to relieve ourselves from blame in what is now known as irregularity in transmission," she said. "We were a day or two ago surprised and mortified to learn that on one occasion these dispatches remained uncalled for until three were on hand." Mrs. Young said they had no idea how many dispatches had gone unsent—or whether any had reached Cleveland at all—but said they felt it their duty "to say we have done our best to serve you."[93]

The Youngs weren't the only ones who ran into problems with their local telegraph operators. In Omaha, at the headquarters of the Army's administrative district known as the Department of the Platte, Assistant Surgeon Samuel M. Horton could not get his observations sent, apparently due to formatting issues. As his superior, Joseph Brown, who served as medical director at the post, said in a letter to Cleveland, Horton "attempted to transmit his reports, to you, but met with so much discouragement at the Telegraph Office."[94]

At St. Louis University, the Reverend F. H. Stuntebeck wrote to Cleveland, acknowledging his confusion over what was expected with his observations. "I do not know exactly what you wish me to send, but I have done what I thought was wanted."[95]

Another educator and minster, the Reverend Cecil Bancroft, principal of the school on top of Lookout Mountain in Tennessee, expressed his willingness to cooperate, so long as Cleveland didn't mind the occasional report coming in late. "We are 2200 ft. + above the sea 1400 above the valley, five miles from the telegraph office," he explained. "We send to town daily, but irregularly, sometimes early, sometimes late. We keep wind, barometer, thermometer, clouds, and duration of storms only. Please inform me by sending the 'Commercial,' if our observations so late and irregular as some of them must be will be reliable to you."[96]

Meanwhile, in Minneapolis, observer William Cheney wrote that he was "willing to cooperate" with Cleveland's request. A businessman and prominent member of the local community, Cheney maintained a weather station at his home, "keeping records of daily temperatures, precipitation and other meteorological phenomena from 1 November 1864 through 30 June 1901."[97] Cheney, however, was somewhat confused by Cleveland's instructions, or lack thereof. "Do you want reports of the observations for each of the three hours, 7 a.m. 2 & 9 p.m. or only the means of each day?" he asked. As for compensation in the form of a daily paper Cleveland had promised, Cheney seemed ambivalent. "I do not know that the daily paper would be of any value to me as I am now in receipt of more papers than I can read," he said, yet he still requested that Cleveland send him the "Daily Gazette, postage paid."[98]

Some observers were eager to help, so long as it did not require any expenditure on their part. "I take considerable interest in meteorological observations and anything I can do which does not involve an outlay of money in the purchase of instruments I am not only willing but anxious to do," wrote O. F. Russell, principal of the Normal Academy in Helena, Arkansas. "I have only the thermometer and am not able to supply myself with the other necessary instruments." Russell asked Cleveland if he could use his connection with the Smithsonian to furnish him with a barometer, as well as wet and dry bulb thermometers and a rain gauge. "There are only two Barometers in our city (I think) & those I cannot get access to or the use of," he added.[99]

Meanwhile, in New Orleans, Robert Foster was hoping he would be compensated for his efforts, to offset the financial difficulties he was facing in having recently been laid off from his job. "I would willingly volunteer my services without remuneration were it not that the insurance company for which I was Marine Surveyor went into liquidation in May last," he wrote. "Since then I have been out of business and having a family to support my pecuniary means are very limited. As you beg to enquire on what terms I would be willing to furnish you with the regular Reports, would $45 per month be too much to ask, or whatever lesser amount, if any, the gentlemen of the Chamber may decide on."[100]

Edward Goldsmith of Memphis told Cleveland he would be taking readings at seven o'clock in the morning, "the hour of 9 a.m. being very inconvenient to me."[101]

At the same time Cleveland began his correspondence to prospective observers, he undertook another venture to solidify the foundation of the meteorological endeavor he was creating. With the help of other like-minded gentlemen of Cincinnati and the surrounding area, he founded a meteorological society known as the Western Meteorological Association, whose objectives were to "to further the interests of meteorological observations by preserving such records for past years as can be obtained; by discussing and establishing laws controlling meteorological phenomena; by discussing meteorological information and exciting an increased interest in this study."[102] Besides Cleveland, the group consisted of doctors, teachers, an engineer, and a printer, among others—all with an interest in furthering the scientific pursuit of meteorology. They met at the home of Cincinnati optician Walter Alden to agree on a set of bylaws and approve a constitution. Dr. John A. Warder was voted president and Cleveland vice president.

Among the actions agreed upon as part of the association's bylaws, the officers resolved "to solicit records of observations from competent persons in every part of the continent, but especially from the valley of the Ohio river." In addition, the association would undertake the printing of blank observation forms to be "furnished to those willing to make regular observation as active members of the association." The instructions provided to the observers would "be not materially different from those recommended by the Secretary of the Smithsonian Institution, and by the Surgeon General of the army." Finally, the bylaws stipulated that "the interest of the association and meteorological science demand the publication of a meteorological bulletin."[103]

Off for the Eclipse

Before Cleveland could begin work on his Weather Bulletin, he took time to indulge in one of the most rewarding experiences of his astronomical career at that point. On August 7, 1869, a total eclipse of the sun was to occur along a path of totality that in the contiguous United States stretched from Montana Territory to North Carolina. Cleveland had decided to organize an expedition to view the phenomenon from a site at Sioux Falls City, formerly occupied by Fort Dakota, in Dakota Territory. While he could have viewed the eclipse in its totality from a spot just south of Lexington, Kentucky, roughly 130 miles south of Cincinnati, Cleveland knew that from an astronomical—and meteorological—perspective the broad plateau bordering eastern Dakota Territory and southwestern Minnesota, known as Coteau des Prairies, would offer a more ideal vantage point. "Among the parties organized to observe the total eclipse of 1869," he later wrote, his "was probably favored above all others in the advantages of having a comparatively elevated station and exquisite atmosphere."[104]

Cleveland's party included William C. Taylor, of the Philadelphia firm Wenderoth Taylor and Brown, who brought with him "an exquisite six-inch telescope," which he had received as a prize at the Paris Exposition Universelle of 1867. Alfred G. Compton, a friend from Free Academy of New York (at that point, the College of the City of New York), also joined, along with I. J. Longstreth of Chicago, James Haines of Waynesville, Ohio, and Robert B. Warder of Champaign, Illinois. Cleveland's brother Robert, who was visiting from New York, rounded out the party and agreed to take meteorological observations and provide assistance to the other party members, as needed. The group met in Cincinnati and left together by train, except for Taylor and Longstreth, who traveled separately and met the rest of the party at Fort Dakota.

"Off for the Eclipse," Cleveland wrote in his diary entry for July 28, as the party set off for their expedition.[105] After spending the first two nights in Chicago, they would make their way to Sioux City, Iowa, arriving on July 31. On August 2, they left for their camp in Dakota Territory. Since it was outside "the settled portions of the United States," Cleveland required a special rider on his life insurance policy, to extend coverage to the unsettled regions of Dakota Territory, inhabited primarily by Native Americans.[106]

"Clouds & mosquitoes," Cleveland noted in his diary on August 3, as the party arrived at camp. A walk to the falls on the Big Sioux River brought on a case of eczema, he noted. The skin condition would plague him at various times throughout his life.[107] On August 4, the party set up their instruments and began making final preparations for the eclipse three days later. That evening, they took time to celebrate with a "gay and festive party."[108]

On the day of the eclipse, clouds began to fill the sky, threatening to squelch their chances of witnessing the event. "Rain and cloud had continued up to a few hours previous to the critical moment, but the atmosphere during the eclipse was of surpassing steadiness and clearness," Cleveland later wrote. "The altitude of the sun at the time of totality was about 40°, the local time 3 ½ p.m., the duration of totality four minutes. No sooner had totality begun than after sketching in most of the prominences as points of reference, I viewed the corona without darkening glasses, and with a magnifying power of probably 120 diameters."[109]

During the critical minutes of totality, Cleveland's view of the eclipse was briefly interrupted by one of the other members of the party, along with "the very rough and faulty stand supporting the telescope."[110] Nevertheless, he was able to make observations and sketches of the finer details of the eclipse, including a "long series of red prominences" that rose above the sun's limb, appearing as "conical masses of pearly light" that resembled "the kilns used in some branches of pottery."[111] As Cleveland continued to peer through the telescope, his companions viewed the eclipse either with the naked eye or with the use of opera glasses.[112]

Years later, at a meeting of the Philosophical Society of Washington on December 2, 1876, Garrick Mallery, an ethnologist whose specialty was Native American sign language and pictographs (and who had also served as executive officer of the Signal Service), read a paper titled "A Calendar of the Dakota Indians." After the reading, one of the members present, John Wesley Powell—who would later become the second director of the U.S. Geological Survey and the founding director of the Smithsonian's Bureau of Ethnology—remarked that that he "did not understand how there could be so many symbols for names of individuals, nor the picturing of the total eclipse of the sun in 1869 as it actually appears, instead of the usual mythological representation of a monster devouring the sun." Cleveland, who was also present at the meeting, spoke up in contradiction to Powell's remarks, noting that during his stay at Fort Dakota in 1869, he and his party "explained the eclipse to numerous Sioux, and probably a hundred of those Indians had occasion to realize that white men knew of the approaching event, and that to them the phenomenon was no mystery." Cleveland described how, on the day of the eclipse, "a party of six or seven warriors lingered about the camp until the progress of the eclipse became evident to the naked eye, when, all their doubts being dispelled, they departed with a shrug of the shoulder and 'Ugh! bad medicine.'" Cleveland concluded his remarks by saying the eclipse "as seen in that high latitude and elevated region, where the Dakotas roam, was impressive and beautiful in the highest degree. The stars, which were thus made visible in the daytime, have been deemed by the Indian chronologist worthy of marking the year 1869."[113]

Weather Bulletin Begins

Cleveland returned to Cincinnati in late August, full of excitement from having witnessed his first total solar eclipse and ready to begin work on issuing the daily weather bulletin he had convinced the Cincinnati Chamber of Commerce to back. On his way back from Sioux Falls City, Cleveland stopped in Chicago for a few days, where he attended a meeting of the American Association for the Advancement of Science.[114] He also hoped to convince members of the Chicago Board of Trade to agree to participate in his weather bulletin project, thus expanding its reach. The Chicago papers had already run an editorial extolling the virtues of Cleveland's endeavors, including an editorial that ran in *The Chicago Tribune* on August 18. In part, it read:

> American railroad and telegraph officials have for a longtime estimated, with considerable certainly, the coming weather, by consulting the despatches pri-

vately received from points to the west and northwest of them. Such predictions, more carefully made and authoritatively published, would have no less value in Chicago and throughout the Northwest, than in Boston, New York and Washington.

Such predictions, the editorial contended, would benefit not only commerce, railroads, farming, and other industries but also "social excursions and picnics." "The prophet who should run the bulletin would certainly have his hands full to keep even with all the fluctuations of our gusty climate."[115]

For his part, Cleveland would not have to concern himself with Chicago's "gusty climate," at least for the time being, as he was unable to persuade the board there to participate in the weather bulletin project. The board's secretary, Charles Randolph, wrote to the Cincinnati Chamber of Commerce on August 21 with the findings of the committee assembled to consider the proposal. "The Committee expressed some doubt of the practical value of such reports to our trade generally, except perhaps at certain limited seasons," Randolph wrote. "And in view of the expense necessarily attending a regular report from a large number of points, it is recommended that no action be taken."[116]

Back in Cincinnati, Cleveland made final preparations before he inaugurated his experimental weather forecasting service, now with the sole backing of the Cincinnati Chamber of Commerce. On August 25, Samuel Covington, one of the members of the committee that evaluated Cleveland's proposal, reported to the larger chamber of commerce board that "Abbe had been authorized to contract for the receipt of daily telegraphic messages from not to exceed sixteen points, with a view to the preparation of his reports of the weather."[117]

Cleveland also needed to secure the cooperation of the telegraph companies, on whose services his observers would rely to transmit their daily reports to him. He made arrangements with the Western Union Telegraph Company "for the use of their line at a nominal price"[118] of twenty-five cents for messages of twenty words or less.[119] With all the pieces in place—the support of the chamber of commerce, the cooperation of Western Union, and his cadre of weather observers willing to report each morning—Cleveland's plan finally was coming to fruition and the nation's first weather forecasting service was about to begin operations.

On the morning of Wednesday, September 1, 1869, Cleveland went to the Western Union office on West Third Street, in downtown Cincinnati, and waited for the first weather reports to come in. He was disappointed when only two reports came in—from Leavenworth, Kansas, and St. Louis—each reporting at seven o'clock that morning. Nonetheless, he looked optimistically on the humble beginning of what he hoped would be a more prosperous endeavor. These two reports "may be taken as an earnest of what is to be," he later wrote, promising that an "increase in the number of stations reported from will be delayed only a few days."[120] A third report—from Chicago—did eventually come in, its transmission being delayed.[121]

With three incomplete sets of observations (no sky condition was reported at St. Louis and no pressure or humidity values from Leavenworth) from stations spanning approximately 550 miles east to west, the inaugural edition of the Weather Bulletin of the Cincinnati Observatory appeared in *The Cincinnati Commercial* on Thursday, September 2. It only reported weather conditions from the three locations from the previous day but did not offer a forecast. The first bulletin also came with a disclaimer of sorts, with Cleveland including the following message beneath it:

> The correspondence and preparatory arrangements for the publication of the Weather Bulletin have been so delayed by the Observatory Expedition for observing the recent eclipse, that the undersigned must needs apologize for the meager appearance of this, the first number of the Bulletin. Within a few weeks at least sixteen important stations will be reported from, and with much fuller detail.[122]

Readers of *The Commercial* had to turn to page eight to find the Weather Bulletin, where it appeared at the top of the page, sandwiched between, on one side, advertisements for Batchelor's Hair Dye and a concoction known as Dr. McConnell's Sarsaparilla and Wild Cherry (which promised a permanent cure from scrofula, a type of tuberculosis), and, on the other side, by the Miniature Almanac, a regular feature of the newspaper presenting, among other information, meteorological observations made by Henry Ware, a local optician. A miscellany of pithy editorial comments and trivial news items were printed beneath the Miniature Almanac, including the following:

> There was a fine display of meteors last night.
>
> The beer jerkers don't like this weather. Neither do paper collar dealers.
>
> The office-grubbers were out in force last night. The primary returns interested them.

> Catherine Hines, a poor widow living on Walnut street, broke one of her ribs by a fall down stairs yesterday.

> The wife of Rev. Mr. Cramer, of Covington, Consul to Leipzig, and brother-in-law of the President, has presented him with a son recently.

The same day that Cleveland's Weather Bulletin made its first appearance in *The Cincinnati Commercial*, the paper published a letter to the editor that at first glance might seem to have come from a would-be competitor of Cleveland's. "To the Editor of the Commercial," it began. "Accompanying you have the weather prophecies of Mr. F. L. Capen and the actual occurrences, day by day, for the last week," the anonymous writer continued. "He made a correct prophecy in one case, that is, on Thursday afternoon, no other." Apparently, Capen's infamous reputation as a forecaster had been established several years prior, during the Civil War, when he wrote to President Lincoln, offering his weather prediction services to the War Department. "It would give me great pleasure to assure you of the fine weather suitable for a visit to the front, or for starting an Expedition fraught with momentous interests to the Country, & not less important in its economical aspects, like the recent Cavalry Movement," he wrote to the commander and chief in a letter dated April 25, 1863. "Please refer me, favorably to the War Department, & I will guarantee to furnish Meteorological information that will Save many a serious Sacrifice." Capen enclosed his card with the letter, adding to his appeal for a commission. "Thousands of lives & Millions of dollars may be saved by the Application of Science to War," he wrote. Lincoln, however, was not impressed. "It seems to me Mr. Capen knows nothing about the weather, in advance," he wrote in response, on April 28. "He told me three days ago that it would not rain again till the 30th of April or 1st of May. It is raining now & has been for ten hours. I can not spare any more time to Mr. Capen."[123] While the letter to the editor of *The Cincinnati Commercial* is not signed, it is possible that Cleveland sent it, as his diary entry one week prior, on August 26, includes mention of a "call from Capen the meteorologist."[124]

While Cleveland did not include a forecast with the version of the first Weather Bulletin published in *The Cincinnati Commercial*, he did produce a forecast, which appeared at the foot of his manuscript version of the September 2 bulletin:

> Easterly and southerly winds prevail. Barometer has begun to fall at Cincinnati, and a storm passing over the southern country will not reach Cincinnati.

> Temperature here on the increase. Cloudy and warm weather this evening. Tomorrow clear.[125]

Despite the confidence conveyed in the comprehensiveness of his first forecast, Cleveland was dubious. "The 1st Prognostication a doubt & a failure?" he wrote in his diary later that day.[126]

The first day's bulletin was also accompanied by a lengthy explanation, which appeared in tiny, six-point type and took up nearly an entire column in the newspaper. In it, Cleveland wrote that the bulletin "proposes to give a complete knowledge of the weather for each day, and to give it in such a form as that one can by a few minutes' reading gain an accurate idea of the weather over the whole country north, west and south of Cincinnati." He described in detail the various elements reported in the bulletin, along with how changes in them could be interpreted to forecast the weather. "The known laws of the changes of the weather enable us from the perusal of these reports, to anticipate by a day at least the general character of the weather in Cincinnati, and indeed in the country for a hundred miles about," he said. "The storms and all other changes in the weather move eastward over the surface of the country. The area covered by the storm may extend three or four hundred miles northward and southward, so that the storm may be first heard from at a station far to the northwest or southwest, even when its center is directly west of us. The movement of the storm eastwardly may be estimated on the average as about twenty miles per hour, or five hundred per day, thus passing over the distances from St. Paul, Omaha, Leavenworth or Little Rock to Cincinnati in twenty-four hours."

Cleveland went on to discuss various principles of meteorological conditions and their relation to storms and local weather, including how the movement of storms could be determined by the upper-level clouds, with movement in the lower layer of clouds being indicative of local disturbances. He also discussed the "cold, clear periods that intervene between successive storms," which he said "are so important to the pork-packers and river men."[127] While they did not publish the Weather Bulletin in its tabular form each day, two other Cincinnati newspapers—the *Daily Gazette* and the *Daily Enquirer*—did include Cleveland's detailed explanation in their September 2 issues. In addition, the *Gazette* published summaries of the observations contained in the bulletin and, when issued, Cleveland's forecasts. These appeared, unceremoniously, beneath optician Henry Ware's meteorological observations for Cincinnati.

On Friday, September 3, the second edition of the Weather Bulletin appeared in *The Cincinnati Commercial*, slightly expanded from the previous day, with two morning reports each from Cincinnati and Chicago, along with early morning dispatches from St. Louis and Leavenworth, and a late evening report from Omaha.[128] Beneath the bulletin ran the notice of the newly formed Western Meteorological Association, complete with its constitution and bylaws.

By September 7, the Weather Bulletin included reports received that morning from Cincinnati, Leavenworth, St. Louis, Chicago, Minneapolis, and Indianapolis, along with late reports from September 6 for Minneapolis, Leavenworth, Indianapolis, and Omaha. That day's bulletin also carried a note pertaining to the observation of rain reported at Cincinnati at ten o'clock that morning. "This rain was predicted on Saturday noon, but heavier than was expected," the note read.[129]

In addition to appearing in the newspaper, handwritten copies of the Weather Bulletin were posted on the bulletin board at the Cincinnati Chamber of Commerce. At the top of the September 7 edition, in Cleveland's handwriting, it read: "Weather Bulletin of the Cincinnati Observatory, Teusday, September 7, 1869." Cleveland was notorious for misspelling the word *Tuesday*, consistently transposing the first two vowels. Apparently, this caught the attention of William H. Davis, a well-known pork packer in Cincinnati who, in reaction to the misspelling or perhaps to the heavier-than-expected rain—or both—added his own commentary, in a line written in pencil at the bottom of the bulletin. "A bad spell of weather for Old Probs," it read, providing, in abbreviated form, the meteorological moniker that would follow Cleveland throughout his life from that point forward. "This established my future very popular name of 'Old Probs,'" Cleveland later wrote.[130] In fact, "Old Probabilities" (or "Old Probs" or "Old Prob") would come to be applied to other officials in the weather forecasting field, as well as more generically to the concept of a weather prognosticator. As Cleveland once told a group of South African scientists, "Although the nickname 'Old Prob' subsequently followed me to Washington, yet by courtesy it has come to be now generally given to the Chief Signal Officer, *ex-officio*."[131] In 1876, author and humorist Samuel Clemens (better known by his nom de plume, Mark Twain) addressed the annual dinner of the New England Society in New York with a speech on the vagaries of New England weather. "Old Probabilities has a mighty reputation for accurate prophecy, and thoroughly well deserves it," he said. "You take up the paper and observe how crisply and confidently he checks off what to-day's weather is going to be on the Pacific, down South, in the Middle States, in the Wisconsin region. See him sail along in the joy and pride of his power till he gets to New England, and then see his tail drop. He doesn't know what the weather is going to be in New England."[132]

The following day, September 8, saw the first printing of the bulletin using a printing press, with each day's edition sequentially numbered beginning on that date.[133] A notice began appearing at the bottom of the bulletin, advertising that printed copies would be furnished to subscribers between noon and one o'clock daily (Sundays excepted) at the rate of $1.50 per month. On September 14, this notice was preceded by an explanation of how to interpret the various weather elements, including a description of the kinds of clouds: "Cirrus, or the highest; Cumulus, or the little noonday clouds—large ones attend thunder storms; Nimbus, or the rain clouds; Stratus, or the stratified clouds of sunset and clearing off storms." There was also a brief statement explaining how changes in cloud type, barometric pressure, temperature, and wind direction could be used to foretell a coming storm: "A falling Barometer, increased temperature and Humidity, and Nimbus or Nimbus Stratus clouds, precede rain and storms. The winds blow toward the center of a storm, or toward the point where the Barometer is below its average height."

On September 22, the Weather Bulletin included its first published forecast, which appeared in the September 23 edition of *The Cincinnati Commercial*. With reports from nine stations for the previous day—some of which were missing critical data—along with two reports from two days prior, Cleveland made the following prediction for Cincinnati:

> The above reports indicate the following weather: Wednesday, September 22, morning cloudy and warm; afternoon not so oppressive; evening clear and cool. Thursday, September 23, morning cloudy and warm; afternoon clear; evening clear and cool. Friday, September 24, morning clear and warm; afternoon hot.[134]

Cleveland's audacity in putting forth this first published forecast was tempered by the fact that the Weather Bulletin for September 23 reported a "Deep Blue" sky for Cincinnati that morning, not "cloudy," as Cleveland had predicted. Also, while the temperature of 72.9 degrees on the morning of the twenty-third could be considered warm, it was nearly ten degrees cooler than that of the morning of the twenty-second. "Weather predictions not well verified," Cleveland wrote as the single entry in his diary for Friday, September 24.[135]

It would be nearly two weeks before Cleveland would attempt another public forecast. On October 6, the following brief forecast appeared beneath the Weather Bulletin for that day:

> The weather reports above given indicate the following weather for Cincinnati: Wednesday, October 6, night, clear and cool. Thursday, October 7, day, clear and warm.[136]

Information gleaned from the following days' bulletins indicates that October 7 saw clear skies in Cincinnati, with a high temperature of 69.8 degrees.

Over the next several weeks, Cleveland's forecasts continued to appear sporadically with the daily Weather Bulletin, becoming, for the most part, more regular and detailed as time went on. By November 8, Cleveland began including the entire list of stations from which he was receiving reports, even if some or all the data for a particular station were missing. The list of stations included:

Cheyenne, Wyoming
Omaha, Nebraska
Leavenworth, Kansas
St. Louis, Missouri
Des Moines, Iowa
Minneapolis, Minnesota
Milwaukee, Wisconsin
Chicago, Illinois
Springfield, Illinois
Cairo, Illinois
Memphis, Tennessee
Little Rock, Arkansas
New Orleans, Louisiana
Nashville, Tennessee
Louisville, Kentucky
Indianapolis, Indiana
Cincinnati, Ohio
Toledo, Ohio
Cleveland, Ohio
Pittsburgh, Pennsylvania

Among the most detailed forecasts Cleveland issued during his Weather Bulletin experiment was the one for Thursday, October 21, which discussed an impending storm from the west:

> From the weather reports above given, we infer that the storm of Tuesday has been immediately succeeded by another, which will probably come from St. Louis and Memphis, arriving here Thursday night, and breaking up on Friday. Clear weather was indicated by the dispatches of Wednesday morning, but those received later in the day gave notice of a storm approaching from the West.[137]

The Weather Bulletin continued to appear in *The Cincinnati Commercial* through December 4, when Cleveland's agreement with the Cincinnati Chamber of Commerce expired, bringing an end to his three-month-long weather forecasting experiment. Cleveland, not content with waiting for a more permanent solution to present itself, decided to take matters into his own hands. "At the expiration of the first three months' trial and while negotiations were still pending with the Western Union Telegraph Company for its permanent continuance," he later said, "I, in order to prevent a break in the series, for six months maintained the Bulletin myself, receiving the dispatches gratuitously from the telegraph employés, and publishing the reports daily, including Sundays, in the newspapers of Cincinnati."[138]

Despite its short-lived existence, Cleveland considered the initial trial of the Weather Bulletin of the Cincinnati Observatory to be not only a success but an important first step toward a larger goal of providing practical weather forecasts, for the benefit of commerce and other interests, for the entire nation. "This was, I believe, the first systematic attempt in the United States to make the weather reports practically useful to our commercial communities."[139] He recalled later having written to his father in New York, telling him, with an uncharacteristic lack of modesty, "I have started that which the country will not willingly let die."[140]

Cleveland was not alone in his assessment of the effort. The 1869 annual report of the secretary of state of Ohio included a section titled "The Importance of Weather Bulletins," perhaps written by Cleveland himself (or certainly based on information he supplied). "To predict the weather is certainly a very unthankful task, but it seemed necessary to attempt this also, in order to complete the ideal of a weather bulletin, and the attempt may be considered as not altogether a failure," it claimed. "On comparing the daily predictions with the weather actually experienced, we find only about five errors per month."[141]

In reflecting on the project years later, Cleveland recalled the fact that this was his initiative; no one had asked or directed him to begin a series of daily weather bulletins. And, yet, he did not lose sight of the fact that he had achieved this milestone while standing on the shoulders of others whose earlier attempts, while unsuccessful, provided the foundation upon which his accomplishments stood. "The Cincinnati Weather Bulletin and predictions of 1869 was really my personal effort to utilize science for the benefit of the people," he said, "but historically it may also be considered as a revival of the reports and maps started by Espy and Henry, under the joint auspices of the Federal Government and the Smithsonian Institution, in 1848, and maintained at Washington with the coöperation of the various telegraph companies until 1861."[142]

Near the end of his life, Cleveland said in an interview that his early forecasts in Cincinnati, while generally accepted and appreciated by the public, drew the ire of some, who felt he had crossed a line and was meddling in the realm of the divine. "I am glad to say that my 'probabilities' were found on the whole to be accurate, though local storms sometimes threw them out of balance, and that confidence in them grew steadily," he said. "Some persons said that I was defying the laws of God and condemned me out of the eleventh chapter and fourth verse of Ecclesiastes, which reads: 'He that observeth the wind shall not sow; and he that regardeth the clouds shall not reap.'"[143] This was clearly an area where Cleveland's dedication to his scientific principles outweighed his adherence to strict religious theology.

Fanny

It was while he was in Cincinnati that Cleveland finally found the love and companionship he had so dearly sought since his days in Russia—in his relationship with a young woman named Frances Martha Neal, known to her family and close friends as Fanny, who became his secretary shortly after his arrival in Cincinnati. She was the half-sister of William Hooper's wife, Mary. Cleveland first met Fanny on July 11, 1868, while paying a visit to the Hoopers following meetings with representatives from the various Cincinnati newspapers.[144] Friends and family would later describe her as "a woman of strong character and personality"[145] who was "beloved by all who knew her."[146]

Fanny was born January 16, 1838, near Hamilton, Ohio, about twenty miles north of Cincinnati. She had a twin brother named Francis (Frank) and, while the two were close growing up, they made a pact as teenagers not to reveal their true relationship to anyone as adults. Apparently, she "considered multiple births bestial, analogous to the multiple births of many animals,"[147] and thus kept the fact from Cleveland, all throughout their lives together, that she and her brother were twins, taking it with her to the grave.

When she was two years old, Fanny and her family moved to Cincinnati. When she was around seven or eight, her father, David Neal, abandoned the family and, unbeknownst to them at the time, went to Indiana to live with his daughter from a previous marriage.[148] "Evidently David Neal thought he could be happier with his first family than with his second," according to Truman.[149] Shortly after that, Fanny moved with her mother, twin brother, and older sister, first to Middletown, Ohio, twenty-five miles northeast of Cincinnati, and then to the small village of Amanda, three miles to the south. A smallpox outbreak in 1863 left the older sister dead and Fanny severely ill. She recovered but developed what was described as "a distinct deafness."[150] In 1854, the family returned to Cincinnati, where Fanny studied dressmaking. She also devoted much of her time to the Presbyterian Sunday schools of Cincinnati, including one that met over a saloon.[151]

Following the Civil War, Fanny's brother managed cotton plantations near Natchez, Mississippi. In 1866, Fanny went to Natchez and spent two years there teaching at a school for African American children, run by the American Freedmen's Aid Commission, which was created in August 1865 by representatives of leading relief organizations for freed slaves. The commission sought as its purpose "the redemption of the freed people from the degradation into which slavery has plunged them, that they may become thoroughly FIT for complete citizenship. No sectional, no partizan, no class interests are sought or recognized."[152]

In 1868, Fanny returned to Cincinnati. She initially lived with her brother and their mother in a farmhouse, until it caught fire and burned down. Awakened by the blaze early in the morning, Frank was able to save his twin sister and their mother from certain death, along with their servant. He and Fanny went back inside to retrieve her trunk containing valuables, along with some furniture. At that time, Fanny moved in with her half-sister, Mary, and her husband, William Hooper. Her mother, who had been sick with cancer, also moved in with them and died within a year.

It was William who suggested that Fanny take up work for Cleveland as his secretary and assistant, shortly after he took over as director of the Cincinnati Observatory. "Father discovered in Miss Neal many of the traits he had also found praiseworthy in Aemelia Struve," Truman wrote. "There was her innate desire to be of service to others, shown in her work for Father. She had the missionary spirit as well, a desire to help the underprivileged, and her years of work at Natchez bore a striking resemblance to Father's Sunday-school work in Pulkova and his church work in Washington."[153]

As the time Cleveland and Fanny spent together increased, so too did their affection for one another. This can be seen in a letter from Cleveland in November 1869. "My Dear Fanny," he wrote, "Having set apart an hour this evening for a little talk with you I shall not relinquish my plan though I am indeed in but very poor writing mood. It's now about nine o'clock; I've been writing all day long—have had neither dinner nor supper—and am now at my desk in the office of the Western Union Telegraph Company, hungry yet happy (at least just now)." In the letter, Cleveland enclosed a photograph of his father and three of his mother (noting that "mothers generally have pictures taken more frequently"). "In transmitting these to you I am parting with some precious keepsakes so you must preserve them carefully and one of these days I will claim them and you too."

When Cleveland wrote his parents in February 1870 to announce that he was getting married, his mother replied with a sense of both astonishment and curiosity. "You may imagine that I was somewhat surprised at what you rather more than intimated in your last letter, about being married next summer," she said. "Are you really in earnest? & if so, why don't you tell us, who it is, or have you not settled the thing? Is she a literary lady, a widow, a spinster, or a blooming young lady—American, or foreign—Baptist or not. Don't be rash or do anything unadvisedly, make a confidante of some of us."[154] His brother Robert wrote in a more sardonic tone. "We understand from your last that your silver wedding will not be more than twenty five years hence—Have we ever met her? For goodness sake don't do as the poet Hooker did and let your landlady choose you a wife."[155] Cleveland's brother Walter seemed downright dumbfounded at the news. "Father tells me that you are really thinking of getting married—that your talk is serious & that acts will before long speak louder than words," he said. "Well now I do declare; you don't say so, do you now, come! I never. A queer idea comes into my head when I think of you & your getting married," he exclaimed.[156] For his part, George Abbe also admitted his surprise at his son's news, but added, "I have no doubt it is all for the best and we are all glad to hear of it and hope it will prove a blessing to both."[157] As the wedding date drew nearer, Charlotte Abbe grew more anxious about the details of the event—and her son's bride-to-be. "You must let us know as soon as you can, what sort of a reception there will be at the wedding, so that I may know, how to arrange myself," she wrote Cleveland on April 11. "Is there any thing I can do for you beforehand? Of course we are all curious to know how the lady looks, & all about her, but may be it is only an idle curiosity—If nothing prevents, we shall soon know."[158]

Cleveland and Fanny were married on May 10, 1870, in Cincinnati. The Reverend Henry Smith, professor of sacred rhetoric and pastoral theology at Lane Seminary in Cincinnati, presided over the wedding, which took place at the home of William and Mary Hooper. Only about a dozen guests were in attendance, including Cleveland's parents and younger brother Walter, who met the bride for the first time the morning of the wedding. Following the ceremony, Cleveland noted "The Ride to Mt. Adams," indicating the newlyweds retreated to the observatory, where they would make their home initially. There was no honeymoon. "The work of the director of the observatory was essential and had to go on," Truman noted, adding, "But the bride and groom were very happy."[159]

Fanny's devotion to her husband went well beyond matrimonial matters. She had been an invaluable partner in his work at the observatory, especially in his efforts to establish the daily Weather Bulletin. According to Truman, "she had been most helpful to father in putting foundation stones under his newly inaugurated ambition to forecast the weather."[160] Among other things, this manifested itself in her assistance in preparing written works related to the endeavor. "Abbe's cramped handwriting was often relieved on the Weather Bulletins and correspondence by a feminine hand," noted Weather Bureau forecaster and historian J. Cecil Alter.[161]

Yet their marriage was not without its challenges, at least in the beginning. In early August, less than three months into their marriage, Fanny wrote a letter to Cleveland, expressing her disappointment in not being with him one particular evening. "My dear Cleve," she wrote, "Why did you not come out this evening? I am so anxious especially as you promised to write every day and then the last words were 'I will go out tomorrow.' Do not keep me in such anxiety."[162]

Shortly after the wedding, Cleveland received a letter from his close friend and confidant Albert Bickmore, who was working as a professor at Madison University (now Colgate University), in Hamilton, New York. "For some days I have been promising myself the pleasure of writing you a hearty note of the most earnest congratulations," Bickmore wrote. "I was only disappointed in one thing—why didn't you send me a photograph of your pretty lady? And now I find myself quite deserted by all my bachelor associates . . . not one left to condole with me!!!"[163] Bickmore, who was lecturing as he continued to get the newly established American Museum of Natural History—which had been officially incorporated the year before—off the ground, confessed that he had "begun to seriously doubt" whether he would ever be married. He would, however, give up his own bachelorhood three years later, when he married Charlotte Bruce. While both men were at the cusp of embarking on the greatest chapters of their professional lives, their personal bond remained strong and the desire to be close left a longing that would remain unfulfilled. "I wish we had an observatory here and that you were one of our faculty," Bickmore wrote wistfully. "May we not hope that such a consummation may be brought about by and by." Bickmore closed his letter to Cleveland with a promise to remain close, if only in spirit. "Never forget that you have a sincere and lasting friend in your [old] confidant."[164]

View of the one-block-long Dutch Street in New York City, as it appeared around the time of Cleveland Abbe's birth in 1838. Colgate & Co., located at No. 6 Dutch Street, was directly across the street from the house at No. 7, where Cleveland was born.

Map of New York City, 1846. New York Public Library Digital Collections

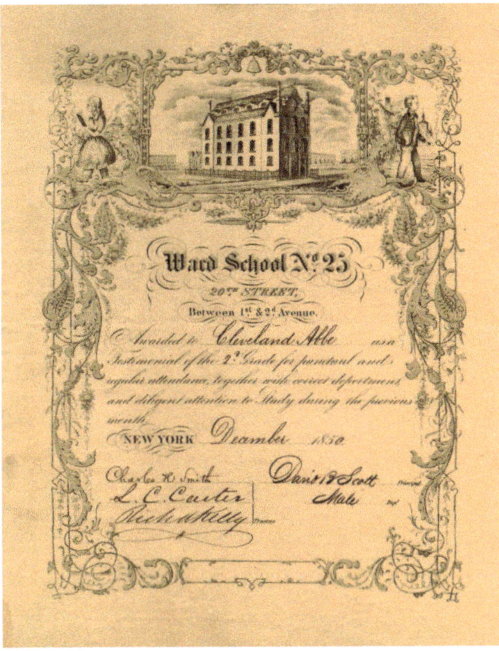

Ward School No. 25
20th STREET,
Between 1st & 2d Avenue.
Awarded to Cleveland Abbe as a Testimonial of the 2d Grade for punctual and regular attendance, together with correct deportment and diligent attention to Study during the previous month.
NEW YORK December 1850

Certificate from Ward School No. 25, awarded to Cleveland Abbe in December 1850 "for punctual and regular attendance, together with correct deportment, and diligent attention to Study during the previous month." Cleveland Abbe Papers, Library of Congress

Cleveland Abbe's weather notebook, 1854. Cleveland Abbe Papers, Library of Congress

Early photograph of Cleveland Abbe, undated. Cleveland Abbe Papers, Library of Congress

Cleveland Abbe, at the time of his graduation from the Free Academy of New York, 1857. Cleveland Abbe Papers, Library of Congress

George Waldo Abbe

Mrs. Charlotte (Colgate) Abbe

Cleveland Abbe

Walter Abbe

William Colgate Abbe

Charles Colgate Abbe

Dr. Robert Abbe

Mrs. Helen (Abbe) Howson

Harriet Colgate Abbe

Members of Cleveland Abbe's immediate family. Abbe and Nichols (1916)

Professor Franz Brünnow, 1860. HS14536, University of Michigan Faculty and Staff Portraits, Bentley Historical Library, University of Michigan

Benjamin Apthorp Gould, from Harper's Encyclopedia of United States History, Vol. IV. Wikimedia Commons

Simon Newcomb, c. 1901. Cleveland Abbe Papers, Library of Congress

Pulkovo Observatory, 1855. Wikimedia Commons

Cleveland Abbe, c. 1865. Cleveland Abbe Papers, Library of Congress

Cleveland Abbe, c. 1865. Cleveland Abbe Papers, Library of Congress

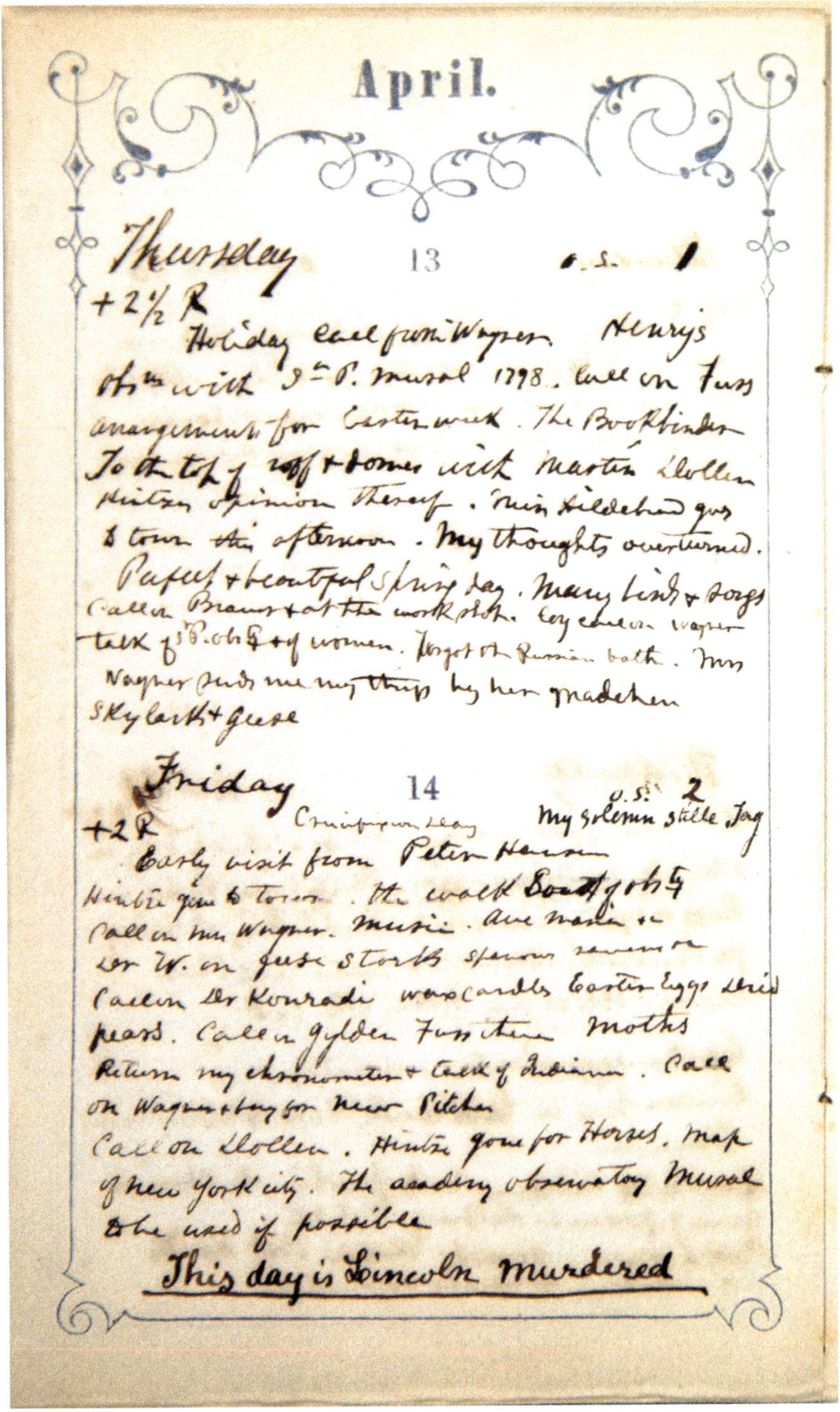
April.

Thursday 13 O.S. 1

+2½ R

Holiday call from Wagner. Henry's obs'n with 3rd P. mural 1798. Call on Fuss arrangements for Easter week. The Bookbinder. To the top of roof + dome with Martin Wollen [illegible] opinion thereof. Miss Hildebrand goes to town this afternoon. My thoughts overturned. Perfect + beautiful spring day. Many birds + songs. Call on Brauer + at the workshop. [illegible] call on Wagner talk of 3P. obs + of women. Forgot the Russian bath. Mrs Wagner sends me my things by her madchen. Skylarks + geese

Friday 14 O.S. 2

Crucifixion day. My solemn stille Tag

+2 R

Early visit from Peter Hansen [illegible] gone to town. The walk [illegible] Call on Mrs Wagner. Music. [illegible] [illegible] W. on [illegible] [illegible] [illegible] Call on Dr Konradi wax candles Easter eggs dried pears. Call on Gylden Fuss there. Moths. Return my chronometer + talk of Indiana. Call on Wagner + Bay for new Pitcher. Call on Wollen. Hintze gone for Horses. Map of New York city. The academy observatory mural to be used if possible.

This day is Lincoln murdered

Page from Cleveland Abbe's diary, in which he records the assassination of President Lincoln on April 14, 1865. Cleveland Abbe Papers, Library of Congress

Correspondence between Cleveland Abbe and his mother during his time in Pulkovo, 1866. Cleveland Abbe Papers, Library of Congress

Passport issued by decree of Tsar Alexander II, allowing Cleveland Abbe to travel freely within the borders of Russia, issued September 1866. Cleveland Abbe Papers, Library of Congress

Otto Struve, 1899. Cleveland Abbe Papers, Library of Congress

Bust of Cleveland Abbe, located at the Cincinnati Observatory, which he directed from 1868–1870. Author photo

The cornerstone of the original Cincinnati Observatory building, which former president John Quincy Adams laid during a dedication ceremony on November 9, 1843. Following the dedication, the original site of the observatory was renamed Mt. Adams in his honor. In 1873, after Cleveland Abbe's tenure as director had ended, the observatory moved to its present location on Mt. Lookout, with the cornerstone relocated to the newly constructed building. Author photo

This 11-inch refracting telescope was purchased by Ormsby MacKnight Mitchel, the original director of the Cincinnati Observatory, in 1842 from the firm Merz and Mahler in Munich. Cleveland Abbe used this telescope, among other instruments, while he served as director of the observatory from 1868–70. It was relocated to the observatory's current site, on Mt. Lookout, in 1873. Author photo

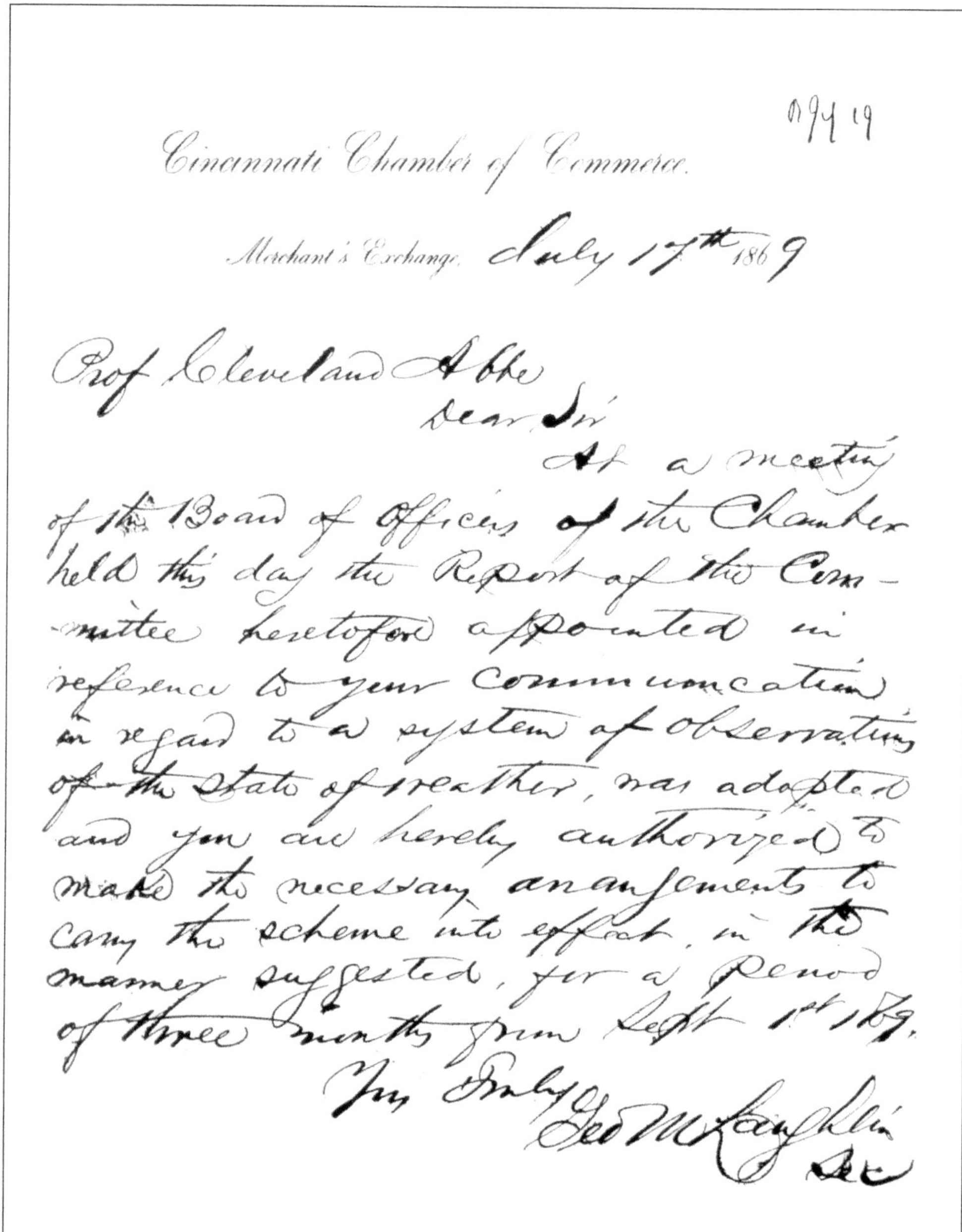

Cincinnati Chamber of Commerce.

Merchant's Exchange, July 17th 1869

Prof Cleveland Abbe

Dear Sir

At a meeting of the Board of Officers of the Chamber held this day the Report of the Committee heretofore appointed in reference to your communication in regard to a system of observations of the state of weather, was adopted and you are hereby authorized to make the necessary arrangements to carry the scheme into effect, in the manner suggested, for a period of three months from Sept 1st 1869.

Yrs Truly

Geo McLaughlin

Sec

Letter from George McLaughlin, secretary of the Cincinnati Chamber of Commerce, to Cleveland Abbe, authorizing him to undertake, with the chamber's support, a system of daily weather bulletins, beginning September 1, 1869.

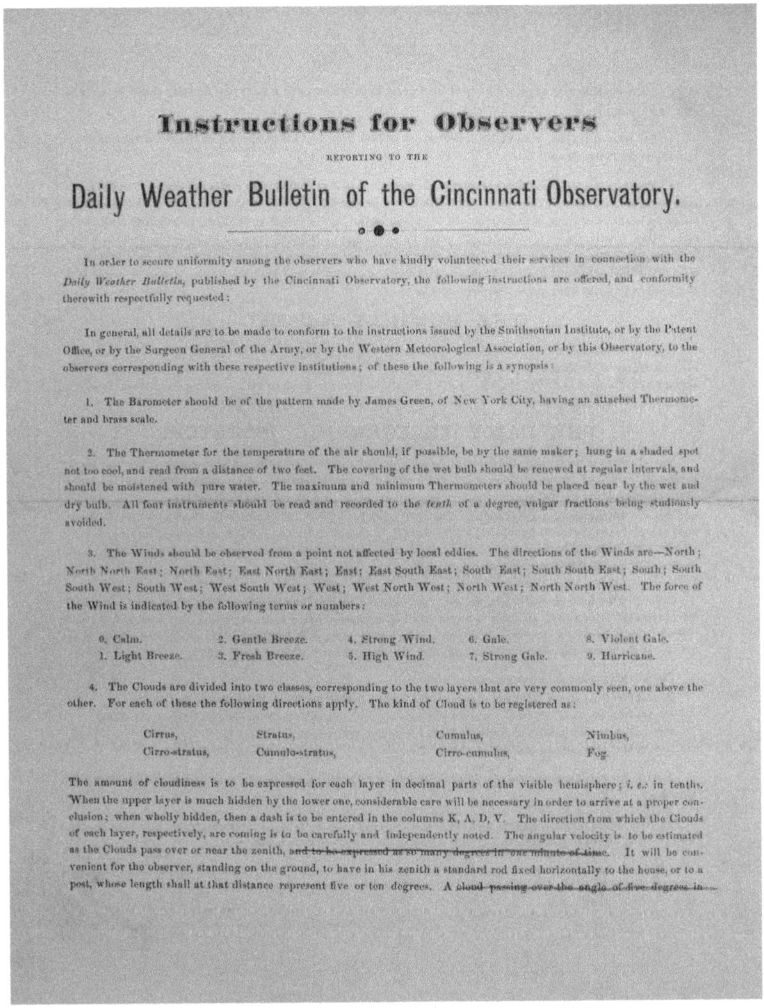

Instructions for Observers

REPORTING TO THE

Daily Weather Bulletin of the Cincinnati Observatory.

In order to secure uniformity among the observers who have kindly volunteered their services in connection with the *Daily Weather Bulletin,* published by the Cincinnati Observatory, the following instructions are offered, and conformity therewith respectfully requested:

In general, all details are to be made to conform to the instructions issued by the Smithsonian Institute, or by the Patent Office, or by the Surgeon General of the Army, or by the Western Meteorological Association, or by this Observatory, to the observers corresponding with these respective institutions; of these the following is a synopsis:

1. The Barometer should be of the pattern made by James Green, of New York City, having an attached Thermometer and brass scale.

2. The Thermometer for the temperature of the air should, if possible, be by the same maker; hung in a shaded spot not too cool, and read from a distance of two feet. The covering of the wet bulb should be renewed at regular intervals, and should be moistened with pure water. The maximum and minimum Thermometers should be placed near by the wet and dry bulb. All four instruments should be read and recorded to the *tenth* of a degree, vulgar fractions being studiously avoided.

3. The Winds should be observed from a point not affected by local eddies. The directions of the Winds are—North; North North East; North East; East North East; East; East South East; South East; South South East; South; South South West; South West; West South West; West; West North West; North West; North North West. The force of the Wind is indicated by the following terms or numbers:

0. Calm.	2. Gentle Breeze.	4. Strong Wind.	6. Gale.	8. Violent Gale.
1. Light Breeze.	3. Fresh Breeze.	5. High Wind.	7. Strong Gale.	9. Hurricane.

4. The Clouds are divided into two classes, corresponding to the two layers that are very commonly seen, one above the other. For each of these the following directions apply. The kind of Cloud is to be registered as:

Cirrus,	Stratus,	Cumulus,	Nimbus,
Cirro-stratus,	Cumulo-stratus,	Cirro-cumulus,	Fog.

The amount of cloudiness is to be expressed for each layer in decimal parts of the visible hemisphere; *i. e.:* in tenths. When the upper layer is much hidden by the lower one, considerable care will be necessary in order to arrive at a proper conclusion; when wholly hidden, then a dash is to be entered in the columns K, A, D, V. The direction from which the Clouds of each layer, respectively, are coming is to be carefully and independently noted. The angular velocity is to be estimated as the Clouds pass over or near the zenith, ~~and to be expressed as so many degrees in one minute of time~~. It will be convenient for the observer, standing on the ground, to have in his zenith a standard rod fixed horizontally to the house, or to a post, whose length shall at that distance represent five or ten degrees. A ~~cloud passing over the angle of five degrees in~~

Instructions for Observers Reporting to the Daily Weather Bulletin of the Cincinnati Observatory. University of Cincinnati, Archives and Rare Books Library

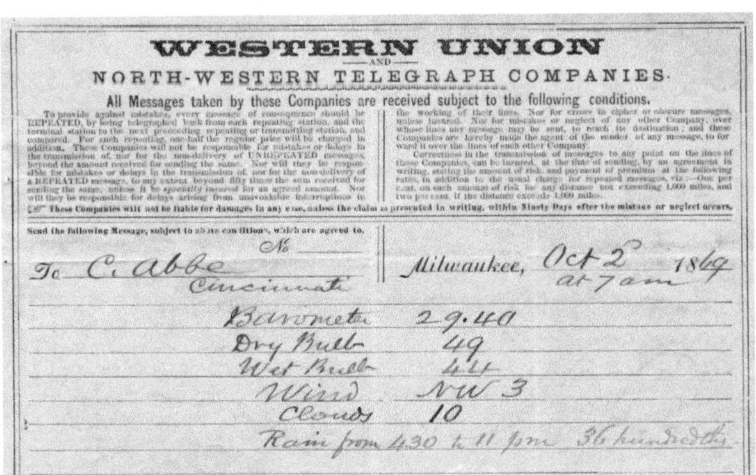

WESTERN UNION

—AND—

NORTH-WESTERN TELEGRAPH COMPANIES.

All Messages taken by these Companies are received subject to the following conditions.

To provide against mistakes, every message of consequence should be REPEATED, by being telegraphed back from each repeating station, and the terminal station to the next preceding repeating or transmitting station, and compared. For such repeating, one-half the regular price will be charged in addition. These Companies will not be responsible for mistakes or delays in the transmission of, nor for the non-delivery of UNREPEATED messages, beyond the amount received for sending the same. Nor will they be responsible for mistakes or delays in the transmission of, nor for the non-delivery of a REPEATED message, to any extent beyond fifty times the sum received for sending the same, unless it be *specially insured* for an agreed amount. Nor will they be responsible for delays arising from unavoidable interruptions in the working of their lines. Nor for errors in cipher or obscure messages, unless insured. Nor for mistakes or neglect of any other Company, over whose lines any message may be sent, to reach its destination; and these Companies are hereby made the agent of the sender of any message, to forward it over the lines of such other Company.

Correctness in the transmission of messages to any point on the lines of these Companies, can be insured, at the time of sending, by an agreement in writing, stating the amount of risk, and payment of premium at the following rates, in addition to the usual charge for repeated messages, viz:—One per cent. on such amount of risk for any distance not exceeding 1,000 miles, and two per cent. if the distance exceeds 1,000 miles.

☞ These Companies will not be liable for damages in any case, unless the claim is presented in writing, within Ninety Days after the mistake or neglect occurs.

Send the following Message, subject to above conditions, which are agreed to.

No. ______

To C. Abbe
Cincinnati

Milwaukee, Oct 2 1869
at 7 am

Barometer 29.40
Dry Bulb 49
Wet Bulb 44
Wind NW 3
Clouds 10
Rain from 430 to 11 pm 36 hundredths

Western Union telegraph sent to Cleveland Abbe from the observer in Milwaukee, with observations for the morning of October 2, 1869. Cleveland Abbe Papers, Library of Congress

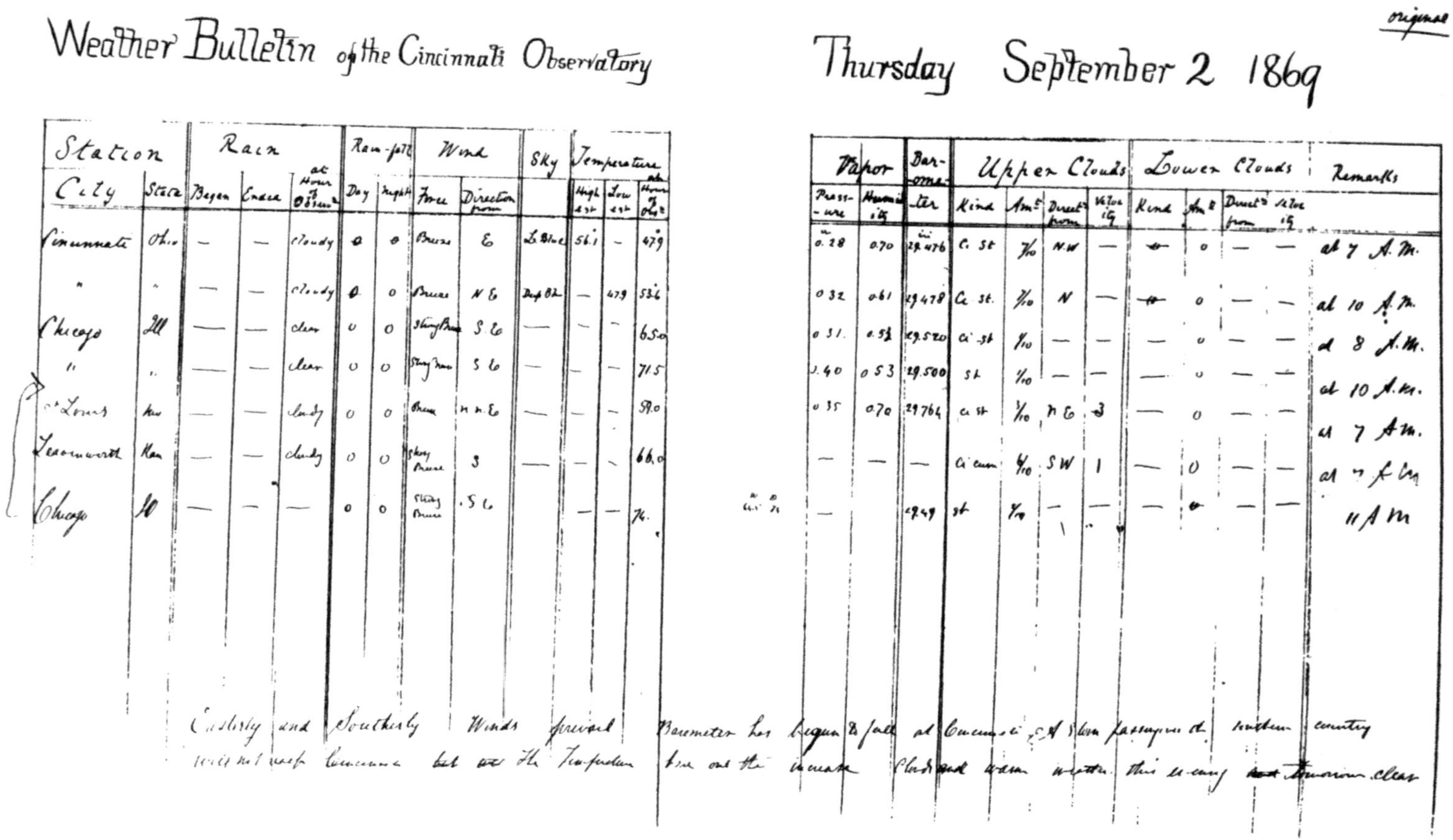

original

Weather Bulletin of the Cincinnati Observatory

Thursday September 2 1869

Station: City	Station: State	Rain: Began	Rain: Ended	Rain: at Hour of Observ.	Rain-fall: Day	Rain-fall: Night	Wind: Force	Wind: Direction from	Sky	Temperature: Highest	Temperature: Lowest	Temperature: at Hour of Obs.	Vapor: Pressure	Vapor: Humidity	Barometer	Upper Clouds: Kind	Upper Clouds: Amt.	Upper Clouds: Direct. from	Upper Clouds: Velocity	Lower Clouds: Kind	Lower Clouds: Amt.	Lower Clouds: Direct. from	Lower Clouds: Velocity	Remarks
Cincinnati	Ohio	—	—	cloudy	0	0	Breeze	E	L. Blue	56.1	—	47.9	0.28	0.70	29.476	C. St	7/10	N.W	—	—	0	—	—	at 7 A.M.
"	"	—	—	cloudy	0	0	Breeze	N E	Deep Bl.	—	47.9	53.6	0.32	0.61	29.478	Ci. St.	7/10	N	—	—	0	—	—	at 10 A.M.
Chicago	Ill	—	—	clear	0	0	Stiff Breeze	S E	—	—	—	65.0	0.31	0.53	29.520	Ci. St	1/10	—	—	—	0	—	—	at 8 A.M.
"	"	—	—	clear	0	0	Stiff Breeze	S E	—	—	—	71.5	0.40	0.53	29.500	St	1/10	—	—	—	0	—	—	at 10 A.M.
St. Louis	Mo	—	—	cloudy	0	0	Breeze	N N E	—	—	—	59.0	0.35	0.70	29.764	Ci. St	3/10	N E	3	—	0	—	—	at 7 A.M.
Leavenworth	Kan	—	—	cloudy	0	0	Stiff Breeze	S	—	—	—	66.0	—	—	—	Ci. cum	4/10	S W	1	—	0	—	—	at 7 A.M.
Chicago	Ill	—	—	—	0	0	Stiff Breeze	S E		—	—	7[illegible]	—		29.49	St	1/10	—	—	—	—	—	—	11 A.M.

Easterly and Southerly Winds prevail. Barometer has begun to fall at Cincinnati & A slow passage of northern country
will not reach Cincinnati but one the Temperature … the increase Cloudy and warm weather this evening ~~and~~ tomorrow clear

Handwritten copy of the Weather Bulletin of the Cincinnati Observatory for September 2, 1869, with Abbe's first public forecast

WEATHER BULLETIN OF THE CINCINNATI OBSERVATORY,

Showing the state of the Weather at points North, West, and South of Cincinnati.

NUMBER 13.] WEDNESDAY, SEPTEMBER 22, 1869. [$1 50 PER MONTH.

PLACE AND TIME OF OBSERVATION.	SKY.	WIND.		VAPOR.		Temperature.	Barometer.	UPPER CLOUDS.				LOWER CLOUDS.				DURING PREVIOUS TWENTY-FOUR HOURS.				
																RAIN OR SNOW.			TEMPERATURE.	
		Force.	Direction.	Pressure.	Humidity.			Kind.	Amount.	Direction.	Apparent Velocity.	Kind.	Amount.	Direction.	Apparent Velocity.	Began.	Ended.	Amount.	Highest.	Lowest.
[7 A.M.] SEPTEMBER 22.			From the	Inches	Per cent.	°	Inches		Tenths	From the	On a scale of 5		Tenths	From the	On a scale of 5			Inches		
Cincinnati, O.,	Light blue.	Calm.		0·66	100	67·4	29·36 stndg.		0			Cir. Str.	9			5 p.m. R.	6 p.m. R.	0·00	82·4	67·0
Louisville, Ky.	Overcast.	Calm.				65·0	29·68 stndg.					Nimbus	8							
Indianapolis, Ind.	Overcast.	Fresh br'ze.	S.W.	0·54	67	73·5	29·42 rising					Nimbus.	10	S.	4			Sprinkle.	68·3	
Chicago, Ill.	Foggy.	Fresh br'ze.	N. E.	0·51	89	63·3	29·33 rising		0				0					0·00	62·4	57·6
Minneapolis, Minn.	Deep blue	Fresh br'ze.	S. E.	0·33	93	54·[illegible]	28·39 falling					Cirrus.	6					0·00		
Omaha, Neb.	Clear.	Breeze	S.			60·0		Cirrus.	A few.	S.								0·00	76·0	54·0
Memphis, Tenn.	Overcast.	Fresh br'ze	E.	0·56	84	67·4	29·90 stndg					Nim. Str.	8					0·00	89·5	64·0
Leavenworth, Kan.	Hazy.	Breeze.	S. E.			64·0						Nimbus.	10	S.W.	1			0·00	76·0	56·0
St. Louis	Light blue	Breeze.	N. E.	0·60	90	66·5	29·79 stndg	Cir. Cum.	2	W.	1	Cum. Str.	6	N.E.	2	6.45 a.m. R.	7 p.m. R.	0·11	69·5	62·0
SEPTEMBER 21.																				
Omaha, Neb.	Clear.	Calm.				64·0		Cirrus.	A few.			Cum. Str.	5					0·00	70·0	54·0
Lookout Mt., Tenn.	Deep blue.	Breeze	S. W.			78·0	28·50 falln'g	Cir. Cum.	1				0					0·00		

The kinds of clouds are: Cirrus, or the highest; Cumulus, or the little noonday clouds—large ones attend thunder storms; Nimbus, or the rain clouds; Stratus, or the stratified clouds of sunset and the clearing off of storms.

The moisture in the air exerts a pressure on the barometer, as given in the Pressure column. The Humidity column shows the per cent. of vapor in the air as compared with what it would hold if saturated. 100 per cent. occurs on very moist days and during rain; 60–80 per cent. on dry days and fair weather.

A falling barometer, increased temperature and humidity, and nimbus or nimbus stratus clouds, precede rain and storms. The winds blow towards the center of a storm, or towards the point where the barometer is below its average height.

The above reports indicate the following weather: Wednesday, September 22, morning cloudy and warm; afternoon not so oppressive; evening clear and cool. Thursday, September 23, morning cloudy and warm; afternoon clear; evening clear and cool. **Friday, September 24**, morning clear and warm; afternoon hot.

Printed version of the Weather Bulletin of the Cincinnati Observatory for September 22, 1869, which included the first published weather forecast

WESTERN UNION TELEGRAPH COMPANY'S

WEATHER REPORT,

For Saturday June 11th 1870

Compiled at the Cincinnati Observatory.

Augusta, Ga.	Cloudy SW 71	Louisville, Ky.	Cloudy SW 68
		Marquette Mich	clear calm plnt
Beaufort, N. C.		Meadville, Penn.	
Bellair, O.		Memphis, Tenn.	Clear W 62
Baltimore, Md.	Cloudy NE 70	Milwaukee, Wis.	Clear N 44
Baton Rouge, La.	Cloudy Calm 94	Mobile, Ala.	" NW 78
Boston, Mass.	Raining NE 58	Montgomery, Ala	Clear — 71
Buffalo, N. Y.	Cloudy NW 65	Morehead City, N. C.	" SW 72
Charleston, S. C.	Clear SW 76	Nashville, Tenn.	Cloudy W 60
Chattanooga, Tenn.		Natchez, Miss.	Clear S 78
Cheyenne, Wy.	Clear NE 74	Newark, O.	Raining E —
Chicago, Ill.	Raining NE 60	New Orleans, La.	Clear S 78
Cincinnati, O.	Cloudy NW 59	New York, N. Y	Raining NE 60
Cleveland, O.	" SE 57	Omaha, Neb.	Clear Calm 68
Columbus "	Raining W 53		
Corinth, Miss.		Oswego, N. Y.	
Denver Col	clear NE 65		
Detroit, Mich.	Cloudy NW 55	Osyka, Miss.	
Fernandina, Fla.		Philadelphia, Penn.	Cloudy NE 63
Fortress Monroe, Va.	Cloudy S 64	Pittsburg, Penn.	Clear N 60
Goldsboro', N. C.		Plaister Cove, N. B.	Hazy NW 66
Green Bay Wis	clear calm plnt		
Greensboro', N. C.	" SW 64	Portland, Me.	Raining E 69
Greenville, S. C.		Raleigh, N. C.	Clear SW 70
Halifax, N. S.	Clear S 60	Richmond, Va.	" W 73
Harrisburg, Penn.		Saginaw, Mich.	Clear [illegible] 59
		Savannah Ga	clear W SW 79
Havana, Cuba.	Clear Calm 81	Selma, Ala.	
Hinsdale, O.		Shreveport, La.	Raining NW 74
		Springfield Mo	" NE 57
Houston, Texas.		St. Augustine, Fla.	
Indianapolis, Ind.	Cloudy NE 58	St. Souis, Mo.	Clear NW 64 74
Jackson, Miss.	Clear SE 66	Tallahassee, Fla.	" W 72
Key West, Fla.	Cloudy SW 82	Vicksburg, Miss.	
Knoxville, Tenn.		Washington, D. C.	Clear SE 72
		Helena	" SW 68
Leavenworth, Kan.	Cloudy NW 62	Wheeling, W. Va.	
Little Rock, Ark.	Clear SE 68	Wilmington, N. C.	Clear S 72

Western Union Telegraph Company's Weather Report for June 11, 1870, with observations compiled by Cleveland Abbe

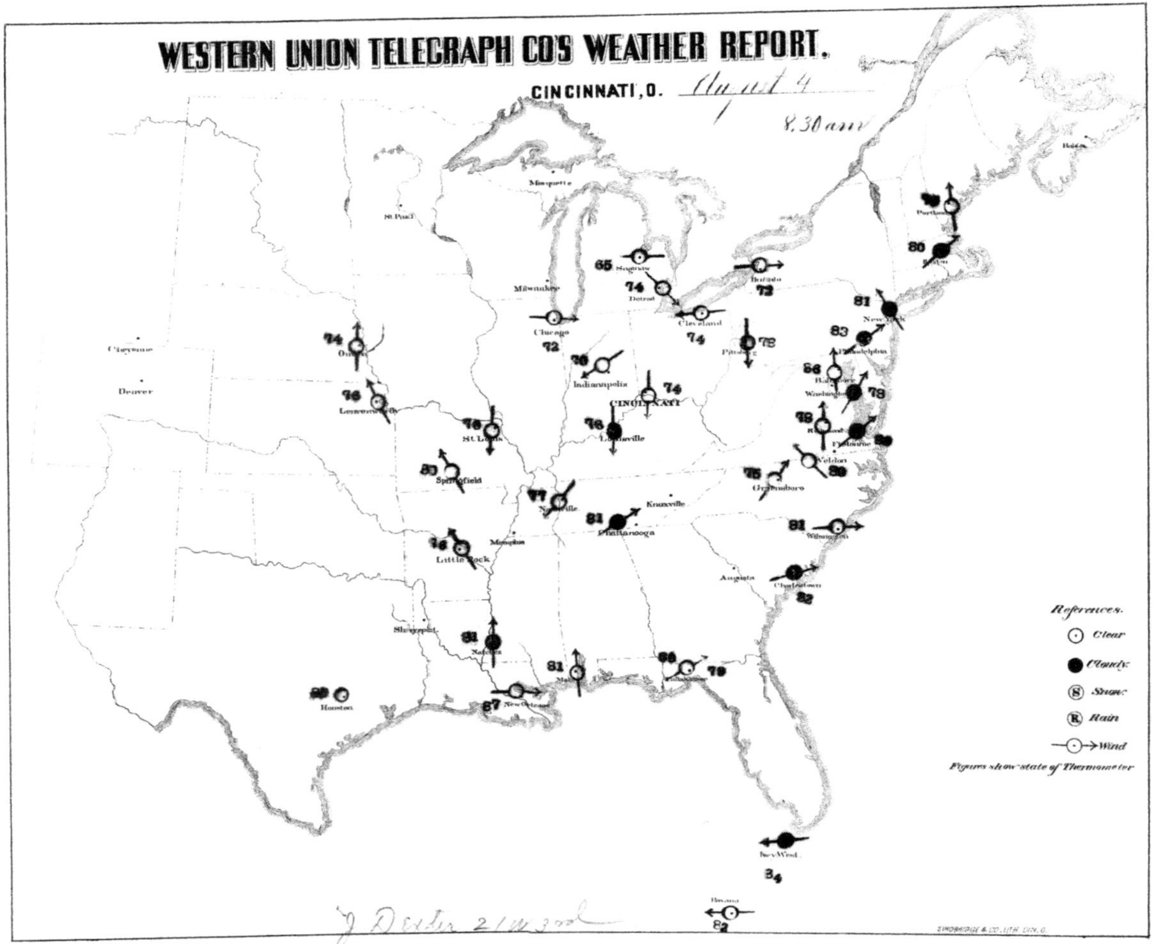

Map Accompanying Western Union Telegraph Company's Weather Report for August 4, 1870. Cincinnati History Library and Archives Printed Works Collection

General Halbert Paine, c. 1863. National Archives

Increase Allen Lapham, c. 1882. Wikimedia Commons

Cleveland Abbe, 1884. Cleveland Abbe Papers, Library of Congress

Frances Martha (Fanny) Abbe, 1875. Cleveland Abbe Papers, Library of Congress

Marriage License.

STATE OF OHIO. HAMILTON COUNTY.

To Any Person Authorized to Solemnize Marriages.

You are Hereby Authorized to Solemnize in said County the Marriage Contract between

Mr. Cleveland Abbe

AND

Miss Frances M. Neal

In Testimony Whereof I the Judge of the Probate Court of said County have hereunto set my hand and seal, this 6th day of May in the year of our Lord One Thousand Eight Hundred and Seventy

Geo. S. Hoeffer [illegible] Probate Judge.

CERTIFICATE of MARRIAGE.

THIS IS TO CERTIFY, that by authority of a License issued by the judge of the Probate Court of said County Mr. Cleveland Abbe and Miss Frances M. Neal were by me legally united as HUSBAND & WIFE on the 8th day of May in the year of our Lord One Thousand Eight Hundred and Seventy

Witnesses:

[illegible] M. L. Hoop[illegible]

Sarah L. Perkins

Julia [illegible]

Henry Smith

Engraved & Published by Moore, Wilstach & Baldwin, Cincinnati.

Cleveland and Fanny's Marriage Certificate, 1870. Cleveland Abbe Papers, Library of Congress

General Albert Myer, c. 1865. Library of Congress Prints and Photographs Division

General William Hazen, c. 1861. Library of Congress, Civil War Photograph Collection

General Adolphus Greely, undated photograph. Library of Congress, George Grantham Bain Collection

Interior of the "Fact Room" of the Signal Office in Washington, D.C., where the weather probabilities are made. Wood engraving from sketches by H. A. Ogden appearing in Frank Leslie's Illustrated Newspaper, March 19, 1881. Library of Congress

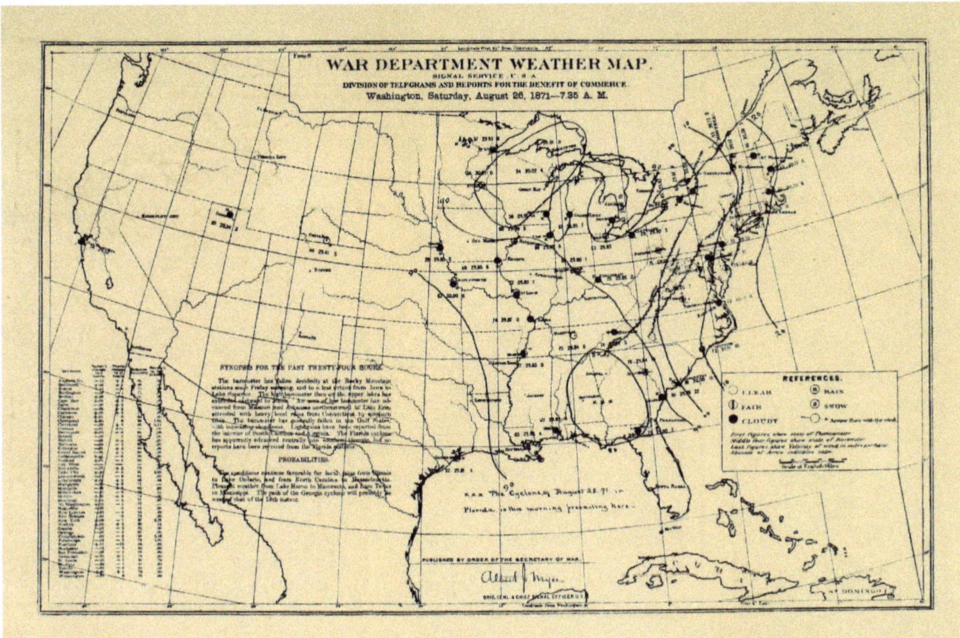

War Department Weather Map, issued by the Signal Service Saturday, August 26, 1871. In addition to observations made at 7:35 a.m. Washington time, the map includes Abbe's synopsis and probabilities for 10:00 a.m. that morning.

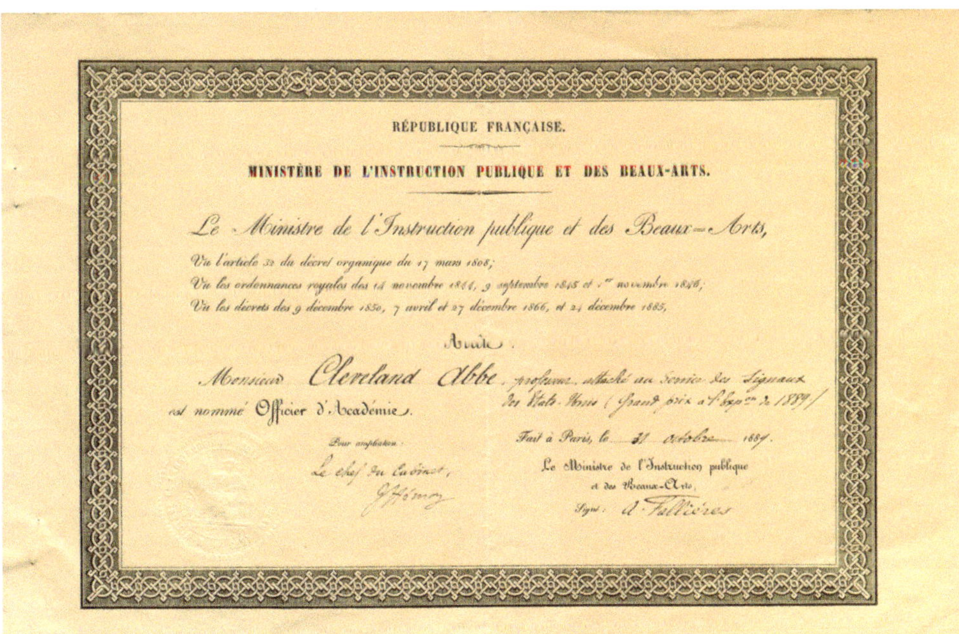

Certificate from the French Ministère de l'Instruction Publique et des Beaux-Arts (Ministry of Public Education and Fine Arts) in Paris, awarding Cleveland Abbe the title of Officier d'Académie, 1889. Cleveland Abbe Papers, Library of Congress

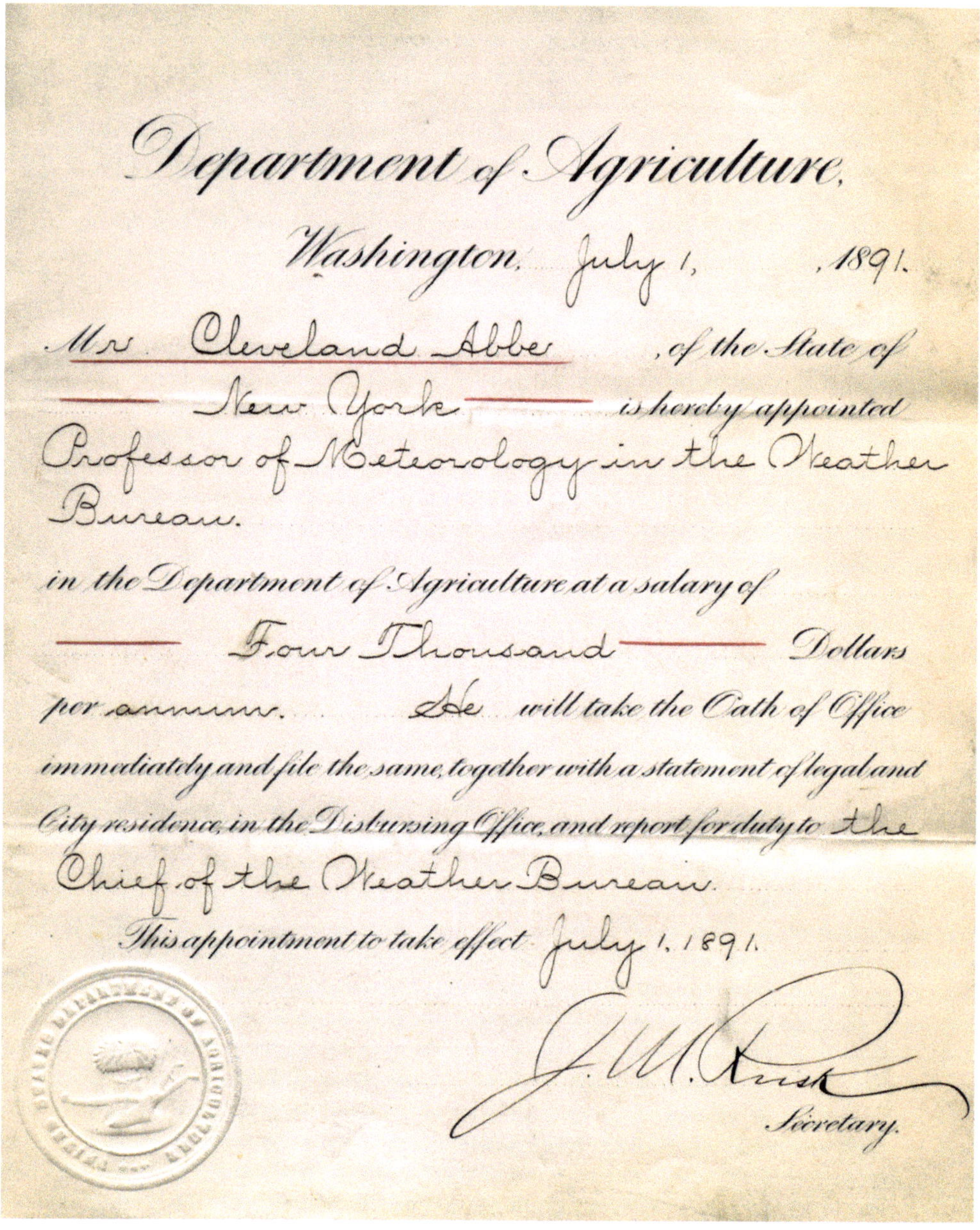

Department of Agriculture,

Washington, July 1, 1891.

Mr Cleveland Abbe, of the State of New York is hereby appointed Professor of Meteorology in the Weather Bureau.

in the Department of Agriculture at a salary of Four Thousand Dollars per annum. He will take the Oath of Office immediately and file the same, together with a statement of legal and City residence, in the Disbursing Office, and report for duty to the Chief of the Weather Bureau.

This appointment to take effect July 1, 1891.

J. M. Rusk
Secretary.

Order signed by Secretary of Agriculture Jeremiah M. Rusk appointing Cleveland Abbe to the position of Professor of Meteorology in the newly established Weather Bureau, at an annual salary of $4,000, effective July 1, 1891. Cleveland Abbe Papers, Library of Congress

Albert Bickmore, undated. Cleveland Abbe Papers, Library of Congress

Professor Mark Harrington, c. 1890. HS15028, Observatory (University of Michigan) Records, Bentley Historical Library, University of Michigan, licensed under CC BY 4.0

Professor Willis Moore, c. 1894. Library of Congress, C.M. Bell Studio Collection

Professor Charles Marvin, 1913. Library of Congress, Harris & Ewing photograph collection

Milwaukee Convention of U.S. Weather Bureau Officials, 1901. Cleveland Abbe is in the front row, tenth from the left. To his immediate right are Secretary of Agriculture James Wilson and Chief of the Weather Bureau Willis L. Moore. To his left is Professor Charles F. Marvin. Cleveland Abbe Papers, Library of Congress

Front of Abbe house at 2017 I Street, NW, Washington, D.C., 1937. Library of Congress, Prints & Photographs Division, HABS DC, WASH, 22-7

Plaque designating the Cleveland Abbe House as a National Historic Landmark. Wikimedia Commons

Cleveland Abbe and his mother, Charlotte Abbe, in the library at 2017 I Street, undated photo. Cleveland Abbe Papers, Library of Congress

Truman, Cleveland Jr., and Will, c. 1880. Cleveland Abbe Papers, Library of Congress

Cleveland and Fanny, in front of 2017 I Street. Cleveland Abbe Papers, Library of Congress

Cleveland Abbe, undated photograph. Cleveland Abbe Papers, Library of Congress

Cleveland Abbe, undated photograph. Cleveland Abbe Papers, Library of Congress

Frances Martha (Fanny) Abbe, undated photograph. Cleveland Abbe Papers, Library of Congress

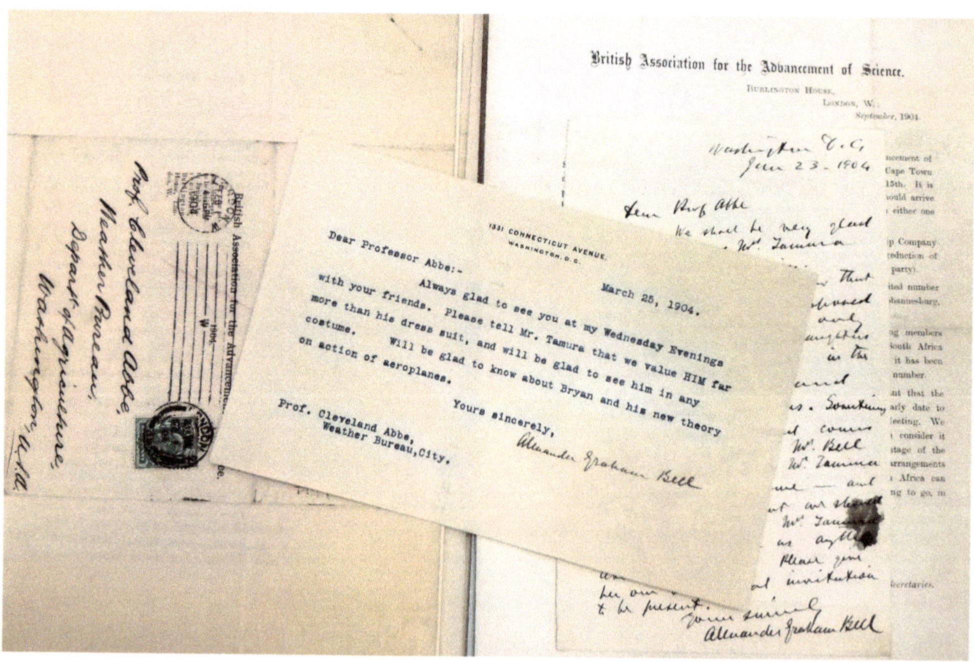

1331 CONNECTICUT AVENUE,
WASHINGTON, D.C.

March 25, 1904.

Dear Professor Abbe:-

Always glad to see you at my Wednesday Evenings with your friends. Please tell Mr. Tamura that we value HIM far more than his dress suit, and will be glad to see him in any costume.

Will be glad to know about Bryan and his new theory on action of aeroplanes.

Yours sincerely,

Alexander Graham Bell

Prof. Cleveland Abbe,
Weather Bureau, City.

Correspondence to Cleveland Abbe from Alexander Graham Bell, 1904. Cleveland Abbe Papers, Library of Congress

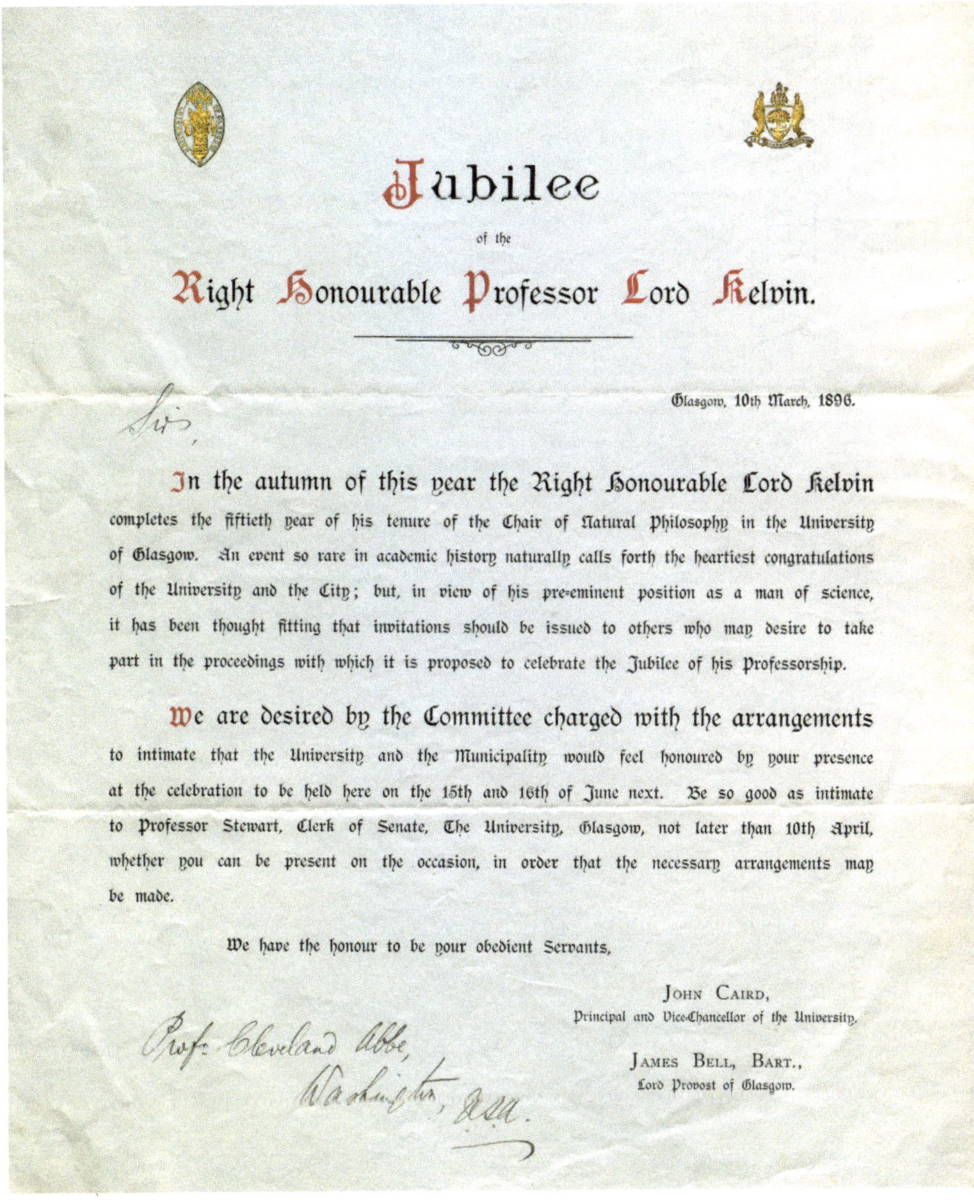

Jubilee

of the

Right Honourable Professor Lord Kelvin.

Glasgow, 10th March, 1896.

Sir,

In the autumn of this year the Right Honourable Lord Kelvin completes the fiftieth year of his tenure of the Chair of Natural Philosophy in the University of Glasgow. An event so rare in academic history naturally calls forth the heartiest congratulations of the University and the City; but, in view of his pre-eminent position as a man of science, it has been thought fitting that invitations should be issued to others who may desire to take part in the proceedings with which it is proposed to celebrate the Jubilee of his Professorship.

We are desired by the Committee charged with the arrangements to intimate that the University and the Municipality would feel honoured by your presence at the celebration to be held here on the 15th and 16th of June next. Be so good as intimate to Professor Stewart, Clerk of Senate, The University, Glasgow, not later than 10th April, whether you can be present on the occasion, in order that the necessary arrangements may be made.

We have the honour to be your obedient Servants,

John Caird,
Principal and Vice-Chancellor of the University.

James Bell, Bart.,
Lord Provost of Glasgow.

Prof: Cleveland Abbe,
Washington, U.S.A.

Announcement formally inviting Cleveland Abbe to take part in the jubilee celebrating fifty years of Lord Kelvin's tenure as chair of natural philosophy at the University of Glasgow, 1896. Cleveland Abbe Papers, Library of Congress

Certificate of honorary membership from the German Meteorological Society. Cleveland Abbe Papers, Library of Congress

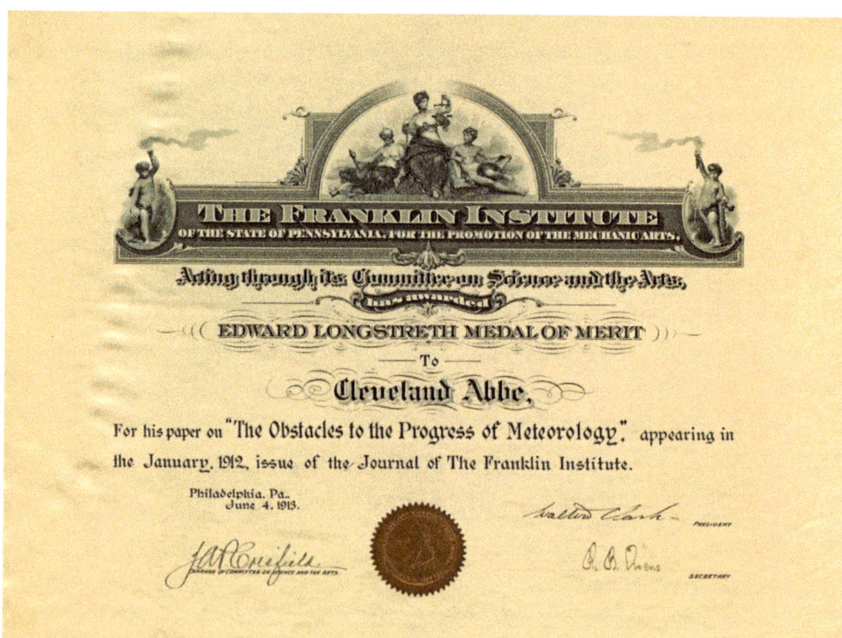

Certificate from The Franklin Institute, awarding Cleveland Abbe with Longstreth Medal of Merit for his paper "The Obstacles to the Progress of Meteorology," 1913. Cleveland Abbe Papers, Library of Congress

Cleveland Abbe, 1909. Cleveland Abbe Papers, Library of Congress

Cleveland Abbe, Cleveland Abbe Jr., and Ernst Cleveland Abbe (Cleveland Jr.'s son), c. 1910. Cleveland Abbe Papers, Library of Congress

Cleveland Abbe on Kebo Mountain, Mt. Desert Island, Maine, 1901. Cleveland Abbe Papers, Library of Congress

Cleveland Abbe in Bar Harbor, Maine, 1901. Cleveland Abbe Papers, Library of Congress

Cleveland Abbe in Bar Harbor, Maine, 1901. Cleveland Abbe Papers, Library of Congress

Cleveland and Margaret's house in Chevy Chase, Maryland. Seated from left: Cleveland, Margaret, Frieda Abbe (Cleveland Jr.'s wife), and a woman identified only as "Sarah P." Cleveland Abbe Papers, Library of Congress

A family gathering at Dog Hill, near Windham, Connecticut, 1911. Cleveland (fourth from left) and Margaret (sixth from left) are pictured along with several of Cleveland's siblings: Helen Abbe Howson (ninth from left), Harriet (Hattie) Abbe (twelfth from left), and Walter Abbe (third from right). Cleveland Abbe Papers, Library of Congress.

Granite memorial marking the graves of Cleveland and Margaret Abbe, Rock Creek Cemetery, Washington, D.C. Author photo

Footstone marking Cleveland Abbe's grave, Rock Creek Cemetery, Washington, D.C. Author photo

CHAPTER FIVE

The Birth of a Weather Service (1869–1877)

> For a year and until assistants could be trained for the work I concocted all of the probabilities myself. I left my office regularly at 2 in the morning and was at my desk again at 9 o'clock.
>
> —Cleveland Abbe, to *The Sunday Star* newspaper, 1916

On the morning of November 12, 1869, the schooner *Arrow* left Muskegon, Michigan, with a load of lumber, bound for Chicago, some 240 miles southwest, on the opposite shore of Lake Michigan. The voyage was uneventful up until late Tuesday, November 16. That night, a fierce gale blew the *Arrow* off course and it ran aground on Grosse Point, near Evanston, Illinois. As the winds increased and the waves crashed against the vessel, the crew clung to the rigging in sheer terror, hoping against all odds for some sort of miracle. As word of the schooner's fate reached Chicago the next morning, a rescue team set out aboard the tug *Alfred Mosher* to save the crew of the *Arrow*. As the *Mosher* neared the ill-fated schooner, it cut loose one of its lifeboats, with seven men aboard. The tiny lifeboat was no match for the towering breakers, however, and after being swamped, it was driven ashore. Unable to provide further assistance, the *Mosher* returned to shore. Hours later, another tug, the *G. W. Wood*, set out for the *Arrow*, with a small, two-masted boat called a yawl. With great difficulty, the yawl was able pull up next to the wreck of the *Arrow* and secure the seven members of its crew. Unfortunately, just as the yawl was about to leave the scene of the wreckage, a huge breaker smashed down upon it, tossing it upside down like a child's toy in a bathtub. The beleaguered crew of the *Arrow*, weakened and unable to swim, perished. Their bodies later washed ashore near Evanston.[1]

The storm that wrecked the *Arrow* was just one in a series of deadly and destructive weather systems that ravaged the Great Lakes in 1869, making it the worst year on record for shipping on the lakes.[2] "A gale of unprecedented fury has raged for the past two days all through the surrounding country," the *Cleveland Leader* reported. "It is not only the severest storm that has been experienced this fall, but for many years no storm has been characterized with such violence."[3]

In Milwaukee, a fifty-eight-year-old civil engineer and surveyor of canals named Increase Lapham took notice of the devastation wrought by storms on the Great Lakes—a subject he had been following closely for years. Lapham, who was born in Upstate New York but eventually settled in Milwaukee, was something of a Renaissance man and self-taught scientist, having studied, written about, or otherwise contributed to such disparate fields as botany, geology, archaeology, and zoology. His interest in meteorology began at an early age. During the fall and winter of 1827, he took daily weather observations, which he recorded in his personal diary. His interest further developed in 1840 when, at the age of twenty-nine, he received a letter from his brother Darius, containing an account of Espy's Law of Storms.[4] Lapham later provided weather observations for Espy and, later, the Smithsonian. He had even lobbied the Wisconsin State Legislature, in 1850, to create a storm warning service.[5] This did not happen and, with the advent of the Civil War, organizing meteorological services took a backseat to defending the Union.

On January 1, 1860, Lapham began a "full series of meteorological observations," including barometric pressure, temperature, wind speed, humidity, precipitation (both rain and snow), and even tide measurements.[6] His dedication to weather observations and to the science of meteorology ensured his place as one of the prospective observers Cleveland Abbe wrote to in August 1869, to recruit for his burgeoning weather observation network. Lapham, however, was unsure he would be able to comply with Cleveland's request. "A pressure of other duties & my inconvenient distance from the Telegraph Office will prevent me from my compliance with the request contained in your letter of the 25th, and hence I have sent it to the president of our Chamber of Commerce with the request that some suitable person may be appointed by that body for the purpose," he wrote.[7] Lapham sent another letter to Cleveland on September 7, however, in which he indicated he would help ensure Cleveland received reports from Milwaukee. "The Pres't. of the Chamber of Commerce here thinks favorably upon your project & reports will be sent to you," Lapham wrote, adding information about the exact location and elevation of his station, as well as observations he made since the first of the month, from which, he told Cleveland, "you can judge whether my reports will be of service."[8] In Cincinnati, Fanny Neal, Cleveland's secretary (who would eventually become his wife), neatly copied Lapham's observations onto a sheet of graph paper for Cleveland.[9]

Despite his efforts, Lapham's observations were not reaching Cleveland in a timely enough manner to be of use, as evidenced by a letter Lapham sent to Cleveland on October 2. "The telegraph boy is so irregular in his calls that I presume you have not found my observations on much value and it seems hardly worth while to continue to do what cannot be done well," Lapham wrote. "He has failed altogether for two days now."[10]

On October 15, Cleveland wrote a letter to Lapham in which he expressed his gratitude for Lapham's assistance with his Weather Bulletin, but he also expressed concerns about the way the observations from Milwaukee were being sent. "At present I must confine this note to a short request that you will please instruct the gentleman who sends me his daily observations to send me only the 7 a.m. obsn and to send it so early that I may be sure of getting it before 10 ½ a.m. of the same day. It should if possible be delivered to the telegraph operator before 9 a.m.," Cleveland wrote, noting the importance of the timeliness with which he received the reports. "The messages that I have received contain the three observations of the day and are received at 10 ½ a.m. of the following day at which hour I visit the telegraph office and compile the daily Bulletin," Cleveland said, adding that "the observations of the previous day have thus lost most of their interest."[11]

Lapham responded to Cleveland four days later, informing him that a new observer from Milwaukee, Louis E. Levy of L. Black & Co., would begin sending weather reports in accordance with Cleveland's instructions. He then took the opportunity to share his excitement with Cleveland over a non-meteorological discovery recently made in his home state. "I send som[e] photographs of our Wisconsin Meteorite which may interest you & entitle me to a representation of yourself!!"[12]

Cleveland and Lapham's correspondence shows an exchange of scientific data and ideas, working toward a similar goal of providing timely, accurate predictions of the weather via telegraphic reports. While Cleveland's motivation was primarily scientific, Lapham's actions were driven by a desire to mitigate loss of life and property. On December 1, Lapham sent Cleveland a "rough projection of the barometrical curve at Milwaukee" during the storm of November 16–19 and included a clipping from the *Milwaukee Sentinel* showing a tabular list of all the vessels—97 in all—lost or damaged during the storm, including the *Arrow*. Lapham added in pencil at the top of the clipping, "No. of lives lost about 60." Lapham proposed that Cleveland could increase the scope and accuracy of his forecasts by increasing the frequency with which he received reports from his network of observers. "If you could add to your present enterprise, hourly telegraphic observations from each station, from the beginning to the ending of each storm, I think it would enable you to predict many of them several hours in advance and by sending to the different Lake ports be the means of saving at least some portion of this great loss of life and property," Lapham said. He went on to say that a friend had "promised to call the attention of the National Board of Trade now in session at Richmond, Va. to the importance of the matter, and I hope for something useful as the result of his effort."[13]

Lapham's friend was Edward Holton, a Milwaukee businessman and politician who represented the city at the National Board of Trade meeting in Richmond. The meeting, held December 1–6, 1869, brought together representatives of local boards of trade, chambers of commerce, and other related bodies "in order to secure unity and harmony of action in reference to commercial usages, customs, and laws."[14] On the third day of the meeting, Holton asked to introduce a resolution, which he requested be referred to the board's executive council for consideration. "I hold in my hand a communication from Dr. Lapham, of my city," he proclaimed, "a man eminent in science, which I will not read, but I will say briefly that it relates to scientific investigations touching the late storm on the lakes, which destroyed in twenty-four hours from a million to two millions of property and many lives. This learned gentleman claims that it is within the scope of science to communicate to ship-masters and navigators a knowledge of the approach of storms, hours before they reach a certain point."[15] Holton said the communication from Lapham included a resolution, which he read:

> *Resolved*, That it is expedient to inaugurate in the United States a system of meteorological observations by communicating telegraphic information of the occurrence of destructive storms and winds, thus preventing much of the present loss of life and property upon the ocean and lakes.[16]

On the final day of the meeting, December 6, George S. Hazard, a representative from Buffalo, submitted a report from a subcommittee of the executive council, to whom Lapham's resolution was referred:

> Whereas, The subject of meteorology with reference to its influence upon the interests of commerce is attracting attention in some parts of the country,

and even with limited experience it has been shown that observations on the changes of the weather foretelling the approach of storms have been attended with good results, and may, with proper encouragement, be made of increased benefit; therefore,

Resolved, That it is expedient to initiate in the United States, a system of meteorological observations to be communicated by telegraph, with a view of predicting the occurrence of destructive storm winds, and thus prevent much of the present loss of life and property upon the ocean and the lakes.

Resolved, That the Executive Council be empowered to recommend to Congress to afford such aid to the different observatories of the country, as will enable the astronomers in charge of them to give necessary time to the subject.[17]

Lapham later suggested that the inclusion of "the different observatories of the country" and "the astronomers in charge of them" was done at the hand of the delegates from Cincinnati[18], which included John Gano, editor of *The Cincinnati Commercial*, which published Cleveland's Weather Bulletin; and William Hooper, secretary of the Cincinnati Astronomical Society, who had been the prime mover in facilitating Cleveland's appointment as director of the Cincinnati Observatory. The resolution passed, but the executive council would not meet again until March 1870.[19]

In the meantime, on December 8, the *Milwaukee Sentinel* published a summary of the devastating shipping season on the Great Lakes—including the destructive storm of mid-November that wrecked the *Arrow*. In reading it, Lapham felt a resolve to take action beyond that of the National Board of Trade and his friend Holton. That same day, he wrote a letter[20] to his congressman, General Halbert Paine, voicing his concern about the increasing losses suffered by the shipping industry on the Great Lakes due to violent storms:

Milwaukee, Wis., Dec. 8th, 1869

Hon. H. E. Paine

Dear Sir,

I take the liberty of calling your attention to the accompanying list of disasters to commerce on our great lakes during the past year and to ask

> whether its appalling magnitude does not make it the duty of the government to see whether anything can be done to prevent at least some portion of this sad loss in future.
>
> Yours truly,
> I. A. Lapham

Lapham enclosed with his plea the summary published by the *Milwaukee Sentinel*, titled "Disasters on the Lakes," along with a memorial—a sort of petition—of his own, in which he made the case for engaging "the services of a competent Meteorologist at some suitable point on the lakes, with the aid of a sufficient corps of observers with compared instruments at stations located every two or three hundred miles towards the west, and the co-operation of the telegraph companies" to track the origin and progress of the destructive storms on the Great Lakes. It began:

> Not only does the interest of commerce and navigation, but also that of humanity itself, demand that something should be done, if possible, to prevent the fearful loss of life and property on our great lakes, such as has recently filled so many newspaper columns with their appalling details. If we could have even a few hours' notice of the approach of the great storms that bring these calamities upon us, much of their mischief might be avoided.[21]

Paine recalled years later how he received the letter from Lapham. "One morning I was pleased to find among my letters a communication from my esteemed friend, Professor I. A. Lapham, of Milwaukee," he said. "He inclosed two numbers of the Milwaukee Sentinel, setting forth in detail the losses of life and property occasioned during two successive years by storms on the northern and northwestern lakes. There were hundreds of casualties, and the aggregate was appalling. He suggested that Congress should do something to prevent these disasters."[22] Paine admitted that he was unsure initially what, exactly, Lapham was asking of Congress, with respect to mitigating losses from the destructive lake storms. "My first impression was that he wanted Congress to restrain the winds; but, upon perusal of his whole letter, I discovered that his plan was to take daily meteorological observations throughout the United States and give notice on the lakes and seaboard of the approach of storms."

According to his account, Paine immediately began work drafting legislation, which he introduced in the House of Representatives as H. R. 579 on December 14:

> *Be it enacted by the Senate and House of Representatives of the United States of America in Congress assembled*, That the Secretary of War be authorized and required to provide for taking the necessary meteorological observations at the military stations in the interior of the continent, and for giving notice on the northern lakes and Atlantic coast, by means of the electric telegraph, of the approach and force of storms.[23]

According to House procedures, the bill was read twice before being referred to the Committee on Commerce and ordered printed, along with a record of the disasters on the lakes during the year. Two days later, on December 16, Paine introduced a slightly revised version of the bill, H. R. 602:

> *Be it enacted by the Senate and House of Representatives of the United States of America in Congress assembled*, That the Secretary of War be authorized and required to take the necessary meteorological observations at the military stations in the interior of the continent and on the northern lakes, and to give notice on the lakes and Atlantic coast, by means of the electric telegraph, of the approach and force of storms.[24]

As with the first version of the bill, this revision was read twice, referred to the Committee on Commerce, and sent to the printer. Once printed versions were in hand, Paine sent copies to several eminent officials in the field of meteorology, namely Professor Elias Loomis (under whom Paine had studied years earlier at Western Reserve College); Joseph Henry, secretary of the Smithsonian; and Surgeon General Joseph K. Barnes.[25]

The House adjourned for its holiday recess on December 22. On January 10, 1870, the day it reconvened, Loomis wrote a brief letter endorsing Paine's legislation, and Lapham's idea. "I have carefully read the memorial of Professor I. A. Lapham, recommending the establishment of a system of observations to give warning of the approach of violent storms, and heartily approve of the object of that memorial," he wrote.[26]

That same day, Joseph Henry sent a letter to Paine in which he expressed his support for the bill. "There can be no doubt from the present state of meteorological science that a properly devised and intelligently conducted system of weather telegrams would be of great importance to the welfare of commerce as well as of much interest to the general public," Henry wrote.

In early January 1870, as Paine's bill was working its way through the legislative process, Cleveland sent a letter to Lapham, conveying his enthusiasm for Lapham's efforts to establish a national system of weather forecasting and storm warning. "I must write to express the pleasure experienced in noticing the energy with which you are pushing the matter of a telegraphic meteorological system of storm warnings," he said, noting the work he was doing in Cincinnati, albeit for differing motivations. "My own labors in the field have been not perhaps so much for the good of the country and advance of meteorology as for the sake of astronomy," Cleveland said. "We can I think, make no more progress in our knowledge of terrestrial and celestial refractions, until we better understand the laws of the distribution of heat and pressure in the atmosphere and our proposed system of signals coupled with a daily bulletin or chart will much help this study."[27]

While Cleveland encouraged Lapham's efforts overall, he expressed concern for the way the proposed system was to be carried out at the hands of military officials. "Now these warnings ought to be based upon observations made by the intelligent telegraph operators or managers of offices or other employees," he argued. "The meteorological observations of the army have generally proved themselves very unreliable and are certainly no better than those that the telegraph operators could easily make." Cleveland said it would "have been wiser" had the bill called for a committee of three experts (he also suggested Henry of the Smithsonian, John Huntington Crane Coffin of the Nautical Almanac Office, and an officer from either the Army or the Navy) to formulate a plan of action. "It would be a pity to see the country swindled with an inefficient meteorological office as it has already enough to do to carry on the naval observatory with the present objectionable system of management," he contended.[28]

Lapham responded several days later, pleased with Cleveland's comments and optimistic that the bill before Congress would prove beneficial in some form. "I am glad to find that you approve of the project of storm predictions, and hope we shall be able to accomplish something even if we do not succeed in <u>all</u> our efforts, or in the manner we could wish. The bill introduced in Congress does not appropriate any money, a defect, which may render it nugatory; though it may do some good," he said. "The bill is now before the Committee of Commerce and may be modified before its final passage, perhaps your view might influence the Committee to give it the right shape."[29]

While there is no record of Cleveland writing directly to the committee, as Lapham suggested, advice did come from the Chamber of Commerce of the State of New York, which appointed a special committee to consider the proposed legislation. On February 3, the committee reported that it was giving its "hearty assent to the passage in Congress of the proposed law, but would respectfully suggest that it should first be so amended that its influences be felt all over our country, and along the Pacific and Atlantic coasts, by every industry and every class of our fellow citizens, as far as convenient and practicable, and not be confined merely 'to the Northern lakes and Atlantic seaboard,' as at present worded."[30]

Paine began working on yet another revision of the bill—this time with the help of Senator Henry Wilson of Massachusetts, chair of the Senate Military Affairs Committee. On February 2, Paine reintroduced the legislation to the House as a joint resolution, H. Res. 143, "to authorize the Secretary of War to provide for taking meteorological observations at the military stations and other points in the interior of the continent, and for giving notice on the Northern Lakes and seaboard of the approach and force of storms."[31]

As Paine later recalled, "I made several ineffectual attempts to secure the passage of the joint resolution by unanimous consent. There was always an objection from some quarter, generally from Indiana. At length I called upon my Indiana friend and explained my measure, begging him to permit it to pass." Apparently, Paine's colleague from Indiana was concerned about the measure put forth in the joint resolution turning into an unwieldy overgrowth of government expense. After securing his colleague's endorsement, Paine once again asked the House to pass the resolution. "To my great astonishment my Indiana friend instantly objected. I hastened across the Hall and reminded him of his promise. He said he had forgotten it, and shouted, 'Mr. Speaker, I withdraw my objection.' That was decisive of the fate of the resolution. If the gentleman from Indiana did not object nobody could. The resolution was adopted by unanimous consent." [32]

That same day, the joint resolution was read a first and second time, by unanimous consent, before the Senate and referred to the Committee on Military Affairs.[33] Two days later, on February 4, Senator Wilson reported that the joint resolution had left the committee without amendment. In bringing it before the entire Senate for consideration, the joint resolution was read three additional times, before being passed. The vice president, Schuyler Colfax, acting as president of the Senate, signed it on February 8 and delivered it to a committee to be presented to the president for his signature.[34]

On February 9, Horace Porter, private secretary to President Ulysses S. Grant, sent a message to the House of Representatives informing them that the president had signed the joint resolution. It officially became codified into law as Public Resolution No. 9, whose final wording read:

> *Be it resolved by the Senate and House of Representatives of the United States of America, in Congress assembled*, That the Secretary of War be, and he hereby

> is, authorized and required to provide for taking meteorological observations, at the military stations in the interior of the continent, and at other points in the States and Territories of the United States, and for giving notice, on the Northern Lakes and on the seacoast, by magnetic telegraph and marine signals, of the approach and force of storms.[35]

With the stroke of a pen, Grant effectively gave birth to the country's first national weather service—only the fourth in existence worldwide at the time to issue forecasts or warnings using the telegraph.[36] In the years following its inception, credit for the establishment of the service would be ascribed—in some cases single-handedly—to everyone from Cleveland to Lapham to Espy to Henry[37] to even Henry L. Dawes, chair of the House Appropriations Committee at the time the joint resolution was passed.[38]

Following Lapham's death in 1875, his daughter Julia worked tirelessly to promote her father's legacy. In 1901, she was able to get a previously unpublished manuscript by her father printed in *Earth and Air*, a monthly journal "published in the interest of the science of meteorology." The journal had advertised the publication of the manuscript—which spanned three issues—as being "from the pen of the late Increase Allen Lapham, best known as the founder of the Weather Bureau."[39] In summarizing the article, the editor of the journal said it shows "how closely the late Dr. I. A. Lapham was associated with the early struggles of the Storm Signal Service, and how it is only through his untiring energies and intense devotion to the science of meteorology that we are enabled to enjoy our present magnificent weather service."[40]

On more than one occasion, Julia Lapham corresponded with Cleveland about the details of her father's career and his contributions to the field of meteorology, as well as the establishment of a national weather service. In a letter to Julia in 1897, Cleveland stated that he felt credit for establishment of the service should go "first and foremost" to General Paine. "Your father helped him greatly," Cleveland said, "as did Professor Henry and Loomis and myself, and many others. Your father proposed, primarily, to start a weather system for Milwaukee and Chicago, like that which I had inaugurated in Cincinnati and had offered to the Chicago Board of Trade; but Mr. Paine saw at once that the project should be taken up by Congress for the benefit of the whole country."[41]

For his part, Lapham acknowledged the pioneering work Cleveland undertook in Cincinnati, in proving the practicality of weather predictions, for providing some of the motivation for his actions in helping secure the legislation. "I was very much encouraged to make this movement by the very efficient and successful effort made by Prof. Cleveland Abbe of the Cincinnati Observatory in 1868 and 1869, in predicting weather changes; showing (as it did) that commercial men already felt an interest in the subject, and that there were persons competent to carry into effect the measures that it might be adopted," Lapham wrote.[42]

Charles Marvin, who served as chief of the Weather Bureau at the time of Cleveland's death, attempted to demonstrate during a speech several months later the extent to which Cleveland credited Lapham's efforts. "No one has been more scrupulously careful than Abbe himself, as can be shown by documentary evidence, to give Professor Lapham the fullest measure of credit for the work done by him which practically ended with the enactment of the law which imposed upon the Secretary of War the task of organizing meteorological observations throughout the United States and northern Lakes and sea-board of the approach of storms," he said.[43]

Perhaps the most fitting sentiment regarding the respective efforts made by Cleveland and Lapham that resulted in the creation of a national weather service came in 1901 from Weather Bureau Chief Willis Moore, who, speaking in Milwaukee at a convention of Weather Bureau officials, gave due credit to both men for their efforts. "Milwaukee and Cincinnati can shake hands over that question," Moore said. "Professor Abbe in Cincinnati, with the aid of the Cincinnati Chamber of Commerce, and Dr. Lapham, in Milwaukee, with the agitation he carried on for years, were the two spirits that moved this Government to take the action that finally resulted in the convention we are holding to-day."[44]

General Myer

With the framework for the country's first national weather service firmly in place, the next steps were to identify where in the secretary of war's purview the responsibility for the new service would fall and to begin its organization.

"Before I finally obtained the unanimous consent of the House to the passage of the joint resolution, a stranger called upon me and introduced himself as Colonel Myer, of the Signal Corps," Paine explained. "He exhibited the most intense anxiety for the success of the measure. It seemed to me that his zeal and enthusiasm marked him as the fit man to launch the new enterprise." According to Paine, Myer's enthusiasm to lead the new weather service was matched by his superior. "As soon as the joint resolution passed, I called upon General Belknap, then Secretary of War, and suggested that he should consider the propriety of assigning Colonel Myer to the duty," Paine said. "He said at once that he had already in his own mind fixed upon Colonel Myer as the officer to commence the work under the joint resolution."[45]

Albert James Myer was a consummate Army officer and a natural leader. "In personal carriage he is every inch a soldier—tall, erect, alert, with the air of command in every look and gesture," read a description in *Frank Leslie's Popular Monthly*. "He is a sharp disciplinarian, but quick to discern and recognize honest merit."[46] Myer made a name for himself developing a system of signaling utilized by the Army during the Civil War. At the time of the joint resolution's passage, he was looking for a way to reestablish the prominence of the Signal Corps, which was formally established in 1860, with Myer as chief signal officer. Following the war, Myer became something of a man without a purpose, or a leader without a corps, with only a single lieutenant and two clerks under his command.[47] After conflict arose in an attempt to recruit telegraphers for the Signal Corps, Secretary of War Edwin Stanton relieved Myer of his command and, in 1864, the Senate failed to reconfirm his position, placing him on inactive duty and putting his military career in a state of limbo.[48] Following a long campaign to restore his position—and dignity—Myer was vindicated in 1866, when President Andrew Johnson ordered Stanton to reinstate Myer as chief signal officer. The following year, Myer received a brevet promotion to the rank of brigadier general. He would receive a full commission as brigadier general on June 16, 1880, just two months before his death.[49]

Myer would officially take control of the newly established weather reporting responsibility Secretary of War Belknap had been given via General Orders No. 29, issued by the Army's adjutant general, Edward D. Townsend, on March 15, 1870. In referring to the joint resolution passed five weeks earlier, the order read: "The Chief Signal Officer of the Army is charged, subject to the direction of the Secretary of War, with the special duties of the observation and giving notice, by telegraph and signal, of the approach and force of storms, under the provision of this resolution." The orders further stated that, since the undertaking was for the benefit of the commerce of the United States, "It is therefore expected that all commanding will afford every facility for its successful discharge; and all scientific establishments, commercial associations, and others are requested to aid, by their co-operation, in its accomplishment."[50]

As a result of the latter part of Townsend's order, Myer sent a letter to Cleveland on March 24, 1870, requesting "any information it may be your pleasure to give as to the plans of observation adopted by the Institution which you represent." Specifically, Myer asked for copies of any printed or written forms, forms of weather reports or maps, a list of the names and stations of correspondents—along with instructions to them—and "generally, whatever you may deem of value for the information of this office."[51]

In his response, Cleveland told Myer that the "late action of Congress authorizing the establishment of a system of Storm warnings cannot but be viewed with much interest by this Institution." He went on to briefly describe the events of the previous two years in establishing a network of weather observers, publishing the Weather Bulletin of the Cincinnati Observatory, and his efforts to support the work of the National Board of Trade in Richmond—and of Lapham in Milwaukee—that resulted in the passage of the joint resolution. Cleveland admitted that the scope of the national-level system of observations and forecasts Myer was charged with establishing would far outweigh the scope of his regional endeavors, centered around Cincinnati. "As the grand scale on which you propose to carry on this meteorological work will quite dwarf our own humbler efforts—if, indeed, it does not entirely supersede them—it is not improbable but that we may make some modification in the system at present pursued," he said.[52] Myer, in reply, told Cleveland it would give him "very great pleasure" to work with him and the observatory "in every practicable way so soon as the undertaking imposed upon the [War] Department has taken such organized form as will enable me to do so."[53]

Before Myer could do anything, Congress needed to allocate funding for the new service, as no appropriations were made as part of the joint resolution. This led Henry to tell Paine that his "troubles would commence" when he reached the Appropriations Committee with his "prayer for money to meet the incidental expenses of the service."[54] As Paine later recalled, however, "Professor Henry's predictions were not verified." After the passage of the joint resolution, Henry L. Dawes, chair of the House Appropriations Committee, sent a request to Secretary of War Belknap, asking for estimates of appropriations required to carry out his new responsibilities in taking meteorological observations. Belknap looked to Myer, as the officer in charge of the new service, to provide an analysis of what appropriations would be necessary. "In view of the novelty on this side of the Atlantic of such combined duties of meteorological observation and telegraphic report as are contemplated by the enactment, it would be a labor of extreme difficulty, and require more time than can well be given, to prepare extended estimates in detail," Myer explained. "I would suggest, therefore, that action under the resolution be limited, until the best modes for its execution shall have been wisely determined. It can be expanded as its utility causes it to be sustained."[55] Myer estimated a total of $15,000 be appropriated for "expenses for the observation and report of storms, by telegraph and signal, for the benefit of commerce on the northern lakes and seaboard" for the fiscal year ending June 30, 1870, and $25,000 for the fiscal year ending June 30, 1871.

On April 20, 1870, the House passed a series of acts providing funds "to supply deficiencies in the appropriations for the service of the government" for the fiscal year about to end. Included with such provisions as "repairing and refurbishing the President's house" and "compensation and mileage for the members of the legislative assembly of the Territory of Utah" was an item titled "Northern lakes and seaboard," which provided "for expenses of the observation and report of storms, by telegraph and signal, for the benefit of the commerce of the northern lakes and seaboard, fifteen thousand dollars."[56] This sum represented a small fraction of the total amount appropriated for the military service for the fiscal year, which exceeded $37 million.[57] "The modesty of this first appropriation is almost ridiculous in view of the munificent appropriations of modern cities," Paine later remarked.[58]

Myer set to work organizing the new service under his command, which he assigned to a newly formed section of the Signal Service known as the Division of Telegrams and Reports for the Benefit of Commerce. He was able to get by, at least initially, with so little in the way of appropriations, as he had much of what he needed—especially in terms of human resources—already at his disposal. As one official later observed, the placement of the new service under Myer's command, within the Department of War, "was in no conceivable sense due to any recognized necessity for military control or military methods in conducting the work, but simply because at that time (1870), without specific appropriations, there were at the disposal of the Secretary of War no better means for carrying out the work."[59]

Myer began staffing his new service in August 1870, drawing upon a pool of personnel "largely made up of sergeants and others from the Army and those who were easily found about Washington. Afterwards recruiting was largely done at the large cities where stations had been located."[60] While the vast majority of the service consisted of officers and enlisted men from military ranks, they were, by and large, ignorant when it came to the scientific principles of meteorology. In fact, they "knew nothing, or but little, about the work," but, due to the simplicity of the instruments they were instructed to read and maintain, the work "was easily managed. It began without difficulty. Some went at once upon stations; others required about five weeks' instruction."[61]

In his first annual report to Secretary Belknap upon taking command of the new service, published in October 1870, Myer laid out a plan of taking meteorological observations he hoped would "give thrice daily a synoptic view of the atmospheric condition over a greater portion of the States and Territories of the United States."[62] The focus would be on timely, synchronous observations, which were to be made three times a day by the observer-sergeants stationed at various posts across the country and telegraphed to the Signal Office in Washington, as well as other stations in the network. Twenty-four stations outside of Washington made up the initial reporting network. With the exception of Omaha, Nebraska, and Cheyenne, Wyoming Territory, the stations were all located east of the Mississippi River, with concentrations along the Great Lakes, as well as the Gulf and Atlantic coasts. Lack of experience and expertise prevented the burgeoning service from attempting to issue forecasts, at least initially. As Myer explained:

> The publication of official deductions or forecasts to be had from the mass of reports received at different centers, involves so much of responsibility, that, while it has been considered, the office has not been willing to enter upon it until it shall have practically tested the promptness with which the reports will be received, and the facts as to the approach and force of storms which synchronous reports, following each other in such close succession, will announce without any effort of anticipation. The fact that an extensive storm is moving in a certain direction, and its movement and its force reported at intervals of a few hours as it reaches the different stations in its course, will, of themselves, be a warning to points further in the track of its probable progress, and a little experience with the study of the "generalizations," which meteorological research has seemed to establish, and which, it is proposed, shall accompany the bulletin reports, together with the synoptic charts exhibited by the meteorological maps displayed, will enable conclusions reasonably correct to be arrived at in the threatened localities. It has been considered wise by this office not to attempt more than this at the outset.[63]

On November 1, 1870, at 7:35 a.m. Washington time, the first reports made by the observer-sergeants of the Signal Service traveled along the telegraph lines—in coded form using a cipher adapted from the one Cleveland developed in Cincinnati—to the Army's Signal Office, located in adjoining buildings at 1719 and 1721 G Street, NW, in Washington, D.C. The new weather service had officially become operational. A week later, Myer was in Chicago, where he agreed to meet with Lapham. Impressed with Lapham's abilities and ambition, Myer offered him a temporary position as his assistant, which Lapham accepted on the spot, with a salary of $167 per month.[64] Lapham's duties placed him in charge of the service's operations in the Great Lakes region, with a duty station at Chicago. Lapham wasted no time getting to work. At noon on the same day Myer hired him, Lapham issued the nation's first official storm warning:[65]

> To Observers along the Lakes
> Bulletin this at once
>
> Noon Chicago Nov. 8, 1870
>
> A High wind all day yesterday at Cheyenne and Omaha. A very high wind reported this morning at Omaha.
>
> Barometer falling with high wind at Chicago and Milwaukee to day. Barometer falling & thermometer rising at Chicago. Detroit Toledo Cleveland Buffalo & Rochester.
>
> High winds probable along the lakes.
>
> J. Mackintosh
> observer

Lapham, who drafted the bulletin, acknowledged the Chicago observer, Sergeant James Mackintosh. Lapham also spent time plotting the observations on "a skeleton map of the weather over the whole country from Boston to Cheyenne and from Duluth to Key West."[66] Lapham's work was not confined to operational activities, however. "In addition to his duties in connection with the preannouncement of storms, this gentleman has prepared a series of valuable tables for this office," Myer noted in his annual report for 1871.[67]

While Lapham thoroughly enjoyed his new position ("Things are going flourishingly here," he wrote his daughter Julia on November 27, three weeks into the job[68]), his advanced age, the demands placed on him by his superiors, and the rigors of work in a strict military environment began to wear on him. At one point, his lack of adherence to protocol, in signing some of his official correspondence as "Assistant Chief Signal Officer" rather than "Assistant to the Chief Signal Officer," led to a letter of admonishment from Garrick Mallery, executive officer of the Signal Service and acting signal officer. "There cannot be, under existing laws, as assistant chief signal officer of the Army, and the adoption of that title has lead [sic] to some misconception which however has hitherto been of no moment," Mallery said. "You see will the propriety of military particularity in a Bureau of the War Department liable to military criticism as regards titles and signatures."[69] When Lapham told Myer in December that he planned to move his office from Chicago to Milwaukee, where his home was, Myer told him that his duty station "cannot under any circumstances" be moved.[70]

Fate intervened on December 16, when Lapham's good friend Byron Kilbourn died at his home in Jacksonville, Florida, naming Lapham as executor of his estate. Lapham wrote to Myer on December 28, telling him it had become necessary for him to go to Jacksonville "without delay" and requesting a leave of absence for the month of January.[71] On his return to Milwaukee, Lapham spent time in Washington, D.C., where, according to a letter to his daughter Julia, he dined "with Gen. Myer at his house on I Street. Having "arranged matters satisfactorily," he said he was no longer to be stationed at Chicago.[72] He would spend the next year engaged primarily in preparing special reports for the Signal Service, including one on the Great Chicago Fire that October, which burned more than two thousand acres, destroying the city's central business district. On May 11, 1872, Lapham received a letter from Lieutenant Henry Howgate of the Signal Service, informing him that his time with the service would be coming to an end. "I am directed to inform you that in view of the limited amount of money at the disposal of this Office for the current year and the consequent necessity for the reduction of its working expenses, the arrangement by which your valuable services have been secured as Assistant to the Chief Signal Officer will terminate at the close of the present month," Howgate wrote. "It is hoped that the Office will be in sufficient funds by that date to liquidate your account in full."[73]

Weather Bulletin Continues

While Myer was organizing his new weather service, Cleveland was struggling to get his burgeoning system of weather bulletins off the ground. His initial run of the Weather Bulletin of the Cincinnati Observatory, backed by the local chamber of commerce, ended in early December 1869. Cleveland, not wishing to see his efforts fade into the forgotten pages of history, decided to take matters into his own hands. "At the expiration of the first three months' trial, and while negotiations were pending with the Western Union Telegraph Company, for its permanent continuance, I, in order to prevent a break in the series, for six months maintained the Bulletin myself, receiving the dispatches gratuitously from the telegraph employees, and publishing the reports daily, including Sundays, in the newspapers of Cincinnati," he wrote of his efforts.[74]

Still, he was struggling to maintain all of the logistical necessities involved in publishing the Weather Bulletin—from coordinating with the observers to laying out the table and dealing with the detailed printing process. In a sense, the arduous enterprise had become something of a beast Cleveland could not tame. At least this is what his brother Robert insinuated in a letter shortly after the end of the trial run, in December 1869. "Instead of holding on to him by the tail with danger of his kicking up I should think it best as you said to dispose of him to some more wealthy owner who could afford to put a strong harness on him while you as being the best master could adjust his yoke and apply the goad."[75]

Beginning on February 9, 1870, the same day President Grant signed the joint resolution authorizing the secretary of war to establish a weather observing and reporting service, Cleveland enlisted the help of Frank Armstrong, manager of the Western Union office in Cincinnati, to breathe new life into the fledgling Weather Bulletin. With Cleveland's meteorological expertise and Armstrong's resources, the Western Union Telegraph Company's Weather Report, compiled at the Cincinnati Observatory, went into effect.[76] It ran ten months, with Armstrong taking over sole responsibility in May of compiling the reports and issuing the Weather Bulletin, "thus relieving the Observatory of all further responsibility."[77] In addition to the tabular bulletin, Armstrong, with Cleveland's initial involvement, began publishing a daily weather map, which ran from late February until mid-December. Using sheets of yellow tissue paper called "flimsies" or "greasers," Cleveland traced an outline of the United States, using a base map placed underneath the sheet, and carefully drew circles—a quarter inch in diameter—around each of the reporting stations. Using a pencil, he shaded in the circles, as appropriate, to indicate stations reporting cloud cover but no precipitation. He then placed the letters "R" or "S," as appropriate, inside the circles of the stations reporting rain or snow. Finally, he drew arrows through the circles to indicate wind direction. Next to each circle was a number, which showed the "state of thermometer" for that location.[78] "The Daily Weather Bulletin and Chart are, therefore, now supported solely by the Western Union Telegraph Company, and must be considered as a very important contribution to meteorology," Cleveland noted in his annual report in June 1870. "It would have been highly to the credit of the Observatory could these publications have been maintained in its own name; but this was impossible owing to the want of funds and assistants."[79]

Cleveland was doing his best to manage the operations of the Cincinnati Observatory—which was becoming increasingly encroached upon by pollution from nearby industrial sources—and to settle into married life. On June 4, 1870, less than four weeks after his wedding, Cleveland submitted his annual report to the Board of Control of the Cincinnati Observatory. "I would remind the Board that the Observatory now possesses not only books and apparatus, but also an element of life and growth within it," he said in his conclusion. "This growth can not now be checked without injury to the future interests of the Observatory. We need a proper location, appropriate buildings, and good assistants—without these, we are hindered and dwarfed. The work of the Observatory can not be satisfactorily carried on in its present condition, though I shall always labor to do my best."

In early July, Cleveland received a letter from his mother. "I don't think marriage has sobered you down much," she wrote, trying her best to be encouraging. "I am glad you are so happy & enjoying yourself so much. It is too bad that your great city can't support that observatory, & I would try & obtain another situation more satisfactory, if I could."[80] Charlotte Abbe seemed as concerned as ever about her son's situation. Just a few months earlier, in December, she wrote him a similar letter of encouragement. "Don't despond Cleveland, you have done your duty, & if that observatory can't be made to work, it's all right, & some thing else will cast up for you—You know where your trust is, & don't allow yourself to become disheartened. The world is large & you are yet young."[81] In March, she wrote another letter urging Cleveland not to overexert himself with his work at the observatory. "Now Cleveland, don't work too hard & injure your health, take some recreation, & don't let your brain be overtaxed—a few weeks at home will do you good, & not think of any thing of work during the time—Can't you do it."[82]

Farewell to Cincinnati

By the fall of 1870, Cleveland had reached a point where he felt he could no longer continue as director of the Cincinnati Observatory. The lack of assistants left him unable "properly to conduct the work undertaken at this Observatory" and necessitated his hiring several young men to serve as astronomical students-in-residence. The buildings and grounds had fallen into such a state of disrepair that, when "it became probable that we must, for several years, occupy the present ill-adapted site and building, it seemed necessary at once to spend enough upon the fences and buildings to ameliorate the neglected appearance of the property." In addition, expenses had been "heavier the past year than heretofore, and must still be heavier the coming year, if the Board of Control attempt to maintain the present establishment in a manner any way creditable to themselves."[83]

On October 8, Cleveland submitted his resignation as director of the observatory. "The culminating evidence of the indifference of the Board of Control is too much," he wrote two days later to his friend Julius Dexter, himself a recently appointed member of the observatory's board.[84] Though disappointed, Dexter understood Cleveland's position and wished him well, but he feared what would become of the observatory in his absence. "I am sorry that the observatory loses your services for without them I almost despair of our doing anything. You have been about all that has kept the Association alive, and even you may not have animated it enough to survive your departure."[85]

With no one to immediately take his place as director, Cleveland's departure resulted in what was essentially a leave of absence from the observatory,[86] as he looked to pursue other ventures. The following week, he accepted a position as astronomer on an expedition to conduct a survey of Panama. His role would be to provide longitudinal coordinates to accurately determine the position of the isthmus, as well as other points along the survey, which was expected to last five or six months. For this, he would receive a salary of $180 per month, plus subsistence.[87] He had planned to take his wife, Fanny, with him and wrote to his father in New York that the pair would be coming for a visit prior to the expedition's departure, which was planned for mid-November. "We shall be glad to see you and Fanny," George Abbe wrote, adding that they "have plenty of room & will do our best to make it pleasant for Fanny."[88] To Cleveland's disappointment, however, he received a letter in late October from Captain Thomas O. Selfridge, who was leading the expedition, that would ultimately change his mind—and the course of his career. "I am sorry to say that it will not be possible for your wife to accompany you," he wrote.[89] This, combined with "a radical difference of opinion" that arose between Cleveland and Selfridge on how to accurately perform the work,[90] left Cleveland with no choice but to withdraw from the expedition. On October 28, Cleveland paid thirty-four dollars for two tickets to New York[91] and he and Fanny set off to spend some time with his parents and ponder what lay ahead.

Myer's Offer

Cleveland's frustration with the state of affairs in Cincinnati and his withdrawal from the Panama expedition left him without an outlet for professional fulfillment but also open to opportunity. For several months, he had been corresponding with General Myer, offering support and encouragement as Myer worked to build the foundation of the weather reporting and storm warning service placed under his command. In September, Myer wrote to Cleveland, seeking his help as an expert in the field—recognizing him as the only person in America at that time who had gained practical experience issuing regular, public weather forecasts, based on a network of observations:

> In view of the duties of the meteorologic investigation and report devolving upon this office, it is desired to obtain from the most competent authorities, the result of their experience in reference to meteorologic phenomena or changes noticed by them as premonitory of high winds, storms etc. at the places where their observations have been chiefly made. It seems not impossible, that something of a local character attaches to such premonitions, if therefore, you can do so without too greatly inconveniencing yourself, you will please favor this office and the department, with a brief collation of such prominent facts or phenomena as you are disposed to regard as of such premonitory character for any locality or division of the United States for which you may regard them as established or if not certainly, probably, established, by observations.
>
> Similar collations obtained from other known meteorologists in different parts of the United States will enable a fair schedule of premonitions to be made, and they cannot fail to be of general utility. It will afford this office much pleasure to acknowledge or reciprocate in any way most satisfactory to yourself, the favor it thus invites.[92]

"I have been told by those who were then on duty under Gen. Myer that immediately upon the passage of the Joint Resolution of February 4, 1870," Cleveland later recalled, "the officers were ordered to make it their first duty to acquire all the meteorology that was available." Cleveland said that Myer and his staff conducted interviews with such meteorological luminaries of the time as Professor Henry of the Smithsonian, Dr. Benjamin F. Craig of the Army Medical Corps, Mr. Charles A. Schott of the Coast Survey, Admiral Thornton A. Jenkins of the Navy, and Professor John H. C. Coffin of the Nautical Almanac Office. "By correspondence with Prof. Loomis of Yale, Dr. Daniel Draper, and Mr. T. B. Maury of New York City, and especially Mr. Lapham of Milwaukee, and myself at Cincinnati, a fund of knowledge, suggestions, forms for observations and telegraph ciphers were acquired, which materially guided in the organization of the meteorological service."[93]

For his part, Cleveland had been sharing information with Myer pertaining to the Weather Bulletin project, including the cipher he had used with his observers to transmit their observations over the telegraph lines using as few words as possible. In early November, Cleveland received another letter from General Myer, expressing his gratitude. "Permit me to express my appreciation of your very courteous communications with this office," Myer wrote. "It will afford me pleasure to cooperate with you in any way so soon, as some experience has shown the best way in which we can do so."[94]

Myer's willingness to cooperate with Cleveland extended well beyond exchanging forms and cipher codes. In early December, Cleveland wrote Myer that he would possibly be staying in New York through the winter. Myer responded, expressing his desire to meet with him personally. "Do you think of visiting Washington?" he asked. "I have much in mind some plans of cooperation with the observatory or in some way with yourself and wish we might meet."[95]

On December 27, Myer wrote another letter to Cleveland. "I would like an appointment to confer with you in reference to your duties of this office," he said. "Can you make it convenient to run over here for a day or two." Myer reiterated that the subject on which he wished to confer with Cleveland "relates to public duties" and that any necessary expenses Cleveland might incur on traveling to Washington, D.C., would be paid by the Signal Office.[96] Cleveland made that trip to Washington, as Myer had requested, on January 3–5, incurring $22.75 in expenses, charged to the Signal Office.[97] There Myer offered him a position as his assistant—only the second civilian (after Increase Lapham) to be hired to work for the new service. His initial salary was set at $250 per month, or $3,000 annually.

Return to Washington

On January 9, Cleveland and Fanny took the train from New York to Washington, D.C. They spent the first night at the opulent Arlington House hotel, located on Vermont Avenue, between H and I Streets, just north of the White House, before finding rooms at a nearby boarding house.[98] On January 12, Cleveland reported for duty at the U.S. Army's Signal Office, on G Street, near the War Department Headquarters. Brevet Major Lemuel B. Norton, in his capacity as acting signal officer, issued General Orders No. 2, which read:

> Professor Cleveland Abbe, having reported for duty, is announced as Assistant in the Signal Service to date from the 3rd instant. He will be respected accordingly.

> Professor Abbe will, as Assistant, have access at any time to the different meteorological books, instruments, records, and papers of this office, or of any Station at which he may be on duty.[99]

Thus, retroactive to January 3, 1871, Cleveland officially joined the ranks of the Signal Service—as a civilian assistant—and began a career that would span more than four decades in the service of the United States.

Cleveland's first order of business was establishing a system of weather forecasts, to be issued three times daily, based on observations taken at 7:35 a.m., 4:35 p.m., and 11:35 p.m., Washington time. Similar to the weather bulletins he had published in Cincinnati, the official products of the Signal Service would consist of two parts: synopses and probabilities. "The synopses consist of a synoptic view of the meteoric condition of the United States, as had from the data received at each regular report," described the Annual Report of the Chief Signal Officer for 1871. "The probabilities are the deductions made by the office, from the data in its possession at the time of each report, as to the meteoric conditions probably to be for the eight hours then next ensuing," the report stated, adding, "Copies of these synopses and probabilities are furnished at the moment of their issue to the different press associations in the United States. They are also printed upon the graphic weather-charts issued by the office."[100]

Cleveland began by producing practice forecasts, "After a month's practice it was decided that my forecast would evidently more than fill the popular expectations, and tri-daily publications began at once."[101]

Meanwhile, in anticipation of the forthcoming forecasts, *The New York Times*, on the front page of its February 13 issue, published a short piece titled "Official Weather Predictions," which offered a preview of what was to come:

> The War Department has concluded to yield to the pressing demands made upon the Signal Office by ship-owners and commercial men generally, for the daily weather for a limited period of time, and will begin the work during the present week, by issuing daily from the Signal Office, Washington, a synopsis of existing weather throughout the country, and the probable change during the succeeding twenty-four hours. This synopsis will be based upon the three daily reports now received, and will be prepared by competent authority. Arrangements are now making to give them a wide and speedy circulation.[102]

The "wide and speedy circulation" of the new forecasts, however, would have to wait. The following day *The Times* noted that "Gen. Myers [sic], Chief of the Signal Corps, has decided to postpone for a few days the synopses of reports of weather and the probabilities concerning it."[103] By February 19, Cleveland and Myer felt confident enough to issue the first official public forecasts for the nation, which were to be published in the following day's papers "with the explicit understanding that it shall not be altered or garbled, and that any paper using it at all will follow the precise wording," according to instructions provided to editors. "There is danger that incorrect or altered reports may greatly mislead the public and bring discredit upon the service. Editors are requested to insist upon the accurate following of the copy."[104] Cleveland's final forecast that day, based on 11:35 p.m. observations, appeared on the front page of *The Times* the following day:

> **Synopsis of Weather Report for the Last Twenty-four Hours.**
>
> The storm of the 18th, which left the East Atlantic coast last night, was followed by a rapid recovery of pressure and high northwest winds. Today a low barometer has prevailed on the Lakes, gradually giving way to the pressure from the South. A pretty decided increase has taken place in the pressure in the southern States, attended by clear weather and clear winds. Humidity has been small in the North-east and on the Atlantic. A steady pressure, with fair weather, holds in the West, but decided fall is reported from San Francisco.
>
> **Probabilities.**
>
> There are no indications of an approaching disturbance in any part of the country. Clear and fair weather is anticipated for to-morrow in the regions south and west of Pennsylvania, clouds and light south and west winds in the Eastern States.[105]

While this first day's forecast may seem a bit lackluster and nondescript in its meteorological messaging, Cleveland's predictions did at times pack more of a punch, so to speak, as the week wore on. For example, his morning probabilities issued on February 24, based on 7:35 a.m. observations, were much more comprehensive in nature—and even included an international component:

> It seems likely that the center of the storm now on Lake Michigan will move to the northeast and the low humidity on the Lakes indicates that compara-

tively little rain or snow will fall except perhaps, in Canada. The southerly winds along the Atlantic induced by the low pressure on the Lakes, will probably bring rain to most points along the coast, above Cape Hatteras.[106]

The probabilities issued that evening, however, based on 11:35 p.m. observations, were markedly terse and general in nature, not to mention a stark contrast to those issued that morning:

> It is probable that fresh or light winds and clear weather will to-morrow prevail over the whole country.[107]

According to the Signal Service reports received at 11:47 p.m. the following day, February 25, as published in the February 26 edition of *The Times*, only ten of the thirty-five stations reported clear weather, with another ten reporting fair weather. Eleven stations reported cloudy conditions, while one reported hazy conditions. Two locations reported heavy rain and one reported light rain.[108]

The apparent discrepancy in the scope and wording of these consecutive forecasts may be explained by a disclaimer of sorts put forth in Myer's annual report to the secretary of war for 1872. "It must be remembered, in apology for the failures, that the duties of the signal service require very rapid action. The reports are no sooner received at this office at the time of each reporting than they must, to meet the demands of the press for speedy publication, be discussed, the deductions made (written out in form) and telegraphed to the different cities in a period of time limited by minutes." The average length of time, according to the report, "from the moment the observations at the stations, near and distant, to that at which the results are reported and telegraphed to the press" was an hour and twenty-five minutes. "An advantage is had in the fact that the reports to be issued follow each other so rapidly—the greatest interval being nine hours—each may be regarded rather as a supplement of the one that preceded it than a solitary report to be made complete from a single series of data."[109]

In its first year of operational weather forecasting, the Signal Service boasted a verification rate with its probabilities of 69 percent. "A higher percentage of verifications results, if allowance is made for the meteoric changes that may have occurred within an hour of the times stated in the predictions." Such "partial verifications," the service claimed, occurred in 21 percent of the cases; "the total of verifications and partial verifications being thus in the proportion of ninety to each one hundred of the predictions announced." Myer cautioned, however, that it was "not deemed advisable that the partial verifications be considered for any practical purposes. It is proper, therefore, to limit the official claim of the office to the fact that 69 per cent. of the forecasts made of record, and published by it, have been verified."[110]

Initially, Cleveland was the sole person responsible for preparing the synopses and probabilities issued three times each day, a task that consumed much of his time during his first year on the job. "For a year and until assistants could be trained for the work I concocted all of the probabilities myself. I left my office regularly at 2 in the morning and was at my desk again at 9 o'clock," he recalled years later.[111]

Cleveland's devotion to his work—and the successful operations of the Signal Service's forecast division—did not go unnoticed by Myer. In his annual report, the chief signal officer heartedly commended Cleveland for having "devoted himself to these duties and to others of the most onerous description with rare fidelity." Myer further noted:

> The favor with which the Synopses and Probabilities issued by the office have been received, and the commendatory expressions of scientific meteorists, sufficiently evidence the skill with which he has discussed the mass of material laid before him. This officer has rendered very valuable assistance in the preparation of the publications of this office—the circulars in relation to the practical use of meteorological reports and weather maps issuing from it. It is believed that some of the rules and generalizations contributed by him to these papers are now for the first time announced.[112]

Myer's report also indicated the sheer volume of reports Cleveland compiled during his first year with the Signal Service. From January 19, 1871, to November 1, 1871, some 846 "detailed sheets of synopses have been tabulated to accompany sheets exhibiting the changes of weather deemed probably for the succeeding day."[113]

As Cleveland labored away at the Signal Office in Washington, D.C., his family in New York took notice—not only of his work but of the emerging news of the service itself, which had become the focus of a somewhat novel fascination for the nation. "I see by the papers that the Signal Service Dept. is quite prominent just now and attracting the notice of the public and likely to become a permanent institution," his father wrote in February. "I hope so for your sake, I should be glad to get a letter from you and know how you are getting along and how you like the position you have & what you hear from Cincinnati."[114]

In fact, Cleveland did hear from Cincinnati and the news was not good. On February 25, he received a letter from James Lofthouse, a laborer at the observatory, informing him that conditions there had continued to deteriorate, causing damage to the facilities and residence—where Cleveland and Fanny still had many of their possessions. "The Observatory roof is bad all over," Lofthouse said. "Rain and snow water comes into the small and the large bed rooms over the parlour and through the floors into the hall and one place into the parlour. But with wash tubs and buckets &c we have kept it away from your furniture." According to Lofthouse, the library sustained the worst of the damage, after very heavy rain pelted the roof throughout an entire night. "It came through in countless solid streams, all the wash tubs, buckets and coal scuttles were instantly called into service and three of us with mops and swabs could not keep it from going through the floor," Lofthouse explained. "So we quit the mops and with brooms swept the stream down the stairs and out at the hall door. We worked desperately to keep the water if possible from the beds in our bedroom under the library. Some did go through but we caught it in dinner buckets &c."[115]

Meanwhile, Cleveland's brother William, writing from Philadelphia, told of a friend who had written to General Myer "with reference to engaging as observer at this point in the matter of meteorological data." William asked Cleveland to provide a reference for his friend. "His enthusiasm is always in the interest of science and a word spoken for him will be acknowledged with gratitude," he wrote.[116]

For her part, Cleveland's mother could not help but worry that her son was overexerting himself and wrote him to express her concern. "I am afraid you are applying yourself too closely to your new business, & can only hope, that you will have less laborious work, when maps & charts are complete, & you can tell at a glance just which way the wind blows." She also passed on news from an old friend. "Mr. Bickmore called on us the last week, for the first time since you left. He did not know, that you were in Washington, but said if you did not stay there it would not be wise in you, as it was a superior position. I told him to write to you. Every one that speaks of you says that you must stay there if you can." Charlotte could not hold back her frustration, however, in pointing out a feature of the Signal Service's meteorological reports of observations—which she attributed to Cleveland—that seemed to cause annoyance. "One gentleman suggests that instead of placing the cities (in your daily reports) in alphabetical order, that you place them in the order they come on the coast & elsewhere, for now we have to look from one end of the column to the other, to find our city & it is a real bother," she complained, adding, "'a hint to the wise,' but I don't want to make your labours any more arduous."[117]

Cleveland's sister Helen, in a letter dated March 18, reiterated the suggestion of how the cities in the weather reports should be listed. "Mr. Smith wanted me to suggest to you that instead of arranging the places in the paper where the observations of the weather are taken alphabetically you arrange them from west to east or south to north," she said. "He thinks we would almost tell the storms ourselves then. Don't you think it is a good idea?"[118]

Robert took the opportunity to give his brother a good-natured teasing when one of his early forecasts failed to verify. "We take great interest in your 'probabilities' and read them the very first thing when we get the paper both morning and evening," Robert wrote Cleveland in early April. "We not only take interest in the same but have great faith in it. So much so, in fact, that when you predicted 'cloudy and rainy' for [the] day before yesterday I carried a big cotton umbrella to college amid clearing up weather and had the pleasure all to myself of marching the same home in the afternoon in sunshine and under bright skies." Robert then went on to praise Cleveland for his achievements and offered his heartfelt encouragement for continued success. "However in five cases out of six you come out right for N.Y. weather," he said, adding, "persevere, and acquaintance will insure accuracy. The magnificent field of the United States, gulf, and Canada, with the telegraphic communication at your command, ought to afford a basis for establishing absolutely accurate predictions." Robert had faith not only in Cleveland's abilities but also in the predictive potential of meteorology in general. "I think there is every reason to believe that very soon one day will tell what two or three of its successors shall be." Still, knowing that Cleveland's original passion lay in astronomy, he tempered his encouragement with the thought that perhaps Cleveland's foray into forecasting would be short-lived. "I, for one, hope you will not be led to abandon astronomy for any other branch of learning; meteorology is perfectly in order, goes hand in hand with astronomy—and may be a splendid provision for a year or two."[119]

Cleveland's work was beginning to earn him a reputation that extended well beyond his immediate family. Benjamin Silliman, founder and editor of the *American Journal of Science and Arts*, wrote to him on June 9, thanking him for an article he had submitted titled "Historical Notes on the Systems of Weather Telegraphy, and especially their Development in the United States," and offered his accolades for the system of national weather forecasts Cleveland had developed. "Allow me to congratulate you on the almost prophetic accuracy of your daily statements of 'Probabilities' which have done more (in connection with the daily bulletin) to command public respect and confidence in Meteorological Service than all that has gone before in the voluminous records of former years," he said.[120]

In another letter, dated July 2, Robert told Cleveland of an alumni meeting he had recently attended at the College of the City of New York. One of Cleveland's classmates, Adolph Werner, spoke on behalf of the class of 1857 "and occupied half his time and more, in speaking of Cleveland Abbe 'our only astronomer, and meteorologist, now predicting weather and forecasting storms for our country etc. etc.' His remarks were received with applause!!!" Robert also recalled a chance encounter that illustrated the growing support for Cleveland's forecasts among an ardent group of users. "Speaking of your weather reports let me tell you that a gentleman whose father has had large experience in ship building, told me, in an entirely disinterested and impartial manner the other day, that two sea-captains with whom he had conversed had told him frequently of the great dependence and reliance they had on the weather reports; storms predicted from the North they avoided by 'laying out' whilst when from the South they kept port," Robert said. "I told him my brother made the predictions (as I often have told many others proudly) and he was at once taken back though pleased and highly interested."[121]

Even as Cleveland was making a name for himself through his work with the Signal Service, there remained uncertainty over his position—especially when it came to his salary—and whether he might return to Cincinnati. "I was sorry I did not see Gen. Myer," Cleveland's father wrote in April, referring to a recent trip he took to Washington, adding, "is there anything new in your office. What about assistants. I think if the matter of salary comes up that it would be well to claim what it was understood you were to have at Cincinnati at least."[122]

Cleveland consulted with his father over the matter, who provided shrewd advice on negotiating with General Myer. "You speak of saying somthing to Gen. Myer about salary on his return," George wrote. "It will require a little diplomacy and if he feels that your services are indispensable to him you can get an increase of pay." George went so far as to suggest that Cleveland invoke his father's apparent displeasure with the situation as a means to remedy it. "It may be well to suggest to him that your father is not quite reconciled to your giving up astronomy," he said, adding "that you have been to a considerable expense in trying to avail yourself of the best observatorys of Europe to perfect yourself in the science and there is no advantage in your present position as the pay is no more than you were to receive at Cincinnati as an astronomer." George was careful not to push his son too hard and reminded him of the value of his current situation. "I think you have a nice position and I would not jeopardize it by trying to get too much at the same time. I have no doubt they will be glad to pay you more than you are now receiving—if they had the idea that you are not satisfied."[123]

A month had gone by and George was growing anxious for news. "I supposed Gen. Myer has returned," he wrote on May 25. "Have you got an assistant? And do things go along pleasantly in your office. What do you hear from Cincinnati—do they say anything about your returning there? This is not my business, but I am interested of course."[124]

Cleveland wrote back, suggesting various options regarding Cincinnati and Washington, D.C., and asking for his father's advice. "After thinking the matter over," George wrote in response, "I should say that if the Cin. Obsty. people put the institution on a good footing, and offer you the position on a salary of $3,000 or more with house and grounds and such a sum for special expenses as will enable you to do the work you wish to on a good and reputable scale I think it would be preferable to the position you now hold with a salary of $5,000."[125] Cleveland's father noted that the position in Cincinnati would allow him to be independent, "at the head of the institution," and afford him time to himself to study and do research. On the other hand, he argued, the government may try to recall him to Washington, D.C., should he decide to go back to Cincinnati. He would, therefore, "have to run a risk one way or the other." George advised his son to keep his cards close to his chest when negotiating with General Myer and not reveal his intentions. "If Myer thinks you have no idea of leaving Washington I would not undeceive him nor would I make a long engagement with him at present," he said. "The Signal Service reports are so satisfactory to the public that I think Myer will not want to make a change of meteorologist."

George's persistent advice paid off. Six months after beginning his position with the Signal Service, Cleveland was able to secure from Myer a 25 percent increase in annual salary, from $3,000 to $3,750.[126] Still, his father seemed to think he could do better. "I think you are quite modest about salary but I suppose you understand best what the funding is," George wrote his son. "I think however your pay is too small for the services rendered but I suppose you will claim an advance when you think you can get it."[127]

Cleveland decided to remain in Washington, D.C., though his decision did not come without a certain amount of angst and self-doubt, as noted by a letter from his mother in early July. "I am glad you have decided to stay in your present position, for the present," she wrote. "I am sorry also, that you so underrate your spirit, or spunk, as you call it—on the contrary, you have, I think quite enough, & I am not alone in my opinion—Any one who by his own efforts has made his way & acquired the reputation that you have, could not be devoid of spirit & decision, & I don't want you to feel that you are at all lacking." Charlotte said she felt it was "praiseworthy" that Cleveland showed restraint and self-control when dealing with others, noting he could "control [his] language" and "not answer back with spirit," as well as his ability to "coolly take every thing into consideration, before deciding, it is the best way in the end."[128]

On August 29, a brief notice appeared in *The New York Times*, under the headline "The Weather Prophet." It read:

> Prof. Abby [sic], who makes up at the Signal Office the synopsis of weather events and probabilities, is Director of the Observatory at Chicago, and is only temporarily engaged at his present work. Some concern is felt at the prospect of this labor falling into the hands of some other person. The trustworthy nature of the predictions has becomes already so well established, that those who know how they have been worked up fear that nobody but the Professor can do the work.[129]

George read the notice and clipped it to send to Cleveland. "I enclose a paragraph cut from the N.Y. Times of 28th, he said, noting, "it is rather amusing at the same time perhaps the writer knows the difficulty in getting someone to fill the place in case you would go to 'Chicago.'"[130] Cleveland's sister Helen saw a similar notice in one of the daily papers and wrote Cleveland that it "has created considerable talk for it was in several papers and most every one seems to have seen it. All are anxious to know if you are going back to Chicago. That is about as straight as papers generally have things."[131]

A Professional Adversary Appears

In June 1871, Thompson B. Maury, a former private in the Confederate Army from Fredericksburg, Virginia,[132] and cousin of famed Navy hydrographer and oceanographer Matthew Fontaine Maury, entered the Signal Service as a civilian assistant. Maury's appointment concerned Cleveland to the point that he considered resigning from the service. Cleveland wrote to his father in New York, who shared his concerns, apparently having received intelligence of his own that suggested Maury would be a threat to Cleveland. "I received your letter of yesterday and am surprised to hear that Maury has got into your office," George wrote, "but before I resigned I would know from Gen. Myer whether he is to be there permanently, and what his position is. If you are to conduct the meteorological department you want those under you that you can manage & those that will be agreeable to you. I doubt that Maury will be either from what I hear of him."[133] In a subsequent letter, Cleveland's father offered a more stern warning regarding Maury. "I would not let Maury steal any of your thunder," he wrote. "I should keep him as far off as possible. I judge from what I have heard that he would have the impudence to ask even Gen. Myer to blacken his boots or do other dirty work."[134]

When an article titled "Weather Prognostics by the People" appeared under Maury's name in the December 1871 issue of the popular magazine *The Galaxy*, it seemed to confirm their suspicions. The article, which *The New York Times* praised as a work that "should be read by every one,"[135] bore a striking resemblance to a work Cleveland had prepared, titled "Suggestions for the Practical Use of Meteorological Reports and Weather Maps," which the Signal Service published as a circular in 1871. The resemblance caught the attention of the editors of *The Nation*, who offered a pointed commentary in their review of magazines for December:

> We do not know who Professor Thompson B. Maury is who writes in the *Galaxy* about "Weather Prognostics by the People," but we would call the attention of the editors of the *Galaxy* to the fact that whoever he may be ought at any rate to be the author of a work called "Suggestions for the Practical Use of Meteorological Reports and Weather Maps"—a valuable little hand-book prepared in the office of the Chief Signal Officer. It teaches how one may read understandingly the weather reports which the Signal Officer has lately been furnishing to the newspapers, and how one may even aid the observers to make their reports fuller and more specific. The *Galaxy* article in its facts and phraseology is rather too close to this hand-book to be pleasing to the author of the latter, unless, as we say, he is Professor Maury, and the credit of the magazine article belongs to him and the credit of the book as well. We dare say that applications by proper persons, as presidents of agricultural societies, editors, and the like, will be answered from the Signal Office of the War Department by the transmission of the circular in question. Meantime, the *Galaxy* article will be found serviceable.[136]

The possibility that Maury had passed Cleveland's work off as his own—and attempted to profit from it—infuriated both George and Robert, such that they were ready to take action. "I have been mad ever since I received your letter to learn that such a shameful thing is connected with the Signal Office as the one who signs his own name to the stolen article in the Galaxy," George wrote. "Myer is almost as bad as he is and I would call his attention to it to see if he sanctions such things. There is one satisfaction [in that] such things bring their own reward—it will only sink him a little lower when he is exposed."[137]

Robert expressed similar resentment at the situation. "As none of our family have yet reached that eminence to which you have arrived among scientific and thinking men—we naturally feel great pride and experience much pleasure in receiving letters from you, and publications or notices of yourself," he said. "And if we feel pride taking possession of our thoughts and minds under such circumstances, we realize also that equally strong sensation (—indignation—) where an insignificant third rate plagiarist steals your 'thunder' and virtually calls it his own. Father has hardly been able today to express that burning indignation and utter disgust which he peculiarly feels toward so mean a specimen of humanity as T. B. Maury." At the same time, Robert cautioned his brother not to be overly trusting of others, even if his own nature leads him to do so. "I fear that you regard the world too honest, like yourself, and believe that invariably 'credit will be given where credit is due,'" he said. "I think that in nine cases out of ten the latter will be true, but I am just as confident that no one should for one moment allow another to gain unlawful spoils."[138]

On Thanksgiving Day, Cleveland wrote to his father, describing a meeting he had with Maury on the matter. "Maury having desired to see me I sent him word at 11 am that I was at leisure. He came to the office looking ill at ease—evidently felt weak & sat down, looking into the fire & proceeded with what I should term an explanation and justification," he said. He went on to describe how Maury had submitted an article the previous summer to *The New York Herald*, but General Myer had wanted something "more popular," so at his request Maury prepared *The Galaxy* article, with the Signal Office furnishing the woodcuts that illustrated it. "That only 3–4 pages were copied and even then full credit was given to the office—it not being proper to mention my name as he would have been glad to have done. The pamphlet indeed having been a public one it was not real plagiarism to copy it," Cleveland admitted.[139]

In an effort to vindicate Cleveland, Robert took it upon himself to visit the publishers of *The Galaxy*, Sheldon & Co., at their New York offices to seek retribution. He learned that the publishers had agreed to pay Maury $200 for the work, but after Cleveland sent them a letter explaining the situation they declined to pay. "Maury gave them the impression or stated that the department consented to the use of your pamphlet in this way—I can't believe that Gen. Myer would conspire with Maury to cheat Sheldon & Co. out of $200 in this thieving way, by agreeing to have Maury put his name to your writing and sell it for original. If he does he is as bad as Maury."[140] Maury continued to work for the Signal Service until 1875, when he retired. He eventually became a correspondent for *The New York Herald*, writing about weather.[141]

A Growing Family and Reputation

In September, Cleveland and Fanny moved to more spacious rooms at 1305 F Street, NW, which was much closer to his work at the Signal Office.[142] "I would like to know how many times you have changed your residence, since you went to Washington, but am real glad that you are nicely fixed now," Charlotte wrote upon learning of the move.[143] It was here, on March 25, 1872, that Cleveland and Fanny welcomed into the world their firstborn son, whom they named Cleveland Jr.

That summer, Cleveland came down with typhoid fever and was forced to take a leave of absence from his duties at the Signal Office. He was absent and sick from July 24 to November 1, 1872.[144] In January 1873, he received a letter from his brother Robert, then in medical school in New York, urging him to pace himself during his recovery. "I certainly believe a respite of a few days would support you for the coming four months which are the hardest on the system," he wrote. "I am surprised that you have been at work so steadily since your recovery—our teachers tell us that it is rare that a man can work his brain with the vigor that was common before typhoid, for a period of six months after the recovery—and your case was a hard one." Robert described how a "quiz" that evening on typhus and typhoid brought to mind Cleveland's case, noting that "on looking over the record of your temp. & pulse for the fortieth time, I was impressed with the idea that your condition was at one time within the limits of great danger for ten days."[145]

On June 1, 1872, Myer authorized an increase in Cleveland's salary to $4,500 per year "as a wholly voluntary act on his part and accompanied with the express statement which he made to me," Cleveland later said, adding, "that he did this in view of the immense services that I had rendered to the Weather Bureau and the country by our first year's successful work and that he wished it to be understood that his meteorologist must be recognized as being on par, in the importance of his work, with the Superintendent of the Coast Survey, the Secretary of the Smithsonian and the Professors of Astronomy at the Naval Observatory."[146]

Cleveland's work during his first years at the Signal Service has been described as "very strenuous."[147] Even after the appointment of assistants—namely Maury and First Lieutenant Robert Craig (who had been with the service since February 1871)—to share in the duties of creating and issuing forecasts,[148] Cleveland's schedule left him with little free time. When a member of the Board of Directors of the Cincinnati Observatory, Lewis Mills, wrote Cleveland in April 1873 to express his concern that Cleveland's "overwhelming duties" prevented him from responding to requests for advice regarding the construction of a new observatory, Cleveland wrote back with admonishment. "My 'overwhelming duties' consist in work that is generally considered to be one of the most responsible labors that any man is engaged in, it occupies me from 9 am to 3 pm, from 6 pm to 8 pm and from 11 pm to 2 am, daily, Sundays included, as these are my regular office hours," he said in response, obviously frustrated at Mills's apparent lack of understanding. "You may judge from this how much leisure or strength I have to do aught else."[149]

The work of Cleveland and his colleagues who prepared the tri-daily probabilities gained the notice of the public and the press and became a fixture in the daily lives of Americans. Their work was so familiar, in fact, that the term "probabilities" itself became synonymous with the government officials—both in Washington, D.C., and posted at stations across the country—engaged in producing and distributing the forecasts and harkened back to the moniker first applied to Cleveland during his days in Cincinnati several years earlier. "Yesterday was a gloomy day," began an editorial in the *New Orleans Republican* on March 31, 1872. "Old Probabilities said it would be, and he seldom misses in his calculations."[150] Another example could be found by readers of the *Wilmington Daily Commercial* in Delaware on November 1 of that year. "We have had a most tempestuous time all Thursday and Friday with the most disastrous effects. 'Probabilities' here put up his red danger flag, by day, and his red lights by night, and those days it blew fearfully."[151] The "red danger flag" and lights referred to a new system of cautionary signals that went into effect in November 1872. As *The New York Herald* reported, "The signal decided upon by General Myer is a square red flag, with a square centre of black, for denoting danger by day, and a red lantern to denote danger by night."[152]

The Evening Star of Washington, D.C., attempted to dispel the myth of a sage "old gentleman," single-handedly penning the predictions from his cloistered quarters at the Signal Office (even though this description, other than the reference to age, could have applied to Cleveland during his first year on the job), but in doing so suggested that Myer, not Cleveland, deserved to be known by the nickname "Old Probabilities":

> The idea which may be entertained by some that the weather prognostications sent out by the signal office daily are really made by a certain old gentleman deeply versed in meteorological lore, and to whom the irreverent appellation of "Old Probabilities" properly belongs, is altogether fallacious. If that name belongs to any one in particular, it ought, perhaps, to attach to Gen. Albert J. Myer, the chief signal officer, under whose general direction weather predictions are made—all except the "Old," which does not apply. Gen. Myer, however, has no direct agency in compelling the daily reports, that work being assigned to three gentlemen—Lieut. Robert Craig, of the United States army, and Professors Cleveland Abbe and Thompson B. Morey [sic]—who alternate in making the daily meteorological forecasts. None of these gentlemen are old men. Lieut. Craig is a graduate of West Point, and is about twenty-eight years of age; Professor Abbe, who was formerly director of the Cincinnati observatory, is but thirty-five, and Professor Morey, who was a few years ago president of a Kentucky college, is about the same age. The professors have no connection with the military service, but are simply employed to aid in compiling the reports. All of these gentlemen are enthusiastic meteorologists, and were selected with a special view to their peculiar qualifications for the positions which they now fill. It will be seen from this statement of facts that "Old Probabilities" is a myth, and that the public is indebted for the daily weather reports printed in the press to three young men, all of whom, as we have before stated, are under thirty-five years of age.[153]

In 1922, a former Signal Service employee named Henry Calver wrote to *The Evening* Star to correct them on the error the newspaper had made half a century earlier. "It so happens I was working in the weather office myself at that time, fifty years ago, assisting the three gentlemen mentioned in the article in question in getting out the weather reports," he said. "Prof. Cleveland Abbe, and not Gen. Myer was really 'Old Prob.'" Calver also pointed out the misspelling of Maury's name.[154]

The term "probabilities" would continue to be used until 1876, when it was changed to "indications," and that term, in turn, was followed by the more familiar "forecasts," which the Signal Service adopted in April 1889.[155]

On October 15, 1873, Cleveland moved his family again, this time to a house at 1825 I Street, NW, which he rented from Mary A. Hoover for $800 per year for a period of two years. Just a few weeks later, on November 1, Cleveland and Fanny's second son was born. It took a while to settle on a name, and there was some disagreement among members of the extended Abbe family. "We all say, don't call [the] baby—Irving—We think Paul, or some solid name, better & more manly," Charlotte wrote several months after the baby was born.[156] Cleveland and Fanny eventually settled on the name Truman, after Truman J. Backus, an "intimate college classmate" of Cleveland's.[157] "Heaven protect the babies!" Robert wrote his brother upon hearing the news. "I'm glad it's a boy, for they are my special favorites. Yours must be brought up to be powerful men in mind and body—and I know they will one day be shining lights."[158]

Both baby Truman and his older brother, Cleveland Jr., suffered from health issues early on, ranging from eczema to gastrointestinal issues. "Your boys are giving you considerable trouble to be sure," wrote Cleveland's brother Robert. "But my firm belief is that the constant appearance of the trouble in them is not due so much to their inheritance of it as to their irregular diet." Robert, who by this time had finished medical school and become a doctor, told Cleveland that babies "should never have potatoes or mixed food put in their stomachs" nor should they ever have "the run of the table." Robert claimed that milk should be the only food given to children until they are "five, six or seven years old." He also advised that the "bowels of the child should invariably be kept open and this can be done perfectly by diluting the milk one half with a mucilaginous drink composed of oatmeal water, made by putting a teaspoonful of oatmeal to a pint of water."[159]

In the same letter, Robert mentioned that their father had brought home the latest issue of *The Phrenological Journal*, a publication by Samuel R. Wells, who, along with brothers Orson and Lorenzo Fowler, had by the mid-nineteenth century created a thriving business dedicated to the pseudoscience. Based on a woodcut portrait of Cleveland that accompanied it, the article attempted to paint a clear and complete picture of his attributes and moral character:

> In our portrait we have the indication of a very fine nature; the temperament is sensitive, the mind very active and exceedingly nice and accurate in all its efforts. The head expands as it rises, being comparatively narrow at the base, and increasing in width all the way to the top. Such a person is a natural theorist and reasoner, and believes that everything in nature has a well ordered cause. Observe the squareness of the upper part of the forehead, Causality and Comparison being very prominent. The side-head at the temples also expands as it rises, indicating large Constructiveness and Ideality, or a capac-

> ity for comprehending combinations, and the ability to invent and study out truth. He has also large Spirituality, which gives an appreciation of the higher forms of truth, and a sense of the life to come, a feeling that, as regards the world and creation,
>
> "All are but parts of one stupendous whole,
> Whose body nature is, and God the soul."
>
> His Veneration gives him a profound sense of creative wisdom and power, a reverence for all that is great and sacred. His Benevolence is strong enough to make him sympathetical, kindly, liberal, and especially tender toward the helpless and the aged. He appears to have a well-developed crown, showing aspiration, self-reliance, the sense of reputation, and a hunger for appreciation by his friends, if not by people generally. He appears to have large Cautiousness, which gives prudence and guardedness; and we think his Combativeness is considerably larger than his Destructiveness; that he has, therefore, enterprise, earnestness, and spirit, without severity, harshness, or cruelty of disposition. He appreciates wit and poetry, philosophy, spirituality, art, refinement, and is capable of winning a position in the intellectual and social circles of life.[160]

The description seemed to depict Cleveland accurately, according to his family. "Mother and the girls say it is perfectly portrayed," Robert said. "I think it a little 'airy.'"[161]

Its sensational nature aside, the article underscored the degree to which Cleveland's life became a matter of public interest. As he rose in prominence in his professional life, he became something of a celebrity. In 1875, he participated in the Grand National Spelling Match, which took place at Lincoln Hall, "one of the finest auditoriums in the Nation's Capital during the nineteenth century."[162] Two separate contests took place in an event whose tickets sold "in a lively manner," according to a brief article that appeared in *The National Republican*. "The first will be between two classes of ladies and gentlemen, led by Professor Cleveland Abbe, meteorologist at the weather bureau, who will spell 'probabilities,'" the newspaper reported.[163] Years later, Cleveland became the subject of a notice in the Personal Intelligence column of *The Washington Post*, after "suffering from the effects of a severe fall on the ice."[164] Even his autograph garnered attention. In 1905, a signed, eight-page letter he had written in 1873 appeared for sale in a magazine for collectors with a price of twenty-five cents.[165]

2017 I Street

By the time Cleveland and Fanny's third son, William, was born, on June 27, 1877, the family had outgrown their quarters at 1825 I Street, NW, and decided another move was in order. On June 20, Cleveland purchased a three-story, red-brick, late-Georgian townhouse at 2017 I Street, NW, just two blocks down the street, for $10,000.[166] The price "was not too great for a man on a small government salary," according to Truman, who also noted there was less demand for such large houses in the years following the Civil War, thus resulting in a more modest price.[167] The property had also experienced some neglect and, before the family could move in, Cleveland saw to several improvements, including the removal of a row of outbuildings behind the house that consisted of "a bake house, a smoke house, an ash house, a privy, and a stable."[168] When moving day finally came, the older two Abbe boys were eager to assist their father in transporting the contents of his voluminous library to their new home. "I well remember the September day we moved in, soon after my younger brother was born," Truman recalled. "My older brother and I thought that we were most helpful as we loaded our toy express wagon with Father's books and made trip after trip from 1825 to 2017 I Street. And in what a confusion of boxes we slept that first night!"[169] As Truman later described:

> Our impressions of the early days were all of good times. We rode velocipedes around the bare floor of the library, the big second floor front room, and we swung in a big rope swing in the second floor back. We remember well the spaces between the wide boards of the floors, into which we used to poke our paper soldiers. There was one very wide crack between the boards just in front of father's desk that we could get at only when father had gone to the office. Whole companies of soldiers would disappear down that crack in one morning. We remember with great pleasure going with father to the Weather Bureau, first at 17th and G Streets, and filling broken thermometers with red alcohol and so making new ones for ourselves. We were not very old when we used to make barometers with old glass tubing, dirty mercury and empty bottles. I could not have been much more than ten years of age when father thought I knew enough about barometers to take a very crude one that I had made at home and at the Weather Bureau and demonstrate its making to the other children at school.[170]

The house had a storied history, having been built by Timothy Caldwell, a wealthy Philadelphia businessman, over a period of years beginning in 1802.

In 1808, Caldwell sold the house to Gideon Granger, who served as postmaster general from 1801 to 1814. Granger sold it back to Caldwell in 1813.[171] Of the many residents who called the house home over the years, the most famous was James Monroe, who lived there during his tenure as secretary of state and, later, as secretary of war under President James Madison. When Monroe became president in 1817, he continued to reside there for several months, as the White House, which had been burned by the British in 1814, was still undergoing reconstruction. One legend has it that Madison, who was at the house during the War of 1812 for a meeting with then Secretary of State Monroe and Secretary of War John Armstrong Jr., was forced to flee the approaching enemy by riding his horse through the halls of the residence.[172]

Caldwell had intended to create "the handsomest house in the capital city,"[173] and his efforts certainly reflect this goal. One of the outstanding features of the exterior is the large, semicircle fanlight, or lunette, above the front door, with three concentric rows of glass, allowing sunlight to filter into the vestibule. This is flanked on the top by an ornamental arch with a scroll keystone at the apex. Narrow pilasters on either side of the door give the appearance of small supporting columns. To the right of the front door are three "six-over-six" double-hung windows, complete with splayed lintels, also adorned with ornamental keystones in the center. A row of four identical windows spans the second-floor exterior. Cleveland added a third floor in 1881, expanding on what had originally been a dormered attic, and added two dormers to the top floor, each with a small fanlight on top.[174] "To those top-floor windows, he often took us boys, in the afternoons, to watch the crows flying back to their rookery in Arlington, or to observe gathering thunderclouds as they moved down over Rock Creek or the Potomac toward the city," Truman said of his days growing up in the house. "It was from those windows that we were first shown the Pole Star, the Great Dipper and the Little Dipper, and occasionally the quivering lights of the Aurora Borealis."[175]

The house contains some twenty rooms, with several added by Cleveland.[176] Many of the rooms feature fireplaces as well as decorative plaster moldings.[177] The staircase joining the first and second floors is festooned with a decorative, bas-relief trim made of stucco in the form of garlands, giving the appearance of vines elegantly climbing up the side. It also features slender balusters and a mahogany banister, which the Abbe boys reveled in sliding down when they did not want to descend the twenty-five steps by foot.[178] One of the larger rooms on the second floor—which spans the entire width of the house—served as Cleveland's library, where he installed custom bookshelves along all the walls to house his voluminous collection of literature on a variety of subjects (though mostly meteorology), along with several complete series of scientific journals, including his prized collection of *Astronomische Nachrichten* given to him by his father years earlier. Atop the bookshelves sat various illustrations of astronomical phenomena, including an early photograph of the moon by the chemist and photographer John William Draper. It was here that Cleveland did most of his work outside of the Signal Office. A standing desk allowed him to "think more clearly and consistently"[179] than when seated.

Works of art could be found throughout the house, from a plaster bust of Julius Caesar atop one of the bookcases in the library to a statue of Venus de Milo in the front hall. Watercolors of English castles adorned the parlor and oil paintings of Cleveland's grandparents hung on the walls of the dining room.

The house became not only the focal point of family life for the Abbes but also a fixture in their social interactions. Cleveland entertained many visitors—including several international meteorologists—and Fanny hosted meetings of the various groups in which she was involved, including The Women's Anthropological Society and the Ladies' Historical Society, where she was known for bringing "a genial method and a spirit of great fairness into all discussions."[180]

The location of both of the Abbe residences on I Street not only provided Cleveland with easy access to work—it took less than ten minutes to walk to the Signal Office on G Street—but also put him in close proximity to the residence of his boss, General Myer, who lived just down the street at 1827 I Street, NW.[181] This arrangement, it seems, proved disagreeable at times. One August evening in 1874, while Fanny and the boys were away on vacation in Upstate New York, Cleveland, who was feeling "particularly & expressly lazy," decided to go to bed at half past seven, hoping to rise early the next morning to work on an article on meteorology he was preparing for the *The American Cyclopedia*. Around eight o'clock, his housekeeper woke him with the news that General Myer was at the front door. Cleveland told her to go downstairs and explain the situation to him. When she did, Myer exclaimed with a laugh, "What? So early!" and promptly left. "Somehow I always feel better when I thus miss seeing him," Cleveland confessed in a letter to Fanny the next day. "I suppose I am foolish & wicked but I can't help pining for freedom & a telescope." Cleveland's apparent disappointment with his position—or his superior—was evident in his recollection of what his Cincinnati friend and observatory board member Julius Dexter had said to him. "Dexter's last letter 'You can come back if you will but say the world' keeps ringing in my ears," he wrote Fanny.[182] "Perhaps some good angel will ere long effect my deliverance. As for my taking hold of my own boot straps and lifting myself off the earth—that is hard to do."[183]

CHAPTER SIX

Science and Service (1878–1908)

> Although the study of science and the pursuit of research is most fascinating and elevating, yet no man should be satisfied therewith. It is right to be content from day to day, but never satisfied. The highest type of man is he who seeks to be most useful to his fellow men.
>
> —Cleveland Abbe, 1911

On July 20, 1878, Cleveland Abbe arrived by train in Colorado Springs on a journey to observe the total solar eclipse of July 29—the first visible in the United States since the eclipse of 1869. Unlike the eclipse of nearly a decade earlier, which only a handful of scientists, including Cleveland, had observed, this eclipse was the astronomical event of the decade and promised to put Colorado—not even two years into its statehood—on the map and at the center of attention.

"Colorado is certainly a wonderland, and can lay special claim to that distinction this year on account of the total eclipse which is billed to come off within its borders the 29th day of next month," read a brief notice in the *Sunshine Courier* of Boulder County a month prior to the event. "Already some enterprising genius has planned a mammoth excursion from the cities on the lakes to witness it, and is advertising it largely. He certainly ought to succeed in his enterprise. Just think of seeing Colorado with a total eclipse thrown in, all in one excursion trip!"[1]

Despite the influx of tourists and pleasure seekers, this was not a vacation for Cleveland. He had gone to Colorado on the orders of General Albert Myer to reach the summit of Pikes Peak "and carry out, at that place, the special instructions received by him from the Chief Signal Officer of the Army in reference to an observation of the total eclipse of the Sun on July

29, 1878."[2] Before he could begin for the summit, however, Cleveland had to attend to the shipment of scientific instruments the Signal Service had sent, which arrived a day earlier. He arranged for a mule train "of about twelve mules or burros" to aid in carrying the equipment up the mountain.

Cleveland found Colorado Springs to be "a surprisingly delightful town." He checked into his hotel, the Crawford House, which billed itself as the "oldest and best hotel in Colorado Springs," boasting a "table equal to any in the state." In a letter to Fanny, he described it as "very pleasant of course it's plain & comfortable." He found the local inhabitants to be "far better" than those he encountered in the small towns of Illinois, Missouri, and Kansas. "They are not farmers at all but merchants, landowners, travelers, &c." He noted there was "an enlarged jolly spirit so that I feel at home & pleased," adding, with a sense of longing, "I know you would be delighted here." He also marveled at the clearness of the sky and purity of the air. "This morning the sky is everywhere as clear as a bell, and the blue is such a deep fine solid blue that it is inspiring to an astronomer to look at it."[3]

In Colorado Springs, Cleveland met up with Samuel Pierpont Langley, director of the Allegheny Observatory in Pennsylvania and a frequent correspondent of his. Langley was the Signal Service's guest on the expedition and was accompanied by a party that included his brother, John W. Langley. Cleveland set off for the summit with Sergeant William Black, the Signal Service observer at Pikes Peak, on the July 22, reaching the Lake House—about halfway up—that evening. The next day, Cleveland completed the trek to the summit, "taking the walk very leisurely," he later reported, "as I hoped thereby to lessen the injurious effect of the rarefied air upon my system."

That same day, Myer, having decided to personally take charge of the Signal Service eclipse expedition, set off from Washington, D.C., accompanied by Lieutenant Henry Harrison Chase Dunwoody, who served as acting signal officer and assistant to Myer.

At the summit, with an elevation of more than fourteen thousand feet, Cleveland found the Signal Service station "to be in a very bad condition" and ordered "tents to be pitched and beds prepared for the night." He employed temporary workers to help in repairing the roof of the station, through which "continual rains and snows" were leaking.

The next several days were spent setting up and preparing a five-inch equatorial refractor telescope—on loan from the Naval Observatory in Washington, D.C.—through which Langley was to make his observations of the eclipse. Everything went well initially, despite the weather. "Rather disagreeable weather, but tents all up and both parties provided for," Cleveland telegraphed Myer on July 25. "Dew-point observations successful. The prevailing weather thus far has been—temperature 45°, cloudy, foggy, and hailing."[4] On July 27, two days before the eclipse, Cleveland telegraphed again that conditions had worsened. "Two snow-storms with gales, endangering tents and instruments. No satisfactory glimpse of sun to-day. Very little progress in preparing for Monday." Just when all hope seemed lost, the umbraphiles' luck turned around, as Sunday—the day before the eclipse—"dawned and continued with a perfectly clear sky, and, of course, very dry air, which continued throughout Monday."[5] Cleveland's luck, however, was about to take a turn for the worse and, over the course of the next day, he would come close to sacrificing himself for the sake of his scientific curiosity and determination.

While several among the parties—including Langley—reported symptoms of "mountain sickness," they were not severely affected by the extreme altitude and thin air. "It was otherwise with myself," said Cleveland, who had been stricken by violent pains throughout his head every day since he arrived on the summit. By Saturday night, the affliction had become unbearable and "had settled into a steady terrible pain in the cerebellum and upper portion of the spinal column." Despite his critical condition, Cleveland refused to leave the summit—or to move at all. "I concluded to lie still throughout Sunday and until Monday noon, thinking that this would be my best preparation for the eclipse of Monday afternoon," he later told Myer, who had since arrived on the summit and ordered that Cleveland be moved. "In this condition you found me Sunday evening, and I cannot doubt but that your order sending me immediately down on a stretcher to the Lake House was absolutely necessary in order to save life."[6]

Early Sunday evening, several members of the eclipse party secured Cleveland to a stretcher and carefully carried him down the side of the mountain. It was midnight before they reached the Lake House—just over ten thousand feet in elevation—where he would spend the night. "Of my own will I certainly would not have left the summit, since I was determined, if possible, to study the solar corona under the unique circumstances of high optical power and pure thin air," he insisted. "It, however, now appears that these observations would have been far less interesting than those that I was able to make with the naked eye at the Lake House."

By noon Monday—the day of the eclipse—Cleveland had been taken out of the house and laid outside, "upon a gentle slope facing southwest, where I studied such phenomena as were visible during totality." Workers hastily assembled a makeshift device around him, consisting of a board nailed to a wooden crossbar, supported by stakes driven into the ground on either side of him. Upon the board was attached a piece of paper, whose plane was nearly perpendicular with Cleveland's line of sight. "My head being propped up, I easily kept my gaze fixed upon the sun during the whole of totality," he later recalled. "By slightly tipping the board about its revolvable horizontal axis I could easily bring the sun to be just visible over its upper edge while I drew in such details as I saw, and that too, as it seemed at the time, with very considerable accuracy. For steadiness, ease, convenience, and accuracy, the whole arrangement was highly satisfactory."[7]

Despite not having any telescope or other optical instruments at his disposal—and with even his stronger spectacles, which he usually wore "when looking for faint stars or other celestial details," left on the summit—Cleveland was able to make detailed observations during the nearly three minutes of totality. As he gazed upward toward the heavens, squinting his eyes with a determination that only the most ardent astronomers could possess, he witnessed sheets of flickering white light dance from the edges of the sun's corona, while flashes of blazing red flames protruded out in various directions at the moment the moon shrouded its celestial companion from earthly view. Like a painter feverishly applying brushstrokes to a canvas while fixated on a fleeting subject, he quickly sketched what he saw on the paper in front of him, capturing as much detail as possible. About an hour after the eclipse had ended, he returned to his bed in the Lake House, "quite tired out."[8]

The following afternoon, Cleveland had recuperated enough to borrow a pony from the proprietress of the Lake House, Mrs. Copley, and descended the mountain trail to Colorado Springs, where he spent the remainder of the week as he waited for the supplies to make their way down from the summit, which were delayed "owing to the scarcity of pack animals." While he waited, he made a side trip to Denver, where he met with several astronomers, comparing notes on the eclipse and other matters. On Monday, August 5, he boarded a train for Washington, D.C., where he arrived four days later and returned to his regular duties at the Signal Office.

Standard Time

One of the issues to which Cleveland devoted much of his time during his early years with the Signal Service was the lack of standardization of timekeeping among observers. Prior to the rise of railroad travel in the early to mid-nineteenth century, few Americans experienced a need to deviate from their local timekeeping, which was dictated by Earth-sun geometry. Farmers, local businesses, and interested citizens alike observed noon at any given day at the time the sun reached its highest point in the sky above them—known as solar noon. The time at which this occurs, however, varies as one travels east or west, crossing different meridians or lines of longitude, across the globe. To account for these variations, local municipalities kept their own local time, which was often calibrated daily based on solar noon.

As Americans began to travel more frequently—and to more distant places—the difference in local time from one location to another presented challenges. It was not uncommon for frequent travelers to carry printed charts or tables displaying the differences in time between major cities in the United States. Cleveland's own pocket diary for 1870, for example, included in one of its introductory pages a table showing the difference in time between New York and various cities lying to the east or west. "When it is 12 o'clock, noon, at New York City, it will be morning at all places *west* of New York, and after noon at all places *east*," the table explained. According to the table, when it was noon in New York, it would be 11:49:38 a.m. in Baltimore, 11:47:53 a.m. in Washington, D.C., and 12:11:50 p.m. in Boston.[9]

The lack of standardized time presented challenges not only to rail travel but also for the collection and analysis of observations of geophysical phenomena, such as weather and the aurora borealis, or northern lights. "Precision of time at all stations was absolutely demanded by the Signal Service system of work," Cleveland wrote, "and the great annoyance caused by the uncertainties in the local standard of time used by our voluntary observers and in a few cases by our regular observers had been peculiarly felt by myself in studies upon the phenomena of thunderstorms, earthquakes, auroras, and meteors."[10]

In 1876, as part of the chief signal officer's annual report, Cleveland presented a detailed report he prepared on the aurora of April 7, 1874, which was visible across the northern United States, from Dakota Territory to Minnesota to Maine (and as far south as Kentucky and present-day Oklahoma), as well as parts of Canada. "In the study of these observations the next step has been to convert all the items relating to local times into a uniform system of Washington time, by applying the proper corrections for longitude," he said. "The errors of the observer's [sic] clocks and watches, and even the standards of time used by them, are generally not stated in their reports, so that the uncertainty of this vitally important matter will be found to throw obscurity upon some interesting features that might otherwise have presented no difficulty."[11]

Cleveland had been interested in standard time since he was director of the Cincinnati Observatory, when he learned "much inconvenience" was felt throughout the city for the want of accurate timekeeping. He reported to the city council that the observatory had "long furnished such time to certain clock makers in this city whenever they have desired it," noting the observatory was "able to furnish the city directly and regularly as often as may be required with the correct time."[12]

In May 1875, Cleveland appealed to Frederick Augustus Porter Barnard, president of the American Metrological Society—a professional organization dedicated to standards of measurement—and convinced him to establish a committee dedicated to the proposal and implementation of standard time. Barnard, who also served as president of Columbia College in New York, appointed Cleveland as chair of the committee, which submitted its report four years later, in May 1879. The report found that some seventy-five standards of time existed across the United States, generally to satisfy the needs of local railroads. To simplify the way time was observed across the country, the committee adopted a system—originally suggested by mathematician Benjamin Peirce—of "standard meridians, exactly four, five, or six hours west of the meridian of Greenwich."[13] Under this system, five zones were suggested, each spaced fifteen degrees of longitude apart, corresponding with the distance Earth rotates in one hour. These were to be known as "Eastern Time," "Atlantic Time," "Valley Time," "Mountain Time," and "Pacific Time." (Ultimately, the "Atlantic" and "Eastern" time zones essentially switched names, while "Valley Time" became what is now known as "Central Time.")

It would take several more years before Cleveland's quest for standard time became a reality. In May 1882, Cleveland drafted a joint resolution that would be passed by both houses of Congress and signed by President Chester A. Arthur, authorizing and requesting him "to call an International Conference to fix on and recommend for universal adoption a common prime meridian to be used in the reckoning of longitude and in the regulation of time throughout the world."[14] Two years later, in October 1884, delegates to the International Meridian Conference—representing more than twenty countries—met in Washington, D.C., with Cleveland serving as part of the U.S. delegation. Among the resolutions adopted at the conference were those stipulating a single prime meridian, which it was decided would be the meridian passing through the observatory at Greenwich, in the United Kingdom, along with the adoption of a "universal day," defined as a mean solar day "to begin for all the world at the moment of mean midnight of the initial meridian, coinciding with the beginning of the civil day and date of that meridian; and is to be counted from zero up to twenty-four hours."[15]

"The adoption of twenty-four successively labeled hours, beginning at midnight and ending at the next midnight, was one of Father's early and continued dreams," Cleveland's son Truman wrote.[16] Cleveland himself saw the achievement as a defining accomplishment of his career. In fact, in a letter to his sister Harriet, written on his fiftieth birthday, in 1888, he described it in an almost spiritual manner, placing it in the context of his own life and mortality. "Time has dealt lightly with me in my youth and now that old age dawns, I expect him to stand at a respectful distance," he wrote. "He knows me in fact, Old Time does—he knows me as one of the great modern reformers of standard time—the one who called the International Congress together to decree that Time shall be no longer, and he has slyly whispered to his minions 'Let Old Abbe have all he wants of it.'"[17]

International Simultaneous Observations

The systems of simultaneous observations that Cleveland began in Cincinnati, which General Myer adapted and expanded nationwide, enabled weather forecasting over relatively large areas of the country for the benefit of commerce and science alike. The obvious extension was to create a system whereby observations from locations in different countries could be taken at the same time—and shared immediately via telegraphic communications—to enable forecasting across even larger areas of the world. In his first annual report upon taking charge of the nation's weather service, Myer alluded to the practicality of such a system. "The idea of a worldwide system of telegraphic weather reports is not as chimerical today as was thirty years ago the workings of the electric telegraph itself."[18]

Cleveland had begun taking steps toward this goal in 1869, as he was organizing his weather observation network in Cincinnati. He sent a note to French mathematician and astronomer Urbain Le Verrier, director of the Paris Observatory and president of the Scientific Association of France, who had established a telegraphic storm warning service for that country in 1863, informing him that he had been authorized to inaugurate a system of telegraphic weather reports from observers to the west and south of Cincinnati, initially comprising twelve stations, but that it was only a beginning. "Mr. Cleveland Abbe intends to give it a greater development, and he expresses the thought that the daily transmission of some meteorological problems of America by the new transoceanic cable would be of great use for France," Le Verrier wrote.[19]

After he began working for the Signal Service, Cleveland enlisted Myer's help in securing the cooperation of other national weather services—primarily in Europe and Canada—to begin exchanging observations taken at the same time. Myer, as Cleveland put it, was able to achieve a "remarkably successful combination of the whole civilized world in the study of the atmosphere as a unit, so that the largest storms could be studied on a scale commensurate with their size and importance."[20] In late 1872, Myer made arrangements with Professor George Templeton Kingston, chief of the Dominion Meteorological Service of Canada, for the exchange of observations made at seven Canadian stations, using the same cipher of coded words employed by the American service.

"To the United States the reports received from the Dominion are like those of vidette stations against the storms moving upon the lake region from the north, and thence traversing the Northern-Middle and Eastern States, and the adjacent sea-coast," Myer reported. "It is to be hoped the system may be extended in the Canadas, and the co-operation be yet closer, this connection of the services becoming the first link in the grand chain of interchanged international telegraphic reports, destined with a higher civilization to bind together the signal-services of the world." In addition to Canada, Myer hoped for a mutual exchange of observations with the islands of the West Indies, once the authorizations of the respective governments were in place, and "before the opening of the stormy spring season."[21]

Cleveland noted the satisfaction of his superior stemmed from seeing the work as an evolution of the original mandate to take meteorological observations across the United States, as well as an extension of the science of weather prediction. "Myer was pleased not only with the grandeur of the undertaking as a natural development of Signal Service work, but because it promised to finally give us some knowledge about the beginning and the ending of the many storms that we saw flitting across the American continent."[22]

In September 1873, Myer traveled to Vienna, to represent the United States at the International Meteorological Congress, which brought together delegates from nations across Europe and as far away as Turkey and China. The goal was to build on the foundation of an international conference held the previous year in Leipzig in order to establish an organization to facilitate the exchange of ideas—and data—between the various countries involved in meteorological work. The Vienna Congress would eventually lead to the establishment of the International Meteorological Organization, which would ultimately become the World Meteorological Organization.

During the seventh meeting of the congress, the chairman, Dr. R. H. Scott, director of the Meteorological Office in London, read aloud a letter from

Myer. "Gentlemen, I have the honour to submit the following proposition," it began. "That it is desirable that, with a view to their exchange, at least one uniform observation of such character as to be suitable for the preparation of synoptic charts be taken and recorded daily and simultaneously at as many stations as practicable throughout the world."[23] The proposal was adopted.

Cleveland recalled the enthusiasm he felt when Myer told him the news. "I shall never forget the pleasure and satisfaction that he evinced when, upon his return to Washington, he said to me: 'I have followed your advice quite closely; I strictly avoided all discussions and controversies as to theories and methods, and stated that we did not care how the observations were made and reduced, provided only they were strictly simultaneous and promptly forwarded.'"[24] Myer said he had obtained assurances from several European weather bureaus that observations would be sent to the United States and had no doubt that others would soon follow suit. "I found all the governments favorably disposed toward the United States, and even more willing to co-operate with us than among themselves," he told Cleveland.

On July 1, 1875, the Signal Service began publishing the *Bulletin of International Simultaneous Observations*, which, beginning in 1877, included daily maps of the Northern Hemisphere. "The data in the bulletins and charts were primarily intended as the basis for studies of the dynamics of the atmosphere and not for climatic study as such, and it is a mistake to treat them from the latter point of view," Cleveland explained. Owing to the amount of time and labor required to collect and process the data, there was an obvious lag between when the observations were taken and when the bulletins were published. Cooperating observers worldwide were instructed to send their observations, by mail, on the fifteenth and final day of each month to the Signal Office in Washington, D.C., where Cleveland "organized a clerical force and rules by which the data were all worked over into a homogeneous system in metric and English measures, the heavy work of getting out the publication daily and regularly proceeded with unerring mechanical accuracy and steadiness year after year."[25] Thus, the first bulletin, published in July 1875, contained observations for January 1 of that year. The final bulletin, published in July 1885, reported observations from June 30, 1884, with "the general rule," according to Cleveland, "being that the bulletin of observations on any date should be published just one year subsequently."[26] The daily charts continued to be published through December 31, 1887. Over the course of this period, Cleveland and his team processed data from some 459 land stations and nearly 600 ships at sea, representing more than five million daily simultaneous observations.[27]

Myer described the outset of the work in his annual report for 1874, extolling the value he foresaw it providing for years to come. "It is not possible, nor is it necessary, here to dwell at length upon the advantages time will develop in the progress of this work. They will readily suggest themselves to any who propose to devote themselves to the studies it will make possible." According to Myer, the work "secures for the United States the wise and cordial co-operation of a world for the solution of questions upon which the United States has entered, and will secure for the world, it is hoped, a better knowledge of the atmosphere and insight into atmospheric changes than has been hitherto possible."[28]

To Cleveland, the endeavor marked a milestone in scientific achievement. "Undoubtedly, the 'Bulletin of International Simultaneous Observations,' which resulted from these efforts of Gen. Myer, represents the finest piece of international co-operation in scientific work that the world had ever seen," he later said.[29] The work garnered attention well beyond the scientific community. In its November 1875 issue, *The Atlantic Monthly* included the bulletin in its monthly review of recent literature. "We see in this the fulfillment of the hope held forth by General Myer in his report on the United States signal service for 1874, that we should soon be able to draw conclusions from a larger area of the earth's surface, and therefore be able to prognosticate with greater certainty of truth," the literary magazine claimed. "Other sciences will gain greatly by this advance in meteorology."[30]

Family Matters

While Cleveland devoted himself tirelessly to his work, he also made time for his family, especially during special occasions, such as birthdays. When his mother, Charlotte, turned sixty-two on March 23, 1879, Cleveland decided a grand celebration was in order. The fact that Cleveland Jr. would turn seven two days later was all the more reason to celebrate. The centerpiece of the celebration, which took place at the house of Cleveland's brother Charlie, in the Le Droit Park neighborhood of Washington, D.C., was an elaborate cake, designed by Cleveland himself, which featured sixty-two candles. The candles on the cake itself were carefully arranged in three tiers—the bottom tier contained eighteen candles; the middle tier, slightly smaller in diameter, held twelve candles; the smallest tier, on the top, featured seven candles, representing young Cleve's age. In the center of the cake, a large, two-foot-tall candle towered above all the others. Twenty-four smaller candles adorned the table, surrounding the cake, to complete the total. In addition to Cleveland, Fanny, and their three sons, those present included Charlie, his wife, and their two children, Cleveland and Charlie's sister Helen, and, of course, Charlotte, the guest of honor.[31] Cleveland regaled the guests with a chronology of the major life events of his mother, along with an original composition in her honor:

Come let us celebrate—here with our families
Her whom we love to call Mother and Friend;
Another festival now we commemorate
Renew our bonds and refresh the hearts love.
Light the bright tapers recalling sweet episodes
Of a young life sailing forth on its voyage;
Tell once again the sweet tales of the olden time;
Tell of events that belong to these latter days;
End with the present—with sixty and two.

Can we not stand up together and singing,
Offer up hymns of the heartiest praise?
Linking our hearts and our voices together
Gaily recalling our dear old lang syne?
All of us join in the words of the chorus
Those are the words that we each love to sing
Even the grand children know the old tune

After the feast there remaineth the blessing;
Blessings upon the good year that's to come,
Be it well filled with the choicest of favors,
End with thanksgivings at home, our sweet home.[32]

Cleveland intended the first verse to be read as the guests gathered at the table for the lighting of the birthday cake, with the second verse recited as everyone joined hands, singing "Auld Lang Syne." This was to be followed by the cutting of the cake, with the final verse spoken as guests joined in a blessing and doxology.[33]

The joy and warmth Cleveland and his family felt that day would be tempered just six months later, with the death of the family's patriarch, George Waldo Abbe, on September 25. At the age of sixty-seven, George had recently gone on a business trip to Colorado to inspect a silver mine in which he had considered investing. After descending to the depths of the mine, he returned to the surface and was overcome by heat. Upon his return to New York a week later, he complained of headaches and neuralgia on one side of his head. For several days, he continued in this state, eventually confined to bed. After the consultation of several doctors, he was eventually diagnosed with hemiplegia—paralysis on one side of his body caused by a ruptured blood vessel in his brain. He had suffered a stroke and the prognosis was grim.

"Little by little father settled into coma—and for two days knew nothing that was said," Robert said. "The last few hours of the last night I was alone with him. To all appearances unconscious, slowly breathing his life away—I could not forbear feeling he must be conscious of what was going on and whispered into his ear tender thoughts I had never spoken to him in life. This was to me unspeakably comforting, and has been so through many years. Who knows that his waiting soul did not know and hear!"[34]

George was buried in the family plot at Greenwood Cemetery in Brooklyn, following a funeral on September 28 whose attendees included former New York Governor Samuel Tilden and former New York City Mayor William Wickham.[35] He was eulogized as much for his benevolence in charity and service as he was for his business endeavors. "His whole life was spent in active work among the poor in the hospitals and in the church, He was a strong Abolitionist, and when the war broke out not only sent his sons in the army, but subscribed liberally for the outfit of others," read one obituary.[36]

As Charlotte mourned the death of her husband of more than forty years, she took solace in the comfort of her children, especially those who still lived with her—Helen, Hattie, and Robert. "Children are a great blessing, when they are brought up with the fear of God, & all do right & honour their parents," Charlotte wrote to Cleveland several years earlier. "Our children are repaying us, for all the anxieties & cares of their childhood, & I trust we may see them all walking in the ways of the Lord." Charlotte died February 19, 1885, from a stroke she suffered at her home on East 20th Street in New York.[37] She was laid to rest in the family plot at Greenwood Cemetery, next to her husband.

General Hazen

For the first decade of its weather observation and forecasting work, the Signal Service was under the direction of General Myer, who had lobbied for the service to be placed under his command at the time Congress was considering the joint resolution introduced by Representative Halbert Paine, at the urging of his constituent and friend Increase Lapham. "In general, the administration of Gen. Myer may be said to have been characterized by a remarkable degree of political sagacity," Cleveland noted, "which enabled him to control the heterogeneous elements out of which he, on the one hand, built up a new military corps in spite of the opposition of the greater part of the officers of the regular Army and, on the other hand, demonstrated the usefulness of this corps by valuable practical work in the interests of every citizen."[38]

Myer's tenure came to an abrupt end when he died on August 24, 1880, following a brief illness.[39] General Richard C. Drum, who served as adjutant general of the Army, assumed the role of acting chief signal officer for several months. His administration "was so far of a temporary nature as to give no opportunity to impress new methods and results upon the Service."[40] In December 1880, General William Babcock Hazen was appointed chief signal officer and took control of the growing weather service Myer had developed.

General Hazen "sought in every way to improve the service"[41] and his style of leadership leaned "strongly toward the encouragement of the employment of a high order of talent in both the military and the meteorological work of the Signal Service."[42]

Scandal and Controversy

Among the changes Hazen attempted was to weed out bad elements from among the ranks of the Signal Service. "His attempts to remove dishonest and incompetent men seem to have made for him many enemies," according to Cleveland. A notable example of Hazen's efforts to rid the service of corruption occurred in August 1881, when Captain Henry Howgate, the Signal Service's disbursing officer, was arrested and charged with embezzlement of more than $100,000—though the amount was later revealed to be as much as $237,000. Howgate, whom Hazen would later describe as "a sort of financial Pooh Bah,"[43] did this by drawing fraudulent checks at the Treasury, supposedly to be paid to telegraph companies. As Howgate's successor, Captain Samuel Mills, explained to Congress several years later, "He would draw and present a check for $40,000 payable to bearer, and he would go to the other counter in the Treasury and buy a draft on New York for $30,000 and put the $10,000 in his pocket, or put it all in his pocket."[44]

Howgate resigned from the Signal Service in 1880, shortly after Myer's death, and at the same time expressed an interest in becoming Myer's replacement as chief signal officer. The following year, information linking

Howgate to the embezzlement came to the attention of Hazen, who ordered an investigation that led to Howgate's arrest. Following his indictment, Howgate awaited trial in a Washington, D.C., jail but escaped during a supervised visit to his home in April 1882. Apparently, he had requested the privilege of bathing in his own bathroom. A deputy marshal and a bailiff accompanied Howgate to his residence on 13th Street. While Howgate supposedly bathed and changed his undergarments, the officers remained in the sitting room with Howgate's daughter, who proceeded to distract them. "Miss Howgate sang for the men in uniform and entertained them so pleasantly that an hour glided by before they requested the young lady to call her father," a local newspaper reported. "She was gone a long time, and then came back pale and excited."[45] Howgate's daughter told the officers she was unable to find her father, at which point they began searching for him.

A boarding house guest next door later told authorities that he heard a carriage speeding down the street, but thought nothing of it until he learned of Howgate's cunning escape, at which point he thought the carriage he heard might have been the fugitive's escape vehicle.[46]

Howgate remained on the lam for twelve years and eventually was caught when a private detective, hired by the government, spotted him in 1894, working at a rare bookstore in New York City. He had been living under the pseudonym "Henry Williams," along with a woman, Nellie Burrell, whom he had met while she was working at the Treasury Department in Washington, D.C., where they began an affair. When the detective arrested him, he is reported to have asked, "You are Captain Howgate, are you not?" to which the fugitive replied, "Yes, I am. I'm Captain Howgate. I'm caught, and I'll go with you quietly."[47]

The Howgate scandal—which made headlines in newspapers across the country—left a pall over the Signal Service, with allegations that others in the service had aided Howgate in his criminal acts. Hazen was forced to make cuts to the service's budget and his leadership suffered as a result.[48]

Another incident that reflected unfavorably on Hazen's leadership involved the enlistment in the Signal Service of William Hallett Greene, who in 1884 became the first African American to graduate from the College of the City of New York—Cleveland's alma mater. Greene, whom one newspaper described as "the colored man whose ambition is to study dry and wet bulb thermometers and the record of high and low barometers, and measure the force of the wind,"[49] tried to enlist in the Signal Service as a private upon graduation, only to have his application denied by General Hazen on the grounds that the only divisions of the Army in which African

Americans could legally serve were the four all-black regiments that existed at the time—the 9th and 10th Cavalry and the 24th and 25th Infantry. "The affirmative legislation, creating the four colored regiments, has always been construed to exclude colored enlisted men from other portions of the army, and this construction has always governed enlistments," Hazen wrote in his defense.[50]

Greene appealed to General Alexander Webb, his college president who had fought at the Battle of Gettysburg (for which he would later receive the Medal of Honor), for help. Webb wrote a letter to Secretary of War Robert Todd Lincoln, who was most displeased with Hazen's decision and decided to intervene on Greene's behalf. Lincoln sent Hazen a pointed letter, offering a personal endorsement of Greene. "Colored men have been Senators and Representatives in Congress, and have occupied many high official stations of an executive character under the National Government," he wrote. Lincoln pointed out that no distinction "is thought of in admitting or instructing them as cadets at the Military Academy or in making them officers of the army after they have graduated," and insisted that "none should be made in admitting them to the Signal Corps in any capacity which they are qualified to fill."[51]

Hazen balked, saying he would only act if ordered to do so. Lincoln then threatened to relieve the Signal Service recruiting officer, Lieutenant Benjamin M. Purssell, of his duty, should he not comply. In response, Purssell said that his "personal feelings and sympathies are all in favor of allowing Greene to enlist in the Signal Corps or any other corps or regiment of the army," but that he felt he did not have the authorization to do so.[52] Lincoln's response was to issue an edict to Hazen:

> The Chief Signal Officer of the army is hereby ordered to give such orders and instructions to officers now or hereafter serving under him as recruiting officers for the Signal Corps of the army as will prohibit the rejection as a recruit by any such recruiting officers of any applicant for enlistment in the Signal Corps on account of color or on account of the African descent of such applicant. The Chief Signal Officer will report to the Secretary of War the action taken under this order with special reference to the application of William Hallet [sic] Greene.[53]

In the end, Greene was accepted as the African American to serve in the Signal Service, having passed his entrance exam with flying colors. He reported for instruction at Fort Myer, Virginia, where Cleveland was one of the instructors of the six-month course on the duties of meteorological observers. Of the original members of Greene's class, two were dismissed, one deserted, and one failed the final exams. Among the eight remaining members, Greene raked second highest.[54]

The Study Room

One example of Hazen's attempts to improve the work—and prestige—of the Signal Service was the creation of a special group dedicated to the investigation of special problems that arose from the everyday work of the service. For this, he would need a cadre of civilian assistants "who should be favorably known for scholarship in meteorology, and who were to be free to pursue such studies, in an uninterrupted manner, as the service demanded."[55] At the center of this group was Cleveland, who had been involved in such work through the various studies he had conducted from time to time since he began his career with the Signal Service.

On January 27, 1881, Hazen issued an order establishing the Scientific and Study Division—what popularly became known as "The Study Room." The goal was to create a separate division within the Signal Service "for the purpose of scientific research and investigation into the laws of meteorology." The division also dealt with questions on matters such as "standard measurements, altitudes of signal stations, and the preparation of tables for the reduction and the conversion of meteorological observations."[56]

"At the beginning, three, and subsequently four, young men were especially engaged to assist me in the work of this room," Cleveland recalled. "The influence of the study room was felt both in and out of the office inasmuch as it was necessary to study innumerable matters bearing on the instruments and work of the stations."[57] Hazen also sought to enlist the help of various specialists employed by organizations outside the Signal Service—a group he referred to as "consulting specialists," which included such luminaries as Samuel Pierpont Langley and Alexander Graham Bell.[58]

Hazen stressed "the importance of infusing into our work every refinement of meteorological science has forced upon me the consideration of how best to combine the practical and scientific, viz: the *art* of observing, recording, and predicting, and the *science* which, by induction explains the phenomena, and, by deduction, investigates the laws on which the predictions must be based."[59]

In the first year after its establishment, the Study Room investigated such issues as standards for thermometers and barometers; the compilation of hygrometric tables for the derivation of dew point from psychrometer readings; the revision of the altitudes of Signal Service stations; the adoption of constants to be used in reducing barometric pressure readings to sea level; the possibility of using Signal Service stations for observations of atmospheric electricity; studies on the force of wind and how best to measure it; investigations into solar radiation and physics, including a study of the absorption of the sun's heat by the atmosphere; the determination of the force of gravity through observations using a pendulum, which relates to the mathematical theory of the motion of air; the preparation of tables for conversions between metric and English units; as well as the application of standard time to the taking of observations by Signal Service observers, an area of particular interest to Cleveland.[60] Many of these investigations continued over a period of years, as Cleveland and his colleagues endeavored to find ways to not only improve the work of the service but also increase the general knowledge of meteorologists in general.

Cleveland and his group also oversaw the Signal Service's library, compiled a bibliography of meteorological works, and initiated the publication of a series of "Professional Papers of the Signal Service," whose titles included "A Report on Tornadoes" by Private John P. Finley (a pioneer in the field of tornado research); "A Chronological List of Auroras" and "Memoir on Isotherms," both by Lieutenant Adolphus W. Greely; and Cleveland's "General Reports on the Solar Eclipse of 1878, July 29."

Much of the work undertaken by the members of the Study Room required more practical investigation, which in 1884 led to the establishment of a laboratory for experimental investigation, headed by Professor Thomas C. Mendenhall, a close friend of Cleveland's who had taught physics at various institutions in Ohio as well as at the Imperial University in Tokyo, Japan. The Study Room and laboratory worked hand in hand and helped establish an esprit de corps among the more practical-minded personnel at the Signal Service's headquarters in Washington, D.C., that set them apart from—and often at odds with—the bureaucrats and military leaders at the upper echelons of the organization.

"The headquarters of the Signal Corps were at that time on 'G Street,' near the War Department, and by a curious chance the two somewhat conflicting elements were housed on opposite sides of the street, the study room, the laboratory, the instrument testing division, etc., being in one building on the south side, while the offices of the Chief Signal Officer and his military aides, the property and disbursing officer, the forecasting officers, etc., were on the north," Mendenhall recalled. "That controversies between the two were on the whole rather infrequent and rarely acute was due, more than to anything else, to Abbe's unfailing good nature and general willingness to be the subject of the obloquy of both sides."[61]

Mendenhall praised Cleveland for his unwavering dedication to the science of meteorology, which, combined with his innate sense of intellectual curiosity and his amiable disposition, allowed him to assign tasks to those under him in a way that promoted a sense of teamwork and comradery. "Certainly if the workers in the study room and in the laboratory were not kept busy enough, it was no fault of Abbe's," Mendenhall asserted. "He had a singularly full and complete knowledge of the state of the science of meteorology in all parts of the world, and was continually suggesting problems that he thought demanded attention. He usually made a short visit in the laboratory every day, and it was humorously regarded as a disappointment when he did not bring us at least one new subject for experimental investigation."[62]

Cleveland's intention with the work of the Study Room was "to increase the accuracy of the work of the whole Service," and, to that end, he felt he had achieved his goal. "The study room accomplished a most important work for the Service in awakening it to the necessity of introducing a higher grade of scientific training and thought and experimental laboratory work; it began to be realized that the Signal Service was no longer able to accept meteorological and physical science as it came from the hands of outside physicists, but that it must itself provide for advanced scientific investigation if the Service was to keep up with the progress of other weather bureaus."[63]

Congress Investigates

In July 1884, Congress established a joint commission—chaired by Senator William Boyd Allison of Iowa—to investigate several scientific bureaus of the federal government, with a view toward increasing the "efficiency and economy of administration" of the bureaus. In addition to the Signal Service, the bureaus investigated included the Geological Survey, the Coast and Geodetic Survey, and the Hydrographic Office of the Navy Department.

The so-called Allison Commission spent more than a year hearing testimony from various individuals associated with the bureaus under investigation and commissioned a report from the National Academy of Sciences on the organization of scientific bureaus in the federal government.

Cleveland was among the key witnesses for the Signal Service portion of the investigation. He met with the commission on three separate occasions in December 1884 and January 1885, providing testimony that generally was favorable to the administration of the Signal Service and General Hazen's leadership.

Cleveland claimed that a transfer to a civilian bureau would result in an increase in cost and a reduction in the quality of service. When asked, for example, what the effect would be on the continuity of the service's record of observations, Cleveland said he thought it would suffer. "There is a certain stimulus to perfect accuracy and uniformity in the present work, due to the knowledge that punishment will follow any failure to do their duty, which would be lacking in a civil organization," he stressed. "For instance, I may say we have no civil organization which can legally order a man to work on Sunday without his consent, and yet our men have to do it. It is supposed a man can do as he pleases on legal holidays, but our rules are that a man shall have a legal holiday only so far as is consistent with his duties in the office."

At the same time, he admitted the majority of the work performed by the Signal Service was not inherently militaristic in nature. "I think the Signal Corps as organized at present is largely for the purpose of doing the meteorological work assigned to it in 1870," he said.

Cleveland was quick to point out that while his seniority in terms of length of service was greater than that of anyone other than the chief clerk, Alexander Ashley (who was Cleveland's first acquaintance when he arrived at the Signal Service in January 1871),[64] he did not outrank anyone among the military personnel of the Signal Service. Cleveland saw himself as being in "only an advisory capacity," as just one of the civilian employees of the service to whom Hazen looked "for special information on any points he wants." Still, he stressed the fact that he felt military rule results in superior performance. "I have done my own duty for years faithfully, I think, but I recognize that there is a certain *esprit de corps* which usually comes with discipline and accountability."

Cleveland attempted to impress upon the committee the progress he and his colleagues at the Signal Service had made in forecasting the weather—especially when it came to the prediction of severe storms. Representative Robert Lowry of Indiana asked Cleveland to elaborate on how certain meteorological indications could be used to predict the occurrence of tornadoes. To illustrate this, Cleveland brought a series of maps that were part of a study of the violent storms conducted by his colleague, Private Finley. Cleveland unfolded the large paper maps on the table in front of the committee members. "Here are several charts," he said, spreading them out across the table. "This first one shows the condition of the weather at 7 a.m. April 1, 1884, in a general way. The barometric pressure is shown by isobars." Cleveland pointed to an area that stretched from eastern Nebraska and northern Kansas into southwestern Iowa and the northwestern corner of Missouri. Across it, the word "LOW" appeared in all capital letters. "Here is the low pressure, which we call a general storm-center, and the winds are seen blowing in toward the center, and also going around it in all directions, making a very well developed—"

"Whirl?" interrupted Representative Theodore Lyman, from Massachusetts.

"Yes; that is the word exactly," Cleveland replied, agreeably. "You see the temperature lines are crowded together there in this place," he said, moving his finger over to an area in Iowa.

"Those dotted lines are the temperature lines?" Lowry asked.

"Yes. You find the line of 60° temperature, and then 20 miles north of it you find the temperature at 55°, and so on," Cleveland explained, motioning toward the eastern half of the country. "In other words, the whole Gulf and Atlantic states are enjoying warm southerly winds, while here, in Iowa," he said as he directed their attention back toward the middle of the country, "is a region where a rapid transition takes place to cold northwesterly winds. We say that this is a place of great temperature-gradient, and of opposing winds."

At this point, Allison chimed in. "This chart shows the storm about 7 o'clock in the morning?"

"Yes," Cleveland said, as he shuffled through the maps. "And here is the 3 o'clock map showing it eight hours afterward. The temperature, as you see, has risen," he explained. "The Sun has poured upon the air and Earth three-fourths of the heat it is to receive during this day. The evaporation from the Earth's surface has thrown a vast quantity of water into the air as invisible vapor, from which large cumulus clouds are now forming over the regions where warm southwest or southeast winds are reported on the map." The congressmen looked on with interest. "Under some of these big cumuli the uprush of warm moist air is sufficient to make them grow rapidly," Cleveland said. "The Sun's heat penetrates a little into their sides and tops and warms them; the rising invisible vapor as it enters them condenses, gives up its latent heat, and warms them. Thus, wherever favoring conditions exist, air is drawn in, gets into a whirl like a whirl of water flowing down through the outlet in a wash basin, and thus originates the principal part of the mechanism of a tornado."

Allison and his colleagues studied the map intently. "You say that chart represents the storm at 3 o'clock?" the chairman asked.

"Yes, sir," Cleveland responded confidently. On this map, the area of low pressure had expanded and moved eastward, now stretching from southeastern Nebraska and northeastern Kansas to Indiana. Cleveland gestured toward this region. "This is the general area of storm or of disturbance of pressure, although it may be only a slight storm of wind or rain yet," he said. He then placed a third map on top of the others. "Here is the 11 o'clock map, and the general storm-center has moved from Illinois eastward to Pennsylvania, and the whole system of winds, isotherms and isobars, moves with it," he remarked. "Now, while this has been going on we find that tornadoes have occurred at these little regions, as indicated along here by the crosses on this fourth map," he said, referring to yet another map that unlike the others had no isobars or isotherms on it but rather a red line connecting dots along the path the storm traveled over the course of several days, along with a number of small cross symbols, which lined up along neat rows across parts of the southeastern United States. "Five to fifty little patches of a mile wide by 100 long, or even only two or three long, along which destructive tornadoes have swept during the afternoon and evening, generally in an eastern or northeastern direction," Cleveland explained. "These paths of destruction do not differ in direction very much from that of the general movement of the wind and the clouds."

"Seemingly disconnected from the other, or main, storm?" Lowry inquired.

"Yes," Cleveland replied, "disconnected in distance, but we see the causal connections." He then produced a sheet of paper with text on it. "Here is a paragraph showing that the destruction of $685,000 worth of property and many lives was caused by these twenty tornadoes on the first day of April, and these were quite ordinary tornadoes—none of them caused such destruction as is often witnessed when one passes over a thriving western town. Most of these occurred in the Ohio valley, Gulf, and North Atlantic states."

"Now, tell us how these storms could be predicted from anything occurring generally throughout those regions," Allison insisted.

Cleveland referred back to the first map. "To understand this you must first look into the history of a day and its tornadoes. The morning map shows us the temperature and moisture over all this section of country," he said, pointing to the map on the table, "south and east from the general storm center." Cleveland looked up from the map at the congressmen. "We know also how much heat will be given to the air by the Sun, and approximately how much moisture will be thrown up into the atmosphere by evaporation from the soil, forests, lakes, etc., in different parts of the country." Cleveland went on to explain how various factors combined to create conditions favorable for tornadoes to develop. "These fundamental data we may get at either by laborious numerical calculation, or more quickly by comparing the record of the previous two or three days, as shown upon our map," he said. "Now, this moist air is almost always moving northeastward, and therefore toward regions of air slightly cooler than itself." The congressmen looked on with interest as Cleveland continued his explanation. "Moreover, the lowest, hottest, and moistest system, being in contact with the ground, frequently meets hills or other obstacles, and is deflected upward, whereby it expands like the gas in a rising balloon and cools according to the laws of thermodynamics, or, again, as midday approaches, the lowest stratum becomes rapidly overheated by contact with the hot ground, and rises up, thereby, as before expanding and cooling." Without missing a beat, Cleveland continued, as if he were delivering a lecture to one of his classes at Fort Myer. "There are thus three, and I might say, two or three other causes operating to cool all the air that is moving eastward over this section of the country on the south and east side of the arc of low barometer. Now, from this cooling results the condensation of invisible vapor into clouds, that if they become large enough will have underneath them the updrafts and whirls of air that constitute tornadoes."

Cleveland paused and looked up at the members of the commission. "You will see, therefore, that the vital question in the prediction of tornadoes is to decide from the morning map, and our knowledge of solar heat and the topography of the country where the regions are favorable to the formation of large cumulus clouds."

Hoping not to lose the attention of his audience, Cleveland began to conclude his remarks. "So far as the winds, temperature, moisture, and barometer are concerned, there is nothing observed on the ground in advance of a tornado that accurately predicts its approach," he admitted. "The prediction is, at present, a deduction from general features, because our stations are from one to three hundred miles apart, and we can only make general predictions, as, for instance, 'Conditions are favorable for severe local storms this afternoon in Ohio.' Our whole service is, at present, organized only for general weather predictions," Cleveland conceded. "Tornadoes a mile wide and ten to fifty miles long slip in between our stations without affecting the general weather conditions. In fact, a tornado is so small an item in comparison with the grand storms, the cold waves, and other great atmospheric changes that we have to deal with, that we have had to devise a special corps of tornado reporters, and are at work on special electrical observations, in order to see if we can promptly make more minute and accurate local predictions a few hours in advance of their approach."

Throughout his testimony, the members of the commission pressed Cleveland on a variety of topics, ranging from his own work in the Study

Room to that of other divisions within the Signal Service to the reliance on government telegraph lines as a means of communication. At times, their questions were pointed and seemed to imply a certain response was desired. Cleveland answered directly and without delving into unnecessary detail, much like an expert witness in a courtroom who had been coached by his attorney.

When asked to compare the weather service in the United States to that of Russia, Cleveland noted that while Russia was vastly larger in territory the number of regular stations in its observation network was roughly equal to that of the United States, with far fewer voluntary observers to augment the official readings. He also cited a fundamental difference in the amount of work done (claiming that Russia only did a tenth of the work undertaken by the Signal Service) and the motivation for the work. "She is *studying* the science of meteorology; we are trying to utilize it for public welfare," he said."[65]

While Cleveland testified that he favored a continuance of military control of the weather service, a group of fellow employees stationed at the main Signal Office in Washington, D.C., disagreed. Writing in an open letter to Congress that appeared in several prominent newspapers[66] the group argued that the *Signal Service* should remain under military control, but "the *Weather Bureau* should not." The group further asserted that Cleveland's desire to maintain the status quo was not altogether altruistic in nature. "Self-interest prompts his opinion," the letter claimed. "If the bureau was transferred, $4,500 per annum would be saved the Government in his salary alone."

Still others testified that military control detracted from the accuracy and efficiency of the service, with reports of officers and sergeants falsifying records. When asked if he regarded the military feature of the service as an embarrassment rather than an advantage, William H. Lamar, who had since left the service, replied, "Most decidedly," adding that "when a man enlists in the Army he is no longer considered a gentleman; and he is cowed continually."

The commission's investigation also found conditions at Fort Myer were sometimes deplorable. William Burrows testified that the food was often inedible, with the meat having "repeatedly been stinky," noting that one officer of the day recorded in the guard report that "he found the stew for breakfast smelling abominably bad and totally unfit for human food."

There were further reports of extreme discipline toward the enlisted men of the Signal Service. In his testimony, Burrows claimed the treatment of the enlisted men under certain officers at Fort Myer was "generally of an oppressive, tyrannical, and insolent character, totally unlike the treatment enlisted men received from the Regular Army Officers." Burrows also alleged that the military training at Fort Myer was "merely a burlesque on military rules and regulations."

Another witness, Edward B. Olney, recalled how a fellow enlisted man had gone AWOL for a number of days, only to return to Fort Myer, where he was placed in the guard house and ordered to work under a sentry. When he refused, he was placed in a small cell with the window darkened. "There was a little grating in the door about eight inches long and perhaps six inches wide, with bars running across the space, which is supposed to give all the ventilation needed." Olney, who was serving on guard duty that day, reported that Lieutenant Greene had ordered the grating on the door be nailed up, so that only an area eight inches long and an inch wide remained for ventilation. When Olney opened the door to give the deserter water, he said that "the smell that came out of there was repulsive. I found him lying down at the door trying to get some fresh air through the crack. He was given no food that day, but only a small quantity of bread and the water we gave him."

Olney testified there was another man, charged with using insulting language directed at the officer in charge, who was confined to the same kind of cell at the same time. Olney said this man had a nervous energy that caused him to cry out in distress from his cell. "He cried out as if he had seen specters or ghosts, showing that his nervous condition was bad," he said.

Yet another witness, J. P. Earnest, testified that the treatment he and others endured at the hands of officers at Fort Myer made him second guess his decision to enlist in the Signal Service. "I think I can say, in all truth, that if we had known what the treatment would be that we have received, none of us would have entered the corps."[67]

When asked how he would deal with the situation, Secretary of War Robert Lincoln said his preference was to place the meteorological operations of the Signal Service under a civilian organization and suggested that Cleveland might be at the head of it. "I would keep the Chief Signal Officer where he is, and have under his supervision throughout the Army of the United States a uniform system of signaling," he testified. "And then I would organize a meteorological bureau, if you choose to call it so, and I would put at the head of that bureau some such man as Professor Abbe, the present professor."[68]

In the end, the members of the Allison Commission agreed that military control over the weather observation and forecasting work of the Signal Service was unnecessary, but they disagreed on what to do about it. While several members, including Allison, were unsure how the work could be improved by placing it under civilian control, other members called for an abolishment of the "corps of soldiers in name who are not soldiers in fact, but a mere uniformed police to watch the weather and watch each other."[69]

Greely Takes Over

By 1886, Hazen's expenditures, coupled with the scandals that marred his administration of the Signal Service, caused one newspaper to report that he would likely be court-martialed. "There has been a wanton waste of public money. Hazen is one of the Garfield Administration pets, all of whom have 'gone wrong,'" the paper criticized.[70]

While Hazen's critics continued to call for changes—including relinquishing military control of the weather service—the status quo prevailed for the time being. Then, on January 16, 1887, Hazen died at his home in Washington, D.C., following a brief illness and what some in the press described as "a diabetic coma."[71] In December 1886, several weeks before Hazen's death and due to his poor health, General Adolphus Washington Greely assumed control of the Signal Service.

A tall, slender man who was distinguished by his wire-rim glasses, full beard, and walrus mustache, Greely enlisted in the Army shortly after the start of the Civil War, at the age of seventeen. He is perhaps best known for the ill-fated Arctic expedition he led to explore Lady Franklin Bay, in the Canadian Arctic near Greenland. The expedition, which began in 1881 as part of the First International Polar Year, ran into trouble when a supply ship failed to reach its camp the following summer. A rescue ship set off for the beleaguered explorers in 1883, but it too failed to reach Greely and his men. In August 1883, Greely made the controversial decision to lead the expedition south from their base camp, in hopes of finding a rescue team or caches of food. Besieged by harsh conditions, the men were forced to abandon their boats and seek refuge on a large ice floe, drifting along the ocean currents, until reaching a point on land where they set up a makeshift camp. Finding only meager caches of food, they suffered greatly as winter came. Starvation, frostbite, and declining morale set in as Greely ordered strict rationing of what little food remained. One of the men, who was caught repeatedly stealing food, was ordered shot by Greely so as not to endanger the lives of the others. By the time a rescue team arrived in June 1884, all but seven of the men had perished. Greely himself was near death. When one of the rescue party inquired, "Greely, is that you?" he reportedly answered, "Yes—seven of us left—here were are—dying—like men."[72] Greely returned home to a hero's welcome, but his accolades were tainted by controversy, with reports of harsh treatment of his men and cannibalism permeating throughout the press.

On February 16, 1887, President Grover Cleveland formally nominated Greely to succeed Hazen as chief signal officer. He was confirmed by the Senate on March 3, receiving with his promotion the rank of brigadier general.[73] Greely was just forty-two and although he would remain chief signal officer for nearly two decades, his time overseeing the nation's weather service would be short-lived.

"During the administration of Gen. Greely the civilian employees of the Signal Service, as well as the lieutenants of the Corps and the lieutenants assigned to the Service from other Army corps, came under the supervision of one who knew every man by name and was intimately familiar with the stations and their work as well as with the relations of Congress to the Service," Cleveland recalled. "His first care was to secure the strictest honesty and economy in matters of finance and property, and next to effect the long-desired organization of the permanent Signal Corps, instead of the temporary makeshifts and special details that had hitherto obtained. So long as such organization was wanting the existence of the Corps was threatened and the meteorological work might at any time pass into other hands."

Pensacola Expedition

In October 1889, Cleveland set off on a seven-month expedition aboard the USS *Pensacola*, a full-rigged Navy steamer, complete with three masts and a crew of three hundred. Officially known as The U.S. Scientific Expedition to West Africa, the expedition's main objective was to observe and document the total solar eclipse of December 22, 1889—Cleveland's third—which was visible across southern Africa. During the course of the long journey, the *Pensacola* traveled to the Azores and Cape Verde, in the central Atlantic, and Sierra Leone and the Gold Coast of Africa, before dropping anchor at Cape Ledo (Cabo Ledo) in Angola to observe the eclipse. Later ports of call included Cape Town, Saint Helena, Ascension Island, and Barbados, before finally returning to New York in May 1890.

For Cleveland, it was also an opportunity to conduct detailed studies of clouds using a special instrument he designed called a nephoscope, which consisted of a rounded mirror with a compass around the edge. The mirror reflected the clouds' movements while the compass indicated their direction.

Cleveland's letters to his wife, Fanny, throughout the expedition reveal both a longing for home during his extended absence and an appreciation for the opportunity it afforded him. To him, it was a sacrifice worth making for the benefit of science. In one of his first letters, written November 1, he detailed what daily life for him was like on the ship:[74]

> My daily life has settled into a routine something like this:
>
> 6^{am} — Called by steward & immediately get into a tub of cold distilled water & rub myself aglow. This 15 minute bath sets me up for the day—it is astonishing how easy it is to do this daily in the moist mild air of the sea & how hard it is to do it in the dry air of Washington. This moist air or the diet or something has kept my eczema down very completely and I have enjoyed perfect health & regularity
>
> 6^{30} -7^{30} — On the after-bridge where I have my meteorological station and observe clouds temperature &c
>
> At 7^{am} — My anemometer is lowered from the masthead read and replaced
>
> 7^{30}-8 — Breakfast—mostly a simple dish of rice or hominy or oatmeal
>
> 8-11 — On the bridge meteorologizing
>
> 11 — Tired out, come into cabin & wash face
>
> 12 — Breakfast official that is to say lunch usually three courses—fish meat & fingerbowls
>
> 1-5^{30} — On deck & on bridge observe clouds & temperature—send up balloons read masthead anemometer at 5 pm get sunset and colors
>
> 5^{30} — Wash face
>
> 6 — Dinner official—during dinner & for an hour after the ship's band plays (a drum and five pieces). After dinner all congregate on the gun deck forward of the cabin around the band & after that we either talk or write or read & laze about.

As the ship sailed along at a leisurely pace of six to seven knots, Cleveland spent his days absorbed in his meteorological work—happy to be away from the strict rules and bureaucracy that dictated life in the Signal Office back in Washington, D.C. One afternoon a rain squall produced "a remarkably fine display of waterspouts."[75] In the evening he passed the time by reading, listening to the ship's band play selections such as the waltz "Le Petit Bleu" by Léopold de Wenzel or works from the Gilbert and Sullivan comic operas "The Princess Ida" and "Patience," or writing to Fanny, who waited patiently for news of her husband, not knowing what fate might have in store for him. "My dear Cleve," she wrote on November 11, "Tonight news came of the safe arrival of the Pensacola at Cape Verde Island, how it cheered my heart to know you were still alive. How often I wanted to write you but it seemed like writing to space, oh it was a terrible feeling but tonight I hear of you I feel I can write."[76]

Fanny had hoped Cleveland would receive her letter before Christmas, but it was just after New Year's Day when he finally got it, along with a letter from his sister Hattie. "I was very pleasantly surprised by these letters for I really felt very much as you did that it seemed like 'writing to space' to send a letter so far and to a country that we in America know so little about," he wrote to Fanny in reply. "When you have travelled as far as this into foreign lands you will however realize that civilization and humanity are everywhere and that we can be just as much at home here as anywhere."[77]

At one point, the separation began to play with Fanny's subconscious to the point that she began to dream about her husband. "I saw you floating away in an air ship the other night. I wanted to go with you but the law was against me, and the captain took the time when I was out to start and I only arrived in time to see the ship float off," she wrote him, adding, "I am very glad you are having this opportunity to make the observations you so much wanted to make."[78]

When the *Pensacola* arrived in Cape Town, Cleveland wrote to Fanny that the city had "the beauty of Washington, the energy of New York, the style & society of Boston & the climate of San Francisco."[79] While there, he gave a talk to the South African Philosophical Society on weather and the weather service. In addition to describing in detail both the history and operations of the Signal Service, he told the audience of the observations he had been making while at sea. "I am at present engaged in a close study of cloud movements on the Atlantic Ocean, and can safely state that without a single exception the clouds have revealed to me the presence of distant storms and the proper steering course to avoid them, and the same may be said of the minor changes in the direction of the wind."[80]

As the expedition neared its completion, Cleveland began to reflect on his journey and what he had accomplished. Writing to Fanny, he wished he could share it all with her. "I wonder if you have any idea where I am—it's all very nice to have to write you from time to time that I am well & busy—but it is very hard to give you any just conception of the many novel experiences I have gone through in order to perfect myself in everything that bears on meteorology & to add to our knowledge whatever I can towards the solution of problems in atmospherics."[81] To Cleveland, the amount of material he had collected—and the amount of time it would require to analyze—seemed daunting but doable. "There's enough work here for two men for a year, to extract all that can be here done for meteorology—pray that I may yet have an opportunity to return & finish my work properly."[82]

By late April, as the *Pensacola* was on its return trip in the Atlantic, Cleveland reminisced about his family back in America, longing to be with them again. "Every Saturday evening at dinner we toast our 'Sweethearts & Wives' so that I seem often to be at home sitting opposite you at the table with our children & friends on either side. I hope this is what will be in about four or five weeks from now by which time our seven months voyage will have ended so that about June 1st we will eat strawberries together with sugar & cream—at least I hope so."[83]

When Fanny received a telegram on May 23 stating that Cleveland had arrived safely in New York, she was ecstatic. "I am so excited I can't write," she exclaimed, adding, "I can't sit still here. I feel like dancing."[84]

With this chapter of his life behind him, it was time for Cleveland to return to his work at the Signal Service. The freedom he felt aboard the *Pensacola* would soon be stifled, he knew, by bureaucratic realities and budgetary constraints. "Only I know I need money and authority with which to prosecute meteorology as it ought to be studied—but I shy off from wasting the labor of arguing for every appropriation before a committee of Congress or a Secretary of War," he wrote Fanny toward the end of his journey, expressing his frustration. "I think the Signal Office will do better in the long run (not immediately) if it has a large infusion of physical & mathematical science—the 'practical' it already has to a large extent & the Army can get it—but it wants more deep students of the laws of the atmosphere. Both Army and Navy are slow & conservative as compared with science & manufacturers & business. They are large bodies & move slowly while science &c deals with the individual and develops him and his work."[85]

While he was on the *Pensacola* expedition, Cleveland received word from Fanny[86] that the French Ministère de l'Instruction Publique et des Beaux-Arts (Ministry of Public Education and Fine Arts) in Paris had awarded him the honorific title of Officier d'Académie. It was a highly prized honor and Cleveland replied with astonishment. "I am still dreaming as to whether that will turn out to be true."[87]

Civilian Control

During Cleveland's absence, the Signal Service had published a work he had prepared before the expedition titled "Preparatory Studies for Deductive Methods in Storm and Weather Predictions."[88] In it, he discussed the physical principles involved in the formation and motion of storms and the practical applications of such principles to the predictions he had made over the years. "In general, it is evident that the progress of the past thirty years in every branch of physical science must now soon produce a natural reaction on meteorology and enable it to take a high stand among the exact and mechanical sciences," he wrote in the introduction.[89]

This was indicative of the type of applied research Cleveland conducted for the Signal Service. "In view of his long service and vast experience in the work of this Bureau, and of his standing as a member of the National Academy of Sciences, Professor Cleveland Abbe has been intrusted with questions of scientific research with a view to the better prediction of storms," Greely noted in his annual report for 1890.[90] "At no time in the history of the Service has the intellectual activity relative to the duties of the Bureau been greater than during the past year," he boasted.[91]

Despite his dedication to the overall mission of the Signal Service, Greely was not always a champion of its meteorological work, especially given the struggle for civilian control that had lingered since the days of the Allison Commission.[92] "General Greely's admission that the weather bureau as existing had certain defects raised a hearty laugh," reported one newspaper, in describing Greely's discussions with senators and other government officials regarding possible transfer of the weather service portion of the Signal Service to a civilian agency. Despite this, he apparently "fairly begged" one senator not to transfer the meteorological portion to civilian control.[93]

At least one newspaper—the *St. Paul Daily Globe*—seemed to revel in making fun of Greely and his apparent lack of meteorological aptitude or awareness. "Some one should stick a red pole in a convenient snow bank in memory of the fact that for once the prediction of Signal Officer Greely has been verified," one critical article, published in January 1890, began.[94] Two months later, the paper was at it again. "Gen. Greely, chief of the signal service, was seen recently on the streets of Washington dressed in a new spring suit and wearing no overcoat," it reported on March 14. "It was snowing at the time. Greely says that the best he can do is to dress according to the calendar."[95]

When President Benjamin Harrison delivered his State of the Union Address to Congress, on December 3, 1889, he finally called for an end to military control of the nation's weather service. "I recommend that the weather service be separated from the War Department and established as a bureau in the Department of Agriculture," he said. "This will involve an entire reorganization both of the Weather Bureau and of the Signal Corps, making of the first a purely civil organization and of the other a purely military staff corps. The report of the Chief Signal Officer shows that the work of the corps on its military side has been deteriorating."[96]

Harrison's recommendation provided a roadmap for lawmakers to proceed with what many had been calling for. When the Fifty-First Congress began its first regular session in December 1889, several bills were introduced that sought to transfer control of the meteorological portion of the Signal Service out of the military and into civilian hands.[97] On December 18, Senator William B. Bate of Tennessee introduced a bill, S. 1454, "to increase the efficiency and reduce expenses of the Signal Corps of the Army, and to transfer the Weather Service to the Department of Agriculture."[98] The bill was read twice and referred to the Committee on Military Affairs. On March 6, 1890, it was reported back with amendments.[99] It was debated and passed the Senate on April 12.[100] Four days later, it was referred to the House Committee on Military Affairs,[101] which referred it to the entire House for consideration on April 23.[102]

During this time, Cleveland was still at sea, on the USS *Pensacola* expedition. On May 8, he received a letter from his friend Thomas Mendenhall, who had since left the Signal Service and had recently been appointed superintendent of the Coast and Geodetic Survey. "You have also heard doubtless that the Weather Bureau is on the verge of being turned into the Agricultural Department, the Bill having passed the Senate—and there is little doubt that it will pass the House—and indeed I think it has General Greely's hearty approval in his case," Mendenhall said. "Everybody on all sides seems to think that the administration will be altogether better under that Bureau than under the War Department."[103]

The House took the bill up for consideration on September 6[104] but quickly decided to defer it. Representative William S. Holman of Indiana said the bill "is of so much importance, relating as it does to a very important branch of the public service, that we ought to take further time to consider it."[105] On September 17, as the House debated the bill,[106] Holman asked Representative Byron M. Cutcheon of Michigan, chair of the Committee on Military Affairs, whether the bill had the support of the secretaries of war and agriculture. "The Secretary of Agriculture is exceedingly anxious for the passage of the bill," Cutcheon replied. "He has been upon the floor within the last eight or ten days urging its passage, and all the friends of agriculture throughout the country are urging it." Then he added, "The Secretary of War is willing and the Chief Signal Officer is anxious for its passage, because he knows he will never have peace any more since the farmers have got after him." This resulted in an outburst of laughter across the House floor.[107] The next day, the House returned the bill to the Senate, with an amendment. Senator Bate, the bill's original author, asked that the Senate not concur with the amendment and requested a conference committee on the disagreeing votes of the two houses.[108] The committee reported its recommendations on September 29, to which the Senate agreed. On October 1, President Harrison approved the act to officially transfer the meteorological portion of the Signal Service to the Department of Agriculture, effective July 1, 1891.[109] The introduction to the act read:

> *Be it enacted by the Senate and House of Representatives of the United States of America in Congress assembled,* That the civilian duties now performed by the Signal Corps of the Army shall hereafter devolve upon a bureau to be known as the Weather Bureau, which, on and after July first, eighteen hundred and ninety-one, shall be established in and attached to the Department of Agriculture, and the Signal Corps of the Army shall remain a part of the Military Establishment under the direction of the Secretary of War, and all estimates for its support shall be included with other estimates for the support of the Military Establishment.[110]

On June 30, 1891, the day before the transfer took effect, Acting Secretary of War Lewis A. Grant signed an order honorably discharging 162 enlisted men from the ranks of the Signal Service. According to the act, the secretary of agriculture, Jeremiah M. Rusk, was obliged to give them preference in filling positions in the newly established Weather Bureau. In addition to the enlisted men, three commissioned officers and the civilian employees of the Signal Service were transferred to the Department of Agriculture.[111] Among the new employees of the Weather Bureau was Cleveland, whose appointment as professor of meteorology earned him a salary of $4,000 per year in the new regime. That same day, General Greely issued a farewell order to the departing men of the Signal Service, which read, in part:

> The Chief Signal Officer knows and fully appreciates the assiduous and invaluable coöperation of the officers of the Army, whose labors in organizing, developing, and operating the meteorological work of this service will never be adequately stated or generally recognized. It is, however, a matter of record that the meteorological system devised by officers of the United States Army has proved to be the most successful service in the world, has

served as a working model and example for other nations, while its unique exhibits have elicited unparalleled commendation. The records of officers who have participated in the work of this service for any prolonged period show the native ability and special adaptability of Army officers ordered to scientific duty for which they had not been educated and which more than one accepted with reluctance.

The Signal Corps collects and distributes an unequaled amount of weather data. In accuracy of collation, in speed of collection from and distribution to distant points, in extent, and in legibility even of its ephemeral publications the service is not only unrivaled, but is not even approached by any other weather service in the world. In attaining this practical excellence many peculiar methods of work and a large number of special mechanical devices were essential to the present success, and the Chief Signal Officer would be wanting in justice did he not acknowledge that far the greater part of these improvements is due to ideas, suggestions, and inventions of the enlisted men.

In parting from the civil employés the Chief Signal Officer feels assured that the new chief in another department will receive from them the same loyal, faithful, and efficient service they has rendered the Government while serving under his orders. The scientific staff have in view important additional duties looking to the extension of the Weather Service in the interest of agriculture and still further development of the science of meteorology. The Chief Signal Officer will follow with deep interest the development on new scientific lines of weather forecasting and the application of meteorology to agriculture, on which grounds this liberal reorganization of the Weather Bureau was planned and carried out.[112]

While there was speculation that Assistant Secretary of Agriculture Edwin Willits, a politician from Michigan, would serve as the chief of the new Weather Bureau,[113] or possibly Professor Francis Nipper of Washington University in St. Louis (whose appointment one newspaper described as "a forgone conclusion"[114]), that honor—and responsibility—fell to Professor Mark Walrod Harrington of the University of Michigan. An academic with wide-ranging interests, Harrington had started his career as assistant curator at the university's Museum of Natural Sciences and was later appointed assistant professor of geology, zoology, and botany, and served as director of the university's observatory. He also spent time working for the Coast and Geodetic Survey in Alaska, studying in Leipzig, and teaching astronomy and mathematics in China. In 1884 he founded the *American Meteorological Journal*, which published a ten-page profile of Cleveland in 1888.

The choice of a scientist over a politician to lead the new Weather Bureau was certainly well received by Cleveland, and initially he prospered under the new regime. In August 1891, both Cleveland and Harrington traveled to Munich to attend the International Meteorological Conference, which took place from August 26 to September 2. They traveled first-class aboard the ocean steamer *Fürst Bismarck*, leaving New York on August 13 and arriving in Hamburg ten days later. While they had missed the Astronomische Gesellschaft[115] conference in Munich in early August, along with the International Geographical Congress in Bern, and the meeting of the British Association in Cardiff,[116] they arrived in Munich in time to attend the majority of the International Meteorological Conference. Cleveland and Harrington were joined by General Greely and Abbott Lawrence Rotch, founder and director of the Blue Hill Meteorological Observatory in Massachusetts. "The presence at the Conference of four delegates from the United States was the occasion of many congratulatory expressions as showing that the United States had no disposition to hold aloof from these important meetings," Harrington wrote to Rusk, "and our intercourse during the week spent at Munich, as well as during the subsequent visits to the respective bureaus, has, we believe, served to arouse a lively interest in, and a more intelligent appreciation of, the work that is being undertaken in Washington."[117]

While in Europe, Cleveland and Harrington also made several other stops, including Vienna, Hamburg, Berlin, Paris, and London,[118] before returning home on the steamer *Columbia*. In Paris, the pair was treated to a visit to the Eiffel Tower, where they made a detailed inspection of the meteorological station atop the famous landmark. They were so impressed that they hoped to make similar measurements from the tower proposed to be built for the World's Fair in Chicago two years later. Harrington noted that "it is only by means of stations on such towers and on mountain tops that we may hope to understand the motions going on within the atmosphere."[119]

Returning to Washington, D.C., Harrington set to work establishing the framework of the Weather Bureau to ensure the continued efficiency and accuracy of the observers, who were no longer under the tight reins of military control. Cleveland, meanwhile, continued his efforts to uphold and strengthen the scientific integrity of the service. Harrington initially encountered little interference in his administration of the Weather Bureau, but that changed soon after the election of 1892, which ousted Benjamin Harrison from power and saw the return of Grover Cleveland to the White House. Two weeks before he had even taken the oath of office for his second, nonconsecutive term, Cleveland announced that Julius Sterling Morton, a so-called "Bourbon Democrat" who favored laissez faire capitalism and strong pro-agriculture policies, would replace Rusk as secretary of agriculture. Morton had previously served as territorial governor of Nebraska and edited the *Nebraska City News*—Nebraska's first newspaper—and is credited with founding the tradition of Arbor Day in the United States. Morton would later establish his own newspaper, *The Conservative*, which billed itself as a "journal devoted to the discussion of political, economic, and sociological questions." The journal was heavily financed by his four sons, especially his son Joy, founder of the Morton Salt company.[120]

Not long after taking office, Morton began a thorough investigation of the various bureaus and divisions of his department, looking for wasted expenditures and seeking out sinecures secured by friends of his predecessor. "Secretary of Agriculture J. Sterling Morton is shaking up the dry bones of the Agriculture Department in a way to make them rattle loudly," *The Sun* reported. "He has long been firm in the belief . . . that large sums of the people's money have been wasted in useless experiments, and that a host of employees have been employed whose services could well be dispensed with."[121] Morton said it was his wish to make the bureau "popular, remove it from the rather high scientific plane to which it has gradually ascended, and bring it down to a level where it would abound in practical work." Morton saw the value and practicality of the forecasts the bureau provided but failed to see the benefit of theoretical or applied research to complement them. "What the people want most," he said, "is the knowledge beforehand of what is to happen, so they can prepare for it, rather than a scientific diagnosis in the line of cause and effect after it is all over."[122]

Morton asked Assistant Attorney General Robert L. Colby to take charge of the investigation into the Weather Bureau. Colby issued his report on May 29, 1893.[123] "While the report makes no specific recommendations it raps the officials of the bureau over the knuckles from beginning to end, particularly the chief, Prof. Harrington," read one account.[124] On June 1, Cleveland received a note from Alexander McAdie, a confidential clerk for Harrington. "Will you please state for the information of the Secretary of Agriculture what your duties are and what services you are performing for the benefit of the public?" it asked. "Officially I am appointed as 'Professor of Meteorology' and my general duties under this designation are the same as they were for many years before the transfer, namely, the seeking out and developing of every possible method of applying modern scientific knowledge to the improvement of the meteorological work of the Weather Bureau besides being always ready for duty on daily weather forecasts," Cleveland said as part of a detailed, nine-page treatise outlining his career and justifying his position. As far as services for the benefit of the public, he added, "I may properly say that my whole life work, official and unofficial, has been given to the practical application, for the benefit of the people, of those branches of science in which I have been interested."[125]

On June 16, Morton wrote directly to Cleveland himself.[126]

June 16, 1893

Prof. Cleveland Abbe,
Weather Bureau

Sir:

Inform me, at the earliest possible moment, what labors you have performed at the Weather Bureau during the past year, and give me in as terse epitome as possible, the beneficent results of your investigations as a meteorologist.

It seems to me that the disbursements of the Weather Bureau for scientists are altogether too extravagant.

State, also, the number of years that you have been in the Government service, and the amount of money that has been paid you during that time, and whether you have been employed or salaried by other institutions during a part, or all of that time.

Respectfully yours,

J. Sterling Morton
Secretary.

Cleveland wrote back the following day, outlining the "very varied duties that have devolved upon" him, which he placed into six general categories:[127]

1. Preparing reports on proper methods of carrying on specific items of work in the Bureau
2. Preparing satisfactory replies to official correspondence with numerous citizens who wish to impose upon the government various erroneous or cranky notions
3. Compilation of data for the use of this Bureau as to what we actually know as to the influence of climates on crops
4. Personal experiments on the growth of corn and wheat under different styles of irrigation or watering

5. Studies on the motions of storms with a view to their better prediction
6. Correspondence relative to the organization of the Meteorological Congress at Chicago

Cleveland had been put on notice, but he was not going to give up easily what he had worked for so diligently. "Knowing as I do, better than almost any man living, the history, the responsibilities, the past work of the Weather Bureau and its future possibilities I do not hesitate to say that the amount of money paid to the half-dozen men who are ordinarily called 'scientists' in the Weather Bureau, is not at all extravagant. The salaries are proper and the men who fill the places are worthy of them," he wrote, adding, in deference to Morton, "You are simply doing what every sound business man approves who invests when he sees a fair prospect of future returns."[128]

Cleveland ended his letter with an emphatic and emotional appeal. "This is the first opportunity that you have given me to speak and I beg to say that my heart and life are in this work of applying meteorology to the benefit of my fellow-citizens," he said. "We have had only a few years in which to develop this subject, but the best students of meteorology throughout the world unite in foreseeing that every year of study opens up the way to still further improvements such as to justify your kindliest regards for our labors in applied science."[129]

In the end, Cleveland's appeals did not satisfy Morton, who was hell-bent on finding ways to cut expenditures and rein in the scientific staff of the Weather Bureau. On July 5, Cleveland received a letter from Israel W. Stone, assistant disbursing officer of the Weather Bureau. "I am directed by the Chief of the Weather Bureau to advise you that the Secretary directs that, from and after July 1st, 1893, your salary as a Professor in the Weather Bureau will be $3,000.00 per annum, with the understanding however that proficiency in forecasting will be necessary for the continuation of your services and the perpetuation of your pay."[130]

Morton calculated that in the time Cleveland had been employed by the government, he had received more than $90,000 in salary. He did not believe, however, that the American people had received a worthwhile return on their investment. "I am convinced that Prof. Abbe is paid more than his services are worth," Morton charged. One of Morton's chief complaints centered around Cleveland's reference to his studies on the motions of storms. "Abbe claims to have discovered a method for determining the future tracks of storms after they have become well-defined and developed," Morton wrote to Harrington. "Then why are the future tracks of storms not added to the weather map from day to day? If his method is established, assured and verified by experience as he claims, putting the future tracks of storms on each day's weather map would greatly enhance the value of weather maps to the general public."[131]

The press did not react kindly to Morton's assault on Cleveland. "The salary of that veteran scientist of international reputation, Professor Cleveland Abbe, is reduced from $4,000 to $3,000, and a brutal letter has been sent to him by Secretary Morton with the evident design of having him resign," read one report.[132] *The New York Times* noted that a "tinge of sarcasm" was apparent in Morton's comments regarding Cleveland's storm motion studies. Still, Cleveland fared relatively well, compared to some of his colleagues. As *The Times* noted, "Messrs. Carl Barus, F. H. Bigelow, and Thomas Russel, professors of meteorology, will be dropped from the rolls this month, with a number of clerks and other employes."[133]

Morton subsequently instituted a system of forecast examinations, whereby the forecast staff of the Weather Bureau was required to prepare practice forecasts daily, based on the morning weather map, during the months when they were not assigned official forecast duties.[134] Major Henry H. C. Dunwoody, who had assisted Morton with his investigation of the Weather Bureau and who had previously opposed funding for research under the Signal Service,[135] oversaw the forecast examinations. Not surprisingly, perhaps, Dunwoody scored highest of all those who participated in the practice forecasts, while Cleveland's performance was deemed subpar. This outraged Harrington, who claimed Dunwoody was "a selfish intriguer and a source of discord in the Weather Bureau" and called for his removal by President Cleveland.[136]

Meanwhile, upset and outraged at the apparent attack on his professional character, Cleveland wrote to several of his friends and colleagues around the country, appealing to them for sympathy and help. "I ought to leave at once and make a strong fight but every one advises against it at present," he told Professor John E. Davies in Wisconsin, who had offered to let Cleveland stay with him during the upcoming meeting of the American Association for the Advancement of Science in Madison. "I do not see that I can be at the meeting of the Association in Madison or of the Congresses in Chicago.[137] I could only talk of Secretary Morton's horrid letter if I came out to see you. In fact I will enclose it and you may judge for yourself what it is to see faithful service and personal worth made the football of political power and ambition."[138]

"It is not likely that I shall please him any better at $3,000 than at $4,000 and I should be much happier elsewhere at any price," Cleveland wrote of Morton to Daniel Coit Gilman, president of Johns Hopkins University. "It seems to me that I shall do best for meteorology if I can get New Yorkers, or others, to help me start a special school of physical and practical meteorology. I presume none of the universities have ready money to spare and, therefore, I must make my own personal appeal to the men whose business interests are specially affected by the weather."[139]

On September 3, Cleveland wrote to Garrick Mallery, the former executive officer of the Signal Service. "I am told that Secretary Morton makes much fun of me to his friends," Cleveland confessed, adding that he would "like to be dealt with fairly and to deal fairly by others." [140]

When reports began to appear in the press that were critical of Morton's actions against the Weather Bureau, the secretary assumed Cleveland had played a role in trying to undermine his authority. Cleveland wrote to Morton, in an attempt to clear his name. "I have lately been much troubled by reading expressions in some newspapers that may be as irritating to you as they are annoying to me. These articles, as you must see, are wholly foreign to my style and nature and are not instigated or favored by me. I am a student and not a politician or newspaper correspondent. I wish to build up meteorology—not to pull down anybody."[141]

While Cleveland was able to hold on to his position—albeit at a reduced salary—Harrington was not so fortunate. By June 1895, the friction between him and Morton had reached a breaking point, with Morton demanding his resignation. When Harrington refused, President Cleveland directed his removal as chief of the Weather Bureau, effective July 1, exactly four years after he began the position. This took a traumatic toll on Harrington and he began to slip deep into mental illness. His condition was not immediately evident to others, however, and he managed to maintain a semblance of stability, at least for a while. Just weeks after his dismissal from the Weather Bureau, he accepted the position of president of the University of Washington in Seattle. "Dr. Harrington is a man splendidly equipped for the duties of his new office," exclaimed Dr. David Jordan, president of Stanford University.[142] Less than two years later, however, Harrington tendered his resignation. According to a letter sent by the board of regents to the university's chancellor, Harrington had "neglected his duties, left them to be performed by others, and proven himself incompetent to fill the office of president of the university."[143]

In 1897, Harrington returned to Washington, D.C., where he hoped to regain his former position as chief of the Weather Bureau, under President William McKinley. Unable to do this, he accepted a position as head of the Weather Bureau's new office in Puerto Rico in 1898. Things did not go well there either. "The climate did not agree with him and he became ill, and the service he rendered, while highly efficient at first, became unsatisfactory," *The Evening Star* of Washington, D.C., reported. After a two-month leave of absence, he was assigned to the bureau's station in Barbados, "which he did not like, and he made an appeal to President McKinley."[144] This was the end of his meteorological career, as he was relieved from duty, never again to work for the Weather Bureau he helped establish. Despondent, he returned to his home, just north of New York City.

One day in October 1899, Harrington left home, telling his wife he had business to attend to in the city. He never returned. For years, his family had no idea of his whereabouts. Then, in 1908, his then-adult son, Mark Raymond Harrington, read an incredible account in a newspaper of a recent admission to the Morris Plains Asylum for the Insane in New Jersey. The mysterious patient apparently had no memory and did not even know his own name but could speak several languages and had a penchant for Latin classics. The younger Harrington had just finished his master's degree in archaeology—having worked for a time while in school at the American Museum of Natural History—and was out West collecting Native American artifacts. He quickly alerted his mother, who contacted the institution and eventually learned the strange man known as John Doe No. 8 was their long-lost relative. Although he denied any knowledge of his family members and called them "imposters," it became known that Harrington's whereabouts during his long absence led him on a sinuous journey across the United States and as far away as England and China. After returning to the United States, he worked a variety of jobs involving manual labor—from a sugar plantation in Louisiana to a logging camp in the Pacific Northwest, where he earned $1.50 a day as a lumberjack.[145] Although he eventually regained his memory enough to know his name, he never left the state hospital in Morris Plains, where he died on September 10, 1926.[146]

Moore Named Chief

In 1895, following Harrington's removal from his post, Secretary Morton made James R. Cook acting chief of the Weather Bureau, until a permanent successor could be named. Speculation arose that Major Henry Dunwoody was the top choice, but as he was still an active member of the military, regulations prevented him from serving as head of a civilian agency. In July, Morton selected thirty-nine-year-old Willis Luther Moore to be the new chief of the Weather Bureau. Moore, who had joined the Signal Service at age twenty-one, rose through the ranks and in 1894 succeeded in a competitive examination to become a professor of meteorology and was assigned to lead the bureau's Chicago forecast district.

In taking charge of the bureau, Moore sought to challenge long-held preconceptions regarding weather forecasting, especially as the Weather Bureau grew in public exposure. "The day has gone by when it was all sufficient for a Weather Bureau official to sit on a high stool beside a long desk poring over papers covered with mysterious hieroglyphics, and look wise but say nothing when a man did venture into his sanctum sanctorum," Moore asserted. "The public is being educated faster than we are if we fail to keep in touch with the world and its ideas."[147]

In 1898, Moore presided over the first Convention of Weather Bureau Officials, held in Omaha. During the morning session on the opening day, as the officials gathered from Weather Bureau offices across the country—some as far as fifteen hundred miles away—Moore took the opportunity to pay tribute to Cleveland, who at that point had dedicated nearly thirty years of his life to the service. "Before proceeding to the consideration of the program, I would say that away back in 1870 there was one who is with us to-day, who laid the foundation of the present weather map, and who, by his own investigations and experimentations, compiled weather charts and made forecasts long before the Federal Government did so," Moore said. "That man has been connected with the Federal Weather Service from the very day of its beginning, and has been an important worker through its whole development. He is a man whom every one of you honors for his scientific attainments, and whom all who know him esteem for his courteous bearing and innate kindness of heart."[148]

While Moore may have exaggerated Cleveland's length of service slightly, he did not underestimate the qualities that underscored Cleveland's characteristic sense of modesty. After Moore finished speaking, he gave the floor to Cleveland to address those in attendance. "Gentlemen, I think you all want to get down to business, and you don't want to hear from me," Cleveland said with humility. "I have been writing a good deal the last five or six years in the *Monthly Weather Review*, and you know just what I would say if I were to say it all over again. The Chief wants to get through with this long program. How he is going to do it, I don't know, but we will begin with paper No. 1."

Monthly Weather Review

When Cleveland addressed his fellow Weather Bureau officials at the convention, he alluded to his work with *Monthly Weather Review*, the journal he helped found a quarter century earlier. Originally consisting of one-page summaries of storms, rainfall, and temperatures across the United States, with accompanying charts, the initial reviews, which date back to July 1872, remained unpublished for wide distribution until 1888, when they were "printed for the purpose of binding up a few sets" of the journal for use in the main Signal Office, as well as several of the larger stations.[149] The first regular issue was published in January 1873, with those from October 1872 through September 1873[150] appearing as an appendix to the Annual Report of the Chief Signal Officer for 1873.[151]

While Cleveland was involved with the first copy and took the initial steps toward the journal's regular publication,[152] the first issues were prepared by a rotating board of editors, consisting of various staff members from the Signal Office (and, later, the Weather Bureau Central Office), who oversaw publication during the first two decades of the journal.[153] "The general rule was that the forecast official for the month prepared the *Review* for that month, but, of course, as a variety of duties multiplied and the scope of the *Review* increased, the work of the editor was often limited to a very general supervision of the work done by the clerks of the Review room," Cleveland later wrote, adding that "the personality of the editor did not enter into the *Review* quite as clearly as it has done during the past few years."[154]

At the time of the Weather Bureau's transfer in 1891, the *American Meteorological Journal*, founded by Mark Harrington in 1884, was the preeminent meteorological journal in the United States. Although its publication continued after Harrington became chief of the Weather Bureau in 1891, the journal struggled to find wide support from either financial backers or subscribers and ceased publication in 1896, allowing the Weather Bureau's *Monthly Weather Review* to claim that title. The journal had already begun expanding its scope by the time Cleveland was named editor in 1893. For Cleveland, it was a chance to engage his own intellectual curiosity on various topics related to meteorology and share that knowledge with as wide an audience as possible. "As the Chief of Bureau has made the Editor largely responsible for the character of the material published in the *Review* he has endeavored, by allowing the greatest freedom of publication, to encourage everyone interested in meteorology to publish his best ideas and to philosophically accept honest and kind criticism when the latter is animated solely by a desire to advance our knowledge of the subject."[155]

Cleveland saw his role as editor as a sort of arbiter of meteorological research, promoting through publication those ideas he deemed worthy or promising, while rejecting those that were without merit or seemed propagandistic in nature. This was, in his mind, an important part of the process in developing scientific advancements:

> The sciences can advance only step by step. No one can tell where or when the next important step will originate. Many humble beginners may suggest good ideas that will be confirmed by more eminent investigators after years of work. We must be careful not to ridicule a new hypothesis, but equally careful not to adopt it as a well established principle for fear lest thereby we may be led astray. There has always been a contest between the dullards and conservatives on one side and the bright theorists on the other. The legitimate use of the imagination is the most important consideration to a man engaged in research, but the illegitimate use of the imagination is very dangerous.[156]

Cleveland said that if he occasionally allowed publication of an item "in which the imagination is more important than the facts," it was not because he was looking to promote some new idea, but rather because he was "confident that the ability of the investigator will eventually enable him to right himself and find his way out of the woods into the clear light of some important truth as yet unknown to us all."[157] At the same time, he justified sometimes rejecting submissions "in which imagination is more prominent than the facts, or in which the facts have been distorted so as to appear to support a preconceived theory," which he attributed to the possibility that "meteorology is overburdened with ill-founded notions, and students must be discouraged from pursuing really foolish or unimportant lines of work while the important problems of meteorology are almost neglected on account of their difficulty."[158] He felt strongly that *Monthly Weather Review* should be "a medium for honest, rational discussion of every important problem of meteorology, whether it be approached from the statistical, the experimental, or the mathematical side. It is not carrying on an unreasonable propaganda."[159]

The changes Cleveland brought to the journal received praise from the scientific community, which welcomed the enlarged format and more diverse content. "There was a time when the *Monthly Weather Review* of our Weather Bureau was anything but an interesting publication, for it contained little besides meteorological summaries and statistics," read a review in *Science* magazine in 1896. "During the past two years, however, under the editorship of Prof. Cleveland Abbe, to whom meteorology in this country owes so much, the *Review* has taken on more of a popular character, and it now presents every month not only the usual tables and summaries, but a considerable number of longer or shorter papers and notes on different meteorological subjects."[160]

Weather Bureau Chief Willis Moore, in his annual report for 1896–1897, also praised Cleveland for his work with the journal. "The scope of the *Monthly Weather Review* has been enlarged and its usefulness increased through the untiring efforts of its editor, Prof. Cleveland Abbe," he wrote. Moore cited Cleveland's "profound knowledge of the mathematics, the physics, and the literature of meteorology," noting that he had "been a modest, loyal, and valuable assistant to the several executive heads of this service. He was the first and is still the senior professor of meteorology." Moore's gratitude toward Cleveland's distinguished service was so high that he added a note in his official report lamenting the fact that the professor's salary should be as low as it was, following the reduction in pay he received several years earlier at the hands of Morton. "I regret to report that to-day the Government, in whose service he has spent twenty-seven years of his earnest life, now pays him but two-thirds of the salary he received on entering its service," Moore said. "At an early day I hope to see his salary restored to, say, $4,000 per annum. He has edited the *Monthly Weather Review* in such manner as to command the admiration of both American and European scientists. Quotations from it are to be found daily in the popular scientific journals of this country and of the world."[161]

Some of the more interesting items Cleveland published in the pages of *Monthly Weather Review* appeared under the heading "Notes by the Editor" and included such titles as: "How Do Rains and Winds Spread Epidemics?"[162] "The Green Colored Sun of September 9–10, 1883,"[163] "The Use of the Search Light in Meteorology,"[164] "Showers of Fish,"[165] "Origin of the Word 'Blizzard,'"[166] and "The Moon and the Weather."[167]

One proposed change to *Monthly Weather Review* that did not take hold occurred in 1878, when General Myer suggested that the journal be translated into French and published as an international edition. "The labor and expense attending this experiment was subsequently found to be prohibitive, but the few copies of this edition that are still to be found in the libraries mark one of the many interesting episodes in the history of the Weather Bureau," Cleveland later recalled.[168]

While the majority of articles and other contributions to *Monthly Weather Review* came from the professors or observers of the Weather Bureau, Cleveland did solicit submissions from outside the organization—and, occasionally, from outside the world of meteorology (though the subject matter was always related to the field). One notable example occurred in late September

1903, when Cleveland wrote to Wilbur Wright, after having learned from Professor Charles F. Marvin, head of the Weather Bureau's Instrument Division, about the experiments Wilbur and his brother Orville had been conducting along the Outer Banks of North Carolina. "It occurs to me that your life on the sand dunes must have given occasion for many observations of little matters that have an interest to meteorology quite apart from the problem of soaring flight," Cleveland wrote. He suggested that some of the material in the pamphlet Marvin had shared with him about the Wrights' work "might be amplified into a very interesting article." He was particularly interested in a study of the soaring of buzzards the brothers made and how it related to ascending and descending currents. "If you can elaborate the meteorological features on pages 11–14 for me, I shall be glad to publish the resulting article in the Monthly Weather Review."[169] Cleveland also took the opportunity to offer his own suggestion regarding the brothers' work. "As regards the problem of flight, is it really necessary to attack the most difficult question at the present moment?" he asked. "Would it not be practicable to devise a flapping machine attached by a trolley to an electric wire overhead so that a man could simply be raised a few feet above the ground and carried along by the flapping, the work being done by the electric current?"[170]

Less than three months later, the Wrights made their mark on history when, on December 17, 1903, they successfully completed the first-ever, powered, heavier-than-air flights along the windswept stretch of beach known as Kill Devil Hills. Wilbur had written to the Weather Bureau in 1899, seeking information on favorable areas to conduct their experiments. Moore responded, enclosing copies of *Monthly Weather Review* for August and September 1899. Based, in part, on tables of average wind speeds published in the journal, as well as correspondence with local Weather Bureau observer Joseph J. Dosher, the brothers settled on Kitty Hawk as the location for their gliding experiments during the winters of 1900 to 1903.[171]

On December 31, 1903, two weeks after their first successful flights, Cleveland again wrote to Wilbur. "In reply to your letter of the 28th inst., I beg to inform you that I would highly appreciate, for publication in the Monthly Weather Review, the photograph to which you refer, showing the course of sand streams in a high wind," he wrote. "The photograph will, I hope, be accompanied by an explanatory note, and will be of great interest because of its bearing on the subject of the movement of sand dunes by the wind, a subject of much practical importance." Cleveland added a note stating that such a contribution to the journal would stand on its own merit and not be considered quid pro quo for the assistance the Weather Bureau had provided.

"Please don't feel obliged to write for the Weather Bureau 'as a matter of courtesy to the Bureau,' I shall accept your articles from a higher standpoint, namely, that of actual contributions to human knowledge." Cleveland ended his letter with a word of encouragement, apparently unaware of the achievement that had recently taken place at Kitty Hawk. "I congratulate you upon the steady prosecution of your experimental research on gliding flight. You are sure to bring out facts of interest and value to everyone."[172] A week later, as word began to spread of the brothers' success, Cleveland decided to help publicize the news. "Prof. Marvin has just shown me the enclosed newspaper clipping, from which I have presumed to make up the accompanying note for the Weather Review, but as I may have made some mistake in this, I beg you to revise it and return in the accompanying envelope," he wrote Wilbur on January 7.[173] Cleveland published an account of the Wright brothers' feat in the December 1903 issue of *Monthly Weather Review*—which appeared in print in early 1904—as a note under the heading, "Meteorology and the Art of Flying":[174]

> During the past four years a series of most interesting experiments have been going on the coast of Dare County, N. C., not far from the Weather Bureau station at Kittyhawk. Here the brothers, Wilbur and Orville Wright, of Dayton, Ohio, have established a camp and all the necessary apparatus for experiments in what is known as gliding flight. The apparatus, which is a form of aeroplane, is launched from the summit of a sand hill, and after making a long glide finally comes to rest on the sands below. After several years of experience and careful study of the currents and winds that blow over the sand hills, the Messers. Wright have applied motor machinery to their aeroplanes. Their success is undoubtedly due in great part to the preliminary careful study of the winds, and for this reason, although machinery is essential, yet we consider that meteorology also has played an important part in their work. Their latest official announcement is that on December 17 four flights were made. The wind record at Kittyhawk was 24 to 27 miles per hour at 30 feet above the ground, but at the flying station it was about 22 miles per hour at 4 feet above ground. These flights were made from the level ground, against the wind, with no assistance from gravity: after a horizontal run of 40 feet the aeroplane rose with the operator on a very gentle incline to a height of 8 or 10 feet from the ground, after which the course was kept as nearly horizontal as the wind gusts and the limited skill of the operator would permit, and the flyer made its way forward with a speed of 10 miles per hour over the ground, or 30 to 35 miles per hour relative to the air. The

fourth flight occupied 59 seconds and the machine few through a distance of 852 feet over the ground, or about three times that distance relative to the wind; it landed earlier than was necessary, owing to a slight error of judgment on the part of operator.

Cleveland concluded with a note from the brothers themselves:

> It had not been our intention to make any detailed public statement concerning the private trials of our powered "Flyer" on the 17th of December last; but since the contents of a private telegram, announcing to our folks at home the success of our trials, was dishonestly communicated to newspaper men at the Norfolk office, and led to the imposition upon the public by persons who never saw the Flyer or its flights, of a fictitious story incorrect in almost every detail; and since this story, together with several pretended interviews or statements, which were fakes pure and simple, has been very widely disseminated, we felt impelled to make some corrections. The real facts were as above.

In July 1893, Cleveland wrote to Theodore Roosevelt, his former neighbor from East 20th Street in New York. At the time, Roosevelt was serving on the U.S. Civil Service Commission. Earlier that year—two months before leaving office—President Harrison issued an executive order placing 314 of the Weather Bureau's observers and local forecast officials under civil service rules.[175] Cleveland asked Roosevelt to prepare an article for him, which the future president declined to do, stating, "I know so little—indeed nothing—of meteorology, that I hardly feel competent to write anything in reference to your scheme."[176]

Meteorology in Schools

The material published in *Monthly Weather Review* also provided valuable material for use in promoting meteorology as a field of study in schools across the country, an area of great personal interest to Cleveland, especially during the latter part of his career in the Weather Bureau. At the convention of Weather Bureau officials in Omaha in 1898, Cleveland posed the question of education to his colleagues. "I have always been curious to know how many of our men have actually done something toward getting meteorology taught in schools. How many of you have had a chance to talk to schools, or colleges, or universities, or to teachers, in any way? Please rise." Nearly everyone in the audience stood up.[177]

Cleveland wrote extensively on the subject of meteorology in schools in the pages of *Monthly Weather Review*, in an effort to bring attention to the growing demand for—and benefit of—teaching weather and climate as a scientific discipline at all levels, from elementary school through university.

"The fundamental principles of nature study are now rapidly spreading throughout this country and must eventually prevail everywhere, for they are founded on correct principles and necessarily bring about successful results," he said. "A child is naturally a learner; he is an inquisitive student and experimentalist. At first he learns by bumps and bruises and through pains and troubles; frequently he actually makes experiments and observes closely and reasons and argues to himself. It is always easier for him to learn by personal experience than by reading books or listening to others tell about things as seen by them." Cleveland argued that by making regular weather observations at schools, teachers could imbue their students with the necessary skills to help them succeed in a variety of subjects, as well as in life in general. "In order to stimulate him to accuracy, he is encouraged to measure and record carefully. The weather lends itself to this method of training quite as easily as any other subject. He may learn a little meteorology, but more important is it that he learn accuracy of observation and correct logical reasoning."

In 1882, Cleveland delivered a series of lectures to future teachers at the Washington Normal School, maintaining his idea "that as we have the weather about us every day it constitutes an admirable subject for youthful observation and study." Cleveland felt that, by teaching the teachers, he could help instill an appreciation for the study of weather in future generations. "In accordance with the principles that were then taught at that Normal School it was necessary for each member of the class to record and analyze her own observations on the subject under consideration, in order, by this personal training, to obtain the experience that is necessary to successfully conduct the classes of children that must eventually come under her care."[178]

In November 1904, Cleveland addressed the Central Association of Science and Mathematics Teachers in Chicago. As he spoke, he hoped to inspire the teachers present to consider integrating problems involving meteorology into their daily instruction. "I regard meteorology not so much as a matter of observation and generalization as a matter of deductive reason," he said. "Our studies have approached the limit of what we are likely to discover by inductive processes. We stand where astronomy stood in the days of La Place. We have had our Galileo and Newton, but we still need other leaders, and you will all agree with me that these must be trained in the schools. They must get their first lessons from you. Twenty or thirty years hence our future masters in meteorology will tell how their feet were turned in the right direction by the teachers of to-day."[179]

Cleveland argued that, while there were some students for whom weather would be a naturally appealing subject, we should not disregard those who seem less interested or find the matter more difficult to comprehend. "In every school I find several boys and girls that have taken a deep interest in the weather and its relations to our lives. They are often asking questions that bear upon it. They appear to observe and understand it better than others. These are they whom I would have you secure for the possible service of the Weather Bureau," he said optimistically. "There are others that often appear dull, but they are not really so; their previous education has perhaps been imperfect, some one has confused their minds with erroneous ideas, of which they can not easily rid themselves," Cleveland contended. "There are others who have not yet awakened to a full interest in intellectual work. In general the school will be benefited by taking up exact and experimental work as compared with inexact, indefinite, texts or phrases."[180]

When it came to higher education, Cleveland, who had assumed the de facto role as "the principal spokesman for the development of meteorological research and training programs,"[181] was equally emphatic and enthusiastic about incorporating meteorology as a subject in colleges and universities across America, which had begun to lag behind its European counterparts.[182] Writing in *The Atlantic Monthly* in 1891, Cleveland made a plea for "recognition by our highest institutions of learning of the claims of terrestrial physics as a distinct department of research and of instruction." Specifically, he said such a department would address problems "in which we consider the land, the ocean, and the atmosphere," in essence, the Earth sciences. "Of all branches of applied science, meteorology, with its weather predictions, is that which at the present moment demands the most serious attention from our universities," he argued. "The professors needed in connection with courses of study preparatory to meteorology are already to be found in several of our universities and technical schools. At these, therefore, it will require but a slight additional labor or expense to conduct the students through a special course in theoretical and practical meteorology and the applications of climatology."[183]

Cleveland claimed that the field was "ripe for the harvest" of skilled, educated professionals and it was up to the institutions of higher learning in America to facilitate the necessary instruction. "So long as our universities make no provision for teaching the new aspect of this science, and confine their courses of instruction to a few remarks on the elementary climatology of twenty years ago, so long must the study of meteorology in America be expected to deal only with the superficial appearance of things, without going to the root of the matter." Given the opportunity to "study the laws of motion of storms and the art of prediction," Cleveland said the young students of physics "will soon make of meteorology a science as exact as is in any way compatible with the complexity of the phenomena."[184]

For his part, Cleveland began a part-time position in 1884 as professor of meteorology at the Corcoran Scientific School at Columbian University (now George Washington University), in Washington, D.C. In 1896, he began lecturing at Johns Hopkins University in Baltimore. He would hold positions at both institutions throughout the remainder of his life. Johns Hopkins, in particular, would hold a special place in Cleveland's life. His eldest son, Cleveland Jr., would attend graduate school there, after graduating from Harvard in 1894.[185] The elder Abbe would later donate to the university the majority of his private library—some two thousand books and journals, thirty-seven bound volumes of charts, and one thousand pamphlets on various topics related to meteorology.[186] This was an attempt, on Cleveland's part, to entice the university to begin conferring doctorates in meteorology—something no school in America had done before. Writing to Daniel Coit Gilman, the university's president, in 1891, Cleveland said, "[I]f it should eventually seem feasible to you to encourage your students and the teachers of the country to select Meteorology as a course of study for the degree of Ph.D. then I shall be glad to help the matter along by transferring to your library the very large collection of weather charts and meteorological literature that I have accumulated."[187] His efforts paid off in 1899 when Johns Hopkins awarded the first American Ph.D. degree in meteorology to Oliver L. Fassig, who had been working at the Weather Bureau's Baltimore office. Cleveland served as a referee of Fassig's dissertation.[188]

Writing in *Monthly Weather Review* in 1903, Cleveland laid out the argument that if meteorologists were ever to advance the state of the science—and, by doing so, the predictability of the weather—the key to their success would lie in a solid educational foundation:

> The gradual development of meteorology has for two hundred years been due to the activity and faithfulness of innumerable observers throughout the world and it has not been supposed that the labor of reading instruments and making weather records required anything but ordinary intelligence, good habits, and perseverance on the part of the observers. Those who have tried to penetrate the laws of atmospheric phenomena generally found the problems

> too difficult and very few profound theories have, as yet, been accepted as satisfactory to the best students. At the present time, however, the so-called practical man is being very hard pushed in order to keep abreast with the progress that is being made by a new race of investigators who are applying to the atmosphere the best that is now known relative to all the laws of physics and mechanics. It will no longer do to say that the practical man is ahead of the theoretical or that the college graduate is inferior to one who is not a collegian. Whatever advance may be made in the practical business operations of the thirty or forty national weather bureaus now in existence; however much they may extend the telegraphic work, and the areas covered by the daily weather maps, or the accuracy and minuteness of the daily weather forecasts, yet, there will always be use for those who are delving deeper and searching further. There is a divine instinct that leads men to strive upward and forward in the realm of knowledge. We are confident that everything is governed by law and that these laws are not beyond our knowledge. Little by little we shall dissipate the ignorance around us; we shall unveil the arcana of the universe; we shall find the work of the observer confirming our theories; we shall honor those leaders of science whose fancies have not led them astray in their efforts to discover the laws of nature.[189]

Cleveland contended that "if education is good for the business man it may also be good for the meteorological observer" and argued that, as improvements are made in understanding the mechanics of the atmosphere, so too must they be made in the education of observers. "Shall we not make better observers in proportion as we study meteorology more thoroughly and learn to appreciate all the fine points that have been brought out by centuries of records and studies?" he asked. "Shall we not make better climatologists by having regard to the rules that govern the legitimate methods of studying statistics, rules that are as rigid as the laws of chance or the play of roulette or cards at the gaming table? Shall we not make better meteorologists by familiarizing ourselves with the laws of physics that pervade the whole atmosphere. The winds and clouds, heat and cold, rain, storm, and drought can not vary, except in obedience to the laws of nature."[190]

Honorary Degrees

Cleveland's own educational record received an august addition in 1888 when he received an honorary degree of L.L.D. (Doctor of Laws) from the University of Michigan, where he had studied astronomy under Dr. Franz

Brünnow and taught physics and civil engineering some thirty years earlier. In June 1896, he received the same honor from the University of Glasgow in Scotland. The conferral of that L.L.D. degree took place as part of an elaborate ceremony celebrating the jubilee of Lord Kelvin, marking fifty years for the esteemed mathematician and physicist as chair of natural philosophy at the university. "It was an occasion almost, if not altogether, without precedent in the annals of science," according to one account.[191] Lord Kelvin himself conferred the degree on Cleveland, along with about a dozen other distinguished scientists and dignitaries—including Professor Simon Newcomb, Cleveland's former boss at the Naval Observatory (the only other American honored). The Abbes stayed with Lord Kelvin and his wife, Lady Kelvin, during their time in Glasgow and, to add to the special honor, Lady Kelvin sewed the scarlet lining of Cleveland's L.L.D. hood herself—an added touch whose elegance was not lost on him.[192] After he arrived home in Washington, D.C., Cleveland received a letter from Lord Kelvin, thanking him for his participation in the event. "I was glad to see that you had got safely home again after coming to see us in Glasgow. It was a great pleasure to me to see you and other friends who were so kind in coming to the Jubilee."[193] In addition to the two L.L.D. degrees, Cleveland received an honorary Ph.D. degree in 1891 from the College of the City of New York, his alma mater, as well as a degree of S.B. (*scientiae baccalaureus*) in 1900 from Harvard, awarded retroactively for the year 1864.

Meteorological Translations

In his quest to help disseminate meteorological research conducted around the world to the widest possible audience, Cleveland took it upon himself to undertake translations of important papers published by foreign scientists. He published three sets of translations—mostly from German—on subjects ranging from atmospheric pressure and rain to the energy of storms to the thermodynamics of the atmosphere. His first collection appeared in the annual report of the Smithsonian Institution for 1877, under the heading "Short Memoirs on Meteorological Subjects."[194] The next two collections, published in 1893 and 1910, were each titled "The Mechanics of the Earth's Atmosphere: A Collection of Translations." Spanning decades of research from leading European minds, Cleveland's translations were an attempt "to introduce English-speaking students of meteorology to the rapidly increasing literature bearing on the fundamental mechanical problems of that science"[195] with a goal of ultimately advancing meteorology through the transfer of knowledge. "There is a crying need for more profound researches into the mechanics of the atmosphere, and believing as I do that meteorology can only be advanced beyond its present stage by the devotion to it of the highest talent in mathematical and experimental physics, I earnestly commend these memoirs to such students in our universities as are seeking new fields of applied science."[196]

Long-Range Forecasts

For years, Cleveland had pondered the possibility of forecasting the weather more than a couple days in advance—and the physical problems associated with it. In 1888, he wrote to his former mentor at Pulkovo Observatory in Russia, Otto Struve, telling him that "the great problem of meteorology is that of the laws of fluid motion a subject on which so many mathematicians and physicists have been at work during the past ten years that we are certainly now on the high road to a successful treatment of the questions that are of practicable importance in hydraulics, and in the movements of the atmosphere."[197]

Cleveland compared the problem of trying to determine the movement of a storm center to that of the movement of a component of a quintuple star, an analogy to which Struve could certainly relate. While Cleveland's love for astronomy had not waned, his professional perspective had changed. "I can hardly read or see anything now-adays without being conscious of looking at it as it were through the atmosphere and with the spectacles of a meteorologist."[198]

Cleveland knew that in order for meteorology to advance as a science the way in which forecasters made their predictions would need to evolve from an inductive-based system to one that was deductive in nature. In the early days of his own forecasting career, with his "probabilities," first at the Cincinnati Observatory in 1869, and, later with the Signal Service from 1871 to 1872, Cleveland had relied on analysis of the formation and movement of areas of high and low pressure—a method known as forecasting by weather "types"—in making predictions more than a few days in advance. By Cleveland's own admission, this method of prediction "is of extremely limited value in weather forecasts."[199]

In 1894, Cleveland published a note in *Monthly Weather Review* titled "The Possibilities of Long-Range Forecasts." In it, he argued that "the only long-range forecasts that we are at present able to make are based upon empirical and very imperfect rules deduced from our study of the accumulated climatological statistics." The best that could be done at the time, he said, was "to chart and study the occurrence of abnormal weather conditions across the globe" and interpret the results in the context of what was known of the mechanics of the atmosphere.[200]

Nearly a decade later, in February 1901, Cleveland gave a series of lectures at Johns Hopkins University on the feasibility of forecasting more than a day or two in advance. He summarized his talks into a paper presented at the American Association for the Advancement of Science meeting that August in Denver, which was published in the December issue of *Monthly Weather Review* with the title "The Physical Basis of Long-Range Weather Forecasts."[201] He pointed out that by "long-range" he was referring "only to the length of time intervening between the date of making a weather prediction and the date when we expect it to be fulfilled."

"At the present time, by the help of the daily weather map, the official weather forecasters of this country, and indeed of every civilized nation on the globe, publish forecasts, in detail, of approaching weather changes, and especially storms, for one and two, or possibly occasionally three days in advance," he pointed out. "These predictions all relate to comparatively minute details for regions that have been charted and studied daily for many years. They merely represent the direct teachings of experience; they are generalizations based upon observations but into which physical theories have as yet entered in only a superficial manner if at all."

Cleveland argued that successfully predicting the weather beyond one or two days required forecasters to look beyond recognizing patterns on weather maps or relying on rules of thumb and truly understand the mechanics of the atmosphere and the physical processes that dictate how it works. "There is a physical basis for all meteorological phenomena," he asserted. "There are laws of mechanics and heat that apply to the atmosphere, and as fast as we acquire the ability to discover these and reason out their consequences we shall perceive that law and order prevail in all the complex phenomena of the weather and the climate."

Cleveland laid out a series of mathematical equations—what have become known as the primitive equations—to simulate physical processes of the atmosphere and describe the various components governing atmospheric motion. "It is to be expected that long before we have attained to what may be called a complete solution of all these equations of condition we shall by means of general theorems have at least obtained some approximately correct ideas concerning the general mechanics of the atmosphere," he wrote.

He also recognized that initial conditions found in the upper and lower parts of the atmosphere represented the greatest uncertainty in carrying out his proposed work. His hope was that upper-air observations made by self-recording instruments attached to sounding balloons—the type of work that was beginning to emerge in Europe at the time—would supplant the historical record of observations made on mountaintops or via manned balloon ascents and help fill in the gaps and provide the necessary data to enable long-range forecasts. "The newer observations are in fact found to be nearly accordant with those indicated by theoretical thermodynamics and hydrodynamics, and it is believed that all the older observations, which gave results contrary to mechanical theory, were really affected by very large errors of observation."[202]

Cleveland's views were ahead of their time, both in terms of the current state of meteorological dogma that existed at the time—at least within the restrictive realm of the Weather Bureau—and in terms of the feasibility of such work, which would require advances in both observational practices and technological capabilities that would come years after Cleveland's death. He realized this and yet felt optimistic that his vision would someday become reality. "While I thus indulge hope in the prospective future high perfection of the science of the weather, I recognize the fact that we must not expect to realize these hopes in this generation. The progress of all science is necessarily slow."[203]

Cleveland concluded his paper by reiterating the necessity for tackling the issue of long-range forecasts through careful, scientific analysis. "We shall arrive at the desired result sooner and better by the study of the mechanics of the atmosphere than by the search for elusive empiric periodicities, and it is in the hopes of inducing some to turn their attention toward this study that I have submitted these views."[204]

Cleveland's paper on long-range weather forecasts has been described as "remarkable" for its "scientific vision."[205] It represented a fundamental paradigm shift in meteorology that was necessary for the evolution from an empirical art to a deductive science. Even the rhetoric Cleveland employed in his text has been cited for allowing him "to position the field's past traditions, and those who supported it, as relics of an earlier, soon to be irrelevant age."[206]

Three years after the publication of Cleveland's seminal paper, a Norwegian physicist named Vilhelm Bjerknes, who was a professor at the University of Stockholm, published his own paper on the subject of long-range forecasting. Appearing in the German-language journal *Meteorologische Zeitschrift*, the paper, titled "Das Problem der Wettervorhersage, betrachtet vom Standpunkte der Mechanik und der Physik" ("The Problem of Weather Prediction, considered from the Standpoint of Mechanics and Physics"), presented a starkly similar view to that of Cleveland's paper. Like Cleveland, Bjerknes argued that a solution to the problem of meteorological prediction required one to know, with sufficient accuracy, both the state of the atmosphere at a given time and the laws by which one successive atmospheric state develops from another.[207] Unlike Cleveland, however, Bjerknes "blandly and prematurely claimed to have at hand the technical means for handling the equations."[208] In fact, it would be years before any attempts were made at numerical weather prediction—and decades before any success.[209]

Although Bjerknes did not mention Cleveland in his work, the two corresponded, and in 1905, while Bjerknes was in New York City to deliver a series of lectures at Columbia University, Cleveland invited him to visit the New York Weather Bureau office. The two chatted for hours before going to dinner, where they "talked meteorology the whole evening."[210] Bjerknes later described Cleveland as "the most charming old man one can imagine, an ageing angel."[211]

Cleveland also invited Bjerknes to Washington, D.C., where he met with Weather Bureau Chief Willis Moore and other officials, and delivered a lecture at the Carnegie Institution titled "Weather Forecasting as a Problem for Mechanics and Physics." This proved successful for Bjerknes, as the institute agreed to fund his research for the next thirty-five years.[212] Although Bjerknes went on to receive much of the credit for establishing the historical foundation of numerical weather prediction—while Cleveland's work went largely unnoticed—Cleveland "did not view or treat Bjerknes as a competitor, but as precisely the kind of young scholar he hoped to attract to meteorology."[213]

Fanny's Death

By the turn of the twentieth century, Cleveland was enjoying relative tranquility and stability, both in his professional life and at home. He had reached a pinnacle with his work at the Weather Bureau and had earned the admiration and respect of his colleagues. All three of his sons had graduated college and were beginning their own careers. Cleveland had time to devote himself to various societies engaged in the dissemination of scientific knowledge. His evenings might be spent at a meeting of the Washington Philosophical Society or the National Geographic Society, of which he was a founding member,[214] or perhaps at one of the "Wednesday Evenings" hosted by Alexander Graham Bell.[215]

In May 1903, Cleveland wrote to his longtime friend Albert Bickmore, reminiscing about their time together in Cambridge four decades earlier and offering his hopeful thoughts on their years ahead. "The forty years that have elapsed since we left Cambridge have brought to you and me little else than happiness and what the world calls—success, but which, in fact, is only the natural outgrowth of the principles that actuated us then and ever since," he wrote. "I think I can see into the future far enough to rest assured that, if we continue as we have begun, we shall enjoy our seventies and perhaps our eighties, as we now do our sixties, and shall be ready to go when the time comes."[216]

That August, Cleveland and Fanny traveled to Ithaca, New York, to visit Cornell University.[217] While there, Fanny was diagnosed with diabetes. The disease, which had been identified as far back as ancient Egypt, was just beginning to be understood by modern physicians and researchers at the turn of the twentieth century. The diagnosis forced the Abbes "to consider the problems of diet, a certain amount of hospitalization, and a definite restriction of her activities."[218] As one contemporary treatise on the disease stated, "Diabetes is a disease in which the expectant plan of treatment is disastrous. It is a disease which never gets well of itself, and always gets worse when not properly treated."[219] Still, the prospects were better for adults who developed the disease, as compared to juvenile patients for whom a diagnosis amounted to a death sentence, with the isolation of insulin as a treatment—and a full understanding of the two types of diabetes that predominately affect the different age groups—still years away. "When the disease appears after middle life, is early recognized and promptly treated, it is ordinarily easily controlled," the medical text assured at the time, "and although it is almost never safe to declare a case of diabetes absolutely cured, it does happen that recovery is so complete that the patient may be left to his own mode of living."[220] In addition to strict restrictions on diet and a regimented physical routine, common treatments at the time included regular doses of opium and arsenic.

To spare her of the work and worry that came with caring for their large house, Fanny went to spend time with their three sons, each of whom had homes of their own at that point. Meanwhile, Cleveland began looking for someone to rent out their home at 2017 I Street, NW, and made arrangements to escape the oppressive heat and humidity of Washington, D.C., during the summer months and work from a location whose climate he felt would be more tolerable.

In the summer of 1908, Cleveland and Fanny traveled to Canton, in northern New York, near the Canadian border, "in order to enjoy the delightful summer climate of this 'North Country.'" There, Cleveland worked out of the local Weather Bureau office, while Fanny relaxed. On June 23, Cleveland Jr. arrived to spend two days with his parents.[221] One month later, on July 24, Fanny finished her lunch and retired to the front porch of the house where they were staying to do some knitting. As she sat quietly, working the needles and yarn, she suddenly felt a sharp pain in her abdomen. In less than an hour she was dead. "It was an easy termination for that diabetes," their son Truman later conceded, "a way that most of us would choose to go."[222] The immediate cause of death was acute indigestion.[223]

Cleveland decided that Fanny would want to be laid to rest with her mother's family at Elmwood Cemetery, in Burlington, Vermont. His son William arrived from New York to accompany Cleveland, along with Fanny's remains, to Vermont. There they were met by Cleveland Jr. and Truman for the funeral, where they grieved for their loss but also celebrated the blessing of her life. "Mrs. Abbe was a woman of unusual culture and nobility of character," read an obituary in an Upstate New York newspaper. "During all her days from childhood up she was unsparing in self-sacrifice for those about her—family, and stranger alike, and many are they that rise up to call her blessed."[224]

A month after the funeral, Cleveland Jr., who had begun working at the Weather Bureau two years earlier and was being groomed to take over as editor of *Monthly Weather Review*, wrote to his father, who was still in Upstate New York, with a plea to return to Washington, D.C., to be looked after by his children. "I wish very much to have you with us if that is possible without being too selfish; of course Truman wishes to have you also and so do Will and Louisa[225] and they all have equal claims on you," he wrote. "For our part, aside from the genuine pleasure it would be to Frieda[226] and Ernst[227] and me, your presence and books in our house (if we can get one) would be of priceless benefit to me in all my work, just as it always has been." Cleveland Jr. was genuinely concerned for his father's well-being and ability to care for himself. "Further, none of your boys and girls like to have you living about the country in the way you are now doing," he argued, urging, "we all know what poor care you take of yourself and we feel that you ought to be at peace somewhere where one really interested on you will attend to your necessary homely comforts in such a way as will not bother you at all yet will keep you among us as long as possible."[228]

The constant attention to Fanny's failing health during her final years—and her eventual death—took their toll on Cleveland and his own health began to fail, requiring an extended stay in the hospital in Ogdensburg, New York.[229] Cleveland Jr. wrote to his father again in September, expressing his concern. "No doubt you are more comfortable in the hospital, but it seems as if you must be often very lonely in spite of the many things you are planning to do," he wrote.[230]

Faced with the prospect of living alone, Cleveland refused the assistance his sons offered to take him in and provide care as he neared his seventieth birthday. "He wanted to be independent," Truman said. "All of us were married, with homes of our own and small growing families, and each offered to share his home with him. But he said he did not care to add to the complexity of our lives."[231]

Yet, as he grieved the loss of Fanny, Cleveland trusted in his abiding faith—and his unending work—to sustain him, unbeknownst that a new chapter of his life was about to unfold, one that would provide a renewed sense of purpose and happiness as he began his eighth decade of existence.

CHAPTER SEVEN

Final Years (1909–1916)

The past has been forgotten
The present soon will be so
past
Then the future will be present
gone
and quickly all be past.[1]
—Cleveland Abbe, 1916

By the beginning of 1909, Cleveland Abbe had returned to Washington, D.C., having just celebrated his seventieth birthday. The auspicious occasion was marked by a congratulatory letter from his colleague, Professor Alexander McAdie, who had since assumed the position of head of the local Weather Bureau office in San Francisco. "I want to offer you my congratulations upon the anniversary of your birthday. A long life filled with good work for the benefit of your fellow men," McAdie wrote. "Feel assured, dear Professor Abbe, that there are many younger men thruout [sic] our country today who hold you in affectionate regard and who remember with gratitude your readiness to help them. Your scientific work speaks for itself and your official duties and positions are known in many lands; but even above these, it seems to me, should be placed today your personal influence in encouraging men to seek the truth."[2]

McAdie's words would certainly serve to lift Cleveland's spirits, though in order to fill the void left by Fanny's death, he knew he would need to find a new partner, someone who could help manage the daily practicalities of life as well as encourage him professionally and serve as a companion with whom he could share what remained of his life. It was a surprise to many, however—including his own family—when Cleveland decided to marry Margaret Augusta Percival, a woman of British descent who hailed from

St. Kitts in the West Indies[3] and who was nearly thirty years his junior. The marriage caused something of a sensation in the press, with accounts varying in their level of detail and accuracy. "New Weather Man Takes Wife on Quiet," read one local newspaper headline.[4] "Aged Professor Weds Suddenly," read another, which also confused Cleveland's first name with his son Truman's (and misspelled it as "Trueman").[5] "A wedding in which Prof. Cleveland Abbe, a noted scientist, formerly of this city, was the bridegroom, has caused a stir of interest in local social and scientific circles," began an article in the *Washington Evening Star*. The article was one of several to state that Cleveland met Margaret while on a scientific expedition to the West Indies some years earlier, claiming "the friendship which sprung up between them ripened into love, with the culmination that they have been made man and wife."[6] A front-page story that ran in New York City's *The Sun* went even further, claiming that the two were distant cousins and that the romance "began eighteen years ago in the West Indies." According to this source, Cleveland "told her if she ever came to the United States he would marry her."[7]

According to Truman, the two met while Cleveland, in his unending quest for genealogical research, visited an older cousin, Mrs. Colgate Gilbert, of Glencoe, Maryland. Margaret was living with Mrs. Gilbert at the time and served as her housekeeper.[8] "She was as much attracted by Father as he was by her," Truman said. "So in spite of the difference in their ages, about thirty years, she gladly accepted the responsibility of caring for him as a life companion, with the sole intention of making his sunset years rosy."[9] Cleveland and Margaret were married during a small, quiet ceremony on April 12—Easter Monday—at St. John's Episcopal Church in Philadelphia, by the Rev. Edward H. Earle, a friend of Cleveland's. "I am sure that the years that followed were among Father's happiest," Truman said. "Margaret gave him a companionship that was most satisfying to him, to us boys, and to herself."[10]

Cleveland's longtime friend and colleague Professor Charles Marvin would later recall how the union invigorated Cleveland, both physically and mentally, with Margaret's relative youth and sense of duty in caring for her husband providing Cleveland with the strength and support he needed to sustain himself. "Abbe entered upon his new happiness with much of the spirit and romance of youth but, yet, with the sincerity and seriousness of maturity. Each found in the other the great need of all humanity, sacred love, completely satisfied, moulding their separate lives into unselfish reciprocal devotion," Marvin said. "There was thus fittingly provided in the tender care and solicitude of this capable wife of a stronger vigor of life than he, both the affection and the attention that were needful when his own bodily strength, which he had so lavishly bestowed in the interests of science and humanity, failed longer to fully sustain him."[11]

Baltimore and Mount Weather

The happiness Cleveland found with Margaret would soon be tempered by hardships. Around the time they were married, Cleveland found himself the recipient of punitive action by Weather Bureau Chief Willis Moore. Cleveland and Moore had sparred over the establishment of a research station at Mount Weather, a one-hundred-acre plot of land in the Blue Ridge Mountains, located about fifty miles west of Washington, D.C. As a result, Cleveland was temporarily reassigned to Baltimore, where he headed the local Weather Bureau office from May to October 1909, and his salary was reduced from $3,000 to $2,500.[12] He continued to serve as editor of *Monthly Weather Review*, with Cleveland Jr. serving as assistant editor, but this too was about to change. The February issue of *Monthly Weather Review*, which was published in mid-May, carried a notice of a major shift in the journal's editorial content. "The Review will hereafter be a monthly report of the weather and climatology of the country, and there will be excluded from its pages everything technical that is not of a purely climatological nature or a current reports of weather conditions." It was also to "contain no mathematical discussion or formulas."[13] Beginning April 1, the Review Room, which Cleveland headed as editor, and all its work were transferred to the Climatological Division of the Weather Bureau. Cleveland's name continued to appear as editor until the July issue, when the changes took effect. His departure as editor of the journal he helped establish and which he grew—with great diligence and care—for more than fifteen years was a low point in his career.

The actions took place during a turbulent time for both the Weather Bureau and Chief Moore. In May 1909, an article titled "Does the Weather Bureau Make Good?" appeared in the popular *Everybody's Magazine*.[14] The article provided a detailed, point-by-point criticism of Moore's weather service, claiming that it was costing American taxpayers too much money for what it delivered and that it lacked progress. It argued the bureau was excessively explanatory ("Thousands of elaborate rainfall charts, snowfall charts, and storm charts, all superbly lithographed, are sent out monthly to men who have no use for them.") and self-defensive as a result of justifying its appropriations, which exceeded those "ever made for any scientific purpose whatever in the history of the world." The services provided were chastised for being overly general and not specific enough to "be of value to the average individual man." There were charges that the bureaucracy was "evasive and intentionally ambiguous" and the bureau offered "no well-founded hope of improvement in local forecasting."[15]

Much of the criticism was directed at Moore, who, among other things, was blamed for the badly busted forecast for William Howard Taft's Inauguration Day on March 4.[16] The official Weather Bureau forecast for the day called for clearing skies and slightly cooler air, despite the fact that a vigorously intensifying winter storm was barreling toward Washington, D.C. Moore reportedly sent a message to Taft the night before the inauguration, "assuring him through the vale of blinding snow that he would take office under cloudless skies, with a flood of sunshine and a temperature of about 40 degrees."[17] In a companion piece that ran in the same issue of *Everybody's Magazine*, Elias B. Dunn, who had headed up the Weather Bureau's New York office until he was forced out "for reasons that were satisfactory to President McKinley and Secretary [of Agriculture] Wilson,"[18] provided a meteorological analysis of the storm's progression and volleyed harsh criticism at Moore for having initially missed it and then blaming others on his staff. "Willis L. Moore, in making this original forecast, was ready to stand in the lime light and take all the credit personally, had it been successful," Dunn said. "After the failure he stated that he did not make the forecast, but that it was made by his able forecasters in the Bureau, and he pushes them forward to stand the brunt of criticism to shield himself—a most despicable act in a man holding a responsible government position."[19] In a rebuke of both articles, the *Pensacola Journal* defended the Weather Bureau and painted Dunn as a disgruntled former employee seeking revenge. "Ever since Mr. Dunn has been ousted from the service he has been helping the newspapers and magazines to find damaging information against the work that was once the pride of his heart; but now, a hornet's nest that stings him to greater indignation every time he pokes it up."[20]

When Moore directed the construction of facilities atop Mount Weather, he did so without notifying Congress of his actions. His critics claimed he installed the weather observatory to double as "an agreeable summer resort in comfortable proximity to Washington, which has a most sultry summer climate."[21] Moore ultimately was exonerated by a report from the House Committee on Expenditures in the Department of Agriculture, in which the committee chairman criticized Moore, only to have his comments removed by the other members and relegated to a minority report.[22]

Following Cleveland's detail in Baltimore, he and Margaret returned to

Washington, D.C., briefly but soon found themselves packing their bags again, this time to be stationed at Mount Weather, the very observatory whose establishment Cleveland recommended against. "We always felt it was that unfavorable report which caused the demotion from editor of the Monthly Weather Review and the transfer to Baltimore," Truman later admitted. "As I recall it, each of the three men who were on that Committee, supposed to report favorably on the Mount Weather Project, was soon transferred out of Washington and then assigned to a turn of winter duty up there on that bleak mountain top."[23] On March 31, 1910, Cleveland and Margaret left the apartment on Columbia Road in Washington, D.C., where they had been residing since returning from Baltimore, and set off for what would be a nearly yearlong stay at the mountain facility, where Cleveland would serve as editor of the *Bulletin of the Mount Weather Observatory*, which had taken the place of *Monthly Weather Review* as the bureau's scientific and technical journal.

In a letter written shortly after their arrival, Cleveland seemed to relish the experience, rejoicing that he and Margaret were "both very well and in good spirits; happier than ever and full of hopes and dreams."[24] He described their journey from Washington, D.C., to their new home in the Blue Ridge Mountains as being "like emigrants seeking their fortunes in the far west." Their train consisted of three cars—one freight car, one smoking car, and one passenger car, which was divided into separate compartments marked "white" and "colored." Cleveland complained how "the whites and blacks are not allowed to sit in the same railroad car—a very artificial and fanciful separation for the car full of whites smells worse and is as full of infectious diseases as the compartment full of honest hardworking blacks." After disembarking from their "horrid conveyance" at the small hamlet of Bluemont, Virginia, they had a chance to observe some of the locals as they purchased provisions—including soap and brooms—at the village store before making the six-mile trek up the mountain to the government reservation. "I myself have a strong liking or an interest in the hardy mountaineers that live near by us," Cleveland said. "Some of the log huts that they live in have been family homes of a century—they are religious and rather set in their sectarianism—they work hard to raise oats and garden vegetables—stick to the idioms and manners of long ago—rough hands and faces but kindly hearts."[25] The somewhat communal living at the observatory on Mount Weather did not seem to bother Cleveland. He and Margaret would share a cottage with another family (each occupying their own floor) and he would enjoy shared meals with the other dozen or so officials, who ate together in the Administration Building. Cleveland looked forward to eventually enjoying private breakfasts of coffee, toast, and eggs with his new wife. "Margaret has fed me so bountifully this past year that I am unusually fat and jolly." Reflecting on their first year of married life together, Cleveland could not have seemed happier. "This is a great change in our life and especially in Margaret's," he said. "She is a most wonderful woman—an angelic wife—a self-forgetful sister and daughter, and deserves all the years of rest & happiness that are opening out in a delightful vista toward the Delectable Land." Ever grateful for the second chance at happiness and fulfillment he had received, he noted that he and Margaret "celebrate daily the wonderful Providence that brought us finally together after years of manifold experiences, each to be a blessing and comfort to the other."[26]

Shortly after returning to Washington, D.C., in 1911, Cleveland wrote a letter to his colleague, Professor Frank H. Bigelow, the Weather Bureau's astronomer and mathematician. In it, he reflected on the struggles he and others in the weather service—going back to the days of General Albert Myer—suffered and how he had tried to do right by his scientific and moral principles. "Of course my highest ambition has been to be useful—not only doing what little I can but stimulating & helping others. Indeed I think the latter is nearer my heart though I have also tried to save others from making mistakes—so as to uphold the dignity & the value of the Weather Bureau & of science as opposed to chicanery." He was not trying to portray himself as a martyr and noted that many others "had suffered more than I," though he acknowledged that failures and setbacks were inherent in the work of the past four decades since the establishment of the government weather service. "Indeed our fascinating love of peaceful study of inert nature is daily interrupted by the need of considering human nature," he said, with a wistful hope for some redemption in what time remained. "My own prayer is that life and health may be spared to finish little works long since delayed and now of historical rather than research interest." Cleveland closed his letter with a sense of optimism and appreciation. "However we must live and hope—live on and hope ever. May you and I, with our wives live peacefully in this world of strife. I am glad very glad that you & she are well & happy."[27]

The Meteorology of the Future

On the evening of Tuesday, March 16, 1909, Cleveland gave a public lecture at Columbia University in New York City titled "Meteorological Problems for the Future."[28] It was part of a series of nontechnical lectures on meteorology sponsored by the university, whose previous installments included talks by Professors Bigelow and Marvin of the Weather Bureau, as well as Chief Moore. With discussions of both the history of weather forecasting and the prospects for long-range predictions, Cleveland's lecture embodied the culmination of all he had accomplished in his professional life over the preceding four decades, and all he hoped might be accomplished in the field of meteorology. "My task to-night is to be as difficult as the problem proposed of old by Pharoah [sic] to Joseph. I am to tell you a dream of the future of science and also the interpretation thereof," he said.

> In the preceding nine lectures, my colleagues have given you some idea of the present state of our knowledge of the atmosphere. Possibly you may have already suspected that we know very little about the air in which we live. You must not think less of the honest scholar when he assures you that what we really know beyond all peradventure is as nothing compared to the unknown ocean of truth still to be explored. I trust that you will sympathize with my enthusiasm over the study of the atmosphere. Does not the wonderful glory of a sunset sky stimulate one to study its causes and to discover what its clouds and colors have to do with the weather of to-morrow? Who can watch the approach or recession of a thunder-storm and not be impressed with the dreadful majesty of its appearance? We may dream of the immensity of space as we contemplate the star-lit sky at night, for the stars are far, far away and men are always dreaming of them—but we can not merely *dream* of the clouds, the weather and the storms; the atmosphere is too near at hand for mere dreams; it forces us to action; it is close to us; we are in it and of it. It rouses us to both study and do; we must know its moods and also its motive forces; we must conquer it in our struggle for existence. Now that our aeronauts Orville and Wilbur Wright have learned to fly, we must learn to utilize the air just as the mariners have learned to utilize the winds and avoid the storms.

Cleveland's words recalled his own journey toward meteorological fulfillment—from his days of wonderment as at boy during summers at Dog Hill, watching the clouds by day and gazing at the stars by night—to his transformation from astronomer to meteorologist during his years in Cincinnati—to his tenure at the Weather Bureau, where, as his colleague William Jackson Humphreys described it, his most useful roles "were those of mentor and propagandist."[29]

Throughout his talk, Cleveland illustrated his points by performing experiments demonstrating various aspects of meteorology. With the help of several assistants, Cleveland held the audience's attention by filling a glass globe with water vapor and allowing it to cool, to simulate the formation of clouds; using a rotating table to demonstrate how the rotation of Earth results in the apparent deflection of objects moving above it through the atmosphere, such as hurricanes and tropical storms; and removing the vertical divisions in a glass box to show how the mixing of cold and warm air causes dynamic interchanges that affect weather.

Cleveland spoke of changes in Earth's climate, postulating that "the great climatic changes that seem to have taken place during geological history must be explained in connection with the corresponding changes that have taken place in the orography of the continents, and the changes in the distribution of land and water." To him, piecing together the interconnected puzzle of the various components of Earth's physical systems—atmospheric, geologic, hydrologic—to the point where the past could be fully understood and the future fully predicted—paved the way not only for the practical task of weather prediction but also the more philosophical goal of increasing human knowledge. "I consider this to be the ultimate end of meteorology, namely, the logical deduction of the climate and the weather for any time and any given configuration of continents and oceans," he proclaimed. "When we have attained this goal; when meteorology has become more truly deductive, then we can pass to the satisfactory discussion of the great problems that we now can merely toy with like children. Then we shall know whether Mars is inhabitable, and whether man could possibly have existed and evolved anywhere on this earth during geological ages preceding the present."

Cleveland concluded his talk by making an almost evangelical plea for the promotion of meteorology as a profession. "The fundamental problem of to-day is to educate men for the work that we see is at hand," he said. "Friends of science and humanity must be found who will provide for the expenses of men able to work on these problems." Cleveland stressed the need for "laboratories, physicists and sympathetic supporters" and suggested that perhaps "the very first step is to provide generous fellowships, securing a support for enthusiastic men who are adapted to these researches. Atmospheric phenomena are not too difficult for us, nor is there any known natural limit to our steady intellectual progress."[30]

Eugenics and Race

Cleveland's lecture at Columbia appeared in print in the January 1911 issue of *The Popular Science Monthly*. The article that preceded it was titled "Euthenics and Eugenics," by Dr. Charles Benedict Davenport, a prominent biologist who was director of the Biological Laboratory at Cold Spring Harbor, Long Island. There, in 1910, he oversaw the establishment of the Eugenics Records Office, which became the focal point in a growing movement in the United States during the early decades of the twentieth century to study what were perceived as inherited traits among humans—and to apply the knowledge gained in an effort to create a better society.[31] "Of late years the reading, thinking public has been awakened to a realization that sickness, poverty and crime are great and perhaps growing evils," began Davenport's article. "It does not seem right that there should always be about 3 per cent, of our population on the sick list, that our alms houses should support over 80,000 paupers, not to mention the hundreds of thousands that receive outdoor relief or are barely able to earn a living; and that there should be 80,000 persons in prison." Davenport further argued that it was unfair "that the nation should have to support half a million insane, feeble-minded, deaf and blind and that a hundred million dollars should be spent annually by institutions in this country for the care of the sick, degenerate, defective and delinquent."[32]

Davenport argued that "when the method of securing strong offspring, even from partially defective stock . . . is widely known, the teachings of science in respect even to marriage matings will be widely regarded."[33] This sentiment was shared widely among Americans of the Progressive Era and gave rise to both the academic study and popular acceptance of the application of science to social engineering. Under the premise of promoting improvements in human society, eugenics found a voice, to varying degrees, in such seemingly unlikely proponents as feminist Margaret Sanger[34] and civil rights activist W. E. B. Du Bois.[35]

While there is no evidence that Cleveland was involved directly in the eugenics movement, which was just beginning to gain popularity in the United States at the time of his death, his deep-seated interest in his own family's history has been used to promote some of the ideals of eugenics in the years following his death. In the introduction to the five hundred–page tome on his family's history, published shortly after his death, Cleveland's motivation for compiling such an exhaustive work of genealogical research is presented as being more than simply a matter of self-interest:

> Professor Abbe had hoped to make this genealogy no mere list of the members of the family. He would have it a contribution to the study of heredity, so has added as much as practicable on the personal characteristics of its members and has included many available photographs. He believes that the

study of any good clean family will bring out facts just as well worth following up for the development of the personality of the nation, as are the facts brought out by the work of criminologists and social workers in the field of the mentally deficient, etc., which show the immense value to a country, of the study of inheritance of traits that increase state expenses for caring for such defectives.[36]

Similar sentiments are found in the writings of Truman, who wrote of his father's "inborn scientific spirit" and felt that heredity was a key factor. "When we look for an answer to that question as to the source of his inspiration, we come back to the question of what makes any great man?" Truman said. "The answer seems to be based on the two great fundamental factors of environment and heredity. No one appreciated the bearing of those two factors better than Cleveland Abbe."[37]

Cleveland's brother Robert also wrote of the influence of heredity he felt was inherent in one's character. "Personality is a composite of every ancestor in one's pedigree. This biologic truth is now universally accepted, and makes all real knowledge of the acts and lives of those who have preceded us in an actual line of descent, a foundation of our own motives for the good and (the) bad in our lives."[38]

In the September 1918 issue of *Eugenical News* (published two years after Cleveland's death), there is a brief item titled "The Families of Abbe and Abbey," which evokes the Abbe family history in suggesting a source of Cleveland's successes in life. "This genealogy furnishes much evidence for the genetic foundations of eminence. Besides many instances of similar abilities occurring in closely related members of the family, it shows lines of marked ability of definite type extending through many generations." It goes on to say, "Many of the characteristics which marked Cleveland Abbe, the meteorologist, appear to be a heritage through his maternal ancestry."[39] The following month's issue of the same journal included a brief article titled "The Field of Genealogy," which also cited Cleveland's family history and its introductory statement as evidence that he "clearly conceived the possible biological uses of genealogy." It portrayed Cleveland's ancestors as "a race of soldiers, path-finders and pioneer settlers" who were "identified with the best influences and prominent in the founding of industrial and educational institutions."[40] Regarding Cleveland in particular, it states:

Cleveland Abbe was himself an illustrious example of this pioneering instinct. Slight in physique, diffident and mild in personal bearing to the

> point of self-effacement, he yet possessed the daring imagination, the energy and enthusiasm in new emprise characteristic of the pioneer. These abilities conceived and put into operation the multitudinous daily observations on which is founded our National Weather Service, and gave him world leadership in turning hitherto untouched resources of untold value to the public weal.

During his travels around the world, Cleveland had occasion to observe race and social constructs that differed from those in America and commented on such differences in his correspondence with family back home. Writing to his mother from Pulkovo in April 1866, Cleveland shared his views on the class divisions that existed in Imperial Russia at the time, but also discussed the issue of immigration in America. "The emigration of German Lutherans & dissenters to America is becoming something more & more important but it is our good element & in a few generations English French German & Negroes will have made us a mightier race than we now dream of," he wrote, adding, "but power is not to be our object—it will be given to us as a trust that we may be able to attain & work out our destiny—which if I rightly apprehend is to lead other nations in the path of self government & righteousness. May we all be true to our mission."[41] Cleveland's views reflected the general sentiment of the time. According to one analysis of U.S. immigration policy in the mid-nineteenth century, "Support for an open immigration policy was strong, though not always vocal. Many Americans sympathized with the refugees and famine victims, and saw their coming as confirmation of the widespread conviction that the United States was in every way superior to Old World countries."[42]

Writing to Fanny from Angola during the USS *Pensacola* expedition in January 1890, Cleveland described the natives as "black uncouth & homely but full of love and kindness," recalling how he spent one evening singing hymns with them while one of the natives played the organ. "They are a jolly happy social people—ignorant of our civilization but with plenty of knowledge of Africa & its peculiarities—a knowledge that I would like to acquire from them for their continental interests are wonderful."[43]

Two months later, while on Ascension Island in the South Atlantic, Cleveland wrote a letter to Truman, who at the time was sixteen years old. He described his experiences on the island of St. Helena, the previous stop on the expedition. He noted that many of the inhabitants of the island were descendants of former slaves—from Africa, Malaysia, Southeast Asia, or India—whose "slight infusion of English blood has made a light colored race that is very good natured and flourishing and willing to work hard but lacking in business energy."[44] Cleveland explained that this last comment referred to the fact that there were "no opportunities for education or business, and no inducement to undertake any extensive work." He went on to describe his belief, in general, of how various ethnic groups interacted with "our Aryan and Semitic ancestors" over a period of thousands of years—a belief prevalent at the time, which held that Indo-European peoples invaded the Indian subcontinent around 1,500 BCE. "Everywhere they found earlier, dark colored, lower, lazier natives whom they called 'the sons of Men' while they called themselves 'the children of God' and from that time until now we have been conquering mixing with & elevating those lower races but most of them died out in the process & left only a little influence or trace on the resulting race." He gave an example of how, in England, the Romans, Danes, and Saxons "pushed out" the Druids, and the Normans later "pushed them, so that England is a mixture of races almost as is the United States." He claimed that in the struggle between races and individuals, "the strongest, wisest & best or those that live in the healthiest or most fruitful regions, triumph and knowing this the English man's rule is to always associate with those that are a little better off than himself—i.e. victor or stronger or wiser."[45] So prevalent was this idea at the time that even Frederick Douglass wrote of it in an essay titled "Aryan Civilization," in which he claimed that "where an inferior race is subdued by one that is superior, but is not destroyed, its customs & beliefs become merged into those of the stronger race, and are made common property. These become the myths & folk tales of all alike, but represent the survival of the underlying savage race."[46]

Back home, Cleveland showed considerable interest in improving the condition of African Americans and looked for ways to lend his assistance, where possible. He spoke at the Bethel Literary and Historical Association, which had emerged as "the principal forum for enlightened discussion on race problems" in the nation's capital.[47] The association, which met at Metropolitan A.M.E. Church, at 1518 M Street, NW, featured such notable speakers as Mary Church Terrell and Frederick Douglass, who delivered his speech "The Race Problem" there in 1890. Cleveland, who spoke at the association several times during the 1880s and 1890s, was described as a "good friend to the society."[48] Meanwhile, as a member of the National Association for the Relief of Destitute Colored Women and Children, Fanny built on the work she had done earlier in her life to help African Americans.[49]

In 1892, Cleveland lent his support to Jennie Dean, a former slave from Virginia who had dedicated her life to improving conditions for fellow African Americans by establishing churches and Sunday schools. After setting her sights on establishing an industrial school for African Americans in Manassas, Virginia, Dean embarked on an ambitious fundraising campaign that lasted nearly a decade. When she wrote to industrialist and philanthropist John D. Rockefeller Sr. in May 1892[50] seeking support, she included a letter of endorsement from Cleveland. "I wish to bring to your attention the enterprise of Jennie Dean a colored Baptist who has built up a large religious movement at Manassas Virginia and now wants to complete this by adding schools and industrial education for her people," he wrote. "She and her coworker Miss Jane Thompson are discreet energetic intelligent and eminently worthy of all the encouragement that you can give them."[51] Frederick T. Gates, Rockefeller's philanthropic advisor—himself a Baptist and former pastor—presented the letters from Dean and Cleveland to Rockefeller, advising him that Dean's enterprise was "not in a position to invite your attention." Gates explained how Dean had visited him in New York and provided all the details of her proposed school but had failed to convince him of its merit or her ability. "Her plan is one of the thousand small, independent, individual enterprises, of well meaning colored people, without experience, and the vaguest possible ideas of the thing undertaken," he said.[52] Despite Rockefeller's lack of support, Dean secured funding for her school with help from others—including another titan of industry, Andrew Carnegie—and chartered the Manassas Industrial School for Colored Youth in 1893.[53]

In February 1900, in his official capacity as editor of *Monthly Weather Review*, Cleveland wrote to Booker T. Washington, founder and president of the Tuskegee Normal and Industrial Institute, who had invited him to speak at a conference. While Cleveland regretted that he was unable to attend, he expressed an interest in Washington's work and offered to send copies of Weather Bureau publications to help in teaching about meteorology and dispelling myths related to forecasting the weather. "From an educational point of view, I suppose that even the *Monthly Weather Review* may contribute a little to the diffusion of knowledge and the elimination of superstition," he wrote, referring to the notion that it was possible to educate farmers about the laws of nature governing the weather in an effort to "rise above the superstitions that really disgrace mankind. If you think a few copies of our popular bulletins, and perhaps of the *Monthly Weather Review* itself, would be profitably used in your schools, I am sure the Chief of the Weather Bureau will be pleased to send them."[54]

In December 1913, Cleveland wrote a letter[55] to his good friend and former colleague Thomas Mendenhall, who had sent Cleveland a congratulatory letter several days earlier for his seventy-fifth birthday:

Douglas Street
Otterbourne
Chevy Chase, Md.

Sunday Dec. 7th

Dear Prof. Mendenhall,

When one receives a spontaneous tribute, such as your night letter of Dec. 3rd, it embarrasses one who knows, that a thousand others have laboured to benefit the world & are equally deserving of praise. "God's rain falls alike on the just & the unjust." He is no respecter of persons.

If I had been forehanded I would have sent you a similar dispatch on the 4th of last October.

From early boyhood I thought over the weather & many other scientific matters.

During 1867–68, after having received all the blessings that a young Astronomer could dream of, I was exceedingly depressed, & was on the point of giving up science, & devoting myself to the elevation of the colored race, but some good spirit saved me from wasting my life & throwing away the special knowledge my parents had given me. But I slowly came to realize that the colored race could only be elevated by centuries of work. That my duty was on the one hand to make my knowledge as useful to the world as possible, on the other, to realize the hopes of my parents, to finish the works I had planned & to prove that I was worthy of the distinguished family into which I had thought to marry.

My inaugural address in Cincinnati reads like that of a young man who needed a fortune to carry out his plans. But in Sept. 1869, I could write to my mother, "I have started a work that the world will not willingly allow to die." No words can tell my surprise when that work was quickly transferred to Washington. At once I turned my thoughts to other plans of usefulness, but it soon became evident by consultation with Prof. Joseph Henry, that I must enter the government service, & sink myself as he had done for many years. So ever since I have been trying to do my share toward demonstrating that man will overcome nature by the steady progress of knowledge. Everyone contributes a little, & the sum total increases slowly year by year. Meanwhile I am greatly comforted by such men as yourself and Marvin, & by the abiding love of those whom I love. Remember me kindly to Mrs. Mendenhall.

Affectionately yours
Cleveland Abbe

It is clear that Cleveland's desire to help improve conditions for African Americans was both deep-seated and longstanding. His depression and struggle for self-identity at the pivotal time in his life he referred to in his letter to Mendenhall—following his return from Pulkovo and prior to his departure for Cincinnati—represented an existential crisis that pitted the charitable ethics embedded in his religious upbringing against the logical reasoning inherent in the fulfillment of his educational promise. Despite the fact that he ultimately chose a life dedicated to scientific pursuit, Cleveland remained steadfast in his conviction to help those he could.

Moore Dismissed

In April 1913, shortly after taking office as president, Woodrow Wilson fired Willis Moore as chief of the Weather Bureau "for alleged irregularities in the conducts of his office." The primary charge was that Moore had misused government funds—and personnel—to help bolster his bid to become secretary of agriculture. Moore, who had survived four administrations, called his ousting "little short of a disgrace."[56] After his removal from office, Moore retreated from public life, eventually moving to Pasadena, California. In 1927 at the age of seventy-one, just fifteen months before his death, he married a twenty-nine-year old woman from Canada.[57] In his place, Professor Charles Marvin, Cleveland's longtime friend and former head of the Weather Bureau's Instrument Division, ascended to the role of chief of the bureau, upon the recommendation of the National Academy of Sciences.[58]

In the months following's Marvin's appointment as chief, *Monthly Weather Review* reverted to its previous form, prior to the introduction of the *Bulletin of the Mount Weather Observatory*, which ceased publication in 1914. Beginning with the January 1914 issue, Cleveland once again saw his name reclaim its former position on the masthead as editor of *Monthly Weather Review*. He immediately resumed his former practice of soliciting articles from a variety of sources, including those outside of the meteorological community. In June 1914, he wrote to conservationist John Muir about the use of tree rings as indicators of climatic change. "Knowing your great interest in the preservation of these trees and in botanical studies in general, I should be glad to publish in the *Monthly Weather Review* a short article by yourself summarizing what we really know about the laws of growth of sequoias or other trees."[59] It is unclear whether Muir ever responded, but no article by him appears in the annals of *Monthly Weather Review*.

Move to Chevy Chase

By August 1913, Cleveland and Margaret decided it was time to change their surroundings and settle into a less hectic life away from the hustle and bustle of urban Washington, D.C. Since returning from Mount Weather two years earlier, they had been living in a small apartment in The Montana, located at 1726 M Street, NW, near the heart of the city. They moved just across the Maryland border to the town of Chevy Chase, where they purchased a small bungalow at 102 E Douglas Street (now Underwood Street) in a neighborhood known as Otterbourne. They moved there at a time when the town was just beginning to emerge as a suburb of Washington, D.C. In 1915 there were scarcely a few dozen homes dotting the town's landscape. Following a building boom in the 1920s, the population began to rise, with nearly a thousand houses built. [60] Cleveland and Margaret began attending services at All Saints Episcopal Church, about a mile down the street, where Cleveland "frequently found inspiration and comfort" during his final years.[61]

The scene was one of idyllic beauty, as told by syndicated newspaper reporter James B. Morrow, who came to interview Cleveland at his home just a few months before he died:

> Among yellow roads, dug through green banks, wild with tangled grasses, vines and flowers, at the northernmost rim of Washington, just over the Maryland boundary, lives Cleveland Abbe in a bungalow shaded by trees.
>
> In his workroom are books, a typewriter and a little brown dog—a friendly little brown dog. Also there are brown chickens in the garden—round, comfortable and glossy brown chickens—seemingly with no fear in their heart of the guillotine.
>
> Thus in the lengthening shadows of his life, amid the songs of birds and the restful silence of the country, the days come and go for Cleveland Abbe. But even so, the world of science is not forgetful or ungrateful and honors from learned societies follow him and cheer him in his retirement.[62]

As the once-frenetic pace of Cleveland's life began to settle into a more leisurely routine, he adopted a more lackadaisical attitude toward life, as he described in a letter to his daughter-in-law Frieda, Cleveland Jr.'s wife. "We must get all the pleasure we can out of this world of work and anxiety. I suppose every day and year ought to be divided into three parts, working, eating and sleeping, but of course smiles and fun, pleasures and jollity may be intersperced [sic] freely."[63]

Accolades and Awards

In January 1912, the Royal Meteorological Society awarded Cleveland the Symons Memorial Gold Medal "for distinguished work in connection with meteorological science." He was the first American to receive the honor. The medal was established in 1901 in memory of George James Symons, a British meteorologist who founded the British Rainfall Organisation. Cleveland and Margaret traveled to London for the ceremony, which took place during the society's annual meeting. In presenting the medal, the secretary of the society read an excerpt of the council's minutes from its meeting of November 15, 1911, which noted that, in his career, Cleveland had "played throughout the part not only of an active contributor, but also of a leader who drew others into the scientific battle and pointed out the paths along which attacks might be successful."[64] When the society's president, Dr. Henry Newton Dickson, made his remarks in presenting the award, he recalled how Cleveland, a quarter century earlier, had helped him earlier in his own career. "I remember the occasion some five and twenty years ago, on which I came, a very raw and budding meteorologist to Washington, and had the privilege of enjoying the hospitality which you so generously offered to those working in the subject; and I remember the strong stimulus which I received from you at that time," he said. "There are very many other meteorologists who must be conscious of owing to you a similar debt. It gives me very great pleasure, Sir, to offer you, on behalf of the Society, this Gold Medal." In accepting the award, Cleveland said that he could not express his emotion but could only thank the society most sincerely for the honor. He said the event would "always be to him a stimulus to future labours," noting they "are all brothers in science, and he was greatly touched to hear from the account read by the Secretary, that they had so closely watched his career and labours in a science of which they had not yet reached the end."[65] While in England, Cleveland visited Gresham's School in Holt, Norfolk. He brought the medal with him and allowed the students in the physics class to examine it. They analyzed its specific gravity, density, and weight in air, among other properties. They determined it was a copper alloy, consisting of 13.13 grams of copper and 139.72 grams of gold, for a total mass of 152.85 grams.[66]

In 1913, The Franklin Institute in Philadelphia presented Cleveland with the Longstreth Medal of Merit for his paper "The Obstacles to the Progress of Meteorology," which the institute published in its journal in 1912. Despite its somewhat discouraging title, Cleveland urged his readers not to feel despondent. "I am not a pessimist," he argued in the paper's introduction, "I see the great work that meteorologists still have before them and that their motto must be that of every student: '*Nil desperandum. Labor omnia vincit.*' Man must never despair."[67]

In April 1916, the National Academy of Sciences bestowed upon Cleveland the Marcellus Hartley Memorial Medal "for eminence in the application of science to the public welfare." Professor William Morris Davis—a geomorphologist who had recently retired from Harvard—gave the nominating speech. "I am glad," he said, "that this medal is awarded for *eminence* in the application of science, for if it were to be awarded for *prominence*, it never could have been given to a man so modest, so retiring, so diffident, as Cleveland Abbe." Davis noted the "warm pleasure" he and others had "in nominating this gentle man, who has so long labored quietly, without ostentation, never intruding himself upon public notice for the display of his learning, to be the recipient of a medal for real eminence in the work that he has done for his country's good."[68]

Cleveland, who was unable to attend the meeting due to illness, asked his friend Charles Marvin—then chief of the Weather Bureau—to accept the medal on his behalf. "Words fail me to speak fully of my deep feeling on this occasion. I can not tell how much I appreciate this great privilege and honor that devolves upon me in accepting this medal for Prof. Abbe, with whom I have been intimately associated for more than 30 years," Marvin said. "During this time we have worked side by side, so to speak, and I have learned not only to hold him in the greatest esteem because of his eminent work in science, but also to love him dearly because of those modest, gentle, and beautiful qualities of character that were just now set out in such touching fashion by Prof. Davis." Marvin told the audience that when he asked Cleveland what he should say in accepting such a prestigious award on his behalf, the senior professor did not hesitate in his modest reply. "Oh, they do too much for me," he said, "they must not forget Henry, Espy, Ferrel, Lapham, and others."[69]

In writing to express his regret that Cleveland was unable to attend, William Henry Welch, president of the National Academy of Sciences, offered a heartfelt congratulations and recalled Cleveland's illustrious career in meteorology, which spanned nearly half a century. "From the inception of your work in this field in Cincinnati in 1868 to the present day you have been the leader in scientific and practical meteorology in this country," Welch wrote. "Your contributions in both directions—theoretical and practical—have been of a high order and have conferred incalculable benefits upon mankind."[70]

Illness and Death

Cleveland's health had been in decline for several months by the time he received the Hartley Medal. On June 4, 1915, he suffered a mild stroke, which left him temporarily paralyzed on his right side. He largely recovered,[71] but the episode forced him to request an extended leave of absence from the Weather Bureau. "The news that Prof. Cleveland Abbe has been under the necessity of taking an extended leave of absence on account of ill health will be received with regret not only by his coworkers in the Weather Bureau, but throughout the scientific world," read an internal statement published by the Weather Bureau, which also appeared in *Monthly Weather Review*. "Through his excellent work and eminence in the application of meteorology he has come to be regarded as the 'dean of the Weather Service.' During this period he has been indefatigable in the pursuit of his favorite branch of science, while his enthusiasm served to enlist the interest of a number of young students who later made their mark in the development of meteorology as a science."[72]

In early 1916, Cleveland requested an extension of his leave of absence from the Weather Bureau. Chief Marvin wrote to him on February 8, informing him that the Department of Agriculture had granted a continuation of his leave through August 4. "Should you so far recover your health earlier as to be able to resume your official duties, which is the earnest hope of your many friends and co-workers in the Weather Bureau, this leave can be terminated without trouble at any time."[73]

Cleveland's condition, however, did not improve. In July, he discovered that a small mole on his abdomen was growing rapidly in size. The mole quickly developed into malignant melanoma—a skin cancer that if not treated in its early stages proves fatal. British surgeon Samuel Cooper was the first to note the importance of early detection of the disease. "The only chance of benefit depends upon the early removal of the disease by operation," he wrote in 1844. Cooper described how, in terms of symptoms, "the disease may at first produce little or no pain; but a sallow complexion, excessive debility, and anasarca frequently come on before its termination."[74]

In Cleveland's case, this prognosis proved to be accurate. "The resultant irritation and great loss of sleep together with the restricted diet imposed by the conditions of his paralysis, drained his strength."[75] That summer, he and Margaret traveled to Maine, where they relaxed on Great Diamond Island, a picturesque spot that was home to an artists' retreat favored in earlier years by Harriet Beecher Stowe and Henry Wadsworth Longfellow.[76] By the time they returned to Chevy Chase in mid-September, Cleveland was "in a greatly weakened condition."[77] He was able to move freely about their house for a few days but soon was confined to bed, unable to sit or lie comfortably except in a single position. While no longer active in public life, his legacy was already beginning to take shape, to which Morrow alluded in his profile:

> Prof. Abbe, therefore, though he is exiled among cardinals, wild canaries, blackbirds, brown chickens and his sociable little dog, is visible, to those who know what he has done, in the forecasts that are printed every day in large and small newspapers throughout the land. He is read in the hurricanes that sweep northward from the West Indies and in the twisting winds that are forged in the southwest.[78]

When it became clear that he would not be able to return to work, Cleveland formally retired from the Weather Bureau in August 1916, upon the expiration of his extended leave of absence. After forty-five years of continuous service to the federal government, his long career had finally come to an end. "The announcement that Prof. Cleveland Abbe, who for some time past has been prevented by the infirmities of advancing years from taking an active part in the work of the bureau, has now definitely retired from official life will awaken a keen sense of personal loss in the minds of his former colaborers," read the notice in the publication *Weather Bureau Topics and Personnel*. "Professor Abbe was not only a tireless and prolific worker in behalf of the science and the public institution to which he dedicated the best years of his life, but he was also, in a very unusual degree, endowed with the faculty of communicating his enthusiasm to others and stimulating their efforts; a faculty that made itself felt both in personal intercourse and through his writings."[79]

Even in his weakened state—as the melanoma progressed along its immutable path—Cleveland applied himself, however possible, toward the pursuit of science. Beginning in late August, he corresponded with the Smithsonian Institution on the translation of a German article about the orbits of meteors in the solar system. From his bed on October 25, Cleveland dictated a letter to Charles D. Walcott, secretary of the institution. "We all agree as to the objection to current terminology of meteors, which is very confusing & if your editor can contribute to its simplification then it will have benefitted that branch of science as it has so many others," he said.[80] It would be his last communication on scientific matters.

Three days later, in the early morning hours of Saturday, October 28, Cleveland passed away quietly at home in Chevy Chase, five weeks shy of his seventy-eighth birthday. Though his body had failed him, his mind "was singularly clear and cheerful even at the last moments."[81] Two days later, his family, friends, and former colleagues filed slowly into All Saints Church to pay their final respects to the man whom many had called the "father of the Weather Bureau." The Reverend Canon Austin officiated the ceremony. Cleveland's brothers Robert and Walter served as honorary pallbearers, along with his brother-in-law Hubert Howson (Helen's husband), Charles Walcott of the Smithsonian, Louis Bauer of the Carnegie Institution, and physicist and mathematician Robert Woodward. Cleveland's three sons, along with Professor Marvin, were among the active pallbearers.

Cleveland was laid to rest in Washington, D.C.'s Rock Creek Cemetery, surrounded by leaves of oak and holly. Buried with him were two items that symbolized his lifelong passion for learning and disseminating knowledge of the world around him. In his hand he held the copy of *The Philosophy of Natural History* given to him by his mother when he was eight years old, and on his shoulders rested the scarlet-lined doctoral hood made for him by Lady Kelvin. His final resting place was marked by a simple granite gravestone, inscribed with his name, the years of his birth and death, and the word *Meteorologist*. As his son Truman recalled, "Those of us who helped select that simple block of polished granite which marks the final resting place for father tried to find an appropriate expression to represent his simplicity of life, his complete contentment with self effacement so long as he could contribute to the progress of truth in his chosen field."[82]

Several decades after Cleveland's death, his friend Bailey Willis, a geologist at the U.S. Geological Survey, wrote a book about his experience leading an expedition to China in the early twentieth century. While describing a visit to Mount Tai (Tài Shān)—one of the five sacred mountains of China—Willis reflected on the simplicity of the monument that stands at the entrance to the Temple of the Jade Emperor. The fourteen-foot-tall monolith of polished granite contains no inscription—a departure from similar shrines whose long expressions denote the Taoist principles of veneration and humility. "The emperor who caused it to be quarried and set up, probably a couple of centuries before Christ, is said to have held that individual fame is insignificant and unworthy before his God, and he would have no inscription," Willis wrote.[83] Truman found significance in this and, relating it to the footstone that served as his father's grave marker, confessed, "We did not do as well as the Emperor, for we did preserve the name and the field of service."[84] The year following his death, a larger granite memorial was erected in the center of the family plot, bearing the names and complete dates of birth and death of Cleveland and, eventually, Margaret.

On October 30, the same day as Cleveland's funeral, Secretary of Agriculture David F. Houston ordered the flags flying above the main building of the Department of Agriculture, along with those atop the Weather Bureau Central Office, flown at half-mast in honor of Cleveland. Professor Marvin wrote to Margaret several days later to let her know "of this unusual and particular mark of honor and esteem shown Professor Abbe, who was recognized as the dean of the Department's scientific staff."[85]

Speaking before the American Philosophical Society six months later, Marvin conveyed his esteem and respect for his friend and colleague and his affection "for the man of gentle and generous ways and a spirit refined and purified by his unselfish promotion of the pleasure and welfare of all around him."[86] He also spoke of Cleveland's devotion both to his faith and to science—two concepts reflected in the National Academy medal Marvin had accepted on Cleveland's behalf shortly before his death. "Coming, as this award did," Marvin said, "from those he counted as his most intimate friends and associates in scientific endeavor and at a time when he recognized that his strength and force were almost spent, it bore the welcome message: 'Well done thou good and faithful servant,' and within the year he entered into the joy of his Master's presence."

Epilogue

Cleveland Abbe's death was mourned by the scientific world for his numerous achievements and the legacy he left in the field of meteorology. As Dr. Charles P. Oliver, of the University of Virginia's Leander McCormick Observatory, wrote shortly after his death, "Professor Abbe's influence upon the present status of meteorology in America is incalculable, and his contributions are far too numerous to begin even to mention. To write out the names of all the scientific societies at home and abroad of which he was a member would alone fill a full page. He was honoured both in Europe and America in nearly every way a scientist could be."[1]

There was controversy, however, in the year following Cleveland's death, with regard to the medal he received from the National Academy of Sciences shortly before he died. Seneca G. Lapham, son of the late Dr. Increase Lapham, wrote a monograph titled "The Origin of the United States Weather Bureau," in which he discussed misconceptions as to the role Cleveland played in the establishment of the nation's weather service. Lapham's criticism lay squarely with the justification language used in making the award, which stated that Cleveland's Medal for Eminence in the Application of Science to the Public Welfare was awarded "for distinguished public service in establishing and organizing the weather service of the United States."[2] Lapham also took issue with an article published in *Scientific American* in

May 1916, just after the National Academy bestowed its award upon Cleveland. The article, titled "How the United States Weather Bureau Was Started" was attributed to "Cleveland Abbe, its Founder and Organizer." In it, Cleveland discussed how he became involved in meteorology, describing in detail the events that took place during 1868 to 1870 while he served as director of the Cincinnati Observatory. One phrase in particular seemed to spark Lapham's ire. In describing the roles that he and others—including William Hooper and John Gano of Cincinnati, as well as Halbert Paine and Increase Lapham of Milwaukee—played in the months leading up to the joint resolution of 1870, Cleveland said, "[W]e each put our shoulders to the wheel, and behold, on February 9, 1870, the Secretary of War was authorized to carry out this new duty."[3] Lapham claimed Cleveland's statement "conveys a very erroneous idea," which created the appearance "that he was an active participant with Dr. Lapham and Gen. Paine in the work preceding the passage of the storm signal bill, which the fact is he was not."[4] Lapham shared his monograph with a local newspaper in Washington, D.C., in an attempt to set the record straight. "The question as to whom is due the most credit for having established the service out of which grew the weather bureau is a controversial one," read an article that appeared in *The Sunday Star* about five months after Cleveland's death.[5] According to *The Star*, Lapham "protested to the National Academy against the reason given for the award of the medal, 'not to the award itself.'"[6]

In the years following Cleveland's death, meteorology evolved as a science in ways that were a natural progression of his work. His vision for long-range forecasts began to be realized through the work of Vilhelm Bjerknes, along with his son, Jacob, and others, who made up the so-called "Bergen School" in Norway. Working with upper-air data such as the type Cleveland collected with Professor Marvin—then head of the Weather Bureau's Instrument Division—in the 1890s,[7] the members of the Bergen School developed a theory that weather systems in the middle latitude regions of the planet develop from the dynamic interactions of contrasting air masses. They named the boundaries of warm and cold air masses clashing with each other "fronts," after the battle fronts of World War I, which was taking place at the time. This proved to be a major turning point in modern meteorology. Spurred by this initial work, Swedish-born researcher Carl-Gustaf Rossby, a student of Bjerknes, further developed the theoretical work of the Bergen School after his immigration to the United States, where he founded the Department of Meteorology at MIT before becoming chair of the Department of Meteorology at the University of Chicago. Rossby's work in the area of large-scale circulation of the atmosphere, combined with his three-dimensional model of the atmosphere, paved the way for modern long-range weather forecasts.

Cleveland's vision for meteorology included not only advances in the science itself—and the expansion of educational opportunities for the individuals who would undertake the work—but also the establishment of a professional society to allow those engaged in the field to meet regularly to discuss problems of interest and share research. In 1898 he wrote a brief "note from the editor" that appeared in *Monthly Weather Review* titled "An American Meteorological Society."[8] In it, he argued for the creation of a society to further the interests of the field. "So far as concerns meteorology and climatology there are countless many features whose development can be especially furthered by local clubs, each of these to embrace the few persons who are especially interested in such matters, and can easily meet together or correspond with each other." Cleveland's vision for such a society stretched beyond political borders and included all of North America and, in fact, much of the Western Hemisphere. "If there is to be a general meteorological society it would be best to have its membership include all America, i.e., the United States and Canada, and as far as possible Mexico, the West Indies, and Central America, since every part of this great region is mutually interested in the weather and the climate of the other parts," he said. Cleveland felt that a society whose membership covered such a large area could "at the best have only an annual or triennial meeting; the interest of the members in each other's work and in the general progress of meteorology must, necessarily, be kept up by means of an efficient meteorological journal whose expenses must be wholly defrayed by the society." Further, he recognized that the goals of an American society of meteorologists relied heavily on the participation of its members in finding practical applications to advance the science. "Meteorological journals or associations and meteorological progress in general will have to be prosecuted in the future as in the past by the sacrifice—say rather, by the devotion—of time and money and personal energies quite independent of the utilitarian aspects of the results that have been or will be attained."

Cleveland's vision was realized two decades later, with the organization of the American Meteorological Society (AMS), on December 29, 1919, in St. Louis (and its subsequent incorporation, on January 21, 1920, in Washington, D.C.), which marked "the beginning of a movement not only to push forward investigations of weather processes and climatic conditions, but also to widen the valuable application of the knowledge already at hand. The great application of meteorology in warfare has shown that there are large possibilities of extending its use much more thoroughly into almost every line of human endeavor."[9]

Cleveland's legacy would be fully interwoven into the fabric of the AMS when in 1963, 125 years after his birth, the society began conferring the Cleveland Abbe Award for Distinguished Service to Atmospheric Sciences by an Individual (the name was later changed to the Cleveland Abbe Award for Distinguished Service to the Atmospheric and Related Sciences). As described in a 1964 issue of the *Bulletin of the American Meteorological Society*, the award "is presented on the basis of activities which have materially contributed to the progress of the atmospheric sciences or to the application of atmospheric sciences to general social, economic or humanitarian welfare."[10] In 1959, several members of the society in Cincinnati banded together to further memorialize Cleveland with the founding of a local chapter, dubbed the Abbe Memorial Chapter, which remained active for a decade.

Outside of the AMS, Cleveland was memorialized in other, very disparate ways. On November 24, 1916, less than a month after Cleveland's death, Weather Bureau Chief Charles Marvin made a recommendation to the secretary of agriculture to officially rename the bureau's suburban meteorological station in Cincinnati in Cleveland's honor. "You will recall that Abbe's work in Cincinnati in 1869–70 demonstrated how a meteorological service like our present Weather Bureau could be organized and conducted, and indicated the very great benefits that would result to commerce, agriculture, and navigation by the collection of simultaneous meteorological observations, the preparation therefrom of a daily weather map, and the dissemination of forecasts and warnings that could be made by these methods," Marvin said in his suggestion to the secretary. "It is apparent that no more fitting tribute could be made to the memory of Professor Abbe than to designate this suburban station as the 'Abbe Meteorological Observatory, Cincinnati, Ohio.'"[11] The change took effect January 1, 1917. Located in a hilltop residential area in the Clifton neighborhood of Cincinnati, the observatory remained in use until 1983, when it ceased operations, eventually becoming a private residence.

A more incongruous tribute came in 1942, when the Oregon Shipbuilding Corporation built a Liberty ship dubbed the SS *Cleveland Abbe* for use by the U.S. Merchant Marines. The ship, which transported cargo during World War II, was eventually scrapped in 1972.[12]

When Cleveland was forced to take a leave of absence from his duties at the Weather Bureau in 1915, his son Cleveland Jr. took his place as editor of *Monthly Weather Review*. He became the permanent editor the following year, upon the elder Abbe's retirement. The promotion would be short-lived, however. In July 1918, Secretary of Agriculture David Houston removed Cleveland Jr. from his post—and from government service altogether. "For the good of the service you are hereby removed from your position as a meteorologist in the Weather Bureau of this department, effective at the termination of July 3, 1918," Houston's order read. Cleveland Jr.'s termination came after a Department of Justice investigation into accusations he harbored "friendly sympathies for the imperial German government" and "friendly sentiments for Germanism," charges he indignantly denied, in spite of having studied in Vienna and having a wife who was a native German. In delivering the news to Cleveland Jr., Marvin reiterated a statement consistent with the wave of anti-German sentiment sweeping the nation at the time. "A searching inquiry of your innermost heart in respect to your attitude toward the United States government must convince you that patriotism and genuine loyalty to the United States are absolutely incompatible with friendly sentiment for Germanism."[13]

Cleveland Jr. went on to find work elsewhere, eventually becoming the scientific editor of volumes of the George F. Baker Non-Resident Lectureship in Chemistry at Cornell University. He died in 1934, at the age of sixty-two.[14] Writing in the *Bulletin of the American Meteorological Society* shortly after his death, Dr. Charles Franklin Brooks, founder of the AMS, said, "Dr. Abbe was a thorough scientist and a perfect editor. As a man who spoke his opinions regardless of consequences, he was, naturally, not popular, though his friends appreciated him for his sincerity."[15]

In 1936, ecologist William S. Cooper and geologist William O. Field named a remote peak in present-day Glacier Bay National Park Mount Abbe, in honor of Cleveland Jr., who published several works on the geography, geology, and climate of Alaska.[16] Cleveland Jr. was preceded in death by his younger brother William, who died in 1928, at the age of fifty. Truman, who went on to have a successful career as a physician and surgeon, died in 1955, shortly before his book about his father was published. He is buried, along with his wife, Ethel, and several of their children, in the Abbe family plot at Rock Creek Cemetery.

Margaret Abbe continued to live at the bungalow in Chevy Chase she and Cleveland had purchased in 1913. There she held luncheons and bridge for her women's club,[17] hosted friends and relatives, and eventually shared the house with her sister, Blanche Percival, with whom she spent the summer of 1929 in the White Mountains of New Hampshire.[18] In January 1930, she held an informal luncheon at her home for Alden Freeman, a cousin of Cleveland, who was an architect and philanthropist as well as heir to the Standard Oil fortune.[19] In 1931, Freeman wrote to Margaret from his opulent Mediterranean Revival mansion, Casa Casuarina, in South Beach, Miami, about a relief portrait of Cleveland he had commissioned from the artist Porter Valparaiso Skinner. "I am very well satisfied of what he did of Professor Abbe," Freeman wrote, adding that he placed the portrait outside the main entrance of his third-floor apartment at Casa Casuarina, "as the most eminent member of my mother's family."[20] Margaret died at home in Chevy Chase on January 7, 1936, at the age of seventy. She was buried next to Cleveland in Rock Creek Cemetery.

Perhaps the most enduring physical legacy of Cleveland's life is his historic home at 2017 I Street, NW, in Washington, D.C., which was added to the National Register of Historic Places in 1969, with the National Park Service designating it a National Historic Landmark in 1976. Shortly before his death in 1916, Cleveland sold the mansion to the Arts Club of Washington, which held the formal opening of its new home on October 10, just two and a half weeks before Cleveland's death.[21] During the Great Depression, the club hosted an annual costume ball that attracted such celebrities as D. W. Griffith, Claudette Colbert, F. Scott Fitzgerald, and Tallulah Bankhead.[22]

In 1923, the District of Columbia Chapter of the Daughters of the American Revolution placed a bronze plaque in front of the house, noting its three most famous residents—President James Monroe, Senator Charles Francis Adams, and Cleveland Abbe. Truman spoke at the plaque's unveiling.[23] He shared his own recollections growing up in the house and spoke of his father's multifaceted career and of his life there from 1877 to 1907. "For those thirty years he gave character to the house," Truman said. "He brought to this house many scientific guests not only from all over this country but from all over the world, and gave them the welcome which the scientific man always feels when he comes in close contact with the man whose whole life is bound up in his work of helping to solve the big problems of the laws of nature and of helping to apply those laws to man's daily life."[24] The house, which played a central role in the life of Cleveland for three decades, stands as a reminder of the man who dedicated his life to science and whose legacy can be found in forecasts for every type of weather—from conditions as mild and gentle as his nature to storms as great as his contributions to the world of meteorology.

Biographical Timeline of Cleveland Abbe

1838	January 16—Frances Martha Neal born near Hamilton, Ohio
	December 3—Cleveland Abbe born in New York City
1850	Enters public school in the first class of Ward School No. 25, on East 20th Street between First and Second Avenues, New York City
1851	Begins college at the New York Free Academy (now City College of New York)
1853	Baptized in the Baptist Church
1857	Receives Bachelor of Arts degree from the New York Free Academy
1858	Studies astronomy under Franz Brünnow and teaches physics and civil engineering at the University of Michigan
1859	Employed as tutor for several months at the Michigan State Agricultural College in Lansing

1860 Receives Master of Arts degree from the New York Free Academy

1860–64 Assists Benjamin Apthorp Gould on longitude determinations for the U.S. Coast Survey in Cambridge, Massachusetts

1862 Enlists in the 44th Massachusetts Volunteers, in hopes of joining the Union Army during the Civil War, only to be rejected after several weeks of training, due to poor eyesight

1864 December—Departs for Russia to study and work as a supernumerary astronomer at the Nicholas Central Observatory in Pulkovo, near St. Petersburg

1865 November 7—Margaret Augusta Percival born in Basseterre, St. Kitts, British West Indies

1866 November—Returns to the United States, having spent nearly two years abroad

1867 Accepts position as aid at the U.S. Naval Observatory in Washington, D.C.

1868 January—Invited to serve as director of Cincinnati Observatory

May—Resigns position at U.S. Naval Observatory

June—Assumes duties as director of the Cincinnati Observatory

1869 July—Receives backing of the Cincinnati Chamber of Commerce to undertake three-month trial in collecting meteorological observations and publishing Weather Bulletin

August 7—Views total solar eclipse from Sioux Falls City, Dakota Territory

September 1—Begins publishing the Weather Bulletin of the Cincinnati Observatory, the first regular comprehensive weather-information service for the general public in America

1870 May 10—Marries Frances Martha Neal

1871 January—Begins work as assistant to the chief signal officer in Washington, D.C., with an annual salary of $3,000

February 19—Issues first published forecast, or "probabilities," for the U.S. Army Signal Service

1872 March 25—Son Cleveland Jr. born in Washington, D.C.

1873 November 1—Son Truman born in Washington, D.C.

1875 Begins work to adopt a system of "Standard Time"

1877 June 27—Son William born in Washington, D.C.

Moves into the historic house purchased at 2017 I Street, NW, Washington, D.C.

1879 September 25—George Waldo Abbe dies at home in New York City

1885 February 19—Charlotte Abbe dies at home in New York City

1888 Becomes founding member of the National Geographic Society

Receives honorary L.L.D. degree from the University of Michigan

1889–90 Detailed as meteorologist on the U.S. Scientific Expedition to West Africa, aboard the USS *Pensacola*

1891 Accompanies Weather Bureau Chief Mark Harrington on trip to attend International Meteorological Conference in Munich

Receives an honorary Ph.D. degree from the College of the City of New York

1893	July—Salary reduced 25 percent, upon orders of Secretary of Agriculture J. Sterling Morton
	July—Named editor of *Monthly Weather Review*
1896	June—Receives honorary L.L.D. degree from the University of Glasgow, Scotland
1900	Receives honorary degree of S.B. (scientiae baccalaureus) from Harvard University, awarded retroactively "as of 1864"
1901	Publishes "The Physical Basis of Long-Range Weather Forecasts," a seminal paper that helps lay the foundation for modern weather forecasting
1906	Awarded the Franklin Medal by the American Philosophical Society
1908	July 24—Fanny dies in Canton, New York
1909	April 12—Marries Margaret Augusta Percival
	May–October—Serves as official in charge of the Weather Bureau office in Baltimore
1910–11	Stationed at Mount Weather, Virginia; serves as editor of the *Bulletin of the Mount Weather Observatory*
1911	Returns to Washington, D.C., after spending nearly a year at Mount Weather
1912	January 17—Awarded Symons Memorial Gold Medal by the Royal Meteorological Society
1913	Purchases house in Chevy Chase, Maryland, where he and Margaret will spend the remaining years of their lives
1915	June 4—Suffers a mild stroke, from which he largely recovers

Requests extended leave of absence from the U.S. Weather Bureau

1916 April 18—Awarded the Marcellus Hartley Medal by the National Academy of Sciences

July—Begins suffering from malignant melanoma; health rapidly deteriorates

August—Officially resigns from the U.S. Weather Bureau

October 28—Cleveland Abbe dies at home in Chevy Chase, Maryland

1928 February 15—William Abbe dies in Plainfield, New Jersey

1934 April 19—Cleveland Abbe Jr. dies in Ithaca, New York

1936 January 7—Margaret Abbe dies at home in Chevy Chase, Maryland

1955 May 2—Dr. Truman Abbe dies in Washington, D.C.

Acknowledgments

This book would not have been possible without the generous support of various individuals and institutions, whose assistance and encouragement are greatly appreciated. First and foremost, I would like to thank the American Meteorological Society—especially Executive Director Keith Seitter, for supporting this project and agreeing to publish this book, as well as AMS Books Managing Editor Sarah Jane Shangraw, whose editorial oversight, critical suggestions, and enthusiasm for the subject helped create a finished product worthy of publication.

As is the case with any historical biography, this book relies heavily on source material from a variety of libraries and archives, which deserve recognition and thanks for their kind support. Chief among these, I would like to thank the dedicated staff at the Library of Congress, especially Jeff Flannery and his team at the Manuscript Division, who dutifully and patiently fulfilled request after request for items from the Cleveland Abbe Papers collection during the three dozen visits I made to the Manuscript Reading Room over the course of more than two years.

I would also like to thank the staff at the Cincinnati Observatory—especially Craig Niemi, John Ventre, and Richard Davis—for their valuable assistance and generosity in hosting me during my visit there, as well as Kevin Grace and his staff at the University of Cincinnati's Archives & Rare Books Library for their assistance during my research trip to Cincinnati.

Others who personally provided valuable assistance include, in no particular order: Scott Gampfer and Jill Beitz at the Cincinnati Museum Center and Cincinnati History Library and Archives; Bethany Antos at the Rockefeller Archive Center; Arthur Carlson at the Worcester Polytechnic Institute's George C. Gordon Library; Jessica Becker at Yale University Library's Manuscripts and Archives; Greg Raml at the American Museum of Natural History Library's Special Collections; William Brown and the staff at NOAA's National Centers for Environmental Information; Leslie Stoecker at the Midwestern Regional Climate Center; Maurita Baldock at the Library of Congress (formerly at the New-York Historical Society); Gail Sansbury at the Chevy Chase Historical Society; Caitlin Moriarty and Sarah McLusky at the University of Michigan's Bentley Historical Library; Lynne Serviss of the HathiTrust User Support Team Member; Olga Tsiopa and Elizaveta Kozlova at Pulkovo Observatory; Marina Ponikarovskaya at the St. Petersburg Branch of the Archive of the Russian Academy of Sciences; the staff at the Patricia D. Klingenstein Library of the New-York Historical Society; and the staff at the District of Columbia Archives.

Special thanks goes to Judith Viggers Nordin of the Arts Club of Washington, D.C., for providing an impromptu tour of the Cleveland Abbe House and sharing some of its rich history with me, and to Stephanie Nolan of St. Paul's Rock Creek Episcopal Parish, for sharing valuable information with me on the final resting places of Cleveland and other members of the Abbe family at Rock Creek Cemetery.

I would be remiss if I did not mention Bob Henson, whose sage advice, counsel, support, and encouragement—not only with this project but throughout my freelance writing career of the past two decades—has been valuable beyond words and without whose help this project would not have gotten off the ground. I also greatly appreciate the comments, discussions, advice, and encouragement of countless other colleagues, especially Lourdes Aviles, Melissa Fleming, Greg Good, Cary Mock, Greg Romano, Bill Hooke, and Jim Fleming.

I would like to express my heartfelt thanks to my family, whose love and support mean the world to me. In particular, I would like to thank my father, who taught me the importance of words and to appreciate the finer points of the English language, as well as my mother, who instilled in me at an early age an interest in science, which grew into a passion—especially for meteorology.

Finally, I cannot express enough my undying love and gratitude to my wife, Sarah, for her patience, love, support, and willingness to undertake this project with me during two of the most exciting—and challenging—years of our lives. Throughout this project, she has been my partner, champion, research assistant, and editor extraordinaire, who along the way has discovered a hidden talent for deciphering hard-to-read nineteenth-century handwriting—especially that of Cleveland Abbe.

References

Abbe, C., n.d.: What I remember about my friends and myself (unpublished manuscript), *Cleveland Abbe Papers, Speech and Article File, Autobiographical Writings*. Manuscript Division, Library of Congress, Box 29.

——, 1858–62: Letters. C. Abbe, 1858–1862. *Cleveland Abbe Papers, General Correspondence, 1850–1916*. Manuscript Division, Library of Congress, Box 2.

——, 1862: Pocket Diary for 1862. *Cleveland Abbe Papers, Diaries, 1862–1889*. Manuscript Division, Library of Congress, Box 1.

——, 1863: Pocket Diary for 1863. *Cleveland Abbe Papers, Diaries, 1862–1889*. Manuscript Division, Library of Congress, Box 1.

——, 1864a: Pocket Diary for 1864. *Cleveland Abbe Papers, Diaries, 1862–1889*. Manuscript Division, Library of Congress, Box 1.

——, 1864b: Cleveland Abbe to Marcia Fessenden. November 24, 1864. *Cleveland Abbe Papers, General Correspondence, 1850–1916*. Manuscript Division, Library of Congress, Box 9.

——, 1865a: Pocket Diary for 1865. *Cleveland Abbe Papers, Diaries, 1862–1889*. Manuscript Division, Library of Congress, Box 1.

——, 1865b: Cleveland Abbe to George Waldo and Charlotte Abbe. January 2, 1865. *Cleveland Abbe Papers, General Correspondence, 1850–1916*. Manuscript Division, Library of Congress, Box 2.

——, 1865c: Cleveland Abbe to George Waldo and Charlotte Abbe. January 17, 1865. *Cleveland Abbe Papers, General Correspondence, 1850–1916*. Manuscript Division, Library of Congress, Box 2.

——, 1865d: Cleveland Abbe to George Waldo and Charlotte Abbe. February 16, 1865. *Cleveland Abbe Papers, General Correspondence, 1850–1916*. Manuscript Division, Library of Congress, Box 2.

——, 1865e: Cleveland Abbe to Charlotte Abbe. March 1, 1865. *Cleveland Abbe Papers, General Correspondence, 1850–1916*. Manuscript Division, Library of Congress, Box 2.

——, 1865f: Cleveland Abbe to Charlotte Abbe. March 15, 1865. *Cleveland Abbe Papers, General Correspondence, 1850–1916*. Manuscript Division, Library of Congress, Box 2.

——, 1865g: Cleveland Abbe to Charlotte Abbe. March 31, 1865. *Cleveland Abbe Papers, General Correspondence, 1850–1916*. Manuscript Division, Library of Congress, Box 2.

——, 1865h: Cleveland Abbe to George Waldo and Charlotte Abbe. April 13, 1865. *Cleveland Abbe Papers, General Correspondence, 1850–1916*. Manuscript Division, Library of Congress, Box 2.

——, 1865i: Cleveland Abbe to Charlotte Abbe. April 14/26, 1865. *Cleveland Abbe Papers, General Correspondence, 1850–1916*. Manuscript Division, Library of Congress, Box 2.

——, 1865j: Cleveland Abbe to Charlotte Abbe. April 28/16, 1865. *Cleveland Abbe Papers, General Correspondence, 1850–1916*. Manuscript Division, Library of Congress, Box 2.

——, 1865k: Cleveland Abbe to Robert Abbe. May 1, 1865. *Cleveland Abbe Papers, General Correspondence, 1850–1916*. Manuscript Division, Library of Congress, Box 2.

——, 1865l: Cleveland Abbe to George Waldo and Charlotte Abbe. May 9/April 27, 1865. *Cleveland Abbe Papers, General Correspondence, 1850–1916*. Manuscript Division, Library of Congress, Box 2.

——, 1865m: Cleveland Abbe to Charlotte Abbe. May 24, 1865. *Cleveland Abbe Papers, General Correspondence, 1850–1916*. Manuscript Division, Library of Congress, Box 2.

——, 1865n: Cleveland Abbe to George Waldo Abbe. May 24, 1865. *Cleveland Abbe Papers, General Correspondence, 1850–1916*. Manuscript Division, Library of Congress, Box 2.

——, 1865o: Cleveland Abbe to Charlotte Abbe. June 7, 1865. *Cleveland Abbe Papers, General Correspondence, 1850–1916*. Manuscript Division, Library of Congress, Box 2.

——, 1865p: Cleveland Abbe to Charlotte Abbe. July 8, 1865. *Cleveland Abbe Papers, General Correspondence, 1850–1916*. Manuscript Division, Library of Congress, Box 2.

——, 1865q: Cleveland Abbe to Charlotte Abbe. July 21, 1865. *Cleveland Abbe Papers, General Correspondence, 1850–1916*. Manuscript Division, Library of Congress, Box 2.

——, 1865r: Cleveland Abbe to Charlotte Abbe. August 1/July 20, 1865. *Cleveland Abbe Papers, General Correspondence, 1850–1916*. Manuscript Division, Library of Congress, Box 2.

——, 1865s: Cleveland Abbe to Charlotte Abbe. August 19/7, 1865. *Cleveland Abbe Papers, General Correspondence, 1850–1916*. Manuscript Division, Library of Congress, Box 2.

——, 1865t: Cleveland Abbe to Charlotte Abbe. September 9, 1865. *Cleveland Abbe Papers, General Correspondence, 1850–1916*. Manuscript Division, Library of Congress, Box 2.

——, 1865u: Cleveland Abbe to Charlotte Abbe. October 1/September 19, 1865. *Cleveland Abbe Papers, General Correspondence, 1850–1916*. Manuscript Division, Library of Congress, Box 2.

——, 1865v: Cleveland Abbe to Charlotte Abbe. October 20/8, 1865. *Cleveland Abbe Papers, General Correspondence, 1850–1916*. Manuscript Division, Library of Congress, Box 2.

——, 1865w: Cleveland Abbe to Charlotte Abbe. November 8, 1865. *Cleveland Abbe Papers, General Correspondence, 1850–1916*. Manuscript Division, Library of Congress, Box 2.

——, 1865x: Cleveland Abbe to Charlotte Abbe. December 10/November 28, 1865. *Cleveland Abbe Papers, General Correspondence, 1850–1916*. Manuscript Division, Library of Congress, Box 2.

——, 1865y: Cleveland Abbe to Charlotte Abbe. December 26/13, 1865. *Cleveland Abbe Papers, General Correspondence, 1850–1916*. Manuscript Division, Library of Congress, Box 2.

——, 1866a: Pocket Diary for 1866. *Cleveland Abbe Papers, Diaries, 1862–1889*. Manuscript Division, Library of Congress, Box 1.

——, 1866b: Cleveland Abbe to Charlotte Abbe. January 18/6, 1866. *Cleveland Abbe Papers, General Correspondence, 1850–1916*. Manuscript Division, Library of Congress, Box 2.

——, 1866c: Cleveland Abbe to George Waldo Abbe. January 19/7, 1866. *Cleveland Abbe Papers, General Correspondence, 1850–1916*. Manuscript Division, Library of Congress, Box 2.

——, 1866d: Cleveland Abbe to Charlotte Abbe. February 6/January 25, 1866. *Cleveland Abbe Papers, General Correspondence, 1850–1916*. Manuscript Division, Library of Congress, Box 2.

——, 1866e: Cleveland Abbe to Charlotte Abbe. February 21/9, 1866. *Cleveland Abbe Papers, General Correspondence, 1850–1916*. Manuscript Division, Library of Congress, Box 2.

——, 1866f: Cleveland Abbe to Charlotte Abbe. March 22/10, 1866. *Cleveland Abbe Papers, General Correspondence, 1850–1916*. Manuscript Division, Library of Congress, Box 2.

——, 1866g: Cleveland Abbe to George Waldo Abbe. March 23/11, 1866. *Cleveland*

Abbe Papers, General Correspondence, 1850–1916. Manuscript Division, Library of Congress, Box 2.

——, 1866h: Cleveland Abbe to Charlotte Abbe. April 5/March 24, 1866. *Cleveland Abbe Papers, General Correspondence, 1850–1916*. Manuscript Division, Library of Congress, Box 2.

——, 1866i: Cleveland Abbe to George Waldo Abbe. April 24/12, 1866. *Cleveland Abbe Papers, General Correspondence, 1850–1916*. Manuscript Division, Library of Congress, Box 2.

——, 1866j: Cleveland Abbe to George Waldo Abbe. May 5/April 23, 1866. *Cleveland Abbe Papers, General Correspondence, 1850–1916*. Manuscript Division, Library of Congress, Box 2.

——, 1866k: Cleveland Abbe to George Waldo Abbe. May 30/June 11, 1866. *Cleveland Abbe Papers, General Correspondence, 1850–1916*. Manuscript Division, Library of Congress, Box 3.

——, 1866l: Cleveland Abbe to Charlotte Abbe. July 6/June 24, 1866. *Cleveland Abbe Papers, General Correspondence, 1850–1916*. Manuscript Division, Library of Congress, Box 3.

——, 1866m: Cleveland Abbe to Elias Loomis. December 12, 1866. *Cleveland Abbe Papers, General Correspondence, 1850–1916*. Manuscript Division, Library of Congress, Box 3.

——, 1867a: Pocket Diary for 1867. *Cleveland Abbe Papers, Diaries, 1862–1889*. Manuscript Division, Library of Congress, Box 1.

——, 1867b: Cleveland Abbe to Clara Barton (with undated reply by Barton to Abbe). January 17, 1867. *Cleveland Abbe Papers, General Correspondence, 1850–1916*. Manuscript Division, Library of Congress, Box 3.

——, 1868a: Pocket Diary for 1868. *Cleveland Abbe Papers, Diaries, 1862–1889*. Manuscript Division, Library of Congress, Box 1.

——, 1868b: Dorpat and Poulkova. *Annual Report of the Board of Regents of the Smithsonian Institution*. Government Printing Office, 370–390.

——, 1868c: Cleveland Abbe to William Hooper. February 1, 1868. *Cleveland Abbe Papers, General Correspondence, 1850–1916*. Manuscript Division, Library of Congress, Box 3.

——, 1868d: Telegraphic Storm Signals. *Journal of the Telegraph*, **1**, 20, September 1, 1868, 1.

——, 1868–72: Day Book. June 1868–March 1872. *Cleveland Abbe Papers, Subject File, 1855–1884, Financial Papers*. Manuscript Division, Library of Congress, Box 16.

——, 1869a: Pocket Diary for 1869. *Cleveland Abbe Papers, Diaries, 1862–1889*. Manuscript Division, Library of Congress, Box 1.

——, 1869b: *Inaugural Report of the Director of the Cincinnati Observatory, 30th June 1868. Annual Report of the Director of the Cincinnati Observatory, 1st May 1869*. Robert Clarke & Co., 48 pp.

——, 1869c: The Resuscitation of the Cincinnati Observatory. *Proceedings of The*

American Association for the Advancement of Science. Seventeenth Meeting, Chicago, Illinois, August, 1868. Joseph Lovering, 172–174.
——, 1869d: Cleveland Abbe to John W. Heimstreet. July 20, 1869. *Cleveland Abbe Papers, General Correspondence, 1850–1916*. Manuscript Division, Library of Congress, Box 4.
——, 1869e: Weather Bulletin of the Cincinnati Observatory, Wednesday, September 1. *The Cincinnati Commercial*, September 2, 1869, 8.
——, 1869f: The Weather Bulletin. *The Cincinnati Commercial*, September 2, 1869, 8.
——, 1869g: Weather Bulletin of the Cincinnati Observatory, Thursday, September 2. *The Cincinnati Commercial*, September 3, 1869, 8.
——, 1869h: Weather Bulletin of the Cincinnati Observatory, Tuesday, September 7. *The Cincinnati Commercial*, September 8, 1869, 8.
——, 1869i: Weather Bulletin of the Cincinnati Observatory, September 22, 1869. *The Cincinnati Commercial*, September 23, 1869, 7.
——, 1869j: Weather Bulletin of the Cincinnati Observatory, October 6, 1869. *The Cincinnati Commercial*, October 7, 1869, 7.
——, 1869k: Weather Bulletin of the Cincinnati Observatory, October 21, 1869. *The Cincinnati Commercial*, October 22, 1869, 7.
——, 1869l: Cleveland Abbe to Frances Martha (Fanny) Neal. November 7, 1869. *Cleveland Abbe Papers, General Correspondence, 1850–1916*. Manuscript Division, Library of Congress, Box 5.
——, 1869m: Cleveland Abbe to Increase A. Lapham. October 15, 1869. *Increase A. Lapham Papers, Correspondence, 1865–1870*. Wisconsin Historical Society, Box 10, Folder 7.
——, 1870a: Pocket Diary for 1870. *Cleveland Abbe Papers, Diaries, 1862–1889*. Manuscript Division, Library of Congress, Box 1.
——, 1870b: *Annual Report of the Director of the Cincinnati Observatory*, June 1870. Gazette Co., 20 pp.
——, 1870c: Cleveland Abbe to Increase A. Lapham. January 7, 1870. *Increase A. Lapham Papers, Typewritten Letters, 1866–1870*. Wisconsin Historical Society, Box 4, Folder 3.
——, 1870d: Cleveland Abbe to Albert J. Myer. March 21, 1870 [copy]. *Cleveland Abbe Papers, General Correspondence, 1850–1916*. Manuscript Division, Library of Congress, Box 5.
——, 1870e: Cleveland Abbe to Julius Dexter. October 10, 1870 [draft]. *Cleveland Abbe Papers, General Correspondence, 1850–1916*. Manuscript Division, Library of Congress, Box 6.
——, 1870f: Cleveland Abbe to John H. C. Coffin and Julius E. Hilgard [draft]. November 16, 1870. *Cleveland Abbe Papers, General Correspondence, 1850–1916*. Manuscript Division, Library of Congress, Box 6.
——, 1871a: Historical Notes on the Systems of Weather Telegraphy. *Am. J. Sci. Arts*, **2**, 81–88.

——, 1871b: Probabilities issued 7:35 a.m. February 24, 1871. *Cleveland Abbe Papers, Subject File, 1855–1884, Weather Synopses and Probabilities.* Manuscript Division, Library of Congress, Box 25.

——, 1871c: Probabilities issued 11:35 p.m. February 24, 1871. *Cleveland Abbe Papers, Subject File, 1855–1884, Weather Synopses and Probabilities.* Manuscript Division, Library of Congress, Box 25.

——, 1871d: Cleveland Abbe to George Waldo Abbe. November 30, 1871. *Cleveland Abbe Papers, Series 2, Assorted Papers, 1871.* Cincinnati Observatory, Box 10, Folder 54.

——, 1872: Observations on the Total Eclipse of the Sun of 1869. *Am. J. Sci. Arts*, **3**, 264–267.

——, 1872–73: Day Book. March 1872-October 1873. *Cleveland Abbe Papers, Subject File, 1855–1884, Financial Papers.* Manuscript Division, Library of Congress, Box 17.

——, 1873: Cleveland Abbe to Lewis E. Mills [draft]. April 7/8, 1873. *Cleveland Abbe Papers, General Correspondence, 1850–1916.* Manuscript Division, Library of Congress, Box 7.

——, 1874a: Cleveland Abbe to Frances Martha (Fanny) Abbe. August 25, 1874. *Cleveland Abbe Papers, General Correspondence, 1850–1916.* Manuscript Division, Library of Congress, Box 7.

——, 1874b: Cleveland Abbe to Rufus King [copy]. October 31, 1874. *Cleveland Abbe Papers, General Correspondence, 1850–1916.* Manuscript Division, Library of Congress, Box 7.

——, 1876: The Aurora of April 7, 1874. *Annual Report of the Chief Signal-Officer to the Secretary of War for the Year 1876.* Government Printing Office, 301–335.

——, 1878a: Cleveland Abbe to Frances Martha (Fanny) Abbe. July 21, 1878. *Cleveland Abbe Papers, General Correspondence, 1850–1916.* Manuscript Division, Library of Congress, Box 8.

——, 1878b: Short Memoirs on Meteorological Subjects. Annual Report: 1877, Smithsonian Institution, 376–478.

——, 1879: Notes relating to the party celebrating 62nd birthday of Charlotte Abbe. *Cleveland Abbe Papers, Subject File, 1855–1884, Miscellaneous.* Manuscript Division, Library of Congress, Box 27.

——, 1881: *Report on the Solar Eclipse of July, 1878.* Professional Papers of the Signal Service, No.1. Government Printing Officer, 178 pp.

——, 1888a: Cleveland Abbe to Otto Struve. October 15, 1888. *Cleveland Abbe Papers, General Correspondence, 1850–1916.* Manuscript Division, Library of Congress, Box 8.

——, 1888b: Cleveland Abbe to Harriet (Hattie) Abbe. December 3/5, 1888. *Cleveland Abbe Papers, General Correspondence, 1850–1916.* Manuscript Division, Library of Congress, Box 8.

——, 1889a: Pocket Diary for 1889. *Cleveland Abbe Papers, Diaries, 1862–1889.* Manuscript Division, Library of Congress, Box 1.

——, 1889b: Cleveland Abbe to Frances Martha (Fanny) Abbe. November 1, 1889. *Cleveland Abbe Papers, General Correspondence, 1850–1916*. Manuscript Division, Library of Congress, Box 8.
——, 1890a: Cleveland Abbe to Frances Martha (Fanny) Abbe. January 3, 1890. *Cleveland Abbe Papers, General Correspondence, 1850–1916*. Manuscript Division, Library of Congress, Box 8.
——, 1890b: Cleveland Abbe to Frances Martha (Fanny) Abbe. January 21, 1890. *Cleveland Abbe Papers, General Correspondence, 1850–1916*. Manuscript Division, Library of Congress, Box 8.
——, 1890c: Cleveland Abbe to Truman Abbe. March 17, 1890. *Cleveland Abbe Papers, Family Correspondence and Related Papers, Truman Abbe, "A."* Manuscript Division, Library of Congress, Box 9.
——, 1890d: Cleveland Abbe to Frances Martha (Fanny) Abbe. March 23, 1890. *Cleveland Abbe Papers, General Correspondence, 1850–1916*. Manuscript Division, Library of Congress, Box 8.
——, 1890e: Cleveland Abbe to Frances Martha (Fanny) Abbe. April 27, 1890. *Cleveland Abbe Papers, General Correspondence, 1850–1916*. Manuscript Division, Library of Congress, Box 8.
——, 1890f: Cleveland Abbe to Frances Martha (Fanny) Abbe. April 29, 1890. *Cleveland Abbe Papers, General Correspondence, 1850–1916*. Manuscript Division, Library of Congress, Box 8.
——, 1890g: Preparatory Studies for Deductive Methods in Storm and Weather Predictions. *Annual Report of the Chief Signal Officer for 1890*, Appendix 15. Government Printing Office, 165 pp.
——, 1891a: Ferrel's Influence in the Signal Office. *Amer. Meteor. J.*, **8**, 342–348.
——, 1891b: International Conferences (typewritten list). *Cleveland Abbe Papers, General Correspondence, 1850–1916*. Manuscript Division, Library of Congress, Box 8.
——, 1891c: Itinerary (typewritten itinerary). *Cleveland Abbe Papers, General Correspondence, 1850–1916*. Manuscript Division, Library of Congress, Box 8.
——, 1891d: A New University Course. *The Atlantic Monthly*, **67**, 16–25.
——, 1891e: Cleveland Abbe to Daniel Coit Gilman. November 21, 1891. *Daniel Coit Gilman Papers, Cleveland Abbe Correspondence*. Johns Hopkins University, Sheridan Libraries, Box 1-1, Folder 2.
——, 1891f: *The Mechanics of the Earth's Atmosphere: A Collection of Translations. Miscellaneous Collections*, No. 843, Smithsonian Institution, 324 pp.
——, 1892a: The Modern Weather Bureau. *Trans. S. Afr. Philos. Soc.*, **6**, 17–30.
——, 1892b: Cleveland Abbe to John D. Rockefeller. April 20, 1892. *Rockefeller Family Archives, Record Group 1, Series C (Correspondence), Subseries O (Office)*. The Rockefeller Archive Center, Box 11, Folder 79.
——, 1893a: Cleveland Abbe to Mark Harrington. June 3, 1893 [copy]. *Cleveland Abbe Papers, General Correspondence, 1850–1916*. Manuscript Division, Library of Congress, Box 8.

——, 1893b: Cleveland Abbe to J. Sterling Morton. June 17, 1893 [draft]. *Cleveland Abbe Papers, General Correspondence, 1850–1916*. Manuscript Division, Library of Congress, Box 8.
——, 1893c: Cleveland Abbe to John E. Davies. August 14, 1893. *Cleveland Abbe Papers, General Correspondence, 1850–1916*. Manuscript Division, Library of Congress, Box 9.
——, 1893d: Cleveland Abbe to Garrick Mallery. September 7, 1893. *Cleveland Abbe Papers, General Correspondence, 1850–1916*. Manuscript Division, Library of Congress, Box 9.
——, 1893e: Cleveland Abbe to J. Sterling Morton. November 14, 1893. *Cleveland Abbe Papers, General Correspondence, 1850–1916*. Manuscript Division, Library of Congress, Box 9.
——, 1893f: Cleveland Abbe to Daniel Coit Gilman. July 29, 1893. *Daniel Coit Gilman Papers, Cleveland Abbe Correspondence*. Johns Hopkins University, Sheridan Libraries, Box 1-1, Folder 3.
——, 1894: The Possibilities of Long-Range Forecasts. *Mon. Wea. Rev.*, **22**, 330–331.
——, 1895a: The Meteorological Work of the U.S. Signal Service, 1870 to 1891. *Report of the International Meteorological Congress, Held at Chicago, Ill., August 21–24, 1893, Under the Auspices of the Congress Auxiliary of the World's Columbian Exposition*, O. L. Fassig, Ed., Weather Bureau Bulletin No. 11, Part II, 232–285.
——, 1895b: How Do Rains and Winds Spread Epidemics? *Mon. Wea. Rev.*, **23**, 295–296.
——, 1895c: The Green Colored Sun of September 9–10, 1883. *Mon. Wea. Rev.*, **23**, 173.
——, 1895d: Meteorology in the Public Schools. *Mon. Wea. Rev.*, **23**, 458.
——, 1897a: Cleveland Abbe to Julia Paine. February 19, 1897. *Increase A. Lapham Papers, Julia Lapham Correspondence 1897–1899*. Wisconsin Historical Society, Box 5, Folder 1.
——, 1897b: The Origin of the Weather Bureau. *Sci. Amer.*, **77**, 182.
——, 1897c: The Use of the Search Light in Meteorology. *Mon. Wea. Rev.*, **25**, 206–207.
——, 1898a: John A. Gano. *Science*, **7**, 123–124.
——, 1898b: An American Meteorological Society. *Mon. Wea. Rev.*, **26**, 64–65
——, 1898c: Origin of the Word "Blizzard." *Mon. Wea. Rev.*, **26**, 562.
——, 1898d: The Moon and the Weather. *Mon. Wea. Rev.*, **26**, 569.
——, 1899a: Origin of the Word "Blizzard." *Mon. Wea. Rev.*, **27**, 18.
——, 1899b: Meteorological Observations at Public Schools. *Mon. Wea. Rev.*, **27**, 550.
——, 1900a: The French Edition of the Monthly Weather Review. *Mon. Wea. Rev.*, **28**, 291.
——, 1900b: Cleveland Abbe to Booker T. Washington. February 7, 1900. *Booker T. Washington Papers, 1853–1946, Part I: Special Correspondence, 1853–1915*. Manuscript Division, Library of Congress, Box 22.
——, 1901a: Mr. Alexander Ashley. *Mon. Wea. Rev.*, **29**, 173.
——, 1901b: The First Number of the Monthly Weather Review. *Mon. Wea. Rev.*, **29**, 176.

——, 1901c: The Moon and the Weather. *Mon. Wea. Rev.*, **29**, 121–122.
——, 1901d: The Moon and the Weather. *Mon. Wea. Rev.*, **29**, 374–375.
——, 1901e: The Physical Basis of Long-Range Weather Forecasts. *Mon. Wea. Rev.*, **29**, 551–561.
——, 1903a: The Observatory of the University. *Mich. Alumnus*, **9**, 419–421.
——, 1903b: Cleveland Abbe to Wilbur Wright. September 26, 1903. *Wilbur Wright and Orville Wright Papers, 1809–1979, General Correspondence*. Manuscript Division, Library of Congress, Box 8.
——, 1903c: Cleveland Abbe to Wilbur Wright. December 31, 1903. *Wilbur Wright and Orville Wright Papers, 1809–1979, General Correspondence*. Manuscript Division, Library of Congress, Box 8.
——, 1903d: Meteorology and the Art of Flying. *Mon. Wea. Rev.*, **31**, 594–595.
——, 1903e: Education of Meteorologists. *Mon. Wea. Rev.*, **31**, 531.
——, 1903f: Cleveland Abbe to Albert Bickmore. May 21, 1903. *Albert S. Bickmore Papers, Correspondence, 1865–1903*, MSS .B5354, Special Collections, American Museum of Natural History Library, Box 1, Folder 1.
——, 1904a: Cleveland Abbe to Wilbur Wright. January 7, 1904. *Wilbur Wright and Orville Wright Papers, 1809–1979, General Correspondence*. Manuscript Division, Library of Congress, Box 8.
——, 1904b: The Introduction of Meteorology into the Courses of Instruction in Mathematics and Physics. *Mon. Wea. Rev.*, **32**, 513–515.
——, 1904c: Cleveland Abbe to Frank Armstrong. April 26, 1904. *Cincinnati Observatory Records, 1842–1970*. University of Cincinnati, Archives and Rare Books Library, Box 3, Folder 12.
——, 1904d: Cleveland Abbe to Frank Armstrong. June 30, 1904. *Cincinnati Observatory Records, 1842–1970*. University of Cincinnati, Archives and Rare Books Library, Box 3, Folder 12.
——, 1906: The Province of the Monthly Weather Review. *Mon. Wea. Rev.*, **34**, 160–161.
——, 1909: Changes in the Monthly Weather Review. *Mon. Wea. Rev.*, **37**, 61–62.
——, 1910a: Copy of unaddressed letter by Cleveland Abbe. April 2, 1910. *Cleveland Abbe Papers, General Correspondence, 1850–1916*. Manuscript Division, Library of Congress, Box 9.
——, 1910b: *The Mechanics of the Earth's Atmosphere: A Collection of Translations: Third Collection*. Miscellaneous Collections, No. 51, Smithsonian Institution, 617 pp.
——, 1911a: Cleveland Abbe to Frank H. Bigelow. July 14, 1911. *Cleveland Abbe Papers, General Correspondence, 1850–1916*. Manuscript Division, Library of Congress, Box 9.
——, 1911b: The Meteorology of the Future. *Pop. Sci. Mon.*, **78**, 21–35.
——, 1912a: The Obstacles to the Progress of Meteorology. *J. Franklin Inst.*, **173**, 55–71.
——, 1912b: The Symons Medal examined by the class in Physics, Gresham School, Holt, Norfolk, January 1912. *Cleveland Abbe Papers, Miscellaneous Notes*. Manuscript Division, Library of Congress, Box 24.

——, 1912c: Cleveland Abbe to Frieda Abbe. November 14, 1912. *Cleveland Abbe Papers, General Correspondence, 1850–1916*. Manuscript Division, Library of Congress, Box 9.

——, 1913: Cleveland Abbe to Thomas C. Mendenhall. December 7, 1913. *Thomas Corwin Mendenhall Papers, 1851–1951*. Worcester Polytechnic Institute, George C. Gordon Library, Box 8, Folder 2.

——, 1914: Cleveland Abbe to John Muir. June 23, 1914. *John Muir Correspondence, 1914*, University of California Berkley, Bancroft Library, Reel 22.

——, 1915: Cleveland Abbe to Allen B. Lincoln. March 26, 1915. *Cleveland Abbe Papers, General Correspondence, 1850–1916*. Manuscript Division, Library of Congress, Box 9.

——, 1916a: Untitled Note. February 10, 1916. *Cleveland Abbe Papers, Subject File, 1855–1884, Miscellaneous*. Manuscript Division, Library of Congress, Box 27.

——, 1916b: A short account of the circumstances attending the inception of weather forecast work by the United States. *Mon. Wea. Rev.*, **44**, 206–207.

——, 1916c: How the United States Weather Bureau Was Started. *Sci. Amer.*, **114**, 529.

——, 1916d: Cleveland Abbe to Charles D. Walcott. October 25, 1916. *Cleveland Abbe Papers, General Correspondence, 1850–1916*. Manuscript Division, Library of Congress, Box 9.

Abbe, C., and Nichols, J. G., 1916: *Abbe-Abbey Genealogy: In Memory of John Abbe and his Descendants*. The Tuttle, Morehouse & Taylor Company, 511 pp.

Abbe, C., E. B. Elliott, H. A. Newton, and C. S. Peirce, 1879: Report of Committee on Standard Time. *Proc. Amer. Metrological Soc.*, **2**, 17–44.

Abbe, C. Jr., 1908a: Cleveland Abbe Jr. to Cleveland Abbe. August 28, 1908. *Cleveland Abbe Papers, General Correspondence, 1850–1916*. Manuscript Division, Library of Congress, Box 9.

——, 1908b: Cleveland Abbe Jr. to Cleveland Abbe. September 13, 1908. *Cleveland Abbe Papers, General Correspondence, 1850–1916*. Manuscript Division, Library of Congress, Box 9.

——, 1915: Professor Cleveland Abbe. *Mon. Wea. Rev.*, **43**, 507.

——, 1916a: Marcellus Hartley Memorial Medal for 1916. *Mon. Wea. Rev.*, **44**, 205–206.

——, 1916b: Symons Memorial Medal for 1912. *Mon. Wea. Rev.*, **44**, 209.

——, 1916c: Cleveland Abbe, 1838–1916. *Mon. Wea. Rev.*, **44**, 517–518.

Abbe, C. C., 1862: Charlotte Abbe to Cleveland Abbe. September 19, 1862. *Cleveland Abbe Papers, General Correspondence, 1850–1916*. Manuscript Division, Library of Congress, Box 2.

——, 1863a: Charlotte Abbe to Cleveland Abbe. April 23, 1863. *Cleveland Abbe Papers, General Correspondence, 1850–1916*. Manuscript Division, Library of Congress, Box 2.

——, 1863b: Charlotte Abbe to Cleveland Abbe. July 6, 1863. *Cleveland Abbe Papers, General Correspondence, 1850–1916*. Manuscript Division, Library of Congress, Box 2.

——, 1863c: Charlotte Abbe to Cleveland Abbe. July 30, 1863. *Cleveland Abbe Papers, General Correspondence, 1850–1916*. Manuscript Division, Library of Congress, Box 2.

——, 1865a: Charlotte Abbe to Cleveland Abbe. February 8, 1865. *Cleveland Abbe Papers, General Correspondence, 1850–1916*. Manuscript Division, Library of Congress, Box 2.

——, 1865b: Charlotte Abbe to Cleveland Abbe. February 21, 1865. *Cleveland Abbe Papers, General Correspondence, 1850–1916*. Manuscript Division, Library of Congress, Box 2.

——, 1865c: Charlotte Abbe to Cleveland Abbe. March 8, 1865. *Cleveland Abbe Papers, General Correspondence, 1850–1916*. Manuscript Division, Library of Congress, Box 2.

——, 1865d: Charlotte Abbe to Cleveland Abbe. March 30, 1865. *Cleveland Abbe Papers, General Correspondence, 1850–1916*. Manuscript Division, Library of Congress, Box 2.

——, 1865e: Charlotte Abbe to Cleveland Abbe. April 13, 1865. *Cleveland Abbe Papers, General Correspondence, 1850–1916*. Manuscript Division, Library of Congress, Box 2.

——, 1865f: Charlotte Abbe to Cleveland Abbe. April 21, 1865. *Cleveland Abbe Papers, General Correspondence, 1850–1916*. Manuscript Division, Library of Congress, Box 2.

——, 1865g: Charlotte Abbe to Cleveland Abbe. May 5, 1865. *Cleveland Abbe Papers, General Correspondence, 1850–1916*. Manuscript Division, Library of Congress, Box 2.

——, 1865h: Charlotte Abbe to Cleveland Abbe. July 1, 1865. *Cleveland Abbe Papers, General Correspondence, 1850–1916*. Manuscript Division, Library of Congress, Box 2.

——, 1865i: Charlotte Abbe to Cleveland Abbe. November 3, 1865. *Cleveland Abbe Papers, General Correspondence, 1850–1916*. Manuscript Division, Library of Congress, Box 2.

——, 1865j: Charlotte Abbe to Cleveland Abbe. November 17, 1865. *Cleveland Abbe Papers, General Correspondence, 1850–1916*. Manuscript Division, Library of Congress, Box 2.

——, 1866a: Charlotte Abbe to Cleveland Abbe. March 2, 1866. *Cleveland Abbe Papers, General Correspondence, 1850–1916*. Manuscript Division, Library of Congress, Box 2.

——, 1866b: Charlotte Abbe to Cleveland Abbe. May 11, 1866. *Cleveland Abbe Papers, General Correspondence, 1850–1916*. Manuscript Division, Library of Congress, Box 3.

——, 1866c: Charlotte Abbe to Cleveland Abbe. June 22, 1866. *Cleveland Abbe Papers, General Correspondence, 1850–1916*. Manuscript Division, Library of Congress, Box 3.

——, 1866d: Charlotte Abbe to Cleveland Abbe. July 30, 1866. *Cleveland Abbe Papers, General Correspondence, 1850–1916*. Manuscript Division, Library of Congress, Box 3.

——, 1866e: Charlotte Abbe to Cleveland Abbe. August 7, 1866. *Cleveland Abbe Papers, General Correspondence, 1850–1916*. Manuscript Division, Library of Congress, Box 3.

——, 1868a: Charlotte Abbe to Cleveland Abbe. January 6, 1868. *Cleveland Abbe Papers, General Correspondence, 1850–1916*. Manuscript Division, Library of Congress, Box 3.

——, 1868b: Charlotte Abbe to Cleveland Abbe. February 3, 1868. *Cleveland Abbe Papers, General Correspondence, 1850–1916*. Manuscript Division, Library of Congress, Box 3.

——, 1868c: Charlotte Abbe to Cleveland Abbe. February 21, 1868. *Cleveland Abbe Papers, General Correspondence, 1850–1916*. Manuscript Division, Library of Congress, Box 3.

——, 1868d: Charlotte Abbe to Cleveland Abbe. March 20, 1868. *Cleveland Abbe Papers, General Correspondence, 1850–1916*. Manuscript Division, Library of Congress, Box 3.

——, 1868e: Charlotte Abbe to Cleveland Abbe. May 5, 1868. *Cleveland Abbe Papers, General Correspondence, 1850–1916*. Manuscript Division, Library of Congress, Box 3.

——, 1869: Charlotte Abbe to Cleveland Abbe. December 25, 1869. *Cleveland Abbe Papers, General Correspondence, 1850–1916*. Manuscript Division, Library of Congress, Box 5.

——, 1870a: Charlotte Abbe to Cleveland Abbe. February 28, 1870. *Cleveland Abbe Papers, General Correspondence, 1850–1916*. Manuscript Division, Library of Congress, Box 5.

——, 1870b: Charlotte Abbe to Cleveland Abbe. March 14, 1870. *Cleveland Abbe Papers, General Correspondence, 1850–1916*. Manuscript Division, Library of Congress, Box 5.

——, 1870c: Charlotte Abbe to Cleveland Abbe. April 11, 1870. *Cleveland Abbe Papers, General Correspondence, 1850–1916*. Manuscript Division, Library of Congress, Box 5.

——, 1870d: Charlotte Abbe to Cleveland Abbe. July 4, 1870. *Cleveland Abbe Papers, General Correspondence, 1850–1916*. Manuscript Division, Library of Congress, Box 6.

——, 1871a: Charlotte Abbe to Cleveland Abbe. February 15, 1871. *Cleveland Abbe Papers, General Correspondence, 1850–1916*. Manuscript Division, Library of Congress, Box 6.

——, 1871b: Charlotte Abbe to Cleveland Abbe. July 2, 1871. *Cleveland Abbe Papers, General Correspondence, 1850–1916*. Manuscript Division, Library of Congress, Box 6.

——, 1871c: Charlotte Abbe to Cleveland Abbe. September 29, 1871. *Cleveland Abbe Papers, General Correspondence, 1850–1916*. Manuscript Division, Library of Congress, Box 6.

——, 1874a: Charlotte Abbe to Cleveland Abbe. April 1, 1874. *Cleveland Abbe Papers, General Correspondence, 1850–1916*. Manuscript Division, Library of Congress, Box 7.

Abbe, E., Ed., 1968: *Letters of George Waldo Abbe and Charlotte Colgate Abbe*. Arnold Printing Company, 39 pp.

Abbe, F. M., 1870a: Frances Martha (Fanny) Abbe to Cleveland Abbe. August 2, 1870. *Cleveland Abbe Papers, General Correspondence, 1850–1916*. Manuscript Division, Library of Congress, Box 6.

——, 1889a: Frances Martha (Fanny) Abbe to Cleveland Abbe. November 11, 1889. *Cleveland Abbe Papers, General Correspondence, 1850–1916*. Manuscript Division, Library of Congress, Box 8.

——, 1889b: Frances Martha (Fanny) Abbe to Cleveland Abbe. December 10, 1889. *Cleveland Abbe Papers, General Correspondence, 1850–1916*. Manuscript Division, Library of Congress, Box 8.

——, 1889c: Frances Martha (Fanny) Abbe to Cleveland Abbe. December 16, 1889. *Cleveland Abbe Papers, General Correspondence, 1850–1916*. Manuscript Division, Library of Congress, Box 8.

——, 1890: Frances Martha (Fanny) Abbe to Cleveland Abbe. May 23, 1890. *Cleveland Abbe Papers, General Correspondence, 1850–1916*. Manuscript Division, Library of Congress, Box 8.

Abbe, G. W., 1860: George Waldo Abbe to Cleveland Abbe. December 14, 1860. *Cleveland Abbe Papers, General Correspondence, 1850–1916*. Manuscript Division, Library of Congress, Box 2.

——, 1865a: George Waldo Abbe to Cleveland Abbe. January 31, 1865. *Cleveland Abbe Papers, General Correspondence, 1850–1916*. Manuscript Division, Library of Congress, Box 2.

——, 1865b: George Waldo Abbe to Cleveland Abbe. June 12, 1865. *Cleveland Abbe Papers, General Correspondence, 1850–1916*. Manuscript Division, Library of Congress, Box 2.

——, 1865c: George Waldo Abbe to Cleveland Abbe. June 30, 1865. *Cleveland Abbe Papers, General Correspondence, 1850–1916*. Manuscript Division, Library of Congress, Box 2.

——, 1866a: George Waldo Abbe to Cleveland Abbe. June 7, 1866. *Cleveland Abbe Papers, General Correspondence, 1850–1916*. Manuscript Division, Library of Congress, Box 3.

——, 1866b: George Waldo Abbe to Cleveland Abbe. September 7, 1866. *Cleveland Abbe Papers, General Correspondence, 1850–1916*. Manuscript Division, Library of Congress, Box 3.

——, 1868: George Waldo Abbe to Cleveland Abbe. January 28, 1868. *Cleveland Abbe Papers, General Correspondence, 1850–1916*. Manuscript Division, Library of Congress, Box 3.

——, 1870a: George Waldo Abbe to Cleveland Abbe. April 9, 1870. *Cleveland Abbe Papers, General Correspondence, 1850–1916*. Manuscript Division, Library of Congress, Box 5.

——, 1870b: George Waldo Abbe to Cleveland Abbe. October 22, 1870. *Cleveland Abbe Papers, General Correspondence, 1850–1916*. Manuscript Division, Library of Congress, Box 6.

——, 1871a: George Waldo Abbe to Cleveland Abbe. February 13, 1871. *Cleveland Abbe Papers, General Correspondence, 1850–1916*. Manuscript Division, Library of Congress, Box 6.

——, 1871b: George Waldo Abbe to Cleveland Abbe. April 4, 1871. *Cleveland Abbe Papers, General Correspondence, 1850–1916*. Manuscript Division, Library of Congress, Box 6.

——, 1871c: George Waldo Abbe to Cleveland Abbe. April 14, 1871. *Cleveland Abbe Papers, General Correspondence, 1850–1916*. Manuscript Division, Library of Congress, Box 6.

——, 1871d: George Waldo Abbe to Cleveland Abbe. April 20, 1871. *Cleveland Abbe Papers, General Correspondence, 1850–1916*. Manuscript Division, Library of Congress, Box 6.

——, 1871e: George Waldo Abbe to Cleveland Abbe. May 25, 1871. *Cleveland Abbe Papers, General Correspondence, 1850–1916*. Manuscript Division, Library of Congress, Box 6.

——, 1871f: George Waldo Abbe to Cleveland Abbe. June 8, 1871. *Cleveland Abbe Papers, General Correspondence, 1850–1916*. Manuscript Division, Library of Congress, Box 6.

——, 1871g: George Waldo Abbe to Cleveland Abbe. June 10, 1871. *Cleveland Abbe Papers, General Correspondence, 1850–1916*. Manuscript Division, Library of Congress, Box 6.

——, 1871h: George Waldo Abbe to Cleveland Abbe. August 30, 1871. *Cleveland Abbe Papers, General Correspondence, 1850–1916*. Manuscript Division, Library of Congress, Box 6.

——, 1871i: George Waldo Abbe to Cleveland Abbe. September 7, 1871. *Cleveland Abbe Papers, General Correspondence, 1850–1916*. Manuscript Division, Library of Congress, Box 6.

——, 1871j: George Waldo Abbe to Cleveland Abbe. November 4, 1871. *Cleveland Abbe Papers, General Correspondence, 1850–1916*. Manuscript Division, Library of Congress, Box 6.

——, 1871k: George Waldo Abbe to Cleveland Abbe. November 21, 1871. *Cleveland Abbe Papers, General Correspondence, 1850–1916*. Manuscript Division, Library of Congress, Box 6.

——, 1871l: George Waldo Abbe to Cleveland Abbe. November 26, 1871. *Cleveland Abbe Papers, General Correspondence, 1850–1916*. Manuscript Division, Library of Congress, Box 6.

Abbe, H., 1863: Helen Abbe to Cleveland Abbe. July 6, 1863. *Cleveland Abbe Papers, General Correspondence, 1850–1916*. Manuscript Division, Library of Congress, Box 2.

——, 1868: Helen Abbe to Cleveland Abbe. June 22, 1868. *Cleveland Abbe Papers, General Correspondence, 1850–1916*. Manuscript Division, Library of Congress, Box 3.

——, 1871a: Helen Abbe to Cleveland Abbe. March 18, 1871. *Cleveland Abbe Papers, General Correspondence, 1850–1916*. Manuscript Division, Library of Congress, Box 6.

——, 1871b: Helen Abbe to Cleveland Abbe. September 12, 1871. *Cleveland Abbe Papers, General Correspondence, 1850–1916*. Manuscript Division, Library of Congress, Box 6.

Abbe, R., 1869: Robert Abbe to Cleveland Abbe. December 11, 1869. *Cleveland Abbe Papers, General Correspondence, 1850–1916*. Manuscript Division, Library of Congress, Box 5.

——, 1870: Robert Abbe to Cleveland Abbe. March 7, 1870. *Cleveland Abbe Papers, General Correspondence, 1850–1916*. Manuscript Division, Library of Congress, Box 5.

——, 1871a: Robert Abbe to Cleveland Abbe. April 5, 1871. *Cleveland Abbe Papers, General Correspondence, 1850–1916*. Manuscript Division, Library of Congress, Box 6.

——, 1871b: Robert Abbe to Cleveland Abbe. July 2, 1871. *Cleveland Abbe Papers, General Correspondence, 1850–1916*. Manuscript Division, Library of Congress, Box 6.

——, 1871c: Robert Abbe to Cleveland Abbe. November 21, 1871. *Cleveland Abbe Papers, General Correspondence, 1850–1916*. Manuscript Division, Library of Congress, Box 6.

——, 1873a: Robert Abbe to Cleveland Abbe. January 15, 1873. *Cleveland Abbe Papers, General Correspondence, 1850–1916*. Manuscript Division, Library of Congress, Box 7.

——, 1873b: Robert Abbe to Cleveland Abbe. November 4, 1873. *Cleveland Abbe Papers, General Correspondence, 1850–1916*. Manuscript Division, Library of Congress, Box 7.

——, 1874: Robert Abbe to Cleveland Abbe. March 27, 1874. *Cleveland Abbe Papers, General Correspondence, 1850–1916*. Manuscript Division, Library of Congress, Box 7.

——, 1924: Personal Reminiscences by Robert Abbe, M.D. *Cleveland Abbe Papers, Family Correspondence and Related Papers, circa 1858–1954, Robert Abbe*. Manuscript Division, Library of Congress, Box 9.

Abbe, T., n.d.: *Cleveland Abbe: Dean of American Meteorologists*. Unpublished manuscript (early draft of *Professor Abbe . . . and the Isobars*). *Cleveland Abbe Papers, Family Correspondence and Related Papers, circa 1858–1954*. Manuscript Division, Library of Congress, Box 10.

——, 1923: To be Read at the Presentation of the Tablet on 2017 I Street. *Cleveland Abbe Papers, Subject File, 1855–1884, Biographical Material*. Manuscript Division, Library of Congress, Box 15.

——, 1955: *Professor Abbe . . . and the Isobars: The Story of Cleveland Abbe, America's First Weatherman*. Vantage Press, 259 pp.

Abbe, T., and H. A. Howson, 1941: *Robert Colgate, the Immigrant: A Genealogy of the New York Colgates and Some Associated Lines*. Tuttle, Moorehouse & Taylor Company, 464 pp.

Abbe, W., 1865: Walter Abbe to Cleveland Abbe. February 17, 1865. *Cleveland Abbe Papers, General Correspondence, 1850–1916*. Manuscript Division, Library of Congress, Box 2.

——, 1870: Walter Abbe to Cleveland Abbe. March 20, 1870. *Cleveland Abbe Papers, General Correspondence, 1850–1916*. Manuscript Division, Library of Congress, Box 5.

Abbe, W. C., 1866: William Abbe to Cleveland Abbe. May 28, 1866. *Cleveland Abbe Papers, General Correspondence, 1850–1916*. Manuscript Division, Library of Congress, Box 3.

——, 1871: William Abbe to Cleveland Abbe. Received February 13, 1871. *Cleveland Abbe Papers, General Correspondence, 1850–1916*. Manuscript Division, Library of Congress, Box 6.

Advertiser, 1896: Lord Kelvin's Jubilee. *The Advertiser* (Adelaide, Australia), August 1, 1896, 1.

Alioth Finance, 2019: FinanceRef Inflation Calculator. Accessed 28 June 2019, http://www.in2013dollars.com/.

Alden, W., 1869a: Meteorological Society Formed. *Cleveland Abbe Papers, General Correspondence, 1850–1916*. Manuscript Division, Library of Congress, Box 5.

Alden, W., 1869b: Walter Alden to Cleveland Abbe. July 21, 1869. *Cleveland Abbe Papers, General Correspondence, 1850–1916*. Manuscript Division, Library of Congress, Box 5.

Alexander, W. H., 1923: *A Climatological History of Ohio*. Bulletin No. 26 of the Engineering Experiment Station of The Ohio State University Bulletin, 745 pp.

Allen, W. F., 1884: History of the Movement by which the Adoption of Standard Time was Consummated. *Proc. Amer. Metrological Soc.*, **4**, 25–50.

Allison Commission, 1886: Testimony before the Joint Commission to Consider the Present Organizations of the Signal Service, Geological Survey, Coast and Geodetic Survey, and the Hydrographic Office of the Navy Department, with a View to Secure Greater Efficiency and Economy of Administration. U.S. Congress, Senate Misc. Doc. 82, 1,104 pp.

Alter, J. C., 1949: National Weather Service Origins. *Bull. Hist. Philos. Soc. Ohio*, 7, 139–185.

The Alumni Association of the University of Michigan Publishers, 1915: News from the Class. *The Michigan Alumnus*, **XXII**, 168.

AMS, 1920: The American Meteorological Society. *Bull. Amer. Meteor. Soc.*, **1**, 1.

——, 1945: The Presidents. Papers Offered in Celebration of the Twenty-Fifth Anniversary of the American Meteorological Society. *Bull. Amer. Meteor. Soc.*, **26**, 235–244.

——, 1964: The Society's Awards. *Bull. Amer. Meteor. Soc.*, **45**, 477–484.

Andreas, T. A., 1885: *History of Chicago from the Earliest Period to the Present Time, Volume II—From 1857 Until the Fire of 1871*. A. T. Andreas Company, 780 pp.

Armstrong, F. A., 1904: Frank Armstrong to Cleveland Abbe. June 28, 1904. *Cincinnati Observatory Records, 1842–1970*. University of Cincinnati, Archives and Rare Books Library, Box 3, Folder 12.

Army and Navy Journal, 1884: Colored Men and the Signal Corps. The United States Army and Navy Journal, and Gazette of the Regular and Volunteer Forces, 21, 956.

Astore, W. J., 2017: *Observing God: Thomas Dick, Evangelicalism, and Popular Science in Victorian Britain and America*. Routledge, 314 pp.

Atlantic Monthly, 1875: Recent Literature. *The Atlantic Monthly*, **36**, 629–630.

Avant, T., 2015: Artifact of the Assassination: The Lincoln Flag and the Gourlay Family. Accessed 27 April 2018, https://www.fords.org/blog/post/artifact-of-the-assassination-the-lincoln-flag-and-the-gourlay-family/.

Bache, A. D., 1852: *Annual Report of the Superintendent of the Coast Survey, Showing the Progress of that Work During the Year Ending November, 1851*. Robert Armstrong, Printer, 559 pp.

Balcerski, T. J., 2019: *Bosom Friends: The Intimate World of James Buchanan and William Rufus King*. Oxford University Press, 352 pp.

Baldock, M., 2011: Egypt on Broadway. New-York Historical Society. Accessed 2 December 2017, http://blog.nyhistory.org/egypt-on-broadway/.

Bancroft, C. F. P., 1869: Rev. C. F. P. Bancroft to Cleveland Abbe. September 1, 1869. *Cleveland Abbe Papers, General Correspondence, 1850–1916*. Manuscript Division, Library of Congress, Box 5.

Bartky, I. R., 1989: The Adoption of Standard Time. *Technol. Cult.*, **30**, 25–26.

Batten, A. H., 1977: The Struves of Pulkovo—A Family of Astronomers. *J. R. Astron. Soc. Can.*, **71**, 345–372.

Batten, A. H., 1988: *Resolute and Undertaking Characters: The Lives of Wilhelm and Otto Struve*. D. Reidel Publishing Company, 258 pp.

Beal, W. J., 1915: *History of the Michigan Agricultural College and Biographical Sketches of Trustees and Professors*. Michigan Agricultural College, 519 pp.

Belknap, W. M., 1870: Report of the Secretary of War, Volume I (as part of House Ex. Doc. No. 1, pt. 2, 41st Congress, 3rd Session). Government Printing Office, 326 pp.

Bell, A. G., 1904: Alexander Graham Bell to Cleveland Abbe. March 25, 1904. *Cleveland Abbe Papers, General Correspondence, 1850–1916*. Manuscript Division, Library of Congress, Box 9.

Bergland, M., and P. G. Hayes, 2014: *Studying Wisconsin: The Life of Increase Lapham, early chronicler of plants, rocks, rivers, mounds and all things Wisconsin*. Wisconsin Historical Society Press, 424 pp.

Berry, J., Ed., 1899: *Proceedings of the Convention of Weather Bureau Officials, Held at Omaha, Nebr., October 13–14, 1899*. Government Printing Office, 184 pp.

Berry, J. and W. F. R. Phillips, Eds., 1902: *Proceedings of the Second Convention of Weather Bureau Officials Held at Milwaukee, Wis., August 27, 28, 29, 1901*. Government Printing Office, 267 pp.

Bickmore, A. S., 1863: Albert Bickmore to Cleveland Abbe. April 10/12, 1863. *Cleveland Abbe Papers, General Correspondence, 1850–1916*. Manuscript Division, Library of Congress, Box 2.

——, 1865a: Albert Bickmore to Cleveland Abbe. January 31, 1865. *Cleveland Abbe Papers, General Correspondence, 1850–1916*. Manuscript Division, Library of Congress, Box 2.

——, 1865b: Albert Bickmore to Cleveland Abbe. May 28, 1865. *Cleveland Abbe Papers, General Correspondence, 1850–1916*. Manuscript Division, Library of Congress, Box 2.

——, 1865c: Albert Bickmore to Cleveland Abbe. November 28, 1865. *Cleveland Abbe Papers, General Correspondence, 1850–1916*. Manuscript Division, Library of Congress, Box 3.

——, 1870: Albert Bickmore to Cleveland Abbe. May 16, 1870. *Cleveland Abbe Papers, General Correspondence, 1850–1916*. Manuscript Division, Library of Congress, Box 5.

——, 1908: *An autobiography, with a historical sketch of the founding and early development of the American Museum of Natural History*. Accessed 24 January 2018, http://digitallibrary.amnh.org/handle/2246/6132.

Bigelow, F. H., 1900: Work of the Meteorologist for the Benefit of Agriculture, Commerce, and Navigation. *Yearbook of the United States Department of Agriculture: 1899*. G. W. Hill, Ed., Government Printing Office, 71–92.

Bjerknes, V., 1904: Das Problem der Wettervorhersage, betrachtet vom Standpunkte der Mechanik und der Physik, *Meteor. Z.*, **21**, 1–7.

Bôcher, M., 1888: The Meteorological Labors of Dove, Redfield and Espy. *Amer. Meteor. J.*, **5**, 1–13.

Bond, W., 1838: *Meteorological Observations of William Bond (1838–1839)*. Historic Climate Diaries and Journals, Environmental Document Access and Display System, Version 2 (EV2), NOAA National Centers for Environmental Information.

Boyd, W. H., 1875: *Boyd's Directory of the District of Columbia, Together with a Compendium of its Governments, Institutions and Trades*. Richard B. Mohun & Co., 624 pp.

Brooklyn Daily Eagle, 1867: The Albany Murder. *Brooklyn Daily Eagle*, June 5, 1867, 2.

Brooks, C. F., 1934: Cleveland Abbe Jr. Necrology. *Bull. Amer. Meteor. Soc.*, **15**, 241–242.

Brown, J. B., 1869: Joseph B. Brown to Cleveland Abbe. August 15, 1869. *Cleveland Abbe Papers, General Correspondence, 1850–1916*. Manuscript Division, Library of Congress, Box 5.

Brown, J. F., 1838: James F. Brown Papers, Vol. 2, *James F. Brown Papers, 1827–1866*. New-York Historical Society. [Available online at http://digitalcollections.nyhistory.org/islandora/object/islandora%3A152395.]

Bruce, J. M, 1914: A Well Rounded Life---Albert Smith Bickmore, LL.D. *Watchman-Examiner*, August 27, 1914, 1159.

Brünnow, F. F. E., 1856: Franz Brünnow to Cleveland Abbe. December 31, 1856. *Cleveland Abbe Papers, General Correspondence, 1850–1916*. Manuscript Division, Library of Congress, Box 2.

——, 1860: Franz Brünnow to Cleveland Abbe. August 9, 1860. *Cleveland Abbe Papers, General Correspondence, 1850–1916*. Manuscript Division, Library of Congress, Box 2.

Calver, 1922: "Old Probabilities." *The Evening Star* (Washington, D.C.), May 3, 1922, 17.

Campbell, J. A., Ed., 1902: *A Biographical History with Portraits of Prominent Men of the Great West*. Western Biographical and Engraving Co., 688 pp.

Capen, F. L., 1863: Francis L. Capen to Abraham Lincoln. April 25, 1863. [Response by Lincoln attached, dated April 28, 1863.] *Abraham Lincoln Papers: Series 1, General Correspondence, 1833 to 1916*. Manuscript Division, Library of Congress, Reel 35. [Available online at https://www.loc.gov/item/mal2313000/.]

Caroli, B. B., 2018: *The Roosevelt Women*. Basic Books, 528 pp.

Cary, F. G., and J. A. Warder, Eds., 1860: Nurserymen's Directory—Kentucky. *The Cincinnatus*, **5**, 12.

Chamber of Commerce of the State of New York, 1870: Reports of Special Committees. *Twelfth Annual Report of the Corporation of the Chamber of Commerce, of the State of New York, for the Year 1869-'70*. Press of the Chamber of Commerce, 32–34.

Chiat, B., 1956: Longitude Determination: An Historical Survey. *Mon. Notes Astron. Soc. S. Afr.*, **15**, 32–34.

Cheney, W., 1869: William Cheney to Cleveland Abbe. July 26, 1869. *Cleveland Abbe Papers, General Correspondence, 1850–1916*. Manuscript Division, Library of Congress, Box 5.

Chicago Tribune, 1869: Bulletin of the Weather. *The Chicago Tribune*, August 18, 1869, 2.

Cincinnati Chamber of Commerce, 1896: History of Weather Bureau Service. *Forty-seventh Annual Report of the Cincinnati Chamber of Commerce and Merchants' Exchange for the Year Ending December 31, 1895*. The Ohio Valley Company, 102–102c.

City of Manassas, 2019: Who Was Jennie Dean? City of Manassas, Virginia. Accessed 11 June 2019: https://www.manassascity.org/2502/Who-Was-Jennie-Dean.

Coiffier, J., 2011: *Fundamentals of Numerical Weather Prediction*. Translated by C. Sutcliffe. Cambridge University Press, 368 pp.

The Collector, 1905. Price List. *The Collector: A Magazine for Autograph and Historical Collectors*, **18** (10), 105.

Columbia Spectator, 1908: Prominent Lectures. *Columbia Spectator*, November 2, 1908, 2.

——, 1909: University Bulletin. *Columbia Spectator*, March 12, 1909, 6.

Commercial Advertiser, 1908a. People in Print. *Commercial Advertiser* (Potsdam Junction, N.Y.), June 30, 1908, 5.

Commercial Advertiser, 1908b. Mrs. Frances M. Abbe. *Commercial Advertiser* (Potsdam Junction, N.Y.), July 28, 1908, 4.

Comstock, G. C., 1922: Biographical Memoir Benjamin Apthorp Gould: 1824–1896. Vol. XVII, *Biographical Memoirs*, National Academy of Sciences, 153–180.

Conner, G., 2004: Nineteenth Century Weather Observers: A Whodunit. *14th Conf. on Appl. Climatol.*, Seattle, WA, Amer. Meteor. Soc., 7.14, https://ams.confex.com/ams/84Annual/webprogram/Paper70253.html.

Cooper, S., 1844: *The First Lines of the Theory and Practice of Surgery; Including the Principle Operations*. Vol. 1. Samuel S. and William Wood, 540 pp.

——, 2012: A Footnote to Florida's Observational History. *2012 AASC Annual Meeting*, Destin, FL, Amer. Assoc. State Climatol., http://coaps.fsu.edu/pub/griffin/Selover/Tuesday%20Afternoon/Session%201/AASC%20Paper.pptx.

Corzine, H. A., 1972: Monthly Weather Review Centennial, 1872–1972. *Mon. Wea. Rev.*, **100**, 517.

Cox, J. D., 2002: *Storm Watchers: The Turbulent History of Weather Prediction from Franklin's Kite to El Niño*. John Wiley & Sons, 252 pp.

Craft, E. D., 1999: Private Weather Organizations and the Founding of the United States Weather Bureau. *J. Econ. Hist.*, **59**, 1063–1071.

Davenport, C., B., 1911: Euthenics and Eugenics. *Pop. Sci. Mon.*, **78**, 16–20.

Day, A., L., 1916: Report of the Annual Meeting. *Proc. Natl. Acad. Sci. U.S.A.*, **2**, 300–308.

Dean, J., 1892: Jennie Dean to John D. Rockefeller. May 9, 1892. *Rockefeller Family Archives, Record Group 1, Series C (Correspondence), Subseries O (Office)*. The Rockefeller Archive Center, Box 11, Folder 79.

Denver Daily Tribune, 1878: The Eclipse and the Weather. *The Denver Daily Tribune*, July 14, 1878, 4.

Desert Weekly, 1893: Washington Items. *The Desert Weekly*, 26, 759–760.

Dexter, E. G., 1904: *Weather Influences: An Empirical Study of the Mental and Physiological Effects of Definite Meteorological Conditions*. Macmillan Co., 286 pp.

Dexter, J., 1870: Julius Dexter to Cleveland Abbe. October 10, 1870. *Cleveland Abbe Papers, General Correspondence, 1850–1916*. Manuscript Division, Library of Congress, Box 6.

Diamond Cove Association, 2014: Great Diamond Island: Artists' Retreat, Island Fort, Vacation Resort. Accessed 15 June 2019, https://www.diamondcove.com/the-cove/history/.

Dickson, N., 2012: Tradition and Humour: the Academic Dress of the University of Glasgow. *Trans. Burgon Soc.*, 12, 10–35.

Döllen, W., 1865: *Jahresbericht dem Comité der Nicolai-Hauptsternwarte*. Printing Office of the Imperial Academy of Sciences, 42 pp.

Dostoevsky, F., 2017: *Crime and Punishment*. A New Translation by Michael R. Katz. Liveright Publishing, 624 pp.

Douglass, F., n.d.: Aryan Civilization. Manuscript and typeset fragments. Frederick Douglass Papers, Speeches, Articles, and Other Writings Attributed to Frederick or Helen Pitts Douglass, 1881–1887. Manuscript Division, Library of Congress, Box 32. [Available online at: https://www.loc.gov/item/mfd.32004/.]

Driver, R. J., 2016: *The Confederate Soldiers of Rockbridge County, Virginia: A Roster*. McFarland. 360 pp.

Dunn, E. B., 1909: The Inaugural Day Storm. *Everybody's Magazine*, **20**, 713–714.

Dunwoody, H. H. C., 1894: Summary of International Observations. *Amer. Meteor. J.*, **10**, 526–527.

Earth and Air, 1901: Earth and Air advertisement. *The Living Age*, **10**, February 23, 1901.

Eliassen, A., 1982: Vilhelm Bjerknes and His Students. *Ann. Rev. Fluid Mech.*, **14**, 1–11.

Emery, A., 1867: Anne Emery to Cleveland Abbe. January 7, 1867. *Cleveland Abbe Papers, General Correspondence, 1850–1916*. Manuscript Division, Library of Congress, Box 3.

Emery, J., 1867: Joseph Emery to Cleveland Abbe. January 15, 1867. *Cleveland Abbe Papers, General Correspondence, 1850–1916*. Manuscript Division, Library of Congress, Box 3.

Espy, J. P., 1841: *Philosophy of Storms*. Charles C. Little and James Brown, 552 pp.

Eugenical News, 1918a: The Families of Abbe and Abbey. *Eugenical News*, **3**, 70–71.

Eugenical News, 1918b: The Field of Genealogy. *Eugenical News*, **3**, 79.

Evening Star, 1872: "Old Prob."—A Popular Delusion Dispelled. *The Evening Star* (Washington, D.C.), April 26, 1872, 1.

——, 1886: Gen. Hazen Testifies. *The Evening Star* (Washington, D.C.), March 24, 1886, 3.

——, 1890: In Fair Clio's Name. *The Evening Star* (Washington, D.C.), July 26, 1890, 9.

——, 1895: Discussion of What the Colored Race Should Undertake. *The Evening Star* (Washington, D.C.), April 4, 1895, 9.

——, 1899: Prof. Harrington Dismissed. *The Evening Star* (Washington, D.C.), July 3, 1899, 1.

——, 1900: Howgate a Free Man. *The Evening Star* (Washington, D.C.), December 28, 1900, 5.

——, 1909a: Prof. Abbe a Bridegroom. *The Evening Star* (Washington, D.C.), April 13, 1909, 7.

——, 1909b: Inauguration Day Marred by Blizzard. *The Evening Star* (Washington, D.C.), March 4, 1909, 15.

——, 1913: Moore Terms His Ousting "Disgrace." *The Evening Star* (Washington, D.C.), April 7, 1913, 1.

——, 1930: Society. *The Evening Star* (Washington, D.C.), January 20, 1930, B-2.

Evening Times, 1897: Slated to Be Diplomats. *The Evening Times* (Washington, D.C.), April 30, 1897, 1.

Fessenden, S. C., 1867: Samuel C. Fessenden to Cleveland Abbe. January 2, 1867. *Cleveland Abbe Papers, General Correspondence, 1850–1916*. Manuscript Division, Library of Congress, Box 3.

Fleming, J. R., 1990: *Meteorology in America, 1800–1870*. Johns Hopkins University Press, 264 pp.

——, 2000: Storms, strikes, and surveillance: The U.S. Army Signal Office, 1861–1891. *Hist. Stud. Phys. Sci.*, **30**, 315–332.

——, 2016: *Inventing Atmospheric Science: Bjerknes, Rossby, Wexler, and the Foundations of Modern Meteorology*. MIT Press, 306 pp.

Fleming, J. R., and S. L. Kaplan, 1996: *Historical Writing on Meteorology: An Annotated Bibliography. Historical Essays on Meteorology, 1919–1995: The Diamond Anniversary History Volume of the American Meteorological Society*, J. R. Fleming, Ed., Amer. Meteor. Soc., 557–580.

Foster, R. W., 1869: Robert W. Foster to Cleveland Abbe. September 3, 1869. *Cleveland Abbe Papers, General Correspondence, 1850–1916*. Manuscript Division, Library of Congress, Box 5.

Free Academy of the City of New York, 1861: Thirteenth Annual Register of The Free Academy of the City of New York, 1861–1862, 101 pp.

Freeman, A., 1931: Alden Freeman to Margaret Abbe. January 2, 1931. *Cleveland Abbe Papers, General Correspondence, 1850–1916*. Manuscript Division, Library of Congress, Box 9.

Fuller, J. F., 1990: *Thor's Legions: Weather Support to the U.S. Air Force and Army*. Amer. Meteor. Soc., 442 pp.

Gallo, N. R., 2004: *Introduction to Family Law*. Thompson Delmar Learning, 513 pp.

Gates, F. T., 1892: Frederick T. Gates to John D. Rockefeller. June 2, 1892. *Rockefeller Family Archives, Record Group 1, Series C (Correspondence), Subseries O (Office)*. The Rockefeller Archive Center, Box 11, Folder 79.

Gingerich, O., 1999: Benjamin Apthorp Gould and the Founding of the Astronomical Journal. Astronomical Journal. *Astron. J.*, **117**, 1–5.

Glassford, W. A., 1885: History, Development, and Organization of the Signal Service, etc. *Testimony Before the Joint Commission to Consider the Present Organizations of the Signal Service, Geological Survey, Coast and Geodetic Survey, and the Hydrographic Office of the Navy Department, with a View to Secure Greater Efficiency and Economy of Administration of the Public Service in Said Bureaus, Authorized by the Sundry Civil Act Approved July 7, 1884, and Continued by the Sundry Civil

Act Approved March 3, 1885. U.S. Senate, Mis. Doc. No. 82, 49th Congress, 1st Session, Government Printing Office, 1886, 462–466.
——, 1892: Synoptical Sketch of the Progress of Meteorology in the United States. *The Amer. Met. J.*, **9**, 151–164.
Goldsmith, E., 1869: Edward Goldsmith to Cleveland Abbe. September 6, 1869. *Cleveland Abbe Papers, General Correspondence, 1850–1916*. Manuscript Division, Library of Congress, Box 5.
Good Government, 1893: Looking Backward and Forward. *Good Government*, **12**, 95–96.
Goode, J. M., 2003: *Capital Losses: A Cultural History of Washington's Destroyed Buildings*. Smithsonian, 539 pp.
——, 2015: *Capital Houses: Historic Residences of Washington D.C. and Its Environs, 1735–1965*. Acanthus Press, 496 pp.
Goodheard, A., 2011: *1861: The Civil War Awakening*. Knopf, 481 pp.
Goodwin, D. K., 2006: *Team of Rivals: The Political Genius of Abraham Lincoln*. Simon & Schuster, 944 pp.
Gould, B. A., 1857: Benjamin Gould to Cleveland Abbe. July 25, 1857. *Cleveland Abbe Papers, General Correspondence, 1850–1916*. Manuscript Division, Library of Congress, Box 2.
——, 1859: *Reply to the "Statement of the Trustees" of the Dudley Observatory*. Charles Van Benthuysen, 366 pp.
——, 1860a: Benjamin Gould to Cleveland Abbe. July 30, 1860. *Cleveland Abbe Papers, General Correspondence, 1850–1916*. Manuscript Division, Library of Congress, Box 2.
——, 1860b: Benjamin Gould to Cleveland Abbe. October 15, 1860. *Cleveland Abbe Papers, General Correspondence, 1850–1916*. Manuscript Division, Library of Congress, Box 2.
——, 1860c: Benjamin Gould to Cleveland Abbe. October 15, 1860. *Cleveland Abbe Papers, General Correspondence, 1850–1916*. Manuscript Division, Library of Congress, Box 2.
——, 1867: Benjamin Gould to Benjamin Peirce (copy). March 28, 1867. *Cleveland Abbe Papers, General Correspondence, 1850–1916*. Manuscript Division, Library of Congress, Box 3.
Greely, A. W., 1887: *Annual Report of the Chief Signal Officer of the Army to the Secretary of War for the Year 1887, Part I*. Government Printing Office, 361 pp.
——, 1890: *Annual Report of the Chief Signal Officer of the Army to the Secretary of War for the Year 1890*. Government Printing Office, 713 pp.
——, 1891: *Annual Report of the Chief Signal Officer of the Army to the Secretary of War for the Year 1891*. Government Printing Office, 781 pp.
Green, C. M., 2015: *Secret City: A History of Race Relations in the Nation's Capital*. Princeton University Press, 422 pp.
Greve, C. T., 1904: *Centennial History of Cincinnati and Representative Citizens*. Vol. 1. Biographical Publishing Company, 1052 pp.

Grice, G. K., Ed., 1991: The Beginning of the National Weather Service: The Signal Service Years (1870–1891) As Viewed by Early Weather Pioneers. National Weather Service, 52 pp. [Available online at: ftp://ftp.library.noaa.gov/docs.lib/htdocs/rescue/wb_historicaldocs/QC861B41991.PDF.]

Gritz, J. R., 2012: But Were They Gay? The Mystery of Same-Sex Love in the 19th Century. *The Atlantic*, 7 September 2012. Accessed 17 February 2018, https://www.theatlantic.com/national/archive/2012/09/but-were-they-gay-the-mystery-of-same-sex-love-in-the-19th-century/262117/.

Guston, D. H., 1994: Congressmen and Scientists in the Making of Science Policy: The Allison Commission, 1884–1886. *Minerva*, **32**, 25–52.

Haines, Z. T., 1863: *Letters from the Forth-Fourth Regiment M. V. M.: A Record of the Experience of a Nine Months' Regiment in the Department of North Carolina in 1862–3*. Herald Job Office, 121 pp.

Hall, A., 1865: Asaph Hall to Cleveland Abbe. June 17, 1865. *Cleveland Abbe Papers, General Correspondence, 1850–1916*. Manuscript Division, Library of Congress, Box 2.

——, 1866: Asaph Hall to Cleveland Abbe. December 14, 1866. *Cleveland Abbe Papers, General Correspondence, 1850–1916*. Manuscript Division, Library of Congress, Box 3.

Hall, J. W., 1870: *Marine Disasters on the Western Lakes, During the Navigation of 1869, with the Loss of Life and Property; Vessels Bought and Sold; New Vessels and Their Tonnage; Also, Those Which Have Passed out of Existence; with the Names of Vessels Laid Up at Various Lake Ports*. W. E. Tunis, 120 pp.

Harper, K. C., 2008: *Weather by the Numbers: The Genesis of Modern Meteorology*. MIT Press, 304 pp.

Harrington, M. W., 1891: *Special Report of Chief of the Weather Bureau to the Secretary of Agriculture*. U.S. Weather Bureau, 26 pp.

——, 1893: Mark Harrington to Cleveland Abbe. July 6, 1893. *Cleveland Abbe Papers, General Correspondence, 1850–1916*. Manuscript Division, Library of Congress, Box 9.

Hart, E. R., 1986: Historic Resources Inventory, Building and Structures, Connecticut Historical Commission. [Available online at http://farmingtonlibraries.org/wp-content/uploads/2015/05/127-Main-Street.pdf.]

Hart, J. S., 1857: *Female Prose Writers of America*. E. H. Butler & Co., 536 pp.

Hazen, W. B., 1881: *Annual Report of the Chief Signal Officer to the Secretary of War for the Fiscal Year Ending June 30, 1881*. Government Printing Office, 1296 pp.

Henry, A. J., 1929: Editors of the Monthly Weather Review. *Mon. Wea. Rev.*, **57**, 63–64.

——, 1930: *Weather Forecasting from Synoptic Charts*. United States Department of Agriculture Miscellaneous Publication No. 71. U.S. Government Printing Office, 80 pp.

Henry, J., 1870: Joseph Henry to Halbert E. Paine. January 10, 1870 (as part of House Ex. Doc. No. 10, pt. 2, 41st Congress, 2nd Session). *Increase A. Lapham Papers,*

Meteorology—Weather Bureau. Wisconsin Historical Society, Box 18, Folder 7.

Henson, P. M., 2015: The Burning of the Smithsonian. Smithsonian Institution Archives. Accessed 18 June 2019, https://siarchives.si.edu/blog/burning-smithsonian.

The Herald, 1869: Jerry Rusk's Successor. *The Herald* (Los Angeles), February 18, 1893, 1.

Herrick, E., 1863: Everett Herrick to Cleveland Abbe. December 1, 1863. *Cleveland Abbe Papers, General Correspondence, 1850–1916*. Manuscript Division, Library of Congress, Box 2.

History Nebraska, n.d.: Morton's The Conservative. Accessed 28 April 2019, https://history.nebraska.gov/publications/mortons-conservative.

Hogan, E. R., 2008: *Of the Human Heart: A Biography of Benjamin Peirce*. Lehigh University Press, 429 pp.

Hooper, W., 1867a: William Hooper to Cleveland Abbe. January 26, 1867. *Cleveland Abbe Papers, General Correspondence, 1850–1916*. Manuscript Division, Library of Congress, Box 3.

——, 1867b: William Hooper to Cleveland Abbe. June 16, 1867. *Cleveland Abbe Papers, General Correspondence, 1850–1916*. Manuscript Division, Library of Congress, Box 3.

——, 1867c: William Hooper to Cleveland Abbe. July 17, 1867. *Cleveland Abbe Papers, General Correspondence, 1850–1916*. Manuscript Division, Library of Congress, Box 3.

——, 1867d: William Hooper to Cleveland Abbe. September 20, 1867. *Cleveland Abbe Papers, General Correspondence, 1850–1916*. Manuscript Division, Library of Congress, Box 3.

——, 1868a: William Hooper to Cleveland Abbe. January 6, 1868. *Cleveland Abbe Papers, General Correspondence, 1850–1916*. Manuscript Division, Library of Congress, Box 3.

——, 1868b: William Hooper to Cleveland Abbe. January 24, 1868. *Cleveland Abbe Papers, General Correspondence, 1850–1916*. Manuscript Division, Library of Congress, Box 3.

——, 1868c: William Hooper to Cleveland Abbe. February 19, 1868. *Cleveland Abbe Papers, General Correspondence, 1850–1916*. Manuscript Division, Library of Congress, Box 3.

——, 1868d: William Hooper to Cleveland Abbe. March 13, 1868. *Cleveland Abbe Papers, General Correspondence, 1850–1916*. Manuscript Division, Library of Congress, Box 3.

Hoover, M. A., 1873: Lease of Mary A. Hoover to Cleveland Abbe for No. 1825 I St. NW. Oct. 15, 1873. *Cleveland Abbe Papers, Subject File, 1855–1884, Financial Papers*. Manuscript Division, Library of Congress, Box 17.

Hough, E., 1909: Does the Weather Bureau Make Good? A Study of the Day-to-day Performance of Our Million-and a-half Dollar Weather Bureau. *Everybody's Magazine*, **20**, 609–621.

House of Representatives, 1869: Disasters on the Lakes [To accompany House bill No. 602], Papers Relative to Losses of vessels on the lakes. Mis. Doc. No. 10., 41st Congress, 2nd Session.

Howell, R., 2007: William H. Greene Was The First Black CUNY Graduate And First Black Member Of U.S. Signal Corps, A Victor And A Victim. City College of New York. Accessed 5 April 2019, http://www1.cuny.edu/mu/forum/2007/04/16/william-h-greene-was-the-first-black-cuny-graduate-and-first-black-member-of-u-s-signal-corps-a-victor-and-a-victim/.

Howgate, H. W., 1872: Henry W. Howgate to Increase A. Lapham. May 11, 1872. *Increase A. Lapham Papers, Correspondence, 1872*. Wisconsin Historical Society, Box 11, Folder 4.

Humphreys, W. J., 1919: Biographical Memoir of Cleveland Abbe. Vol. VIII, *Biographical Memoirs*. National Academy of Sciences, 469–508.

Hussey, W. J., 1912: A General Account of the Observatory. *Publications of the Astronomical Observatory of the University of Michigan, Volume 1*. University of Michigan, 3–36.

Indianapolis Journal, 1890: The Weather Bureau and Signal Corps. *The Indianapolis Journal*, October 7, 1890, 2.

——, 1902: A Freak of Fate. *The Indianapolis Journal*, February 14, 1902, 3.

International Meridian Conference, 1884: *International Conference Held at Washington for the Purpose of Fixing a Prime Meridian and a Universal Day*. Gibson Bros., 212 pp.

Ithaca Daily Journal, 1903: Short Stories Purely Personal. *The Ithaca Daily Journal*, August 5, 1903, 6.

Jackson, K. T., Ed., 2010: *The Encyclopedia of New York City: Second Edition*. Yale University Press, 1582 pp.

Jacobson, T. C., 2009: *Charity & Merit: Trinity School at 300*. University Press of New England, 432 pp.

James, M. A., 1987: *Elites in Conflict: The Antebellum Clash Over the Dudley Observatory*. Rutgers University Press, 301 pp.

Jensen, B., 2015: The Assassin's Assassin. *Washingtonian*, **50** (7), 62–123.

Kellogg, J. H., 1881: *Plain Facts for Old and Young*. Segner and Condit, 512 pp.

Kelvin, 1896: Lord Kelvin to Cleveland Abbe. December 1, 1896. *Cleveland Abbe Papers, General Correspondence, 1850–1916*. Manuscript Division, Library of Congress, Box 9.

Kenaston, C. A., 1863: Professors, Instructors and Superintendents. Second Annual Report of the Secretary of the State Board of Agriculture of the State of Michigan, for the Year 1863, 71 pp.

Klotz, O., 1916: Otto Klotz to Charles F. Marvin. November 8, 1916. *Cleveland Abbe Papers, Subject File, 1855–1884, Biographical Material*. Manuscript Division, Library of Congress, Box 15.

Koelsch, W. A., 1981: Pioneer: The First American Doctorate in Meteorology. *Bull. Amer. Meteor. Soc.*, **62**, 362–367.

Kovel, R. and T. Kovel, 2000: Lamps Burned Lard in Mid-1800s. *Los Angeles Times*, 17 June 2000. Accessed 19 November 2017, http://articles.latimes.com/2000/jun/17/home/hm-42012.

Lapham, I. A., 1869a: Increase A. Lapham to Cleveland Abbe. September 1, 1869. *Cleveland Abbe Papers, General Correspondence, 1850–1916*. Manuscript Division, Library of Congress, Box 5.

——, 1869b: Increase A. Lapham to Cleveland Abbe. September 7, 1869. *Cleveland Abbe Papers, General Correspondence, 1850–1916*. Manuscript Division, Library of Congress, Box 5.

——, 1869c: Increase A. Lapham to Cleveland Abbe. October 2, 1869. *Cleveland Abbe Papers, General Correspondence, 1850–1916*. Manuscript Division, Library of Congress, Box 5.

——, 1869d: Increase A. Lapham to Cleveland Abbe. October 19, 1869. *Cleveland Abbe Papers, General Correspondence, 1850–1916*. Manuscript Division, Library of Congress, Box 5.

——, 1869e: Increase A. Lapham to Cleveland Abbe. December 1, 1869. *Cleveland Abbe Papers, General Correspondence, 1850–1916*. Manuscript Division, Library of Congress, Box 5.

——, 1869f: Increase A. Lapham to Halbert E. Paine. December 8, 1869. *Increase A. Lapham Papers, Typewritten Letters 1866–1870*. Wisconsin Historical Society, Box 4, Folder 3.

——, 1870a: Increase A. Lapham to Cleveland Abbe. January 12, 1870. *Cleveland Abbe Papers, General Correspondence, 1850–1916*. Manuscript Division, Library of Congress, Box 5.

——, 1870b: Letter from Increase A. Lapham accepting the temporary position in the Signal Office. November 8, 1870. *Increase A. Lapham Papers, Correspondence, Sept.–Dec. 1870*. Wisconsin Historical Society, Box 11, Folder 1.

——, 1870c: Weather Bulletin issued by Increase A. Lapham. November 8, 1870. *Increase A. Lapham Papers, Weather Bureau Reports and Labels, 1870–1871*. Wisconsin Historical Society, Box 19, Folder 1.

——, 1870d: Increase A. Lapham to Julia Lapham. November 27, 1870. *Increase A. Lapham Papers, Correspondence, Sept.–Dec. 1870*. Wisconsin Historical Society, Box 11, Folder 1.

——, 1870e: Increase A. Lapham to Albert J. Myer. December 28, 1870. *Increase A. Lapham Papers, Correspondence, Sept.–Dec. 1870*. Wisconsin Historical Society, Box 11, Folder 1.

——, 1871a: Increase A. Lapham to Julia Lapham. February 3, 1871. *Increase A. Lapham Papers, Correspondence, Jan.–July. 1871*. Wisconsin Historical Society, Box 11, Folder 2.

——, 1871b: Letter written by Dr. I. A. Lapham, in response to one from Prof. Cleveland Abbe, who was preparing a magazine article. March 1871. *Increase A. Lapham Papers, Meteorology—Weather Bureau*. Wisconsin Historical Society, Box 18, Folder 7.

Le Verrier, U. J. J., 1869: Nota—Cincinnati (Amérique). *Bull. Hebd. Assoc. Sci. de France*, **6**, 100.

Leslie, F., Ed., 1878: The United States Signal Service. *Frank Leslie's Popular Monthly*, 6, 337–345.

Lewis, D. L., 2000: *W. E. B. Du Bois, 1919–1963: The Fight for Equality and the American Century*. Henry Holt and Company, 715 pp.

Lincoln, A. B., Ed., 1920: *A Modern History of Windham County, Connecticut*, Volume 1. S. J. Clarke Publishing Company, 920 pp.

Linehand, J., Ed., 1990: *The Town of Chevy Chase: Past and Present*. The Town of Chevy Chase, Montgomery County, Maryland, 77 pp.

List, L. L., and M. S. Dix, Eds., 1989: *The Papers of Jefferson Davis*, Volume 6: 1856–1860. Louisiana State University Press, 840 pp.

Lofthouse, J. B., 1871: James B. Lofthouse to Cleveland Abbe. February 20, 1871. *Cleveland Abbe Papers, General Correspondence, 1850–1916*. Manuscript Division, Library of Congress, Box 6.

Loomis, E., 1866: Elias Loomis to Cleveland Abbe. December 13, 1866. *Cleveland Abbe Papers, General Correspondence, 1850–1916*. Manuscript Division, Library of Congress, Box 3.

——, 1870: Elias Loomis to Halbert E. Paine. January 10, 1870 (as part of House Ex. Doc. No. 10, pt. 2, 41st Congress, 2nd Session). *Increase A. Lapham Papers, Meteorology—Weather Bureau*. Wisconsin Historical Society, Box 18, Folder 7.

Loomis, E. J., 1896: *An Eclipse Party in Africa: Chasing Summer Across the Equator in the U.S.S. Pensacola*. Roberts Brothers, 218 pp.

Ludlum, D. M., 1969: The Espy-Redfield Dispute. *Weatherwise*, **22**, 224–261.

Madison Daily Leader, 1891: Politics Not Right. *The Madison Daily Leader* (Madison, S.D.), July 3, 1891, 1.

Majkik, Z. P., C. A. Platt, and M. Meister, 2011: Calculating the Weather: Deductive Reasoning and Disciplinary *Telos* in Cleveland Abbe's Rhetorical Transformation of Meteorology. *Quart. J. Speech*, **97**, 74–99.

Mallery, G., 1870: Garrick Mallery to Increase A. Lapham December 20, 1870. *Increase A. Lapham Papers, Correspondence, Sept.–Dec. 1870*. Wisconsin Historical Society, Box 11, Folder 1.

MARD, 2015: Cleveland Abbe. MARAD Vessel History Database. Maritime Administration. Accessed 22 June 2019, https://vesselhistory.marad.dot.gov/ShipHistory/Detail/1009.

Marvin, C. F., 1916a: Charles F. Marvin to Cleveland Abbe. February 8, 1916. *Cleveland Abbe Papers, Series 14, Assorted Papers, 1912–1916*. Cincinnati Observatory, Box 11, Folder 73.

——, 1916b: Charles F. Marvin to Margaret Abbe. November 3, 1916. *Cleveland Abbe Papers, General Correspondence, 1850–1916*. Manuscript Division, Library of Congress, Box 9.

——, 1917: Cleveland Abbe, 1838–1916. *Proc. Am. Philos. Soc.*, **56**, ix–xix.

Maxwell, J. C., 1859: *Saturn's Rings*. Macmillian and Co., 71 pp.

McAdie, A. G., 1891: Alexander McAdie to Cleveland Abbe. June 1, 1892. *Cleveland Abbe Papers, General Correspondence, 1850–1916*. Manuscript Division, Library of Congress, Box 8.

——, 1908: Alexander McAdie to Cleveland Abbe. December 5, 1908. *Cleveland Abbe Papers, General Correspondence, 1850–1916*. Manuscript Division, Library of Congress, Box 9.

McKeen, J., 1849: Annual Report of the County Superintendent of Common Schools, for the City and County of New-York. *Annual Report of the Superintendent of Common School of the State of New York*, 159 pp.

Mendenhall, T. C., 1890: Thomas C. Mendenhall to Cleveland Abbe. May 8, 1890. *Cleveland Abbe Papers, Series 10, Pensacola Expedition, 1889–1890*. Cincinnati Observatory, Box 10, Folder 7.

Meteorological Committee, 1874: *Report of the Proceedings of the Meteorological Congress at Vienna*. E. Stanford, 97 pp.

Miller, E. R., 1930: Tradition Versus History in American Meteorology. *Mon. Wea. Rev.*, **58**, 65–66.

——, 1931a: The Evolution of Meteorological Institutions in the United States. *Mon. Wea. Rev.*, **59**, 1–6.

——, 1931b: New Light on the Beginnings of the Weather Bureau from the Papers of Increase A. Lapham. *Mon. Wea. Rev.*, **59**, 65–70.

——, 1933: American Pioneers in Meteorology. *Mon. Wea. Rev.*, **61**, 189–193.

Millikan, F. R., 2007: Joseph Henry: Father of the Weather Service. Smithsonian Institution. Accessed 15 June 2018, http://siarchives.si.edu/oldsite/siarchives-old/history/jhp/joseph03.htm.

Monmonier, M., 1999: *Air Apparent: How Meteorologists Learned to Map, Predict, and Dramatize Weather*. University of Chicago Press, 309 pp.

Moore, W. L., 1897: *Report of the Chief of the Weather Bureau, 1896–97*. Government Printing Office, 431 pp.

Morning Journal and Courier, 1887: General Hazen Dead. *New Haven Morning Daily Journal and Courier*, January 17, 1887, 3.

Morris, M. B., 1918: An Old Washington Mansion (2017 I Street Northwest). *Rec. Columbia Hist. Soc.*, **21**, 114–128.

Morrow, J. B., 1916: Prof. Abbe Tells of his First "Weather Forecast." *The Sunday Star* (Washington, D.C.), June 4, 1916, Part 4, 8.

Morton, J. S., 1893a: J. Sterling Morton to Cleveland Abbe. June 16, 1893. *Cleveland Abbe Papers, General Correspondence, 1850–1916*. Manuscript Division, Library of Congress, Box 8.

——, 1893b: J. Sterling Morton to Cleveland Abbe. June 20, 1893. *Cleveland Abbe Papers, General Correspondence, 1850–1916*. Manuscript Division, Library of Congress, Box 8.

——, 1894: *Report of the Secretary of Agriculture*. Government Printing Office, 608 pp.

Mott, L. F., Ed., 1916: Cleveland Abbe. *City Coll. Quart.*, **12**, 165–178.

Murray, J., 1865: *A Handbook for Travellers in Russia, Poland, and Finland*. New Ed., Rev. John Murray, Albemarle Street, London, 282 pp.

Myer, A. J., 1870a: Albert J. Myer to Cleveland Abbe. March 24, 1870. *Cleveland Abbe Papers, General Correspondence, 1850–1916*. Manuscript Division, Library of Congress, Box 5.

——, 1870b: Albert J. Myer to Cleveland Abbe. March 25, 1870. *Cleveland Abbe Papers, General Correspondence, 1850–1916*. Manuscript Division, Library of Congress, Box 5.

——, 1870c: Albert J. Myer to William W. Belknap. February 17, 1870 (as part of House Ex. Doc. No. 162, 41st Congress, 2nd Session). *Executive Documents Printed by Order of the House of Representatives During the Second Session of the Forty-First Congress, 1869–70*. Vol. 7. Government Printing Office, 993 pp.

——, 1870d: *Annual Report of the Chief Signal Officer Made to the Secretary of War for the Year 1870*. Government Printing Office, 41 pp.

——, 1870e: Albert J. Myer to Cleveland Abbe. September 20, 1870. *Cleveland Abbe Papers, General Correspondence, 1850–1916*. Manuscript Division, Library of Congress, Box 6.

——, 1870f: Albert J. Myer to Cleveland Abbe. October 27, 1870. *Cleveland Abbe Papers, General Correspondence, 1850–1916*. Manuscript Division, Library of Congress, Box 6.

——, 1870g: Albert J. Myer to Cleveland Abbe. December 10, 1870. *Cleveland Abbe Papers, General Correspondence, 1850–1916*. Manuscript Division, Library of Congress, Box 6.

——, 1870h: Albert J. Myer to Cleveland Abbe. December 27, 1870. *Cleveland Abbe Papers, General Correspondence, 1850–1916*. Manuscript Division, Library of Congress, Box 6.

——, 1871: *Annual Report of the Chief Signal Officer to the Secretary of War for the Fiscal Year Ended June 30, 1871*. Government Printing Office, 172 pp.

——, 1872: *Annual Report of the Chief Signal Officer to the Secretary of War for the Year 1872*. Government Printing Office, 292 pp.

——, 1873: *Annual Report of the Chief Signal Officer to the Secretary of War for the Year 1873*. Government Printing Office, 1109 pp.

——, 1874: *Annual Report of the Chief Signal Officer to the Secretary of War for the Year 1874*. Government Printing Office, 403 pp.

Nalty, B. C., and M. J. MacGregor, 1981: *Blacks in the Military: Essential Documents. Scholarly Resources*, 367 pp.

Nation, 1871: Magazines for December. *The Nation*, **13**, 359.

National Association for the Relief of Destitute Colored Women and Children, 1895: *Thirty-Second Annual Report of the National Association for the Relief of Destitute Colored Women and Children for the Year Ending January 1, 1895*. Judd & Detweiler, 20pp.

National Board of Trade, 1869: *Proceedings of the Second Annual Meeting of the National Board of Trade, Held in Richmond, December 1869*. Baker, Cotter & Co., 362 pp.

National Geographic, 1888: Members of the Society. *The National Geographic Magazine*, **1**, 94–98.

National Park Service, 1963: Timothy Caldwell House. Data Pages from Historic American Buildings Survey. Accessed 6 March 2019, https://cdn.loc.gov/master/pnp/habshaer/dc/dc0000/dc0014/data/dc0014data.pdf.

——, 1975: National Register of Historic Places Inventory—Nomination Form: Timothy Caldwell House-Monroe-Adams-Abbe House. Accessed 6 March 2919, https://npgallery.nps.gov/NRHP/GetAsset/NHLS/69000289_text.

——, 1997: National Historic Landmark Nomination: Cincinnati Observatory. Accessed 4 November 2018, https://npgallery.nps.gov/NRHP/GetAsset/57209ca2-0c5c-4059-9681-1cad140ff5c9.

——, 2015: The Brownstone Townhouse of Theodore Roosevelt. Accessed 7 November 2017, https://www.nps.gov/thrb/learn/historyculture/brownstone.htm.

——, 2018: Mount Abbe. Glacier Bay National Park. Accessed 22 July 2019, https://www.nps.gov/glba/learn/historyculture/abbe.htm.

National Republican, 1875: The Spellers. *The National Republican*, March 31, 1875, 4.

——, 1882: Where's Howgate?. *The National Republican*, April 14, 1882, 1.

Nebeker, F., 1995: *Calculating the Weather: Meteorology in the 20th Century*. Academic Press, 255 pp.

New Orleans Republican, 1872: A Sad Catastrophe. *New Orleans Republican*, March 31, 1872, 4.

New York Daily Tribune, 1844: The Magnetic Telegraph—Its Success. *New York Daily Tribune*, May 27, 1844, 1.

——, 1879: Obituary. George Waldo Abbe. *New York Daily Tribune*, September 26, 1879, 2.

New York Herald, 1869: The Great Storm. *The New York Herald*, November 20, 1869, 8.

——, 1871: The New Cautionary Signals. *The New York Herald*, October 21, 1871, 4.

——, 1879: Funeral of George Waldo Abbe. *The New York Herald*, September 29, 1879, 11.

New York Times, 1860: Breach of Promise Case. *The New York Times*, October 20, 1860, 2.

——, 1864: General City News. *The New York Times*, December 8, 1864, 8.

——, 1869: The Storm on the Lakes. *The New York Times*, November 22, 1869, 1.

——, 1871a: Official Weather Predictions. *The New York Times*, February 13, 1871, 1.

——, 1871b: The Weather Predictions. *The New York Times*, February 14, 1871, 5.

——, 1871c: Synopsis of Weather Report for the Last Twenty-four Hours. *The New York Times*, February 20, 1871, 1.

——, 1871d: Meteorological Record. *The New York Times*, February 26, 1871, 1.

——, 1871e: The Weather Prophet. *The New York Times*, August 29, 1871, 1.
——, 1871f: December Magazines. *The New York Times*, November 25, 1871, 2.
——, 1878: A Russian Princess' Tale. *The New York Times*, February 26, 1878, 3.
——, 1893: Weather Bureau Reforms. *The New York Times*, July 13, 1893, 10.
——, 1894: H. H. Howgate Found at Last. *The New York Times*, September 28, 1894, 2.
——, 1895: A Presidential Removal. *The New York Times*, July 3, 1895, 5.
——, 1909: Prof. Moore Exonerated. *The New York Times*, March 3, 1909, 13.
——, 1927: Prof. Willis L. Moore. *The New York Times*, December 13, 1927, 23.
——, 1934: Cleveland Abbe Jr. Dies in Ithaca at 62. *The New York Times*, April 30, 1934, 21.
Newcomb, S., 1866a: Simon Newcomb to Cleveland Abbe. December 19, 1866. *Cleveland Abbe Papers, General Correspondence, 1850–1916*. Manuscript Division, Library of Congress, Box 3.
——, 1866b: Simon Newcomb to Cleveland Abbe. December 22, 1866. *Cleveland Abbe Papers, General Correspondence, 1850–1916*. Manuscript Division, Library of Congress, Box 3.
——, 1867a: Simon Newcomb to Cleveland Abbe. January 23, 1867. *Cleveland Abbe Papers, General Correspondence, 1850–1916*. Manuscript Division, Library of Congress, Box 3.
——, 1867b: Simon Newcomb to Cleveland Abbe. March 16, 1867. *Cleveland Abbe Papers, General Correspondence, 1850–1916*. Manuscript Division, Library of Congress, Box 3.
——, 1867c: Simon Newcomb to Cleveland Abbe. April 9, 1867. *Cleveland Abbe Papers, General Correspondence, 1850–1916*. Manuscript Division, Library of Congress, Box 3.
——, 1874: Some Talks of an Astronomer. *Harper's New Monthly Magazine*, **49**, 693–707.
——, 1903: The Outlook for the Flying Machine. *The Independent*, **55**, 2508–2512.
Norberg, A. L., 1978: Simon Newcomb's Early Astronomical Career. *Isis*, **69**, 209–225.
Norton, L. B., 1871: Signal Service General Orders No. 2. Issued by Bvt. Major Lemuel B. Norton. January 12, 1871. *Cleveland Abbe Papers, General Correspondence, 1850–1916*. Manuscript Division, Library of Congress, Box 6.
Nye, E. W., 2019: Pounds Sterling to Dollars: Historical Conversion of Currency. Accessed 28 June 2019, https://www.uwyo.edu/numimage/currency.htm.
Oliver, C. P., 1917: Obituary of Cleveland Abbe. Report of the Council to the Ninety-Seventh Annual General Meeting. *Mon. Not. R. Astron. Soc.*, **77**, 290–292.
Pacific Commercial Advertiser, 1886: More Official Scandals. *The Pacific Commercial Advertiser*, February 13, 1886, 2.
Paine, H. E., 1888: Letter of Halbert E. Paine to Senator Henry L. Dawes, September 18, 1888. Senate, Tuesday, September 18, 1888. *Congressional Record*, **19**, 8675.
The Parish of Calvary-St. George's, 2017: Parish History. Accessed 25 November 2017, https://www.calvarystgeorges.org/new-page/.

Peirce, B., 1867: Benjamin Peirce to Cleveland Abbe. March 20, 1867. *Cleveland Abbe Papers, General Correspondence, 1850–1916*. Manuscript Division, Library of Congress, Box 3.
Pensacola Journal, 1909: The Weather Service is of Great Value to the Entire Country. *The Pensacola Journal*, May 9, 1909, 1.
Philosophical Society of Washington, 1880: Minutes of the 114th Meeting, December 2, 1876. *Bull. Philos. Soc. Wash.*, **2**, 90–94.
Porter, J. G., 1893: *Historical Sketch of the Observatory of the University of Cincinnati*. Board of Directors of the University of Cincinnati, 15 pp.
Potter, S., 2003: The Wright Weather. *Weatherwise*, **56** (6), 16–23
——, 2013: Retrospect: December 17, 1903: Wright Brothers' First Flight. *Weatherwise*, **66** (6), 10–11.
——, 2019: Retrospect: March 4, 1909: Inauguration of William Howard Taft. *Weatherwise*, **72** (2), 10–11.
Portland Daily Press, 1887: Death of Gen. Hazen. *Portland Daily Press* (Portland, Maine), January 17, 1887, 1.
——, 1888: "It is said that General Greely fairly begged . . ." *Portland Daily Press* (Portland, Maine), July 13, 1888, 1.
Raines, R. R., 1996: *Getting the message through: A Branch History of the U.S. Army Signal Corps*. Government Printing Office, 464 pp.
Radzinsky, E., 2006: *Alexander II: The Last Great Tsar*. Translated by A. Bouis. Simon and Schuster, 480 pp.
Redfield, W. C., 1831: Remarks on the Prevailing Storms of the Atlantic Coast of the North American States. *Am. J. Sci. Arts*, **20**, 17–51.
——, 1838: *Meteorological Journal*. Meteorological Manuscripts Collection (MS 349), Manuscripts and Archives, Yale University Library, Box 3, Folder 16.
Reingold, N., 1963: A Good Place to Study Astronomy. *Q. J. Curr. Acquis.*, **20**, 211–217.
——, 1964: Cleveland Abbe at Pulkowa: Theory and practice in the nineteenth century physical sciences. *Arch. Int. Hist. Sci.*, **17**, 133–147.
Roberts, B., 1864: *A Manual of Instructions for Enlisting and Discharging Soldiers*. J. B. Lippincott & Co. 276 pp.
Rodman, S., 1838: *Meteorological Observations of Samuel Rodman (1834–1853)*. Historic Climate Diaries and Journals, Environmental Document Access and Display System, Version 2 (EV2), NOAA National Centers for Environmental Information.
Roff, S. S., A. M. Cucchiara, and B. J. Dunlap, 2000: *From the Free Academy to CUNY: Illustrating Public Higher Education in New York City, 1847–1997*. Fordham University Press, 146 pp.
Roosevelt, T., 1893: Theodore Roosevelt to Cleveland Abbe. July 16, 1893. *Cleveland Abbe Papers, General Correspondence, 1850–1916*. Manuscript Division, Library of Congress, Box 9.
Rufus, W. C.: 1951: The Department of Astronomy. *The University of Michigan: An Encyclopedic Survey*, W. B. Shaw, Ed., Univ. of Mich. Press, 442–465.

Russell, O. F., 1869: O. F. Russell to Cleveland Abbe. September 3, 1869. *Cleveland Abbe Papers, General Correspondence, 1850–1916*. Manuscript Division, Library of Congress, Box 5.

Savannah Morning News, 1884: A Negro as An Observer. *The Savannah Morning News*, September 30, 1884, 1.

Schley, W. S., and J. R. Soley, 1885: *The Rescue of Greely*. Charles Scribner's Sons, 277 pp.

Science, 1918: The Weather Bureau and Dr. Cleveland Abbe. *Science*, **48**, 64–65.

Shillito, J., L. B. Harrison, J. Dexter, W. Hooper, E. Sargent, R. R. Springer, P. Neff, L. Fletcher, R. Mitchell, Hoover, Pumphrey & Co., R. King, S. Davis Jr., H. Probasco, G. K. Shoenberger, J. Kilgour, L. E. Mills, T. D. Lincoln, A. Taft, 1868: Pledge to support Cleveland Abbe for three years. *Cincinnati Observatory Records, 1842–1970*. University of Cincinnati, Archives and Rare Books Library, Box 1, Folder 4.

Seattle Post-Intelligencer, 1895: Harrington is Head. *The Seattle Post-Intelligencer*, August 27, 1895, 3.

Selfridge, T. O., 1870a: Thomas. O. Selfridge to Cleveland Abbe. October 10, 1870. *Cleveland Abbe Papers, General Correspondence, 1850–1916*. Manuscript Division, Library of Congress, Box 6.

——, 1870b: Thomas. O. Selfridge to Cleveland Abbe. October 17, 1870. *Cleveland Abbe Papers, General Correspondence, 1850–1916*. Manuscript Division, Library of Congress, Box 6.

Seller, M. S., 1982: Historical Perspectives on American Immigration Policy: Case Studies and Current Implications. *Law and Contemporary Problems*, **45**, 137–162.

Shaw, N., 1916: Prof. Cleveland Abbe. *Nature*, **98**, 332.

Sherwood, I. R., 1870: *Annual Report of the Secretary of State to the Governor of the State of Ohio for the Year 1869*. Columbus Printing Company, 320 pp.

Shipherd, J. R., 1865: *The American Freedmen's Aid Commission*. [Handbill]. The American Freedmen's Aid Commission, 4 pp.

Silliman, B., 1871: Benjamin Silliman to Cleveland Abbe. June 9, 1871. *Cleveland Abbe Papers, General Correspondence, 1850–1916*. Manuscript Division, Library of Congress, Box 6.

Sketch of Cleveland Abbe. 1888. *Pop. Sci. Mon.*, **32**, 400–408.

Smithsonian Institution, 1872a: Annual Report of the Board of Regents of the Smithsonian Institution, Showing the Operations, Expenditures, and Condition of the Instruction for the Year 1867, 506 pp.

——, 1872b: Annual Report of the Board of Regents of the Smithsonian Institution, Showing the Operations, Expenditures, and Condition of the Instruction for the Year 1868, 473 pp.

Soodalter, R., 2014: The Plot to Burn New York City. The Opinion Pages. *The New York Times*. Accessed 28 June 2019, https://opinionator.blogs.nytimes.com/2014/11/05/the-plot-to-burn-new-york-city/.

St. Martin, T., 2005: Life of William Cheney. *History of Weather Observations,*

Minneapolis/St. Paul, Minnesota, 1854–1955, G. K. Grice, P. Boulay, Eds., Midwestern Regional Climate Center. Accessed 11 December 2018, https://mrcc.illinois.edu/FORTS/histories/MN_Minneapolis_Grice_Boulay.pdf.

St. Paul Daily Globe, 1884: Ambitious Greene. *St. Paul Daily Globe*, September 29, 1884, 1.

——, 1890a: Passed In Review. *St. Paul Daily Globe*, January 13, 1890, 2.

——, 1890b: Personal Points. *St. Paul Daily Globe*, March 14, 1890, 4.

Stark, R. B., 1955: Robert Abbe: Pioneer in Plastic Surgery. *Bull. N. Y. Acad. Med.*, **31**, 927–950.

State Hermitage Museum, 2018: The Acquisition of Leonardo da Vinci's "Madonna and Child" ("The Litta Madonna"). Accessed 16 August 2018, https://www.hermitagemuseum.org/wps/portal/hermitage/explore/history/historical-article/1850/Madonna+Litta/?lng=en.

State of Michigan, 1860: Report of the Board of Regents of the University of Michigan. Twenty-Third Annual Report of the Superintendent of Public Instruction of the State of Michigan, with Accompanying Documents, for the Year 1859, 412 pp.

Steinem, G., 1998: Margaret Sanger. *TIME*, 151, 93–94.

Stillson, J. O., 1898: Correspondence. *Am. J. of Ophthalmol.*, **XV**, 5, 153.

Stone, I. W., 1893: Israel W. Stone to Cleveland Abbe. July 5, 1893. *Cleveland Abbe Papers, General Correspondence, 1850–1916*. Manuscript Division, Library of Congress, Box 9.

Struve, N., 1865: Nikolai Struve to Cleveland Abbe. October 24, 1865. *Cleveland Abbe Papers, General Correspondence, 1850–1916*. Manuscript Division, Library of Congress, Box 2.

Struve, O., 1942: The Poulkovo Observatory (1839–1941). *Sky Telesc.*, **1**, 4, 3–4, 19.

Struve, O. W., 1864: Otto Struve to Cleveland Abbe. June 25, 1864. *Cleveland Abbe Papers, General Correspondence, 1850–1916*. Manuscript Division, Library of Congress, Box 2.

——, 1866: Otto Struve to Cleveland Abbe. November 29, 1866. *Cleveland Abbe Papers, General Correspondence, 1850–1916*. Manuscript Division, Library of Congress, Box 3.

——, 1895: *Wilhelm Struve: Zur Erinnerung an den Vater den Geschwistern dargebracht von Otto Struve*. Druck der G. Braun'schen Hofbuchdruckerei, 79 pp.

Stuntebeck, F. H., 1869: Rev. F. H. Stuntebeck to Cleveland Abbe. September 1, 1869. *Cleveland Abbe Papers, General Correspondence, 1850–1916*. Manuscript Division, Library of Congress, Box 5.

The Sun, 1893: Jerry Rusk's Successor. *The Sun* (New York, N.Y.), March 26, 1893, 6.

——, 1909: Cleveland Abbe Married. *The Sun* (New York, N.Y.), April 13, 1909, 1.

Sunday Star, 1916: Beautiful New Home of the Arts Club of Washington. *The Sunday Star* (Washington, D.C.), October 8, 1916, Part 4, 1.

——, 1917: Gives Dr. Lapham Founder's Credit. *The Sunday Star* (Washington, D.C.), March 11, 1917, Part 2, 1.

——, 1923: Tablet Unveiled at Monroe House. *The Sunday Star* (Washington, D.C.), June 24, 1923, Part 1, 13.
——, 1929: Social Festivities in Chevy Chase Homes Varied and Charming. *The Sunday Star* (Washington, D.C.), September 29, 1929, Part 3, 7.
——, 1932: Philadelphia Woman Is Guest of Daughter in Chevy Chase Homes. *The Sunday Star* (Washington, D.C.), October 16, 1932, Part 3, 4.
Sunshine Courier, 1878: "Colorado is certainly a wonderland. . . ." *Sunshine Courier* (Boulder County, Colo.), June 29, 1878, 2.
Swanson, F., 2016: The Fault in His Stars. *Collections*, **3**, 8–11.
Talman, C. F., 1916: Prof. Cleveland Abbe. *Weather Bureau Topics and Personnel*, August 1916, 1–3.
Townsend, E. D., 1870: General Orders No. 29. Headquarters of the Army, Adjutant General's Office. March 15, 1870. *Increase A. Lapham Papers, Meteorology—Weather Bureau*. Wisconsin Historical Society, Box 18, Folder 7.
Twain, M., 1910: *Mark Twain's Speeches*. Harper & Brothers, 433 pp.
Tyson, J., 1904: *A Treatise on Bright's Disease and Diabetes, with Especial Reference to Pathology and Therapeutics*. P. Blakiston's Son & Co., 381 pp.
United States of America, 1870: *Acts and Resolutions of the United States of America Passed at the Second Session of the Forty-First Congress, December 6, 1869–July 15, 1870*. Government Printing Office, 480 pp.
Unknown, 1909: New Weather Man Takes Wife on Quiet. [Unknown Newspaper], April 13, 1909. *Cleveland Abbe Papers, Subject File, 1855–1884, Biographical Material*. Manuscript Division, Library of Congress, Box 15.
U.S. Army Surgeon/Sergeant Observer, 1838: *Diary of the Weather at Fort Columbus, New York, for the quarter ending the thirty-first day of December 1838*. Pre-Weather Bureau NARA Collection, Environmental Document Access and Display System, Version 2 (EV2), NOAA National Centers for Environmental Information.
U.S. Census Bureau, 2017: Census Instructions. Accessed 19 November 2017, https://www.census.gov/history/www/through_the_decades/census_instructions/.
U.S. Congress, 1870: Meteorological Observations. *Congressional Globe*. 41st Cong., 2nd Sess. 973.
——, 1871: Northern lakes and seaboard. *Statutes at Large*. 41st Cong., 2nd Sess. 90.
——, 1889a: Meteorological Observations. *Congressional Record*. 51st Cong., 1st Sess., 21, Part 1.
——, 1889b: Meteorological Observations. *Congressional Record*. 51st Cong., 1st Sess., 21, Part 2.
——, 1889c: Meteorological Observations. *Congressional Record*. 51st Cong., 1st Sess., 21, Part 4.
——, 1889d: Meteorological Observations. *Congressional Record*. 51st Cong., 1st Sess., 21, Part 10.
——, 1889e: Meteorological Observations. *Congressional Record*. 51st Cong., 1st Sess., 21, Part 11.

——, 1891: Northern lakes and seaboard. *Statutes at Large*. 51st Cong., 1st Sess. 653.

U.S. Department of Agriculture, 1915: Professor Abbe. *Weather Bureau Topics and Personnel*, August 1915, 2.

——, 1916: The Abbe Meteorological Observatory. *Weather Bureau Topics and Personnel*, November 1916, 5–6.

U.S. House, 1869a: H.R. 579, A Bill To authorize the Secretary of War to provide for taking meteorological observations at the military stations in the interior of the continent, and for giving notice on the northern lakes and Atlantic seaboard of the approach and force of storms. 41st Congress, 2nd Session. Accessed 13 January 2019, https://memory.loc.gov/cgi-bin/ampage?collId=llhb&fileName=041/llhb041.db&recNum=2204.

U.S. House, 1869b: H.R. 602, A Bill To authorize the Secretary of War to provide for taking meteorological observations at the military stations in the interior of the continent, and for giving notice on the northern lakes and Atlantic seaboard of the approach and force of storms. 41st Congress, 2nd Session. Accessed 13 January 2019, https://memory.loc.gov/cgi-bin/ampage?collId=llhb&fileName=041/llhb041.db&recNum=2246.

U.S. Navy, 1870: *Astronomical and Meteorological Observations Made at the United States Naval Observatory During the Year 1867*. Government Printing Office, 550 pp.

——, 1871: *Astronomical and Meteorological Observations Made at the United States Naval Observatory During the Year 1868*. Government Printing Office, 494 pp.

U.S. Senate, 1870a: *Journal of the Senate of the United States of America*. 41st Cong., 2nd Sess., 185.

——, 1870b: *Journal of the Senate of the United States of America*. 41st Cong., 2nd Sess., 203.

——, 2018: The Impeachment of Andrew Johnson (1868) President of the United States. Accessed 18 June 2019, https://www.senate.gov/artandhistory/history/common/briefing/Impeachment_Johnson.htm.

USNO, 2018: A Brief History of the Naval Observatory. Accessed 28 October 2018, https://www.usno.navy.mil/USNO/about-us/a-brief-history.

Van Horne, J., 1869: John Van Horne to Cleveland Abbe. September 6, 1869. *Cleveland Abbe Papers, General Correspondence, 1850–1916*. Manuscript Division, Library of Congress, Box 5.

Venable, W. H., 1894: Cincinnati, Past and Present. *History of Cincinnati and Hamilton County, Ohio: Their Past and Present*, S. B. Nelson & Co., 50–79.

Ward, R. D., 1896: Current Notes on Meteorology. *Science*, **4**, 937–939.

——, 1917: Cleveland Abbe (1838–1916). *Proc. Am. Acad. Arts Sci.*, **52**, 827–829.

Washington Post, 1886: Personal Intelligence. *The Washington Post*, January 20, 1886, 2.

——, 1888: Story of Murder Bay. *The Washington Post*, July 8, 1888, 9.

Washington Times, 1909: Aged Professor Weds Suddenly. *The Washington Times*, April 13, 1909, 1.

Weber, G. A., 1922: *The Weather Bureau: Its History, Activities and Organization*. D. Appleton and Company, 108 pp.

Weekly Gazette, 1878: The Coming Eclipse. *The Weekly Gazette* (Colorado Springs), July 16, 1878, 6.

Welch, W. H., 1916: William Henry Welch to Cleveland Abbe. April 16, 1916. *Cleveland Abbe Papers, General Correspondence, 1850–1916*. Manuscript Division, Library of Congress, Box 9.

Welles, G., 1868: Gideon Welles to Cleveland Abbe. *Cleveland Abbe Papers, General Correspondence, 1850–1916*. Manuscript Division, Library of Congress, Box 3.

Wells, S. R., 1874: Cleveland Abbe, the Meteorologist of the Signal Service Bureau—with Portrait. *The Phrenological Journal and Life Illustrated*, **58**, 213–215.

Wheeling Intelligencer, 1893: Conspirator Morton. *Wheeling Intelligencer*, July 17, 1893, 1.

White, R. D., 2003: *Roosevelt the Reformer: Theodore Roosevelt as Civil Service Commissioner, 1889–1895*. University of Alabama Press, 264 pp.

Whitesell, P. S., 2003: Detroit Observatory: nineteenth-century training ground for astronomers. *J. Astron. Hist. Heritage*, **6**, 69–106.

Whitnah, D. R., 1961: *A History of the United States Weather Bureau*. University of Illinois Press, 267 pp.

Williams, G. H., 2014: *The Liberty Ships of World war II: A Record of the 2,710 Vessels and Their Builders, Operators and Namesakes, with a History of the Jeremiah O'Brien*. McFarland & Company, Inc., 372 pp.

Willis, B., 1949: *Friendly China: Two Thousand Miles Afoot Among The Chinese*. Stanford University Press, 312 pp.

Willis, E. P., and W. H. Hooke, 2006: Cleveland Abbe and American Meteorology, 1870–1901. *Bull. Amer. Meteor. Soc.*, **87**, 315–326.

Wilmington Daily Commercial, 1872: Storms at Cape May. *Wilmington Daily Commercial*, November 1, 1872, 1.

Witkowski, J. A., and J. R. Ingils, Eds., 2008: *Davenport's Dream: 21st Century Reflections on Heredity and Eugenics*. Cold Spring Harbor Laboratory Press, 298 pp.

Wortman, R. S., 2000: *Scenarios of Power: Myth and Ceremony in Russian Monarchy, Volume Two: From Alexander II to the Abdication of Nicholas II*. Princeton University Press, 580 pp.

Wyeth, J. J., 1878: *Leaves from a diary written while serving in Co. E, 44 Mass., Dep't of No. Carolina, from September 1862 to June 1863*. L.F. Lawrence & Co., 114 pp.

Yale Law Center, 2008: First Inaugural Address of Abraham Lincoln. Accessed 26 January 2018, http://avalon.law.yale.edu/19th_century/lincoln1.asp.

Yacovone, D., 1990: Abolitionists and the Language of Fraternal Love. *Meanings for Manhood*, M. C. Carnes, C. Griffen, Eds., University of Chicago Press, 85–95.

——, 1998: Surpassing the Love of Women: Victorian Manhood and the Language of Fraternal Love. *A Shared Experience: Men, Women, and the History of Gender*, L. McCall, D. Yacovone, Eds., NYU Press, 195–221.

Young, E., 1869: Eliza Young to Cleveland Abbe. October 4, 1869. *Cleveland Abbe Papers, General Correspondence, 1850–1916*. Manuscript Division, Library of Congress, Box 5.

Young, L., 1869: Lawrence Young to Cleveland Abbe. July 26, 1869. *Cleveland Abbe Papers, General Correspondence, 1850–1916*. Manuscript Division, Library of Congress, Box 5.

Notes

Author's Note

1. Miller (1930)

Preface

1. Marvin (1917).
2. Henry (1930).
3. Klotz (1916).
4. T. Abbe (1955).
5. Fleming and Kaplan (1996).

Prologue

1. This phrase, from the book of Numbers in the Bible, was given to Morse by Miss Annie Ellsworth, daughter of U.S. Patent Commissioner Henry L. Ellsworth. Annie's mother, who knew that Morse was a deeply religious man, suggested the phrase.

2. New York Daily Tribune (1844).

Chapter One: Early Years (1838–1860)

1. The U.S. Army maintained a network of some 450 locations across the country where regular meteorological observations were taken beginning in the early 19th century (and in some cases even earlier). These data are being digitized as part of the "Forts" project funded through the NOAA Climate Data Base Modernization

(CDMP). The Forts data are available from the Midwest Regional Climate Center (MRCC) and the NOAA National Centers for Environmental Information (NCEI).

2. Bond (1838).

3. Rodman (1838).

4. Brown (1838).

5. U.S. Army Surgeon/Sergeant Observer (1838).

6. Redfield (1838). Redfield's journals, which span the years 1831–1861, represent what is perhaps the most complete and accurate record of weather conditions in New York City at the time, with observations made five times daily—at 6 a.m., 10 a.m., 2 p.m., 6 p.m., and 10 p.m. In addition to readings of his thermometer and barometer, Redfield kept records of the "attached temperature," taken from a thermometer attached to his barometer and used to correct the barometer's readings for temperature. He also noted the direction and strength of the wind, the direction from which clouds were moving, as well as present weather conditions and general remarks. The final year of the record was kept by his son, John Howard Redfield, and includes observations made in both New York and Philadelphia.

7. Abbe and Howson (1941) give the address of Cleveland's birth as number 8 Dutch Street, but most other sources put it at number 7 Dutch Street.

8. This and the following recollections are from an unpublished and undated autobiographical manuscript titled "What I remember about my friends and myself" (Abbe n.d.), which according to Reingold (1963) was composed in 1888 or 1889.

9. Jackson (2010).

10. An early version of badminton.

11. Abbe (n.d.).

12. R. Abbe (1924).

13. T. Abbe (1955).

14. Abbe and Nichols (1916).

15. Abbe and Nichols (1916). In another case, Samuel lent his name to a petition signed by several "respectable inhabitants" of Salem, testifying to the good character of their neighbor Rebecca Nurse, who was accused of witchcraft. Despite this, Nurse ultimately was found guilty and sentenced to death. A monument erected in 1892 includes the names of 40 neighbors who came to Nurse's defense, including Samuel Abbe(y). R. Abbe (1924) asserts, "It would be unlike any of the descendant Abbes to have anything to do with thoughtless shallow transient cults."

16. Abbe and Nichols (1916).

17. For more on Williams's involvement in the Amistad episode, see Hart (1986).

18. Abbe and Howson (1941).

19. Abbe and Nichols (1916).

20. "His parents had determined to shape him for the ministry, but with his independence of mind and a head full of stories of violent weather conditions, it is little wonder that he eventually found himself at the threshold of the unexplored field of weather study." (T. Abbe 1955)

21. Abbe (n.d.).

22. Abbe (n.d.).

23. Abbe (n.d.).

24. Abbe (n.d.).

25. The Roosevelt house, which was originally numbered 33 East 20th Street, was—like the Abbe house—renumbered by 1867, to number 28. For more information about the site of Theodore Roosevelt's birthplace, see National Park Service (2015).

26. R. Abbe (1924).

27. Caroli (2018).

28. R. Abbe (1924).

29. Originally Calvary Church, now Calvary-St. George's. According to The Parish of Calvary-St. George's (2017), other early parishioners included Chester A. Arthur, John Jacob Astor, Edith Wharton, J. P. Morgan, and Eleanor Roosevelt and other members of the Roosevelt family.

30. Stark (1955).

31. Stark (1955).

32. E. Abbe (1968).

33. According to E. Abbe (1968), this was Andrew Fink Jr., George's brother-in-law.

34. According to E. Abbe (1968), this was Eliza Taintor Abbe, sister of George, who married Henry Walcott.

35. Giles Taintor, George's cousin under whom he was employed after arriving in New York.

36. E. Abbe (1968).

37. E. Abbe (1968).

38. Abbe and Howson (1941).

39. McKeen (1849).

40. T. Abbe (1955).

41. Astore (2017).

42. T. Abbe (1955).

43. Dr. Henry Abbott, a British physician who became an avid collector of Egyptian antiquities after spending time in Cairo and who later displayed his collection at the Egyptian Museum, located at 659 Broadway. For more, see Baldock (2011).

44. Abbe (n.d.).

45. T. Abbe (1955).

46. Hart (1857).

47. While it's unknown exactly which copy of Smellie's *Philosophy of Natural History* Cleveland Abbe possessed, his son Truman (T. Abbe 1955) indicates his mother gave it to him "at the age of eight," and Abbe (n.d.) notes an inscription from his mother with the date "April 1, 1847"—both of which would be consistent with the 1846 edition.

48. Abbe (n.d.).

49. According to T. Abbe (1955), "That little volume of Smellie's *Philosophy of Natural History* he always held sacred, the greatest treasure in his vast library. After his death, it was placed in his hand and buried with him."

50. Abbe (n.d.).

51. Lincoln (1920).

52. Abbe (1915), writing to Allen B. Lincoln, who was gathering information for an "Old School Week" celebration in Willimantic, Connecticut, in June 1915.

53. T. Abbe (1955).

54. Abbe (n.d.).

55. Mott (1916).

56. Sketch of Cleveland Abbe (1888).

57. Roff et al. (2000).

58. Abbe (1865t).

59. German astronomer Ernst Friedrich Wilhelm Klinkerfues.

60. Abbe (n.d.).

61. T. Abbe (1955).

62. T. Abbe (1955). Apparently, Cleveland's father suggested teaching mathematics as a suitable alternative to stargazing.

63. As T. Abbe (1955) describes, "The watch was fashioned in the current style, open face, key winding, but as thin and as accurate as the best watches of today."

64. Sketch of Cleveland Abbe (1888).

65. Abbe (1916). In addition to the other pioneers in meteorology described in the text, "Merriam" refers to Ebenezer Meriam, the so-called "sage of Brooklyn Heights," an amateur weather forecaster whose predictions were published in the New York *City Commercial* beginning around 1850.

66. According to Fuller (1990), there was little compliance with Tildon's order initially, owing to the ongoing War of 1812. Following a reorganization of the Army's medical service in 1818, Tildon's successor, Dr. Joseph Lovell, issued a similar order and by 1825 there were "surgeons at eighteen forts taking weather observations," with the number increasing to ninety-seven reporting posts by 1853.

67. Millikan (2007).

68. Bôcher (1888). An interesting side note is that Bôcher's article, published in the *American Meteorological Journal* in 1888, was originally written as an essay for the Bowdoin Prize competition during his senior year at Harvard; it received second place.

69. For more on Espy, Redfield, and the "Storm Controversy," see Fleming (1990) and Ludlum (1969), among others.

70. Redfield (1831).

71. Espy (1841).

72. Ludlum (1969).

73. Abbe (n.d.).

74. Abbe (1916c).

75. Abbe (1903a).

76. Abbe (n.d.).

77. Brünnow (1856).

78. Abbe (1903a).

79. Hussey (1912).

80. Jacobson (2009).

81. Abbe and Nichols (1916).

82. E. Abbe (1968).

83. T. Abbe (1955).

84. E. Abbe (1968).

85. T. Abbe (1955).

86. The *Leatherstocking Tales* (Cleveland erroneously spelled it as two words) is a series of five novels by James Fenimore Cooper set in the frontier of New York State, the most famous of which, *The Last of the Mohicans*, was first published in 1826.

87. Abbe (n.d.).

88. State of Michigan (1860).

89. T. Abbe (1955).

90. Abbe (1945).

91. Kovel and Kovel (2000).

92. The Alumni Association of the University of Michigan Publishers (1915).

93. Beal (1915).

94. Smithsonian Institution (1872b).

95. Abbe (n.d.).

96. Abbe (n.d.).

97. U.S. Census Bureau (2017). "Between 1790 to 1870, the duty of collecting census data fell upon the U.S. Marshals. A March 3, 1879, act replaced the U.S. Marshals with specially hired and trained census-takers to conduct the 1880 and subsequent censuses."

98. Abbe (n.d.).

99. Rufus (1951).

100. Brünnow (1860).

101. Asaph Hall Sr., a student of Brünnow's who would go on to achieve worldwide fame as an astronomer, most notably for his discovery of the moons of Mars, Phobos and Deimos, in 1877.

102. Dr. C. H. F. Peters, director of the Hamilton College Observatory in Clinton, New York.

103. Whitesell (2003).

104. Abbe (n.d.).

105. Abbe (n.d.).

106. Free Academy of the City of New York (1861).

107. The Abbes' maid.

Chapter Two: Cambridge (1860–1864)

1. Abbe (n.d.).
2. Gould (1857).
3. Gould (1860a).
4. Gould (1860b).
5. Gould (1860c).
6. Abbe (n.d.).
7. James (1987).
8. James (1987).
9. Comstock (1922).
10. Comstock (1922).
11. List and Dix (1989).
12. Gould (1859).
13. Chiat (1956).
14. Bache (1852).
15. Abbe (1862).
16. See T. Abbe (1955), p. 57, which excerpts a letter Cleveland wrote to his mother in September 1865, while in Pulkovo.
17. Abbe (n.d.). A few pages later in the same manuscript, Cleveland refers to his "superior and friend, Dr. B. A. Gould," with the words "and friend" later crossed out by hand.
18. Abbe (n.d.).
19. Maxwell (1859).
20. Abbe (n.d.).
21. Abbe (n.d.).
22. Abbe (n.d.).
23. Reingold (1963).
24. Abbe (n.d.).
25. Bruce (1914).
26. Bickmore (1908).
27. G. W. Abbe (1860).
28. Yale Law Center (2008).
29. Bickmore (1908).
30. Abbe (n.d.).
31. Haines (1863).
32. Wyeth (1878).
33. T. Abbe (1955).
34. Wyeth (1878).
35. Recounted by T. Abbe (1955); Cleveland noted this in his diary.
36. Stillson (1898).
37. Roberts (1864).
38. Abbe (n.d.).

39. Abbe (n.d.).

40. C. C. Abbe (1862).

41. Bickmore (1863).

42. Yacovone (1998).

43. Yacovone (1998).

44. Yacovone (1990).

45. Balcerski (2019) argues that, in the case of Buchanan and William Rufus King, "the surviving evidence neither supports a definitive assessment of either man's sexuality, nor the occurrence of a sexual liaison between them." Rather, he argues "that their relationship conformed to an observable pattern of intimate male friendship prevalent in the first half of the nineteenth century. Gritz (2012) provides the examples of Garfield, who in 1858 (the year he married his wife, Lucretia, and some two decades before he became president) wrote to his college friend Harry Rhodes, saying, "I would that we might lie awake in each others arms for one long wakeful night," and Lincoln, who as a young man shared a bed with his close friend Joshua Speed for four years, the latter writing to Lincoln in 1842, "You know my desire to befriend you is everlasting—I will never cease, while I know how to do any thing." For more on James Garfield and Harry Rhodes, see Goodheard (2011); for more on Abraham Lincoln and Joshua Speed, see Goodwin (2006), among others.

46. T. Abbe (1955). Truman Abbe, in recounting several of his father's diary entries for 1864, notes: "The next day (July 14) we find: 'Agassiz expels Bickmore,' and again 'Sleep with Bick,' which shows the close friendship between the two men during those years in Cambridge."

47. Quoted in T. Abbe (1955). This was a letter written about six months after his arrival in Pulkovo, Russia.

48. T. Abbe (1955).

49. Abbe (1858–62).

50. Abbe (1863). Cleveland notes in a diary entry for November 12, 1863, that he "received letters, etc." from Thirza, most likely an indication of her returning the many letters he had sent her over the years, thus ending their relationship once and for all.

51. T. Abbe (1955).

52. Gallo (2004).

53. New York Times (1860).

54. C. C. Abbe (1863a). In a postscript to this letter, Cleveland's mother made an odd request of him: "As a favor I ask you to burn all my letters. I am ashamed of them."

55. C. C. Abbe (1863c).

56. Abbe (1866d).

57. C. C. Abbe (1863b).

58. H. Abbe (1863).

59. C. C. Abbe (1863c).

60. R. Abbe (1924).

61. Abbe (n.d.).

62. T. Abbe (1955).

63. T. Abbe (1955).

64. T. Abbe (1955) says the kiss was for Marcia, though the entry in Cleveland's pocket diary does not indicate who the recipient was.

65. Abbe (n.d.).

66. O. Struve (1942).

67. Abbe (n.d.).

68. O. W. Struve (1864).

69. Abbe (1864b).

70. The receipt for the overcoat is in Container 17 of the Cleveland Abbe Papers at the Library of Congress. Cleveland's account book for 1862–65, also in Container 17, also records this purchase.

71. Abbe (1864b).

72. New York Times (1864).

73. Abbe (1864a).

74. Abbe (n.d.).

75. As told in T. Abbe (1955).

76. Abbe (1864a).

77. Abbe (n.d.).

Chapter Three: Pulkovo (1864–1866)

1. Abbe (1865b).

2. Abbe (1865b).

3. Abbe (1864a).

4. T. Abbe (1955).

5. Abbe (1865b).

6. Abbe (1865b).

7. Abbe (1865b).

8. Abbe (1865b).

9. Abbe (1865b).

10. Abbe (1865b).

11. Abbe (n.d.).

12. Abbe (1865b). Although Cleveland used the incorrect definite article "Der" instead of "Die," this translates literally as "The machine is sick."

13. Abbe (1865b).

14. Murray (1865).

15. Abbe (n.d.).

16. Dostoevsky (2017).

17. See, for example, Wortman (2000), who quotes the diary of one of Alexander II's advisors, Prince D. A. Obolenskii, as saying of Alexander, "The most powerful of all sovereigns of Russia, the most beloved and popular of Tsars, no longer believes in his power or in the benefit of the reforms he has accomplished."

18. Radzinsky (2006).

19. Abbe (1866i). Cleveland wrote to his mother about the attempt on Tsar Alexander II's life, saying, "This monumental escape of the Czar must be considered as a high boon to the Empire for his of all often appears to be laboring for the best welfare of his people in opposition to old customs & the interests of noble families. He is far more loved than his predecessor and more worthy of such love."

20. Abbe (1865b).

21. Abbe (n.d.).

22. Abbe (n.d.).

23. Abbe (n.d.).

24. Abbe (1865r).

25. In his diary for Monday, January 2, 1865 (O.S. December 21, 1864), Cleveland writes: "Droshky ( ) for Pulkovo wrong road and long drive through village."

26. Abbe (n.d.).

27. Abbe (1865b).

28. Abbe (1865c).

29. Abbe (1865b).

30. Abbe (1865b).

31. Döllen (1865). Döllen's text was originally published in German; a translation is presented here.

32. Abbe (1865u).

33. Abbe (1865q).

34. Fraulein Hildebrand (sometimes spelled "Hildebrandt") was a governess for Mr. Hintze, the intendant and librarian of the Pulkovo observatory at the time. In a letter to Abbe, Nikolai Struve (1865) mentions that she hails from the city of Goldingen, located in present-day Latvia and known locally as Kuldīga.

35. Abbe (1865q).

36. Abbe (1865d).

37. According to T. Abbe (1955), the samovar presented to Cleveland as a Christmas present disappeared at some point after his return to America but was replaced in 1914 by Mrs. Döllen's daughter, Hannchen, with one used by Emilie Struve in St. Petersburg.

38. Abbe (1865d).

39. Abbe (1865d).

40. Abbe (1868b).

41. Abbe (1865n).

42. Historic currency conversions are complicated, especially given the fact that in 1865 Russia relied on both silver ruble coins and paper money, which was valued differently. Murray (1865) gives a conversion rate of fifty rubles equaling approximately £6. This coincides with Cleveland's letter to his father (Abbe 1865b) in which he suggests his father send him "four or five hundred roubles, say £60 yearly." Thus,

Cleveland's salary of twenty-five rubles a month would be the equivalent of about £3 in 1865. Nye (2019) presents a historical currency calculator that converts £3 in 1865 to $330.72 in 2019. Alioth Finance (2019) shows $21 in 1865 as being worth $329.93 in 2019.

43. Abbe (1865c).

44. Abbe (1865r).

45. Abbe (n.d.).

46. Abbe (1865c).

47. Abbe (1865c).

48. Abbe (1865f).

49. Abbe (1865d).

50. C. C. Abbe (1865d).

51. Abbe (1865l).

52. Abbe (1865l).

53. Abbe (1865h).

54. Abbe (1866i).

55. Abbe (1865j).

56. August Wagner, senior astronomer and vice-director at Pulkovo.

57. Abbe (1865j).

58. Abbe (1865e).

59. Abbe (1865e).

60. Abbe (1865q). Several months later, Cleveland writes his mother, saying that, ". . . more than this was my regret that in the Minister's ball at St. P. I was unable to accept my invitation to dance with the princess Suvaroff of which I have written you before." For more information about Princess Suvarov (Suvaroff), including an interesting firsthand account of an attempt to blackmail her while staying in New York, see New York Times (1878).

61. Abbe (1865e).

62. C. C. Abbe (1865c).

63. A nickname for the suit coat worn as part of a tuxedo, with long tails in the back.

64. W. Abbe (1865).

65. Abbe (1865d).

66. Abbe (1865e).

67. Abbe (1865e).

68. Abbe (1865e).

69. Abbe (1865i).

70. Literally a "Great Guests' Court."

71. This refers to the fairs that were commonplace in the 1860s, organized by local communities to benefit the U.S. Sanitary Commission, a relief agency created by federal legislation but organized by private efforts to assist wounded Union Army soldiers during the Civil War.

72. Abbe (1865j).
73. State Hermitage Museum (2018).
74. Abbe (1865v).
75. Abbe (1865v).
76. Abbe (1866j).
77. Abbe (1865r).
78. Abbe (1865h).
79. C. C. Abbe (1865g).
80. Abbe (1865m).
81. Abbe (1865p).
82. Abbe (1865q).
83. Abbe (1865o).
84. In a letter to his mother (Abbe 1865s), Cleveland writes of "how unpleasantly our little community has divided itself into cold and unsympathizing horizontal strata. It was not so twenty years ago and I improve every opportunity to break through the self imposed harsh and unhappy stiffness. People thrown together as are the forty or fifty here cannot afford to lose all the pleasures of society and live like hermits."
85. Abbe (1865p).
86. Abbe (1865q).
87. Abbe (1865p).
88. Abbe (1865p).
89. Abbe (1865g).
90. Abbe (1865f).
91. Abbe (1865g).
92. C. C. Abbe (1865f).
93. Abbe (1866d).
94. Abbe (1865o).
95. Abbe (1865p).
96. Abbe (1865p).
97. Abbe (1865u).
98. Abbe (1865u).
99. Roff et al. (2000).
100. C. C. Abbe (1866b).
101. G. W. Abbe (1865a).
102. C. C. Abbe (1865a).
103. C. C. Abbe (1865e).
104. Goodwin (2006).
105. Avant (2015).
106. Abbe (1865j).
107. C. C. Abbe (1865e).
108. C. C. Abbe (1865g).
109. Abbe (1865l).

110. Abbe (1865l).

111. Abbe (1865n). Cleveland was referring to Thomas "Boston" Corbett, the Union Army soldier who fatally shot John Wilkes Booth on April 26, 1865, against the explicit orders of his commanding officer. Corbett immediately gained fame as a hero, but it was fleeting. Several years later, he was working as a doorkeeper for the Kansas State Legislature when he suddenly turned on the legislative body, holding it hostage at gunpoint. He was arrested, tried, and committed to a state mental hospital in Topeka, Kansas, from which he escaped in 1888 and disappeared. Rumors surfaced years later, placing Corbett in Hinckley, Minnesota, where he supposedly perished in the Great Hinckley Fire of 1894. For more on the incredible story of Boston Corbett, see Jensen (2015).

112. Hall (1865).

113. Abbe (1865x).

114. C. C. Abbe (1865a).

115. C. C. Abbe (1866a).

116. C. C. Abbe (1866a).

117. Abbe (1865n).

118. Abbe (1865n).

119. G. W. Abbe (1865b).

120. Abbe (1865o).

121. C. C. Abbe (1865h).

122. Abbe (1865k).

123. Do not despair; perseverance is victorious.

124. Cleveland is referring to an elaborate plot by the Confederacy to burn New York City in November 1864. While a small band of rebels succeeded in setting ablaze several hotels across the city, as well as the Barnum's Museum, the damage was limited and there was no loss of life. For more on this event, see Soodalter (2014).

125. Abbe (1865n).

126. Abbe (1865y).

127. Abbe (1865y).

128. C. C. Abbe (1866c)

129. Abbe (1866l).

130. Abbe (1865s).

131. Abbe (1866e).

132. Abbe (1866e).

133. Abbe (1865t).

134. Abbe (1865t).

135. C. C. Abbe (1865j).

136. Abbe (1865y).

137. Abbe (1866c).

138. Abbe (1865w).

139. Abbe (1865a).

140. Murray (1865), which also described Tsar Alexander II as "a keen and experienced sportsman, and passionately fond of bear-shooting, and every winter adds several skins to his already numerous trophies. Bears, as well as elk and wolves, are often shot within 40 miles of St. Petersburg."

141. Abbe (1865y).

142. Abbc (1865a).

143. Abbe (1866a).

144. Abbe (1866b).

145. Abbe (1866b).

146. Abbe (1866b).

147. Abbe (1866b).

148. Abbe (1866e).

149. Abbe (1866h).

150. Abbe (1866g).

151. Bickmore (1865a).

152. Bickmore (1865b).

153. C. C. Abbe (1865i).

154. Abbe (1866h).

155. Abbe (1866h).

156. Abbe (1866f).

157. Abbe (1866f).

158. Abbe (1866f).

159. Abbe (1865v).

160. Abbe (1865v).

161. G. W. Abbe (1865c).

162. G. W. Abbe (1866a).

163. Bickmore (1865c).

164. 1 Corinthians 7:9.

165. Bickmore (1865c).

166. Kellogg (1881).

167. Abbe (1866c).

168. Abbe (1866c).

169. O. W. Struve (1895).

170. Abbe (1865s).

171. Abbe (1865w).

172. Abbe (1865w).

173. Abbe (1866i).

174. G. W. Abbe (1866a).

175. C. C. Abbe (1866d).

176. C. C. Abbe (1866e).

177. W. C. Abbe (1866).

178. Abbe (1866k).

179. Abbe (1866k).
180. Abbe (1866k).
181. Abbe (1866k).
182. Abbe (1866a).
183. Abbe (1866a).
184. Abbe (1866a).
185. Abbe (1866a).
186. Abbe (1866a).
187. G. W. Abbe (1866b).
188. Abbe (1866a).
189. T. Abbe (1955).
190. O. W. Struve (1866).
191. Abbe (1889a).

Chapter Four: Cincinnati (1867–1870)

1 Abbe (n.d.).
2. Abbe (1866m).
3. Loomis (1866).
4. Hall (1866).
5. Newcomb (1866a).
6. Newcomb (1866a).
7. Newcomb (1866a).
8. Newcomb (1866b).
9. Newcomb (1867a).
10. Newcomb (1867b).
11. Peirce (1867).
12. Gould (1867).
13. Newcomb (1867c).
14. Abbe (1867a).
15. Fessenden (1867).
16. Abbe (1867b).
17. For more on the Smithsonian fire of 1865, see Henson (2015).
18. Smithsonian Institution (1872a).
19. Abbe (n.d.).
20. USNO (2018).
21. U. S. Navy (1870).
22. Newcomb (1903).
23. Norberg (1978).
24. T. Abbe (1955).
25. Abbe (n.d.).
26. Abbe (1867a).
27. Washington Post (1888).

28. Abbe (1867a).
29. T. Abbe (1955).
30. T. Abbe (1955).
31. Abbe (n.d.).
32. Although Cleveland never indicated directly in his writings the name of the mysterious woman he befriended aboard the steamer on his voyage home from Europe in November 1866, she is believed to be Emma Gregory, who sailed from her native England to America on the same ship as Abbe to live with her sister and brother-in-law, Anne and Joseph Emery, in Cincinnati. Anne Emery wrote a letter to Cleveland on January 7, 1867, in which she thanked him for the kindness he showed her sister (A. Emery 1867). Further evidence comes from the manifest of the steamer SS *Erin*, which arrived at New York on from Liverpool on November 15, 1866, the same date Cleveland indicates in his diary that he arrived home. While a "Charles Abbe" (likely a misspelling of Cleveland's name) is listed in the main section of the ship's manifold, there is a "Miss E. Gregory" and a "Mrs. Reighley" (with a daughter "Nelly") listed traveling in the Saloon section of the ship. This is consistent with Cleveland's diary entry for November 4, 1866, in which he makes reference to a "Madame _____ [bound] for Cincinnati & Mrs. _____ & Nelly [bound] for Warren, Ohio." Later, in his diary entry for November 15, Cleveland makes reference to a "Miss Gregory & Mrs. Reighley."
33. A. Emery (1867).
34. (Abbe n.d.).
35. J. Emery (1867).
36. J. Emery (1867).
37. Hooper (1867a).
38. Abbe (n.d.).
39. Porter (1893).
40. National Park Service (1997).
41. Hooper (1867b).
42. Hooper (1867c).
43. Hooper (1867d).
44. Abbe (1867a).
45. Hooper (1868a).
46. Hooper (1868b).
47. Shillito et al. (1868).
48. Abbe (1869b).
49. C. C. Abbe (1868a).
50. G. W. Abbe (1868).
51. Abbe (1868c).
52. Hooper (1868c).
53. Hooper (1868d).
54. C. C. Abbe (1868c).
55. C. C. Abbe (1868b).

56. C. C. Abbe (1868b).
57. Brooklyn Daily Eagle (1867).
58. C. C. Abbe (1868d).
59. U.S. Senate (2018).
60. C. C. Abbe (1868e).
61. T. Abbe (1955).
62. Welles (1868).
63. Abbe (1869b).
64. Abbe (1868a).
65. The first meeting of the Society of the Cincinnati—which derives its name from Lucius Quintus Cincinnatus, a fifth-century Roman who left his farm to lead troops in battle—took place in 1783 at Mount Gulian, the Verplanck family home in Fishkill, New York. This is the same location where freed slave James F. Brown recorded in his diary that "the weather has been very fine for the season" the day Cleveland was born, 55 years later.
66. Venable (1894).
67. T. Abbe (1955).
68. Abbe (1868a).
69. H. Abbe (1868).
70. Abbe (1869b).
71. Abbe (1869b).
72. Abbe (1866k).
73. Abbe (1869b).
74. Abbe (1869b).
75. Batten (1988).
76. Abbe (1869b).
77. Abbe (1869b).
78. Abbe (1898a).
79. Cleveland's letter to Gano of July 29, 1868, was reprinted that fall in the *Journal of the Telegraph* (Abbe 1868d), with a few variations from the version reprinted in Humphreys (1919). Most notably, the version reprinted in Abbe (1868d) includes a sentence that reads, "It seems certain, that at least in the case of a great storm, we may arrive at a greater degree of certainty in these predictions than is obtained in England and France where only seven-tenths of the predictions are verified." In Humphreys (1919), this sentence reads, ". . . than is attained in England and France, where only three-tenths of the predictions are verified." Whether this difference in the verifications of European forecasts is due to a typographical error (perhaps from relying on an earlier draft of the letter) is unknown. However, other sources seem to indicate that the higher value of European verifications is correct. In Cleveland's subsequent letter to Gano, dated May 7, 1869, for example—which is cited in both Humphreys (1919) and Alexander (1923)—he describes the British system as "failing in only a small percentage of cases."

80. Abbe (1869b).
81. Alter (1949).
82. Alter (1949).
83. Alter (1949).
84. Cincinnati Chamber of Commerce (1896).
85. McLaughlin's letter is reproduced in Alter (1949).
86. Cincinnati Chamber of Commerce (1896).
87. Morrow (1916).
88. Cincinnati Chamber of Commerce (1896).
89. Abbe (1869d).
90. Cary and Warder (1860). According to the 1860 U.S. Census, Lawrence Young owned real estate valued at $70,000, with another $29,000 of personal estate.
91. Conner (2004).
92. L. Young (1869).
93. E. Young (1869).
94. Brown (1869).
95. Stuntebeck (1869).
96. Bancroft (1869).
97. St. Martin (2005).
98. Cheney (1869).
99. Russell (1869).
100. Foster (1869).
101. Goldsmith (1869).
102. Alden (1869a).
103. Alden (1869a).
104. Abbe (1872).
105. Abbe (1869a).
106. T. Abbe (1955).
107. T. Abbe (1955).
108. Abbe (1869a).
109. Abbe (1872).
110. Abbe (1872).
111. Abbe (1872).
112. Abbe (1872).
113. Philosophical Society of Washington (1880).
114. T. Abbe (1955).
115. Chicago Tribune (1869).
116. Alter (1949).
117. Cincinnati Chamber of Commerce (1896).
118. Abbe (1870b).
119. Van Horne (1896).
120. Abbe (1869f).

121. T. Abbe (1955).

122. Abbe (1869e).

123. Capen (1863).

124. Abbe (1869a).

125. Alter (1949).

126. Abbe (1869a).

127. Abbe (1869f).

128. Abbe (1869g).

129. Abbe (1869h).

130. Abbe (1916d). In Abbe (1904c), he asks Frank Armstrong, former manager of the Cincinnati office of the Western Union Telegraph Company, "Who as it first invented the term, 'Old Probs'? Was it not A. T. Goshorn, or William or Henry Davis, September, 1869. Seems to me I can remember putting up a daily bulletin with my crooked handwriting cramped by using the stencil and manifold process." In his response, Armstrong (1904) said, "That sobriquet was given to Prof. Cleveland Abbe by the few of us in the Western Union Office engaged in the Weather business. I remember distinctly that when the Government took charge of this weather business and the paper gave credit to General Myers and dubbed him 'Old Probs' I took exceptions and wrote I think to the Press some communications. The original old Probs was Cleveland Abbe, and no one else and that is where all credit belongs."

131. Abbe (1892a).

132. Twain (1910).

133. Alter (1949).

134. Abbe (1869i).

135. Abbe (1869a).

136. Abbe (1869j).

137. Abbe (1869k).

138. Abbe (1886a).

139. Abbe (1886a).

140. While the actual letter cannot be found, Cleveland referred to it several times over the years, including during his testimony before the Allison Commission. At times, his recollection varied as to whether the letter was to his father, mother, or both parents.

141. Sherwood (1870).

142. Abbe (1898a).

143. Morrow (1916).

144. T. Abbe (1955) mentions this date as being the first meeting between Cleveland and Fanny. Abbe (1868a) says "left items at the above offices," referring to *The Commercial*, the *Gazette*, and the *Enquirer*, and then "off to the Hoopers" before mentioning "Miss Neale."

145. Marvin (1917).

146. T. Abbe (1955).

147. T. Abbe (1955).

148. T. Abbe (1955).

149. T. Abbe (n.d.).

150. T. Abbe (n.d.).

151. T. Abbe (n.d.).

152. Shipherd (1865). The handbill describing the founding principles of the American Freedmen's Aid Commission went on to say, "That the black population may not *stain* the white population, it is proposed to confine the color to the cuticle, cleansing away ignorance, vice, and degrading poverty, and redeeming to society the millions already redeemed to nominal manhood. In the interest of the nation as one nation, in the interest of the people as one people, in the steadfast faith that it can never advantage one citizen to permit another to miss of the highest standard of manly attainment, the Commission proposes to do whatever its national constituency may permit, to give effect to the Proclamation of Emancipation, and to the Amendment of the Constitution."

153. T. Abbe (1955).

154. C. C. Abbe (1870a).

155. R. Abbe (1870). English poet Richard Hooker (1554–1600) is said to have made the "fatal mistake" of marrying his landlady's daughter.

156. W. Abbe (1870).

157. G. W. Abbe (1870a).

158. C. C. Abbe (1870c).

159. T. Abbe (1955).

160. T. Abbe (n.d.).

161. Alter (1949).

162. F. M. Abbe (1870a).

163. Bickmore (1870).

164. Bickmore (1870).

Chapter Five: The Birth of a Weather Service (1869–1877)

1. The wreck of the *Arrow* and failed attempts to save its crew are described in Andreas (1885) and New York Times (1869), among others. Some accounts say the tug *Wood* sent two lifeboats to rescue the crew of the *Arrow*, with one of the boats swamped before reaching the schooner, and three of the men from the lifeboat later swimming ashore and reporting the captain of the *Arrow* and his six men were washed overboard and drowned.

2. According to Hall (1870), "The season just closed [1869] has been far more disastrous to the Lake shipping than any previous on record, and exceeding those of any other by 786."

3. Excerpted in New York Herald (1869).

4. Miller (1931b).

5. Bergland and Hayes (2014).

6. Bergland and Hayes (2014).

7. Lapham (1869a).

8. Lapham (1869b).

9. The sheet of graph paper with the copied observations in preserved with Lapham's original letter and observations in Container 5 (General Correspondence, 1850–1916) of the Cleveland Abbe Papers at the Library of Congress. On it, there is a handwritten note, in pencil, which says: "[Handwriting of F M Neal later Abbe]."

10. Lapham (1869c).

11. Abbe (1869m).

12. Lapham (1869d).

13. Lapham (1869e).

14. National Board of Trade (1869).

15. National Board of Trade (1869).

16. National Board of Trade (1869).

17. National Board of Trade (1869).

18. Miller (1931b).

19. Miller (1931b).

20. Lapham (1869f).

21. House of Representatives (1869).

22. Paine (1888).

23. U.S. House (1869a).

24. U.S. House (1869b).

25. Miller (1931b).

26. Loomis (1870).

27. Abbe (1870c).

28. Abbe (1870c).

29. Lapham (1870a).

30. Chamber of Commerce of the State of New York (1870).

31. U.S. Congress (1870).

32. Paine (1888).

33. U.S. Senate (1870a).

34. U.S. Senate (1870b).

35. United States of America (1870).

36. Dutch meteorologist Christoph Buys Ballot, director of the Royal Meteorological Institute of the Netherlands, inaugurated a storm signal service for that country on June 1, 1860. The following year, British Admiral Robert FitzRoy began issuing forecasts for a government department that would eventually become the UK Met Office. And in 1863, French mathematician and astronomer Urbain Le Verrier, perhaps best known for his discovery of the planet Neptune in 1846, established a storm warning service, with the backing of the French government, based out of the Paris Observatory, where he served as director.

37. Miller (1930).

38. In a profile of Dawes's son, Chester M. Dawes, Campbell (1902) erroneously claims that Henry L. Dawes "founded the system of daily weather reports in 1869, at the suggestion of Professor Cleveland Abbe, and established the first bureau."

39. Earth and Air (1901).

40. As quoted in bibliography of Weber (1922).

41. Abbe (1897a).

42. Lapham (1871b).

43. Marvin (1917).

44. Berry and Phillips (1902).

45. Paine (1888).

46. Leslie (1878).

47. Fleming (2000).

48. Fleming (2000).

49. Raines (1996).

50. Townsend (1870).

51. Myer (1870a).

52. Abbe (1870d).

53. Myer (1870b).

54. Paine (1888).

55. Myer (1870c).

56. U.S. Congress (1871).

57. Belknap (1870).

58. Paine (1888).

59. Glassford (1885).

60. Glassford (1885).

61. Glassford (1885).

62. Myer (1870d).

63. Myer (1870d).

64. Lapham (1870b).

65. Lapham (1870c).

66. Lapham (1870d).

67. Myer (1871).

68. Lapham (1870d).

69. Mallery (1870).

70. Bergland and Hayes (2014).

71. Lapham (1870e).

72. Lapham (1871a).

73. Howgate (1872).

74. Abbe (1871a).

75. R. Abbe (1869).

76. Alter (1949)

77. Abbe (1870b). Cleveland's report, dated June 1, states, "The daily compilation of this Bulletin for the newspapers was undertaken two weeks ago by the Cincinnati Office of the Western Union Telegraph Company, and will so continue, thus relieving the Observatory of all further responsibility," indicating that Armstrong, as manager of the Cincinnati office of Western Union, would have assumed responsibility sometime in May. Abbe (1904d) also mentions May 1870 as when Armstrong took over.

78. Alter (1949) provides a more detailed description of the preparation of the daily weather maps published by the Cincinnati office of the Western Union.

79. Abbe (1870b).

80. C. C. Abbe (1870d).

81. C. C. Abbe (1869).

82. C. C. Abbe (1870b).

83. Abbe (1870b).

84. Abbe (1870e).

85. Dexter (1870).

86. See, for example, Newcomb (1874).

87. Selfridge (1870a).

88. G. W. Abbe (1870b).

89. Selfridge (1870b).

90. Abbe (1870f).

91. Abbe (1868–72).

92. Myer (1870e).

93. Abbe (1895a).

94. Myer (1870f).

95. Myer (1870g).

96. Myer (1870h).

97. Abbe (1868–72).

98. Abbe (1868–72).

99. Norton (1871).

100. Myer (1871).

101. Abbe (1916d).

102. New York Times (1871a).

103. New York Times (1871b).

104. Myer (1871).

105. New York Times (1871c).

106. Abbe (1871b).

107. Abbe (1871c).

108. New York Times (1871d).

109. Myer (1871).

110. Myer (1871).

111. Morrow (1916).
112. Myer (1871).
113. Myer (1871).
114. G. W. Abbe (1871a).
115. Lofthouse (1871).
116. W. C. Abbe (1871).
117. C. C. Abbe (1871a).
118. H. Abbe (1871a).
119. R. Abbe (1871a).
120. Silliman (1871).
121. R. Abbe (1871b).
122. G. W. Abbe (1871c).
123. G. W. Abbe (1871d).
124. G. W. Abbe 8(1871e).
125. G. W. Abbe (1871i).
126. T. Abbe (1955).
127. G. W. Abbe (1871j).
128. C. C. Abbe (1871b).
129. New York Times (1871e).
130. G. W. Abbe (1871h).
131. H. Abbe (1871b).
132. Driver (2016).
133. G. W. Abbe (1871f).
134. G. W. Abbe (1871g).
135. New York Times (1871f).
136. Nation (1871).
137. G. W. Abbe (1871k).
138. R. Abbe (1871c).
139. Abbe (1871d).
140. G. W. Abbe (1871l).
141. Cox (2002).
142. Abbe (1868–72).
143. C. C. Abbe (1871c).
144. Abbe (1872–73).
145. R. Abbe (1873a).
146. Abbe (1893b).
147. T. Abbe (1955).
148. Myer (1872) states: "Professor Cleveland Abbe, assistant, First Lieutenant Robert Craig, acting signal-officer and assistant, and Professor Thompson B. Maury, assistant, have alternated in preparing the official deductions of the Office, besides performing such other duties in connection with the reductions of observations as have been found desirable."

149. Abbe (1873).

150. New Orleans Republican (1872).

151. Wilmington Daily Commercial (1872).

152. New York Herald (1872).

153. Evening Star (1872).

154. Calver (1922).

155. Henry (1930).

156. C. C. Abbe (1874a).

157. T. Abbe (1955).

158. R. Abbe (1873b).

159. R. Abbe (1874a).

160. Wells (1874).

161. R. Abbe (1874a).

162. Goode (2003).

163. National Republican (1875).

164. Washington Post (1886).

165. The Collector (1905).

166. The Recorder of Deeds land transaction records in the District of Columbia Archives show two deeds transferring this property to Cleveland, both from heirs of Francis Markoe Jr., the previous owner, who purchased the house from Timothy Caldwell, the original owner, in 1838. One deed is from Virgil Maxcy Markoe, for the consideration of $1,400 (Liber 859, Folio 325), and the other from Mary G. Markoe, et al., for the consideration of $8,600 (Liber 859, Folio 328). Cleveland also wrote to his daughter-in-law Frieda in 1912, "It took us ten years to pay off the $10,000 that we once owed on 2017 I." (Abbe 1912c).

167. T. Abbe (1955).

168. T. Abbe (1955).

169. T. Abbe (1955).

170. T. Abbe (1923).

171. National Park Service (1963).

172. Morris (1918). T. Abbe (1955) offers a slightly different version of the story, with "a mounted messenger, sent by President Madison to warn the Monroes, and his wife who was staying with them."

173. Morris (1918).

174. Morris (1918). An annotated copy by the author, which is part of the Cleveland Abbe Papers of the Library of Congress, contains a handwritten note initialed by the author, stating, "This information was furnished me by Prof. Abbe himself but his son told me his father added the 4th floor to the back building only so the front is as originally built."

175. T. Abbe (1955).

176. Morris (1918).

177. National Park Service (1975).

178. T. Abbe (1955).

179. T. Abbe (1955).

180. Evening Star (1890).

181. Boyd (1875).

182. Cleveland contemplated a return to Cincinnati as late as 1874. On October 31 of that year, he wrote to Rufus King, president of the University of Cincinnati, which was taking over the observatory. "In reference to my return to Cincinnati I must frankly say that I always expected to do so until I found on the occasion of the transfer of the Observatory to the University that there was no provision made for my continuance as Director," he wrote (Abbe 1874b). Cleveland included a list of conditions that would have to be met in order for him to return as director of the observatory. These included an assurance of a permanent income of $6,000 for the "special use" of the observatory, independent of the director's salary. There were also stipulations relating to the control of the observatory's budget and the hiring of its staff, as well as to the construction of new facilities and the condition of the instruments. Cleveland also said he would not be able to leave Washington, D.C., before July of the following year. In the end, the university trustees solicited applications from various prominent astronomers and selected Ormond Stone as director, who served from 1875 until 1882.

183. Abbe (1874a).

Chapter Six: Science and Service (1878–1908)

1. Sunshine Courier (1878).

2. Abbe (1881). Page 29 includes Cleveland's orders, which were issued to him by First Lieutenant H. H. C. Dunwoody.

3. Abbe (1878a).

4. Abbe (1881).

5. Abbe (1881).

6. Abbe (1881).

7. Abbe (1881).

8. Abbe (1881).

9. Abbe (1870a).

10. Abbe (1895a).

11. Abbe (1876).

12. Abbe (1869b).

13. Abbe et al. (1879).

14. International Meridian Conference (1884).

15. International Meridian Conference (1884).

16. T. Abbe (1955).

17. Abbe (1888b).

18. Myer (1870d).

19. Le Verrier (1869). Translated from the original French.

20. Abbe (1895a).
21. Myer (1872).
22. Abbe (1895a).
23. Meteorological Committee (1874).
24. Abbe (1895a).
25. Abbe (1895a).
26. Abbe (1895a).
27. Dunwoody (1894).
28. Myer (1874).
29. Abbe (1895a).
30. Atlantic Monthly (1875).
31. T. Abbe (1955).
32. Abbe (1879).
33. Abbe (1879).
34. R. Abbe (1924).
35. New York Herald (1879).
36. New York Daily Tribune (1879).
37. Abbe and Howson (1941) list Charlotte Abbe's cause of death as "apoplexy."
38. Abbe (1895a).
39. Hazen (1881).
40. Bigelow (1900).
41. Bigelow (1900).
42. Abbe (1895a).
43. Evening Star (1886).
44. Allison Commission (1886).
45. Evening Star (1900).
46. National Republican (1882).
47. New York Times (1894).
48. Grice (1991), Whitnah (1961).
49. St. Paul Daily Globe (1884).
50. Savannah Morning News (1884).
51. Army and Navy Journal (1884).
52. Nalty and MacGregor (1981).
53. Savannah Morning News (1884).
54. Conner (2012), Howell (2007). While Greene eventually was allowed to enlist in the Signal Service and passed his training with distinction, his tenure in the service was short-lived and fraught with discord. He was initially stationed to Pensacola, Florida, where the observer in charge, Sgt. McGowan, protested his arrival to their superiors in Washington, D.C. The officials in Washington, D.C., responded by reassigning McGowan to Washington, D.C., and demoting him, thus leaving Greene in charge of the station in Pensacola. Later that year, Greene himself was demoted and ordered to report to Rochester, New York, where he suffered at the hands of his

immediate superior, as well as a Signal Service station inspector, who accused him of such acts as falsifying reports and gambling. This ultimately led to his discharge from the service. Howell (2007) goes into detail about Greene's life, before, during, and after his time in the Signal Service.

55. Bigelow (1900).

56. Hazen (1881).

57. Abbe (1895a).

58. Hazen (1881).

59. Hazen (1881).

60. Hazen (1881).

61. Quoted in Humphreys (1919).

62. Quoted in Humphreys (1919).

63. Abbe (1895a).

64. Abbe (1901a). Ashley, whose official title was chief of the Division of Correspondence and Records, was first detailed to the Office of the Chief Signal Officer in 1861 and, after being discharged from the Army in 1863, appointed as a civilian clerk and eventually assisted General Myer with the formation of the meteorological service placed under Myer's command. In addition to reviewing all scientific papers, he prepared and printed lists of all scientific documents, which Abbe found to be "a great convenience for reference in the daily work of the office."

65. Allison Commission (1886).

66. According to Allison Commission (1886), the letter, titled "An answer to General Hazen's circular criticising Secretary Lincoln's right and competency to judge what is for the best interest of his Department" and signed by "The U.S. Weather Observers," was "published in full in *The New York Times*, the *New York Tribune*, *Springfield Republican*, *Brooklyn Eagle*, Rochester papers, *Buffalo Gazette*, and *Globe-Democrat*."

67. Allison Commission (1886).

68. Allison Commission (1886).

69. Guston (1994).

70. Pacific Commercial Advertiser (1886). The newspaper reported the Signal Service was one of a handful of agencies in the federal government marred by scandal under Garfield's administration.

71. See, for example, Morning Journal and Courier (1887) and Portland Daily Press (1887). Other sources cited Hazen's apparent affliction with Bright's disease, which was also reported by John P. Finley of the Signal Service, who, according to Grice (1991), accompanied Hazen several days earlier to a reception for the diplomatic corps at the White House. "It was a cold day and the evening set in with snow and high winds," according to Finley, noting that Hazen, in full uniform, had only the protection of his military cape and became "quite ill" after being "much exposed on the White House portico." Just days later, Hazen was confined to bed, where "at times his pains were so violent that he had to be held down in bed, and his death was agonizing in the extreme."

72. Schley and Soley (1885).
73. Greely (1887).
74. Abbe (1889b).
75. Abbe (1889b).
76. F. M. Abbe (1889a).
77. Abbe (1890a).
78. F. M. Abbe (1889b).
79. Abbe (1890b).
80. Abbe (1892a).
81. Abbe (1890d).
82. Abbe (1890d).
83. Abbe (1890e).
84. F. M. Abbe (1890).
85. Abbe (1890f).
86. F. M. Abbe (1889c).
87. Abbe (1890d).
88. Abbe (1890g).
89. Abbe (1890g).
90. Greely (1890).
91. Greely (1890).
92. As Fuller (1990) points out, "Although impetuous, Greely did not defend Signal Corps meteorology. At best, he took an ambiguous stand on the long-simmering congressional belief that the nation's weather service should be in civilian, not military, hands." Whitnah (1961) states, "From all outward appearances it might be concluded that Greely was now anxious to lose the meteorological branch of his organization."
93. Portland Daily Press (1888).
94. St. Paul Daily Globe (1890a).
95. St. Paul Daily Globe (1890b).
96. U.S. Congress (1889a).
97. On December 5, 1889, Senator Algernon S. Paddock of Nebraska introduced a bill (S. 652) "providing for the transfer of the Signal Service Bureau to the Department of Agriculture." On December 18, Representative Edwin H. Conger of Iowa introduced a bill (H. R. 282) "transferring the weather service of the United States Signal Service Bureau to the Department of Agriculture."
98. U.S. Congress (1889a), 215.
99. U.S. Congress (1889b), 1,958.
100. U.S. Congress (1889c), 3,341, 3,343.
101. U.S. Congress (1889c), 3,452.
102. U.S. Congress (1889c), 3,753.
103. Mendenhall (1890).
104. U.S. Congress (1889d), 9,814.
105. U.S. Congress (1889d), 9,815.

106. U.S. Congress (1889d), 10,178.

107. U.S. Congress (1889d), 10,179.

108. U.S. Congress (1889d), 10,199.

109. U.S. Congress (1889e), 10,772.

110. U.S. Congress (1891).

111. Harrington (1891).

112. Greely (1891).

113. Indianapolis Journal (1890).

114. Madison Daily Leader (1891).

115. Astronomical Society

116. Abbe (1891b).

117. Harrington (1891).

118. Abbe (1891c).

119. Harrington (1891).

120. History Nebraska (n.d.).

121. The Sun (1893).

122. New York Times (1893).

123. T. Abbe (1955).

124. Desert Weekly (1893).

125. Abbe (1893a).

126. Morton (1893a).

127. Abbe (1893b).

128. Abbe (1893b).

129. Abbe (1893b).

130. Stone (1893).

131. Morton's letter is excerpted in Harrington (1893).

132. Wheeling Intelligencer (1893).

133. *New York Times* (1893).

134. Morton (1894).

135. Whitnah (1961).

136. Whitnah (1961).

137. Cleveland is referring to the Congress on Meteorology, Climatology, and Terrestrial Magnetism—more commonly known as the International Meteorological Congress—held August 21–24 in Chicago. It was one of a series of congresses held from May until October in the city's Memorial Art Palace, under the auspices of the Congress Auxiliary of the World's Columbian Exposition.

138. Abbe (1893c).

139. Abbe (1893f).

140. Abbe (1893d).

141. Abbe (1893e).

142. Seattle Post-Intelligencer (1895).

143. Evening Times (1897).

144. Evening Star (1899).
145. Indianapolis Journal (1902).
146. Swanson (2016).
147. Berry (1899).
148. Berry (1899).
149. Abbe (1901b).
150. Abbe (1901b).
151. Myer (1873). See also Henry (1929).
152. Abbe (1901b).
153. Abbe (1901b) states, "The first copy and the initial steps toward the regular publication were taken by the present Editor [Abbe], but subsequent numbers were prepared by various officials, alternately." Henry (1929) says that while "there is no official record of the responsible editors of the Review during the régime of the military weather service; it was the custom at that time for the official who had served as 'indications' officer to have editorial charges of the Monthly Weather Review during the month immediately following his tour of duty on the indications work as it was then called." Corzine (1972) says Cleveland "is credited with initiating and guiding the *Review* through its early years. For the first 20 years, however, the *Review* was compiled and edited by a board of officials under the direction of the Chief Signal Officer."
154. Abbe (1901b).
155. Abbe (1906).
156. Abbe (1906).
157. Abbe (1906).
158. Abbe (1906).
159. Abbe (1906).
160. Ward (1896).
161. Moore (1897).
162. Abbe (1895b).
163. Abbe (1895c).
164. Abbe (1897c).
165. Abbe (1905).
166. Abbe (1898c), Abbe (1899a).
167. Abbe (1898d), Abbe (1901c), Abbe (1901d).
168. Abbe (1900a).
169. Abbe (1903b).
170. Abbe (1903b).
171. Potter (2003), Potter (2013).
172. Abbe (1903c).
173. Abbe (1904a).
174. Abbe (1903d).
175. Good Government (1893), White (2003).
176. Roosevelt (1893).

177. Berry (1899).

178. Abbe (1895d).

179. Abbe (1904b).

180. Abbe (1904b).

181. Koelsch (1981).

182. As Harper (2008) describes, "In Europe, meteorology held the same 'rank' as astronomy in academic institutions, and research on its theoretical underpinnings was carried out at several academic institutions in Norway, Germany, and England. But in the United States, the top academic institutions did not treat meteorology as a topic on par with any physical science."

183. Abbe (1891d).

184. Abbe (1891d).

185. Koelsch (1981).

186. Koelsch (1981).

187. Abbe (1891e).

188. Koelsch (1981).

189. Abbe (1903e).

190. Abbe (1903e).

191. Advertiser (1896).

192. T. Abbe (n.d.), T. Abbe (1955). For more about the history of academic regalia at the University of Glasgow, see Dickson (2012).

193. Kelvin (1896).

194. Abbe (1878b).

195. Abbe (1910b).

196. Abbe (1891f).

197. Abbe (1888a).

198. Abbe (1888a).

199. Abbe (1901e).

200. Abbe (1894).

201. Abbe (1901e).

202. Abbe (1901e).

203. Abbe (1901e).

204. Abbe (1901e).

205. Willis and Hooke (2006).

206. Majkik et al. (2011).

207. Bjerknes (1904).

208. Willis and Hooke (2006).

209. As Coiffier (2011) describes, "Between 1916 and 1922, the Englishman Lewis Fry Richardson tried to solve weather forecast equations by numerical methods. He even made a 6-hour forecast by hand, although it proved quite unrealistic." He further describes how, "Finally, in 1950, Jule Charney, the Norwegian Ragnar Fjörtoft, and John von Neumann made the first numerical weather prediction."

210. Fleming (2016).

211. Fleming (2016).

212. Eliassen (1982).

213. Willis and Hooke (2006).

214. National Geographic (1888).

215. Bell (1904) wrote to Cleveland saying, "Always glad to see you at my Wednesday Evenings with your friends."

216. Abbe (1903f).

217. Ithaca Daily Journal (1903).

218. T. Abbe (1955).

219. Tyson (1904).

220. Tyson (1904).

221. Commercial Advertiser (1908a).

222. T. Abbe (n.d.). In published form, T. Abbe (1955) simply says, "It was a very easy termination for diabetes."

223. Commercial Advertiser (1908b).

224. Commercial Advertiser (1908b).

225. Louisa Hart Howson, William's wife.

226. Frieda Dauer, Cleveland Jr.'s wife.

227. Ernst Cleveland Abbe, Cleveland Jr. and Frieda's son.

228. C. Abbe Jr. (1908a).

229. Marvin (1917) refers to "a severe illness following his constant and patient attention to the needs of his first wife in her last illness." C. Abbe Jr. (1908b) mentions a letter from his father from Ogdensburg and of him being in the hospital.

230. C. Abbe Jr. (1908b).

231. T. Abbe (1955).

Chapter Seven: Final Years (1909–1916)

1. Abbe (1916a). T. Abbe (1955) describes, "The double wording at the end of the third and fourth lines of the quatrain were left as above, no words being scratched out. The words in alignment probably were his first thought; the words above, his suggestion for possible improvement."

2. McAdie (1908).

3. According to the 1910 U.S. Census, Margaret immigrated to the United States in 1892.

4. Unknown (1909).

5. Washington Times (1909).

6. Evening Star (1909a).

7. The Sun (1909).

8. T. Abbe (n.d.).

9. T. Abbe (1955).

10. T. Abbe (1955).

11. Marvin (1917).

12. T. Abbe (1955).

13. Abbe (1909).

14. Hough (1909).

15. Hough (1909).

16. For more on the forecasts surrounding Taft's inauguration, see Potter (2019).

17. Evening Star (1909b).

18. Pensacola Journal (1909).

19. Dunn (1909).

20. Pensacola Journal (1909).

21. Hough (1909).

22. New York Times (1909).

23. T. Abbe (n.d.).

24. Abbe (1910a).

25. Abbe (1910a).

26. Abbe (1910a).

27. Abbe (1911a).

28. The title of Cleveland's lecture, as it appeared in a notice in the *Columbia Spectator* (1908) advertising the series when it was first announced, in November 1908, was "Outstanding problems of meteorology." Four days before the lecture, the *Columbia Spectator* (1909) advertised it as "Meteorological Problems for the Future." The published version, which appeared two years later in *The Popular Science Monthly*, was titled "The Meteorology of the Future." See Abbe (1911b).

29. Humphreys (1919).

30. Abbe (1911b).

31. For more on Davenport and his work at Cold Spring Harbor, see Witkowski and Inglis (2008).

32. Davenport (1911).

33. Davenport (1911).

34. According to Steinem (1998), Sanger "adopted the mainstream eugenics language of the day, partly as a tactic, since many eugenicists opposed birth control on the grounds that the educated would use it more. Though her own work was directed toward voluntary birth control and public health programs, her use of eugenics language probably helped justify sterilization abuse."

35. As Lewis (2000) points out, "Although he had steadfastly denounced the Nordic eugenics movement launched from Cold Spring Harbor, Long Island, as racist and an insult to democracy, Du Bois's views about family eugenics were a quite different matter. As far as his own flesh and blood were concerned, he believed that genes were destiny."

36. Abbe and Nichols (1916).

37. T. Abbe (n.d.).

38. R. Abbe (1924).

39. Eugenical News (1918a).

40. Eugenical News (1918b).

41. Abbe (1866i).

42. Seller (1982).

43. Abbe (1890a).

44. Abbe (1890c).

45. Abbe (1890c).

46. Douglass (n.d.).

47. Green (2015).

48. Evening Star (1895).

49. National Association for the Relief of Destitute Colored Women and Children (1895).

50. Dean (1892).

51. Abbe (1892b).

52. Gates (1892).

53. City of Manassas (2019).

54. Abbe (1900b).

55. Abbe (1913).

56. Evening Star (1913).

57. New York Times (192).

58. AMS (1945).

59. Abbe (1914).

60. Linehand (1990).

61. Humphreys (1919).

62. Morrow (1916).

63. Abbe (1912c).

64. C. Abbe, Jr. (1916b).

65. C. Abbe Jr. (1916b).

66. Abbe (1912b).

67. Abbe (1912a). The Latin phrase translates as "Never despair. Work conquers all."

68. C. Abbe Jr. (1916a).

69. C. Abbe Jr. (1916a).

70. Welch (1916).

71. C. Abbe Jr. (1916b). T. Abbe (1955) states that the stroke occurred in 1916.

72. U.S. Department of Agriculture (1915), C. Abbe Jr. (1915).

73. Marvin (1916a).

74. Cooper (1844).

75. C. Abbe Jr. (1916c).

76. Diamond Cove Association (2014).

77. C. Abbe Jr. (1916c).

78. Morrow (1916)

79. Talman (1916). Although most contributions to Weather Bureau Topics and Personnel were not credited to a particular author, a copy of this issue in the Cleveland Abbe Papers at the Library of Congress includes a handwritten notation attributing it to Charles Fitzhugh Talman, Librarian of the Weather Bureau.

80. Abbe (1916d).

81. Marvin (1917).

82. T. Abbe (1949).

83. Willis (1949).

84. T. Abbe (n.d.).

85. Marvin (1916b).

86. Marvin (1917).

Epilogue

1. Oliver (1917).

2. Day (1916).

3. Abbe (1916c).

4. Sunday Star (1917).

5. Sunday Star (1917).

6. Sunday Star (1917).

7. See chapter 17 of T. Abbe (1955).

8. Abbe (1898b).

9. AMS (1920).

10. AMS (1964).

11. U.S. Department of Agriculture (1916).

12. MARD (2015), Williams (2014).

13. Science (1918).

14. New York Times (1934).

15. Brooks (1934).

16. National Park Service (2018).

17. Sunday Star (1932).

18. Sunday Star (1928).

19. Evening Star (1930).

20. Freeman (1931). Freeman's mansion changed hands several times after his death in 1937, eventually being purchased in 1992 by Italian fashion designer Gianni Versace, who was shot and killed in front of it in 1997.

21. Sunday Star (1916).

22. Goode (2015).

23. Sunday Star (1923).

24. T. Abbe (1923).

Index